Commitment to Care

Commitment to Care

An Integrated Philosophy of Science, Education, and Religion

by

DEAN TURNER

THE DEVIN-ADAIR COMPANY

OLD GREENWICH, CONNECTICUT

The Devin-Adair Company
143 Sound Beach Avenue
Old Greenwich, Connecticut 06870

International Standard Book Number 0-8159-5216-3
Library of Congress Catalog Card Number 77-78421

Design and Typography by Modern Typographers, Inc., Clearwater, Florida
Printed in the United States of America by
Christian Board of Publication, St. Louis, Missouri

The epigraph on p. 3 is from "Two Tramps in Mud Time,"
from *The Poetry of Robert Frost*, edited by Edward Connery Lathem,
copyright 1936 by Robert Frost. Copyright © 1964 by Lesley Frost Vallantine.
Copyright © 1969 by Holt, Rinehart & Winston.
Reprinted by permission of Holt, Rinehart & Winston, Publishers.

For My Mother

whose life is a hymn to love.
Thank you for your care and forgiveness.
I shall always feel your precious grace.
In all time to come, I can never repay you.

And in memory of Greg
1951–1971
You lived with a careful heart.

Eye hath not seen nor ear heard,
neither hath entered into the heart of man,
the things which God hath prepared for them that love Him.

I Corinthians 2:9

Contents

Contents

Foreword

FOR THREE DECADES the philosophical arena has been largely abandoned by Christian intellectuals and left to the dominion of secular thinkers who seem heartily imperturbable in their despair. In this book, Dean Turner has penetrated behind the "urbanity, sophistication, and erudition" on the face of modern atheism and exposed it for the irrationality and "axiological despair" that it actually is. This is not another of those superficial "Bible bookstore" volumes that have deluged the literary market but that can never reach into the agnostic's mind and heart. Neither is it another of those unsympathetic, emotional diatribes against atheists. Instead, this work is a tour de force in philosophical tectonics. *Commitment to Care* is an epic feat.

The reader will find in these pages three important philosophical and scientific breakthroughs: (1) a radically new concept and definition of objectivity, (2) a brilliant reconstruction (Christianization) of the philosophy of quantum mechanics, and (3) a revolutionary redevelopment (Christianization) of the physics and philosophy of space and time. At last, here is a compelling alternative to positivist philosophy of science, and to the entrenched orthodoxy of relativity physics. In addition to this is a penetrating analysis of evil that goes beyond that of Hume, Leibniz, and Kant—in fact, beyond any contemporary writer on this topic, to our awareness. Turner's concept of *rationale* (his criterion for distinguishing between sense and nonsense with regard to anything) in our judgment lays a foundation for a possible new era of progress in philosophy.

Equally importantly, Turner removes the quackery, misology, and misoneism from conventional Christian apologetics. He brings the real Jesus—the profoundly simple, and simply profound Jesus—into clear view. He finds evident in the teachings of Jesus "the most practical epistemology in the history of philosophy." He uses Jesus' "theory of knowledge based on *need*" as the bricks and mortar for building a radically new and integrated philosophy of science, education, and religion.

Most books written on religion bear little conversion power for persons with questioning and reflective minds. And unfortunately, many books written by scientists on the subject of God treat it in a manner virtually devoid of factual sophistication and logical rigor. For three thousand years western religion has had cycles of belief and unbelief, of growth and disorder. The practice of religion and morals has been based largely upon inspired and venerable authority, or upon the assumption of such authority. Destructive philosophers have always sneered at this way of knowing, the way of faith. At intervals in history, these wreckers get a wide hearing and weaken or even destroy whole societies. During the last 2500 years philosophy has usually meant disaster to churches and their cults. To protect themselves from its possible deleterious influences, churchmen have reacted defensively and kept critical philosophy out of the churches. The cultivation of logical habits of thinking is generally impaired by rigid orthodoxy or mystification in any field, be it science or religion. The destructive philosophers have been aided by many errors and excrescences in the dogmas of even the most magnificent and proud old churches. In this book, Turner has dramatically shifted the balance in philosophy to the creative and constructive side. Reason and religion should be inseparable, each vastly strengthening the other. Turner has carried the battle into the sceptics' camp, turning his command of logic, science, and epistemology against such heretofore sacrosanct figures as David Hume and Albert Einstein, among others. He has advanced traditional religious and scientific realism to a new level of sophistica-

Foreword

tion. He has refined and advanced the design argument for God's existence, welded it together with his powerful "concept of rationale," and brought the combination to bear on philosophy of science in such a manner that it may never again be the same. He offers us a way out of the secular humanism which has bogged down our public schools.

Commitment to Care is the kind of work that can do what philosophy *ought* to do—"influence the direction in which civilization moves." The purpose of the Christian Scholars Foundation is to discover and assist those exceptionally distinguished thinkers whose perspectives can lift the thought of mankind upward. In this age of widely prevailing apprehension and doubt, Turner offers an irrefragible case for belief. *Commitment to Care* is a remarkable achievement. It can strengthen the hope, broaden the vision, and deepen the faith of Man.

We endorse this volume with pride.

CHRISTIAN SCHOLARS FOUNDATION

Box 7128, Provo, Utah 84602

Preface

ALFRED NORTH WHITEHEAD observed that the history of religion in the western world has been a long, undignified retreat. That may be because religionists were defending the indefensible. But the indignity of defending nonsense has occurred on both sides of the religious question. Today, explosions and implosions of data in the exact sciences, and radical new theoretical constructs in mathematics and formal logic, have been accompanied by philosophical fragmentation.

Dr. Turner's constructive and creative synthesis is not, as is the fashion, specialized nay-saying or cautious quibbling. It is a large-scale challenge to traditional assumptions in the West—philosophical, theological, scientific. The book is a many-leveled argument for the startling thesis that "The ultimate clue to the universe is love." I say startling because rigorous thinkers, both religious and a-religious, have taught, as an axiom, that the natural order of the universe is utterly indifferent to Man, to his little purposes and fleeting projections of wish. Even C. S. Lewis could say in tragic moments that the universe appeared to be "the mean trick of a

Preface

spiteful imbecile," thus denying belief in some sensible order or purpose and affirming a diabolical conspiracy.

Today, scientific naturalists say uniformly, with Professor George Wald of Harvard, that "Life happens. But still it cannot happen." The chances against our being here are of "slight, unimaginable improbability" (in the phrase of P. T. Matthews). Yet we are here. Turner's thesis is not simply a warmed-over version of the argument from, or for, the design that seems apparent in Man. For Turner, the building blocks of the universe (atoms, living cells, cosmic principles, mathematical and logical laws—even "oneness") reflect rational purpose. But that is not all. In the very places where men most strongly claim that God is absent, his care and concern are always present. Jesus of Nazareth is present in pain, in perpetual need, and in love.

The universe that emerges in Turner's analysis will be unfamiliar to the orthodox in science, philosophy, and religion. Turner's is a straightforward refusal to accept any popular conclusions that philosophers derive from self-defeating premises, for example, the notion that reality must be absurd because the laws of thought are confounded in certain rigged mathematical paradoxes. For Turner, atheists are fully justified in disbelieving in the classical god. Such a god does not exist. The timeless, changeless, complete utopian Deity revered in ancient and modern times is, for Turner, an idol. The Living God is intimate with space and time, and has lasting needs. He does not transcend our pain. His needs (and likewise ours) become a *sine qua non* of the true, the good, and the beautiful. Turner shows that the concept of need is at work in the systems of other philosophers, theologians, and scientists without their being aware of it. He insists on the splendid blasphemy of affirming the Divine need to continue creating throughout infinity.

In all this, there is a realistic approach to theodicy: the God who is in coexistence with other beings is powerful but also delimited—i.e., limited by the freedom of his creatures, as well as by the conditions innate in the infinite multiverse. For those who will reach beyond methodological blinders and subjective disbelief, the Loving Person whose care and influence pervades reality can be found. Turner insists that this requires no leap of faith, no resort to paradox or absurdity (Kierkegaard's or Russell's) and no romanticizing (as in Pascal or in William James). Shining through reality as revealed by the precise sciences, and by tough-minded thinking, is a God

xiv

who is committed to care. The reality of His love is not simply projected but is discovered by His creatures.

Commitment to Care turns out to be commitment to the heart of reality.

TRUMAN G. MADSEN
DIRECTOR, JUDAEO-CHRISTIAN STUDIES CENTER
BRIGHAM YOUNG UNIVERSITY

Part I

A Philosophy of Care

1

Care in Objectivity

Only where love and need are one,
And the work is play for mortal stakes,
Is the deed ever really done
For Heaven and the future's sakes.

Robert Frost

THE ULTIMATE CLUE to the universe is love.

The ultimate reality in which the universe is grounded is the abiding love of a Supreme Being who cares for himself and all his creatures.

Today, there are pessimists in all quarters who disagree with this. Philosophers and psychologists abound who insist that the ultimate reality is lovelessness, unreason, and death. Atheists and agnostics tell us that the universe is nothing but an accident; i.e., everything in it that occurs or exists does so simply happenstance, and ultimately there is no reason whatever for the world to exist. As they see it, no human being's life is grounded in any permanent reason, purpose, or love. Our lives ultimately are grounded in nothing but chance, which means that, in the end, we really do not have a chance.

Most people have no difficulty whatever in imagining a reason and purpose that informs the existence and behavior of the sun and the earth. Without the earth, and a sun to provide energy to produce and sustain life on it, clearly there could be no earth with

3

life on it. This is of course tautological and is unspeakably simple. Yet, it is also unspeakably profound, except perhaps to some philosophical scrooge who cannot see that it is better for an earth to exist with life on it than for no earth with life on it to exist at all.

As for the existence of the billions of other stars and planets (maybe an infinite number of them in a cosmic multiverse), their existence ultimately must have the same rationale as our earth and sun, namely, to constitute an intelligible world order in which God can progressively create and love more creatures and be loved by them.[1] Not to mention the *beauty* that resides in the universe for God and his creatures to behold. The idea of infinite beauty without an infinite mind to behold it is aesthetically unacceptable, and makes no sense. Comparatively speaking, we finite persons with our limited capacity to observe and appreciate the world can see only a confined amount of beauty in it. One should think big, however, and imagine the existence of an Infinite Creator who can appreciate all the beauty that exists to be seen. Actually, there would be no "allness" for God, in the sense of a final limitation, and He would experience nothing less than infinite joy and beauty in the accomplishments of his creative love and reason. However, I am not suggesting that God's experience would be limited to only joy and beauty. Far be it from me to imagine that God knows no struggle, suffering, disappointment, and tragedy.[2]

Most of my atheist friends regard simple affirmation of reason and purpose in the universe as a projection of mere wishful thinking. They call it naive "animism," uncritical "anthropomorphism," or simply "irrelevant speculation," since the concept of God by its all-encompassing broadness can lend itself to no kind of empirical study or strict verification (or so they tell us). Even when a concept of God is logically coherent and violates no known scientific facts, and even when it serves the practical purpose of making persons feel more at home in the universe, my atheist colleagues generally maintain that religion nonetheless can never appeal to the truly scientific spirit for the simple reason that it lacks the cogency of a theory that can be subjected to empirical testing and proof.

In this book, I am not interested in merely pitting my religious sentimentality against the irreligious, or nonreligious, sentimentality of my atheist and agnostic friends. By all means, let me meet them on their own grounds and agree to draw only logical conclusions from the demonstrable facts of the precision sciences. The sciences have uncovered a superabundance of independent evidence for the existence of God. There is no necessity for a "leap of faith" in order to affirm God's existence, once one looks without prejudice at the hard facts in the very structure of reality, and is able to reason about those facts logically. The evidence for God's existence is overwhelming, and we can ignore it only on pain of lowering our bucket into an empty well. The recognition of God's existence is *categorically essential* to a rational philosophy of life, there being no alternative to it but intellectual suicide and despair.

Not that I would diminish the value of faith. Whether one holds genuinely to his affirmation of God through faith, or arrives at it primarily through a knowledge of the structure of the universe, is not worth debating if his affirmation of God makes him a better and more devoted person. But in my business as a philosophy teacher, I always encounter people who say that they would like to believe in God, but can't, and I am addressing myself in this book primarily to them. The proposition that God exists (when He is rationally defined) cannot but demand assent from the objective and rational mind.

However, one reservation is in order here. There is an important psychological fact that should not be overlooked. Communication of an effective proof of God to the doubter presupposes that he is unsatisfied with his doubt and is looking for a way out of it. Of course, the atheist would say that I am expecting him to assume a prejudice against his own sincere position, which can hardly be fair. And that is in a manner of speaking exactly what I am doing. For it happens to be a fact that the person who feels willfully indisposed towards God will never see any significance in any kind of proof of God, no matter how compelling the objective facts and logic in the case may be. In the matter of personal care for God (or the absence of it), I cannot presume to offer something meaningful to the *professional* atheist who is predisposed to reject any reasoned case for God, regardless of what its argumentative merits may be. The hard facts and logical reasons for God's existence will say nothing to the individual who is by decisive personal preference and emotional disposition an atheist in heart and mind. It is imperative to realize that objectivity in such a question as God's existence, and its implications for man's destiny, is impossible without the cooperation of the willing and feeling subject.

5

Objective truth in some ways must bind, delimit, and govern the subject even when the subject closes his eyes to the very truths that his existence depends upon. But even the most obvious facts are not compelling to closed or distorted minds. No truth can be seen clearly by those who decisively do not want to see it and deliberately refuse to open up to it. Jesus did not speak empty words in alluding to those who have eyes but will not see, and to those who have ears but will not hear.

One apodictic truth that the sciences are categorically dependent upon is the reality of order in the universe. If nature did not operate in a predominately lawful and ordered way, there would be only chaos with nothing constant, and hence no predictability, which is precisely what makes the sciences possible. What is more, it is this selfsame predictability (predicated on nature's laws plus man's ability to look openly inward) that makes personal identity, integrity, sanity, and a sense of dignity possible. In a chaotic world without even a basic order, no one could ever establish and sustain a sense of identity, integrity, and sanity. For without that basic predictability of how nature will operate, and of how oneself and other human beings will behave, the cultivation of that *inner* order conducive to positive identity and integrity would never be possible. Even so, I am familiar with numerous scientists and philosophers who in the name of objectivity consistently refuse to acknowledge that there is any *necessary* or reliable order whatever in nature. But any practical man will readily observe a blatant inconsistency between the theory of these intellectuals and the order which they personally demand of the world *in practice*. Such individuals can maintain their own identity and sanity only by taking the same advantage of that very order in nature from which the rest of us mortals derive our livelihood and sense of joy in living. I can hardly count the occasions when I have heard philosophers and would-be philosophers make ordered arguments to prove that there is no real order in the world. And once one does succeed in convincing such persons that there is order in the world, they then proceed to argue that order only proves that there is order; it does not prove that any order is necessary or nonaccidental, or that a Cosmic Agent exists who can perform the act of ordering the universe. I find it downright curious, that so many university intellectuals try to make ordered arguments to prove that there is no essential order in the universe, or no reason for order. One explanation for this, I suspect, is that in a universe constituted ultimately of meaningless "chance" no one should have to be burdened with the necessity to face definite and binding obligations to either himself or God. A pure-chance world would guarantee an ultimate escape from all burdens and duties.

In this book, I hope to demonstrate that the essential aspects of reality in both nature and human nature cannot possibly be derived from chance, nor be reduced to chance, nor be made intelligible and meaningful by any theory of chance. The only ultimate alternative to God is consummate absurdity, which to the rational mind is no viable alternative at all. It is hopelessly suicidal reasoning to try to show rationally that reality is ultimately irrational. No one can give a logical reason to argue that reality ultimately is devoid of logical reason. There is no value in arguing that nothing in the universe is essentially and permanently valuable. Nor can the voice of love (the kind of love that acts responsibly to enrich, propagate, and conserve its own sacred meaning) ever argue that reality ultimately is loveless. Certainly, responsible *care* cannot argue, as atheism does, that reality ultimately is devoid of care (God).

There are no rational or loving arguments against God. There are rational and loving arguments against irrational and loveless definitions and concepts of God; but, if one's concept of God is empirically and logically plausible, i.e., if it will hold up under all logical and factual analysis, then certainly, one can find in his vision of God an inviolable foundation for abiding hope and love, which unquestionably is an objective need in our lives. Nonetheless, finding a foundation for this hope presupposes care. Any objective truths about the nature of care, the necessity for care, and the intrinsic value of constructive care can be found only by the individual who does care. Quite simply, the atheist who is in love with his atheism will remain an atheist. A person has to care for God, feel a need for Him, see the inadequacy of what atheism has to offer, and be reaching out for God before he can ever find Him. Belief in God is belief in the ultimate dominion of reason and ideals in the universe. Belief in God is belief in the sacredness of life and the permanent conservation of its intrinsic values. Belief in God is belief in the ultimacy of care.

The argument that our lives are grounded in a divine and permanent care always will prove meaningless to whoever will not care for such care. Because of the very nature of divine care, no one can approach the question of its ultimacy and dominion in the universe objectively without himself caring. An objective inquiry into the nature and value of care presupposes care, requires care, and is impossible without caring. A careful faith in God is faith in the ultimate value and demands of righteous care. Care is discovered only by care. Care is upheld and necessitated by care. And the value of care is accessible to the understanding only through care. In questions of love or care, objectivity must transcend that vapid neutrality or "impartiality" of *scientism*—that uncaring kind of agnosticism which, because of its very lack of care, can gain no significant insight into the final nature and value of care in the world. The road to understanding the ultimacy of care in the world (God) is closed to those who will not care to share this understanding. Interest is essential to take this road. *Disinterest* moves one nowhere in the search for God, anymore than it can move a man in a quest for a woman. That a man can find meaning in God without caring for Him is objectively as impossible as his finding meaning in a woman's love without caring for a woman. In fact, there never is any experience of positive meaning in life at all except where there is positive care. Without some positive care in the spirit, there can be no receptacle for positive value or meaning.

In his "disinterest" and "detachment of conviction," even the scientist in his laboratory can never discover anything worth knowing except insofar as he cares to discover, acts to discover, and has faith that his care will lead to the discovery of something worth caring about. It is hardly logical, and neither is it empirically sensible, to suppose that a seeking care can find its fulfillment in empty "chance" data in the world that are in and of themselves devoid of reason and purpose. To make sense, any concept of objectivity must presuppose a complementarity between intelligibility in the objective data of the world and man's quest for intelligibility in the world. It is unthinkable that we can find reason and purpose informing the objective data of the world, if those data are in fact destitute of reason and purpose. Either the universe is purposefully designed in such a way as to bring life into existence, and to provide the basic wherewithal to meet the needs of life, or it is not. There can be no gainsaying the fact that human beings have essential life needs, which could never possibly be fulfilled in a universe not designed to meet life needs. Man unquestionably has a need to find meaning in his life. He has a need to discover intrinsic values, and to find ways and means to conserve those values. Certainly, our needs are doomed to frustration unless we exist in a universe that ultimately is informed with the kind of meaning and value that is necessary to fulfill our needs. Any notion of objectivity is self-defeating if it presupposes, as the atheists would have it do, that the objective facts of the world outside of man's mind are inherently uninformed with meaning and value. Surely I need not labor the point, that no subject can find *objective* meaning in merely happenstance "facts" that by definition have no meaning, except what this or that subject arbitrarily reads into them in passing. If we study the history of science, we find that the greatest scientists invariably have insisted on the categorical necessity for faith in the intelligibility of the universe. Which means, according to creative thinkers in the class with Galileo, Copernicus, Newton, Kepler, Maxwell, Schrödinger, Compton, and Millikan, that the universe itself must be rationally designed or else man could never experience a rational relationship with it. It is unimaginable that we could discover rational meaning in the world if there were no rational meanings informing its structure. How, indeed, could we ever find rhyme or reason in a merely happenstance order inherently empty of rhyme and reason? Meaningful care is always *for* something of value, and is itself constituted of value. An objective person cannot rationally care for carelessness. He cannot sincerely claim to find reason and meaning in a concept of objectivity that would remove all reason and meaning from the objective realities of the universe. The one thing that all great scientists have insisted on is that the universe is constituted of a uniformity, symmetry, and reasoned structure that is complementary to man's need and quest for rational meaning in the world. No objective person would ever presume to find meaning in an objectively meaningless world. Nor would he presume to sustain any hope in a world defined as essentially hopeless.

In this work, I begin with one elementary fact. To put it simply: no rational person can *care* for a concept of objectivity that when taken seriously would frustrate *care*. All meaning and value in life ultimately is located in care, and can be sustained only by care. No person could sustain his care in a universe "designed by chance" to stymie and mock his care. One need not care for the "objectivity" of the atheist, which in essence would mock our very need and care.

Objective care is constituted of intrinsic value and meaning and is the very entelechy of life. That an original universal carelessness somehow accidentally produced beings who care is a useless notion that honors no fact or need. We can afford to settle for nothing less than a philosophy of the primacy and permanency of *care* in the very heart of reality. Neither in his scientific nor religious life can a man function effectively to fulfill his real life needs without care. Truly objective care is the will to discover, conserve, and propagate the intrinsic values and meanings of life.

Real objectivity is care; it is care that is both rational and faithful to real needs. Objectivity does not consist only in observing bald facts and describing them. It consists in seeking value and meaning inherent within the facts that is complementary to our life needs. A point I shall reiterate in this book is that a need is always *for* something, and for something of value. Otherwise, it is inconceivable that one could have any need for it. Theists and atheists alike agree that objectivity is a concern for the truth. But my primary premise in this book is that meaningful and valuable objectivity can consist only of *care* for the *value of needed* truth.

As much as anyone else, most atheists would insist that man needs the truth. But I think a practical man would insist that we need only honor those truths, or accept as ultimate truth, that which will safeguard, honor, and meet our needs.

The concern for reason and facts without positive faith (i.e., *care* for truths of *value*) is like having an automobile with no place to go. Likewise, a professed concern for the value of objectivity without a positive faith in the reasonableness and value of ultimate truth, is like needing to go somewhere with no way to go. Either without the other is scientism or blind religiosity. By definition, agnosticism can never fulfill man's need to discover divine care. For the agnostic simply refuses to care; he is waiting for care to impose itself on him through "overwhelming facts," which is purely a waste of time, since in fact, no truth can ever overwhelm any mind which refuses to *care* for the facts, or to be governed by the meaning informing the facts. Jesus once implied that the kingdom of heaven cannot be taken by force. But neither can it be taken by doubt. All the evidence of care in the universe cannot fulfill the spiritual needs of a person who will not care for such care. And this certainly is dependent on one's will. Facts without a will to care for value and meaning in the facts is like foods without a hungry stomach to turn and digest them. And equally, care for facts without value to meet needs is like a hungry stomach with an empty cupboard. Objective understanding never depends on bald facts and logical abstractions alone. Objective proof always hinges on the receptiveness of a seeking and careful mind. Openness of mind, as defined by the agnostic with no care for the value of needed truths, clearly can be of no value to a human being because it is the absence of care for value. Openness of mind is of value only when it is openness to truths of value that can fulfill need. Surely, no man's mind need be open to ideas that would needlessly depress or diminish him, or ruin him. Neither need he open his mind and heart to any kind of philosophy that would cause needless suffering or harm.

"But I must say," said a critical colleague, "that your notion of objectivity is a *petitio principii*; you are using the things that you personally care about to justify the things that you care about, which is purely subjective."

Such an accusation is an oversimplification of my position, since it is my purpose in this work to set forth a position that can do justice to our real life needs as human beings. But my response to his Latin is *pur et simple*: there is no need for either objectivity or subjectivity except insofar as it can meet real life needs. There is no need to believe what one does not need to believe, and no need to know what one does not need to know. And certainly, there is no need to believe that ultimate truth is not worth knowing.

As a matter of objective fact, care is always an expression of purpose. That any scientist or theologian can discover a meaningful truth that serves no purpose whatever, or is informed with no purpose whatever, is objectively impossible. No one can find meaning in a bald datum that is totally uninformed with reason and purpose. It is only reason and purpose (care) that can inform any datum with meaning. An objective person can care meaningfully for a datum (fact, truth, or reality) only if that datum is *informed* with some care, or is an expression of care.

Throughout the present work, I shall assume that the concept of objectivity must be utilitarian to humanity. The idea that a person should study the world scientifically, but shun his own need and desire to make sense out of it; or, that he should not care

11

to find in its structure the real *meaning* essential to fulfilling his real life needs, is to say the very least a specious and questionable way to define intellectual objectivity. It happens to be an objective fact that any scientist is primarily a person, and only secondarily a scientist. As a person, any scientist has aspirations, ideals, and needs that always pervade his motives, objectives, and methods in whatever scientific work he is doing. That any person, in the name of science, can sensibly ignore the objective truth about his needs in the world is impossible, Nobel Prize winning scientists notwithstanding. Our real life needs as persons are objective facts, which no sensible philosophy of objectivity can overlook in the idolatrous name of science. The needs of a person are just as much a part of objective reality as are the "impersonal" facts of physics and mathematics. The idea that a person can construct a sound philosophy of science irrespective of his care to find a rationale for his existence in the world is plainly demonic. A human being's need to find a rationale for the existence of the universe, and for his life within it, is an *objective* fact that must be included in any sensible philosophy of science. What is more, a person's need to find sacred values in life, and reliable ways and means to permanently conserve them, is also an objective fact that it is witless for any scientist to ignore. Any intellectual or technical discipline must exist to fulfill personal *needs*, or else there is admittedly no need for it to exist at all. Precisely the same must be said for objectivity. Objectivity must center around the objective truths and facts about needs, and ways and means of fulfilling those needs, or there is no need for objectivity whatever.

In this book, I shall argue that *the ultimate objective truth in the universe is care.* Namely, the divine care of God, for whom we do, in objective fact, have a real need, and for whom, in objective truth, we ought to care.

There is no need for a definition of objectivity that would in any way neglect, ignore, or abuse real life needs.

To be sound, any true philosophy of objectivity must be grounded in an awareness of essential life needs, and in the liberal use of imagination, creative speculation, and faithful action to fulfill those needs.

That the ultimate criterion of objectivity is *need* is a fact which I wish to bring to the attention of the traditional theologian, as well as to the ice-hearted agnostic scientist. History certainly has proven that religious faith without critical objectivity can be blind, incompassionate, dangerous, and downright destructive. I believe that the carelessness of professional agnosticism is fulfilling no real life need whatever. But it is unquestionable that much religiosity in the world not only is ignorant of some of our most essential life needs, but is contemptuous towards them, and abusive of them— even in the name of God. Agnosticism and atheism offer humanity no hope. Professional pessimism is devoid of truly objective care. But then, the same can be said about much religion that is practiced in the world today. Much religious life is shallow, cheap, and lacking in the kind of care that is objective and constructive. Just as care ought to be objective (grounded in an enlightened awareness of our real life needs), so must the definition of objectivity be grounded in need, and be careful about need.

No matter what kind of truth we are talking about (be it aesthetic, scientific, or moral truth), there ultimately can be only one practical and intelligent criterion for defining any value-judgment terms, and that criterion is *need*. All meaningful value-judgment terms always come in opposites, e.g., true-false, wise-foolish, just-unjust, reasonable-unreasonable, beautiful-ugly, constructive-destructive, good-evil, etc. In any instance of making value judgments, we can make them objectively only insofar as we make them on the basis of an understanding of our real life needs, and the needs of others. By an objective definition, good is that which fulfills real life need, and evil is that which stymies or frustrates real life need. For otherwise, what need is there for the good? The greatest good is that which fulfills the greatest need. The supreme moral ideal is: every individual ought to seek that alternative to act on that will bring about the greatest amount of need fulfillment, and the least amount of need frustration, into life as a whole (i.e., into the life of God, man, and all other creatures) on a long range basis. Needless to say, it often is difficult for a person to find out, in a given complex situation, what that alternative is; and once finding it out, one may experience extreme difficulty in acting on it in practice. But the difficulty of implementing the ideal in action does not undermine the validity of it in principle. We can never trust or respect any individual who does not affirm this ideal, or who does not try to meet the real needs of others while acting to gratify his own personal desires. Wise behavior is that which fulfills real need, or else what need is there to be wise? Foolishness is foolishness because it stymies or frustrates real need. For if this were not the case, what need would anyone have not to be foolish? Beauty is beauty because it fulfills real life need; or else, what need has anyone for the experience of beauty? Ugliness is that which mocks or abuses need. Reasonable behavior fulfills need, and unreasonable behavior foils it, etc.

Of course, a little explanation is in order if one is to argue that need also must be the criterion for defining truth and falsehood. For example, someone might object: "But what if a person is caught in a burning house under conditions that make it impossible for him to escape, and he is doomed to die? In this case, Is it not obvious that he does not need to die, but the *truth* is he is going to die anyhow, and does this not prove that the truth does not necessarily correspond with our needs?"

Answer: there is unmistakably a need for reality to be structured in such a way that evil is possible as well as good, for reasons that I shall explain in the chapter on Evil. We often are caught in situations where our immediate needs cannot possibly be fulfilled by the conditions that prevail. But ultimately, or on the long range view, there is a perfectly cogent explanation of the need for such situations to be possible, just as there are reasons to explain why there ultimately is always a way to meet our need to eventually get out of an evil situation. If the fact is certain that a man is accidentally going to burn to death in a fire, then he has to accept that fact; he needs to face the situation as it actually is. But at the same time, he needs to believe that reality is structured in such a way as to guarantee that ultimately he can escape from the situation that is presently stymieing his needs. Certainly, he does not need to be done in forever by a fire; no one has a need to be destroyed, or to be transformed into a non-person, for there is intrinsic value in being a person; and, as I shall show in the chapters on Evil and on Jesus, there is a need for the conservation of that value, and a need to believe in it. No need whatever can be fulfilled by believing that ultimate truth is needless or blindly structured incompatibly with our needs.

Note that I am using the word "need," not "desire." We often need things we do not desire, just as we often desire things we do not need. There has to be an objective criterion we can use (or, ideally, that an enlightened person would use) to distinguish between justifiable and unjustifiable kinds of desires. That criterion

14

is *need*. An alcoholic may feel that his dominant need is for another drink; whereas in fact, that is only his desire, and he is confusing his subjective desire for objective need. What he really needs is to unshackle himself of his habit of drinking, in order that he can regain his self-possession and restore his ability to act effectively to fulfill his life. Fulfilling one's life means fulfilling one's needs.[3] Hitler desired to extinguish the Jewish people, but he did not need to do it, and the Jewish people did not need to be annihilated. By acting on such a morbid and unwise desire, Hitler ended up stymieing his own fulfillment and that of untold numbers of others. All along, reality was structured in such a way as to guarantee that he would fail in such a pursuit. A teacher may desire to fail a student who has the audacity to question the validity of his judgment when he is in error, but the student does not need to be failed in such case, and the teacher does not need to be so insecure. Here is a certainty we can depend upon: when we act contrary to our own real life needs, we inevitably suffer needlessly for it. To be intelligible, philosophy must categorically presuppose that the ultimate principles of reality are the kind of principles that are *needed*, that ultimate truth is informed with reason and purpose, and is keyed with the capacity to meet the needs of life. We must presuppose this not only for the sake of intelligibility, but for the sake of our hope and joy, that we may feel truly at home in the universe instead of like aliens.

Many philosophers and psychologists object to need as the ultimate criterion for judging objectivity. But this is precisely the reason that so many modern ideologies fail to help mankind: they isolate ultimate "truth" from need—and consequently perpetuate all kinds of useless and harmful ideas in the name of "truth."

Let me make one point clear right now, however: I do not wish for my position to be equated with the pragmatic romanticism of the American philosopher William James. Someone put the question to James: "Why do you believe in God? Is it from some argument?" And James responded: "Emphatically, no." Then the person asked James: "Or [do you believe] because you have experienced His presence?" And James answered, "No, but rather because I need it, so that it 'must' be true."[4]

James' response to these questions has been severely criticized by sceptics, and in some respects quite realistically and rationally. I do not want my philosophy of need to be compared with James',

15

insofar as he pragmatically denied that there are any ultimate or intrinsic needs and values that human beings can have definite knowledge of; and thus, in effect, he ended up equating real needs with mere wishful thinking. A very tart criticism has been levied against James' view by the American philosopher Dickinson S. Miller. Says Miller:

As for "I need it, so that it 'must' be true," he who feels that because we need something we shall have it has not learned the first lesson of philosophy, even the first lesson of life. It is just because our desires and preferences do not of themselves magically control reality, and because our fate depends on steering aright with reference to reality, and not to dreams, that we must learn in framing our conception of things, as in our grade of civilization we have not yet learned, to keep our eyes on fact alone. "The will to believe" is the will to deceive oneself; it is the will to regard something as true which is doubtful. . . .

It is easy to imagine that, because we are availing ourselves of "the right to believe" only in the supernal realm of religion, of something behind the scenes and higher than the affairs of daily life, these considerations do not apply, that we are escaping from the sphere in which we have to be careful as to fact; that here we are at a place where our assumptions can do us good but cannot do us harm. How remote from the truth! It is just because religious faith is to affect our action that James would have us accept it. *How* is it to affect our action? That depends wholly on the particular belief we form. The conception of God, for instance, that we have actually formed in our strand of civilization has largely tended to confirm the Tradition of Passivity, the fatalism of the multitude, the assumption that the course of events is exclusively in the hands of God. "The longer I live," said an Archbishop of Canterbury, "the more it is borne in upon me that we cannot modify the course of history." "God's mighty purpose," says another Archbishop of Canterbury, "does not depend on our paltry contribution. It is for our sakes . . . that He invites us into the fellowship of His activity." At a peace conference, for example, it is then only for the spiritual education of the participating statesmen that God has invited them there to take part; they cannot modify the course of history; His mighty purpose does not depend on their paltry contribution. Our conception of God does profoundly affect our intelligence, our sense of the need of learning how to control life, and our actual fate. James' own belief was not the above, but his belief did, I think, tend to mislead life.

To be sure, any belief that leads us to form definite expectations which continue to be realized is to that extent true. The question is, how great is that extent; how much of the belief is proved true by the corroborations that occur? A true element in belief, encouraged by such confirmation, may carry on its shoulders a large and a harmful element of untruth associated with it. The pressing *need*, in the interest of human fate, is to get the truth in the faith dissociated from the untruth.[5]

I am quite aware of how deceptive, unrealistic, and naive can be "the will to believe," of which Miller spoke. But it should be obvious that Miller himself is unconsciously appealing to *need* as the ultimate criterion for distinguishing between good and bad concepts of objectivity and truth. Certainly, he is trying to show the harm that can be done by the "will to believe" when it is based on false notions about God, human nature and needs, freedom of the will, history, and man's role in influencing his own destiny. In essence, he is objecting to James' "will to believe" on the grounds that it can result in naive beliefs that do "harm." Now clearly, when Miller uses the word "harm," is he not implying that some need has been violated or abused? Where no need has been violated or abused, has any real harm been done?

Miller alludes to the "harmful element of untruth" of certain kinds of ideas that have no foundation in anything except the will to believe. Certainly, this is not my viewpoint at all; for I must insist, contrary to James, that there are *intrinsic* needs in life and nature, and such needs are *objective truths* or *facts*; they are intrinsic elements of objective reality—indeed, are the most *important* truths or facts that we can ever understand. Those needs to which I refer are inestimably vital truths or facts which only spiritual pikers can equate with capricious desires or mere wishful thinking. As one of James' harshest critics, Miller must himself agree with this, as I have indicated by italicizing his own repeated use of the word "need." It is unfortunate, however, that he himself is confused as he is unable to see a distinction between "desires and preferences" and real "needs" (his own words). While attacking James' appeal to ambiguous and undefined need, Miller is himself unable to criticize intelligently without appealing directly to need. He is apprehensive about "the will to regard something as true which is doubtful"; but manifestly, he is himself dependent upon need as the criterion for distinguishing between what is to be sensibly doubted and what is to be sensibly believed.

If the same question put to James were put to me: Why do you believe in God? Is it because you have experienced His presence;

or is it from some argument? My answer would be: "Emphatically *yes*"—and that argument I shall put forth in this book.

I also want to avoid having my viewpoint equated with that of Blaise Pascal. In his book *Pensées (Thoughts)*, this seventeenth century Frenchman treats the affirmation of God's existence empirically as merely a practically wise gamble ("wager"). According to Pascal, we can never, by reasoning, really *know* that God exists, for there simply can be no way to rationally discern his existence as a fact. In essence, Pascal is saying: "Try believing, it will make you happier; it feels good, fulfills your heart's longings; and anyway, what can you lose in this life by believing if it turns out afterward that you were wrong?" Pascal insists that there is everything to gain by having faith that God exists, and nothing to lose. Yet quite illogically, he also insists that there is a *risk* in believing because of the certainty of what can be lost if God does not exist. He speaks of the uncertainty of what can be gained because of the uncertainty of God's existence. Going around in a circle, he says:

If there is a God, He is infinitely incomprehensible. . . . He has no relation to us. We are therefore *incapable of knowing* either what he is or if he is. This being so, who will dare to undertake to resolve this question? Not we who have no relation to Him. . . . God is, or He is not. . . . Your *reason* is no more offended in choosing one than the other. . . . If we must not act except on a certainty, we ought not to act in behalf of religion, for religion is not certain. . . . *Nothing is certain.* . . . It is not certain that we shall see tomorrow, but it is certainly possible that we may not see it. We cannot say as much about religion. It is not certain that it is true; but who will venture to say that it is certainly possible that it is not true?[6]

I intend no irreverence toward Pascal. He was a very faithful and devoted Christian of substance. But it is impossible to make logical sense out of his reasoning about God's existence since, in his pragmatic position, he cannot avoid contradicting himself time and again. No person with a logical mind can say, "Nothing is certain," and then at the same point argue that he has "wagered for something certain and infinite." There is an unquestionable incongruity between the notions of certainty and risk. If something is certain to happen, or certain to be, then there is no way to argue realistically that it may fail to happen, or fail to be. Moreover, once a person insists that nothing is certain, thereafter he can never speak meaningfully of any certainty at all.

Care in Objectivity

Pascal is famous for his aphorism, "The heart has its reasons which reason knows not"—which is attractive rhetoric, but divides in two the man of reason and the man of feeling. Pragmatism undermines any possibility of religion for the whole man because it simultaneously presumes to doubt what it presumes to affirm. However sincere a Christian, the great French thinker overlooked Jesus' obvious teaching that there can never be any credible questioning of the existence of God. Like James, he is telling us that there is no *truth* about God that can be rationally *known*, as though God is such a bungling Creator that He cannot endow his children with enough intelligence to ever recognize his existence as a logical necessity and a fact.

In "The Sentiment of Rationality" James tells us that

At most, the command laid upon us by science to believe nothing not yet verified by the senses is a prudential rule intended to maximize our right thinking and minimize our errors *in the long run*. In the particular instance we must frequently lose truth by obeying it; but on the whole we are safer if we follow it consistently, for we are sure to cover our losses with our gains. It is like those gambling and insurance rules based on probability, in which we secure ourselves against losses in detail by hedging on the total run. But this hedging philosophy requires that [the] long run should be there; and this makes it inapplicable to the question of religious faith as the latter comes home to the individual man. He plays the game of life not to escape losses, for he brings nothing with him to lose; he plays it for gains; and it is now or never with him, for the long run which exists indeed for humanity is not there for him. Let him doubt, believe, or deny, he runs his *risk*, and has the natural right to choose which one it shall be.[7]

Hence clearly, James as well as Pascal regards the assent to God's existence as a gamble involving a "risk," rather than as an intellectual and moral necessity for the knowledgable man. I must reject both their positions as merely pragmatic and arbitrary, or, as their critics have very wisely put it, as merely "romantic." God is no clumsy second-rate creator unable in his weakness to give us sufficient intelligence to discern his presence in the world. In effect, Pascal and James are admitting that there is no *compelling reason* why we *should* choose to affirm God's existence rather than to be atheists. This admission cannot be allowed by anyone who considers his relationship with God to be a relationship with knowable truth.

19

Even so, when James said, "I need it, so it must be true," he was not really wrong. In the primordial, objective sense of need as I treat it in this book, James was right. It is unfortunate that both he and Pascal never developed a mature insight into the objective nature of need, and never saw need as the ultimate truth at the center of real intellectual objectivity. Thus, they give the crassly pragmatic impression that we must *ignore truth*, or presume not to deal in any definite truth at all, in order to affirm the reality of God's presence in the world.[8]

Pascal and James thus were pikers. If they had resorted to something more substantial than mere desires or expedience, then they would have achieved philosophical coherence and truth. They did not claim enough for the reality and urgency of need. In denying that the ultimate principles of reality can be known, they discredited both the capacity of God's mind and man's. Consequently, instead of taking an effective stand in behalf of our real intellectual and moral needs, they actually belittled them.

Professional atheists and agnostics regard the need to care for the ultimacy of care in the universe as intellectually and morally irrelevant. In the following chapters, let us examine the broad structure of reality, to see what evidence there is of *care* informing the order of things in the world.

2

Care in Atomic Action

Anything as well ordered and perfectly created
as is our earth and universe must have a Maker,
a Master Designer. Anything so orderly, so perfect, so precisely balanced, so majestic as this
creation can only be the product of a Divine
Idea. . . . There must be a Maker; there can be
no other way.

Wernher von Braun

I LIVE IN A TWO STORY, red klinker brick, English Tudor
home. Not only is its beauty precious to me, but I feel altogether inadequate to express my appreciation for the reason and
purpose informing the laws of nature that hold it together. It is
inconceivable to me that so flimsy an idea as mere "chance" could
create and sustain this shelter for my family.

Can anyone conceive of my house having come into existence,
or having evolved into what it is simply happenstance, i.e., "accidentally" or "by chance," without any guiding reason or purpose?
Literally, can anyone sincerely *imagine* my house existing without
some designer planning it and some builder constructing it? Of
course, no one can imagine this. That the house I live in could
have come into being happenstance is absolutely inconceivable,
both theoretically and practically. When pressed with hard facts,
even my most devoutly atheistic friends have acknowledged that
my house cannot possibly be a product of blind chance. By their
own admission, they cannot conceive of such a fine piece of architecture coming into existence without an architect designing and
building it for a reason and purpose. Yet, how strange it is, these

21

same atheists say that they *can* conceive of the *universe* having evolved into what it is just "accidentally by chance." Architecture is a practical, precision science. I have never met an architect who would claim that a sound structure in a house or building can be reliably left to mere chance. A building that is not informed with laws and principles (i.e., sound architectural reasoning and purpose) simply cannot be depended upon to stand and to endure stress. The universe is an infinitely more complex, organized, and majestic work of architecture than is my little brick house. The structure of my house is informed with a few physical, architectural, and engineering principles and laws. It is informed with simple laws of geometry, mechanics, electricity, etc. How much more ordered the universe is has been proven beyond reasonable doubt by the precision sciences of mathematics, astronomy, astrophysics, and many others.

The study of the universe has discovered hundreds upon hundreds of laws of nature, all of which are organized, unified, and ordered to an unspeakably high degree of logical harmony or perfection. All of these laws are logically interrelated in such a way as to constitute and sustain a world order that obviously is a Rational System. Such a System cannot possibly be accounted for by the mere Principle of Blind Chance, which really is no principle at all.

According to most atheists, anyone must grant the reality of the precision sciences, i.e., that no one could study the laws of nature unless there were in fact laws of nature operating in us, and around us, to be studied. Yet, atheists state that order in the universe only proves that there is order in the universe; it does not prove that there is some Cosmic Agent who can guarantee order by always performing the act of ordering the world. Admittedly, all this order in the world is something our very lives and sanity depend upon; nonetheless, the atheists tell us, it ultimately is something that cannot be depended upon at all, for the simple reason that it is not there for any necessary reason or purpose, but is only an accident, offering no solid basis whatever for hope.

The arbitrary position of the atheist is shown in his evasion of the simplest facts. The laws of nature cannot possibly be derived from chance. Logically, the only thing that can be inferred from chance is chance, which means nothing definite whatever. As the atheists define it, chance is a mere empty abstraction; chance is not an existing Agent, endowed with God-like creative powers, whereby it could create an ordered universe informed with logical reason. Creation is, in fact, an *act*. But as the atheists define it, it is nothing more than a fuzzy abstraction, and abstractions cannot act. Only an existing agent (an actor) can act; and only a Cosmic Agent, endowed with infinite intelligence (the ability to reason and to act rationally) could conceivably perform the act of creating a universe and inform it with reliable order and predictability. No amount of evasion of facts, nor loose play with logic, can make plausible the notion that reason and purpose can be derived from nothing, or from a jejune abstraction called "chance." In plain truth, reason and purpose can never be found except in an intelligent agent, i.e., a *mind*. In essence, the atheists are espousing what simply can never be logically believed, namely, that all this logical order in the universe, which makes knowledge, identity, and sanity possible, is there without there being the slightest logical *reason* for it to be there, and without it serving any logical *purpose* whatever.

If a person can believe this, then surely, he can believe *anything* he wishes. And if one can believe anything so totally devoid of reason, then certainly he could believe in God if he wanted to, since he would need no logical *reason* to believe in God. For if the universe can exist without any reason whatever, then so can God.

The logical man will ask, How can all this logical order exist in the world without there being even a single *logical reason* why a world should exist? Invariably, my atheist colleagues answer: "Well, that's just the way it is. *Somehow*, things just exist and happen, without there being any ultimate or necessary reason why anything should ever exist or happen."

The atheist reserves this kind of intellectual arbitrariness exclusively as a luxury for himself alone. For certainly, he never will allow me the same privilege. I can indeed say: God can *somehow* exist, for if anything at all can exist inexplicably, then so can God. I have yet to find any atheist who would allow me to intellectually justify belief in God's existence by appealing to the word "somehow." Yet, every atheist I have ever met has insisted that "somehow" the universe was put together logically for no logical reason or purpose—which is an assumption enjoying not a smidgen of empirical evidence or logical support. If a quantum, an electron, an atom, a grain of sand, a human being or a universe could exist

23

accidentally for no reason (which is absurd), then so could God, for that certainly would be no less absurd. If a finite mind can exist "by chance," there is no conceivable reason why an Infinite Mind cannot also "chance" to exist.

In point of fact, there is a logical necessity for an Infinite Mind to exist. The existence of any finite mind that has an origin in time must be contingent and derived; and logically speaking, all derived effects have to be derived from some source, or necessary cause. Which is precisely the point at which atheism collapses logically, since it postulates the existence of a universe constituted exclusively of derived effects, but denies the reality of a necessary source from which such effects can be logically derived. From the standpoint of logic, the only thing that can be derived from nothing is nothing, which really is no derivation at all. A sourceless world of purely contingent or derived effects would be the essence of absurdity. Certainly, such a world can never be offered as a foundation for a hopeful philosophy of life. If the atheists are consistent, they can offer no rationale for any sort of philosophical system whatever. For by its very terms, atheism defines the whole of reality as an accident, which means precisely an effect absolutely devoid of reason and purpose. There can be no logical rationale for the point of view that reality ultimately is devoid of a logical rationale. This is a patent contradiction in terms. A person cannot logically appeal to what he himself insists can never be logically appealed to.

Precisely what is wrong with atheism is its demonic contradiction and despair. Both emotionally and intellectually it leaves us with nothing to appeal to in the crisis of dying, or in the crisis of conserving the sacred values of life. In fact, the end result of the atheistic line of reasoning is that ultimately nothing is sacred. For how, indeed, can a logical person derive the sacred from the assumption that reality ultimately is absurd, that nothing exists that has any intrinsic or eternal value?

Just as finite space cannot conceivably exist without infinite space (Who can imagine an edge to space, beyond which there is no more space?), the existence of a finite mind can be derived only from an Infinite Mind. That a finite space can be derived from utter spacelessness is logically impossible and categorically unimaginable. And we can say exactly the same thing for mind, reason, and purpose. For logically, no effect can be derived from nothing, nor be derived from a cause that has absolutely nothing in common with the effect. A finite mind can never be derived from mindlessness, but only from an Infinite Mind. God must create finite minds by dividing his own Infinite Mind, in the causal process of making others out of Himself. We are made in his image, and on a finite scale we are constituted of the same primordial essences of which He himself is constituted. As God thinks, feels, imagines, remembers, chooses, and acts creatively on an infinite plane, we possess these same capacities and can perform the same acts, but only on a finite basis. All of us have the spark of the divine within us. We are made out of God. We are not, as the atheists so faithfully proclaim, made out of nothing, nor out of dead matter that comes out of nothing "by chance."

We know from common-sense intuition, as well as from logical analysis, that the act of reasoning can be performed only by a mind. An act of reasoning is never performed by nothing. Neither can it be performed by a glob of tissue which, by definition, is constituted of nothing but a massive series of purely coincidental electro-chemical activities totally uninformed with reason and purpose.

Recently in my classroom, I observed an atheist give a lecture on the origin of life in the universe. The young gentleman accounted for the existence of life on earth in the following manner:

The physical sciences have proven that the origin of life probably is traceable to a gigantesque glob of pure hydrogen gas. This globe of gas somehow exploded and set off a physico-chemical (nuclear) process that, given eons of time, eventually created billions of stars and planets. In the early history of the universe there were no planets with conditions on them conducive to life. However, as the ocean waters and the atmosphere of the earth cooled, chemical and physical conditions began to make possible many accidental combinations of atoms, some combining in sufficiently large and unique aggregates as to produce tiny bits of primordial life slime. The terms "primordial slime" simply refer to the use of amino acids in the construction of complex proteins essential to organic matter. As eons passed, the molecules of "primordial slime" accumulated in larger and more organized aggregates until they chanced to produce one-celled animals containing chemical mechanisms for self-sustenance and conservation. By the same process of blind accidentality and survival of the fittest, these one-celled creatures developed a strong capacity to propagate their species through division and segre-

25

gation. Then later, they began to divide and unite into multicellular organisms of a great variety of types. As yet more time passed, they evolved into highly ordered creatures containing a variety of tissues and organs. By chance, mechanisms were developed to produce cooperation between different cells and organs to sustain a functioning nervous system and brain. After many millions of years, accidental combinations of molecules produced tissues and organs of such sophistication that they gave origin to Man, i.e., a being who can refract his environment and cybernate himself.

After this gentleman's lecture in the class, the students and I put several questions to him about the nature of a person or human being. His answers clearly indicated that, by his definition, a person is nothing but an exceedingly intricate conglomeration of atomic accidents that somehow, after untold numbers of chance mutations in the evolution of organisms, has come to produce thoughts, feelings, reasons, and purposeful acts. To him, mind is purely chemical; the study of mind is only the study of the more sophisticated or complex processes of organic chemistry. The original atomic forces of the universe are "generated accidentally out of nothing by chance." These forces are categorically blind and impersonal. They know nothing at all about what they are doing and do not care. But "somehow," as the result of billions of years of chance occurrences in the Great Cosmic Accident, this blindness has produced that rare and strange phenomenon we call a human being, or a creature who cares.

To sum up, the young atheist was saying in effect: universal purposelessness has "somehow" accidentally produced purpose; universal lifelessness has "somehow" accidentally produced life; and universal meaninglessness has "somehow" accidentally produced meaning.

That this is the atheistic viewpoint became unmistakably clear as the young gentleman responded to my questions in particular. I should like to use his name for the above quote, but cannot, for to do so without his permission would be unethical. There is no problem, however, since it is readily documentable that his way of thinking represents that of the orthodox atheistic viewpoint in biology today. The most up-to-date and influential presentation of the atheistic position is found in the writings of the French biochemist Jacques Monod, whose book *Chance and Necessity* I shall review at length in Chapter 8 the present work. Monod specifically tries to prove that meaning ultimately is generated by blind chance out of utter meaninglessness, life out of total lifelessness, and purpose out of total purposelessness. But this viewpoint certainly is not unique to Monod. Rather, it is the position of atheistic materialism in general, which is evident in the writings of the most influential atheist philosophers and biologists in the western world, e.g., Bertrand Russell, George Gaylord Simpson, and Julian Huxley. Huxley insists that Man is a being of purpose, but that he has originated purely by chance in an inherently purposeless world order. Purpose "does not enter into the basic machinery of the evolutionary process," and consequently, "God is no longer a useful hypothesis." Setting forth atheism as a religion, Huxley declares: "For my part, the sense of spiritual *relief* which comes from rejecting the idea of God . . . is enormous," and "God . . . must be abandoned if further religious progress is to be made."[1]

Now, any thinking individual must ask, Does this atheistic concept of the creation of life in the world really make sense?

Before answering this question, one first has to ask and answer one of the most fundamental of all philosophical questions, namely, What is it that makes something make sense? Certainly, there must be some objective criteria for making valid distinctions between viewpoints that make sense and viewpoints that do not. I submit to my reader that what makes something make sense is its having a *rationale*. If something exists, its just being there *de trop* does not make it make sense. In order for it to make sense, its being there must have a *rationale*. If something happens, the event's just occurring *de trop* does not and cannot make sense. When something happens, what makes it make sense is the fact that the event has a rationale. And of what does a rationale consist?

A rationale must consist of three things: (1) a reason, (2) a purpose, and (3) a cause. If something exists, its being makes complete sense to us only if we can find a reason for it to be, and find some purpose with which it is informed, or which it serves. If we can see no reason for it to be there, then *eo ipso*, its being there cannot seem reasonable; and, if we can see no purpose in its being there, then *eo ipso*, its existence seems purposeless, which is the very essence of absurdity or gross senselessness in both our intellectual and emotional life. In addition to having a reason and purpose, an effect makes sense to us only if it has a discernible logical cause.

27

Logic demands that there be two types of effects in reality: (1) effects which have causes that precede them in time (these are commonly labeled contingent or derived effects), and (2) effects which exist immutably and necessarily, i.e., the things that are *essential* to an intelligible world order and simply cannot fail to be. These latter effects, or phenomena, are necessary because they are logically indispensable to intelligibility, which is simply to say, no logical world order or world view could possibly exist without them. Such effects are commonly labeled as absolutes. These effects have their own built-in cause, which means that their being there is not temporary, not derived, and not dependent upon anything exterior to them or preceding them in time. They have to have always been there, must be there now, and must be there forever; or else, the world would be inherently senseless because, without them, there could be no inherently true criteria for making valid distinctions between necessary and unnecessary behavior, just and unjust motives, true and false ideas and propositions, rational and irrational ways of reasoning, etc. These absolutes are found in the laws of logic, the laws of mathematics, and in the ultimate laws of psychology, ontology, and morality. For example, without such absolutes, moral certainty could never be possible. And if moral certainty was never possible (i.e., if there were no essential or necessary moral ideals inscribed in the Cosmic Scheme of Things), then it would follow logically that there is no ideal that either could or should command anyone's allegiance. Without absolute truths, there could be no necessity whatever. No way of acting would be necessarily justifiable or unjustifiable. No way of thinking would be necessarily rational or irrational. And no way of living would be necessarily any better or worse than any other way of living. In short, in a world without absolutes all judgments and behavior would be purely arbitrary, since there could be no objective basis whatever for making valid distinctions of any kind.

If we took seriously the notion that there are no absolutes, we would end in sheer nihilism, which would leave us no ground whatever on which to objectively defend or refute any viewpoint of any sort. We could make no compelling case for or against anything because no viewpoint could have any basis in *binding* fact or truth. Without absolutes, what *truth* could possibly exist and bind? Without necessary truths, how could we have a meaningful concept of progress, or of moral and intellectual enlightenment? Surely, the concepts of progress and enlightenment presuppose that some ways of living are necessarily better (or worse) than others. And in turn, this presupposes that there are some indisputable facts (objective truths) about human nature and needs, and about the nature of the world, that can be definitely and certainly learned.

All this adds up to say that *beings* and *actions* make sense only if they are produced by, guided by, or informed with some kind of logical reason, purpose, and cause. For example, when I walk into the university auditorium to lecture, my just being there *de trop* does not make sense, either to myself or to the students in the bleachers. The students must find a logical *reason* and *purpose* in my being there, and a reason and purpose for their being there also, before our being there together can make either intellectual or emotional sense. They must connect their being there, and my being there, with some needs and preceding facts (causes) in order for their present moment of experience to make real sense. Only by connecting the effects in their present experience to past facts and needs (as causes of their present behavior) can they integrate the *now* with the *then* to sustain and expand their own identity, integrity, and dignity. In a world without logical connections (causes and effects), and without logical reasons and purposes, personal identity and sanity would be impossible simply because meaningful distinctions would be impossible. No one could distinguish between the past, present, and future, nor distinguish between himself and others. Neither could he distinguish between truth and falsehood.

What makes something make sense is the material it offers us to answer two questions: Why? and How? Only a reason and purpose can answer the question Why? For example, Why am I writing this book? Obviously, the book is not writing itself. Action never performs itself. To make sense, action has to be generated by an act*or*, for a reason and purpose. Action has to be *for* something, or it makes no sense at all. Making no sense at all means having no rationale whatever.[2]

My reason for writing this book is my awareness of the reality of my *need* (and that of the reader). The reader and I need something of each other, or else writing and reading this book would be needless, thus senseless. A person's purpose is his intention to honor or fulfill some desire or need. Objectively speaking, intelli-

29

gible or sensible purpose is grounded in some real life need. In Chapter One, I mentioned that we sometimes desire what we do not need, just as we sometimes need what we do not desire. Sensible desire is desire that is grounded in real life need, e.g., the need to love and be loved, the need for integrity, reasonableness, creative self-expression, security, etc. Desire that is not grounded in some real life need, or that unjustifiably frustrates, abuses, or violates real life need, is *ipso facto* needless, and hence makes no sense. My *reason* for writing this book is my recognition of my need to think, to express myself creatively, and to organize a coherent philosophy of life. Also, I need to grow by putting myself on the line and inviting friendly criticism of my ideas. I need to have a dialogue of feelings and ideas with both myself and others. I need communion with other minds. My *purpose* in writing this book is to fulfill that need (not to mention the need for royalties, or a little cash wherewithal to more abundantly live).

Then comes the question, How? When it is finished, this book will be an effect in reality. Its existence will make sense because it will have a rationale, which means, it will be informed with the answers to two questions: Why? and How? The *why* I have answered already, in citing the reason and purpose that informs the book's being. And the *how?* It is answered by citing the causes that brought the book into being. I exist, endowed with the capacity to write books. I freely acted to utilize that capacity; I acted on the logical possibility that I could write the book, I gathered the necessary materials (pens, paper, typewriter, desk, etc.), then manipulated those materials, or acted on them, to bring the book into being. Books do not bring themselves into being. Like all derived effects, they are *caused* to come into being. All the factors that entered into bringing the book into being serve to answer the question, How? Thus, the existence of the book makes sense because its existence can be explained. A sensible explanation consists of a logical and factual answer to the questions, Why? and How?

Now, apply the concept of rationale to the criticism of atheism as a philosophy that is inadequate for rational *care*.

All of my students judge me, and they demand that my ideas and behavior in the classroom make sense. Likewise, I judge them, expecting them to make sense in the way they talk and act. In fact, if we are sane we carry this expectation into all of our relations with each other, and into our relations with the world. We expect the world to make sense. We expect the very structure of reality to make sense. Indeed, we have to in order to relate with reality sensibly, to establish and sustain a positive identity and the will to live. I have difficulty understanding how my atheist colleagues (some of whom are the harshest critics I know of human behavior) can make such strenuous demands for sensible behavior from others, while they themselves simultaneously insist that the whole of reality ultimately makes no sense, period. Most of them insist that there are no necessarily valid laws of logic of any kind, that "all things are relative," that there are no absolute or necessary truths at all. Yet, they are always the first ones to point out a contradiction in my thinking; they are the ones to pounce me the hardest when I am "reasoning illogically" on some issue that affects them. Also, they insist that ("since nothing is absolute") no judgment about right and wrong is ever necessarily true. Yet, when one listens awhile to these persons talk, one finds them to be amongst the most vociferous moralizers in the community, with the most condemnatory attitude toward people whose behavior they deem "irrational" or "immoral." If the atheist relativists are right, then what obligation have I to be rational in a world in which nothing can be known about rationality? What obligation have I to make sense in a world that ultimately makes no sense at all? In a world with no necessary truths, there could be no basis for a successful or legitimate defense of my acts. *Prima facie*, in such a world no one either could or should offer a rationale for his behavior.

What have we to gain by presupposing that ultimately everybody loses? What sensible contribution do we make to the conservation of values, if we insist that there are no sacred values that can and should be permanently conserved? What point do we make in insisting that life eventually adds up to no point at all?

Earlier, I alluded to an atheist's lecture on the origin of life in the universe as an accident. In the same speech he addressed himself to human destiny on the long range basis. Said he:

As the impersonal forces of nature brought us blindly into being, they inevitably, with no feeling about it at all, will destroy all of us as they destroyed all those who went before us. The second law of thermodynamics and the principles of quantum mechanics prove that there is a devolutionary process at work in the world. All stars are radiating away their energy, which seems to become more or less randomly dis-

31

tributed throughout space. As current theory has it, our sun eventually will expand enormously and envelop the earth. When that happens, the earth with conditions on it that support life will no longer exist. There can be no life then, just as in the beginning there absolutely was no life. If we are to be realists we simply have to adjust to this fact. We have to accept the fact that life and hope appear only momentarily in a chance world. Then life is inevitably and permanently quenched like a candle light that has burned out forever.

When couched in such artistic rhetoric as this, despair can sound rather charming. Nonetheless, it remains despair and has nothing whatever of positive value to help us fulfill our real life needs. Only the desire for charming rhetoric can be fulfilled by such nonsense; the need for the conservation of life's sacred values can be fulfilled only by the actual conservation of such values, which is impossible without a care that represents its own needs in positive faith and action.

The young atheist's despairful rhetoric readily reminded me of the famed Bertrand Russell. Russell described Man as a mere "accident in a backwater," of such trifling value that it is no wonder he is what "might be expected to result from a fortuitous origin."[3]

Said Russell:

That Man is the product of causes which had no prevision of the end they were achieving; that his origin, his growth, his hopes and fears, his loves and his beliefs, *are but the outcome of accidental collocations of atoms*; that no fire, no heroism, no intensity of thought and feeling, can preserve an individual life beyond the grave; that all the labours of the ages, all the devotion, all the inspiration, all the noonday brightness of human genius, are destined to extinction in the vast death of the solar system, and that the whole temple of Man's achievement must inevitably be buried beneath the *débris* of a universe in ruins—all these things, if not quite beyond dispute, are yet so nearly certain, that no philosophy which rejects them can hope to stand. Only within the scaffolding of these truths, only on the firm foundation of unyielding despair, can the soul's habitation henceforth be safely built.[4]

The above lamentations are found in Russell's heralded essay, "A Free Man's Worship." I should credit him for excellence as a writer, for indeed his essay is a masterpiece of rhetoric, as is often the case in the sophisticated expression of sick despair in modern philosophy. However, the question here is not rhetorical, for fancy rhetoric does not necessarily make sane and wholesome philosophy.

Care in Atomic Action

The real question is: Does the point of view of atheist despair actually make sense? Russell himself insisted that there was no contradiction between his simultaneous emphasis on the necessity to be gloomy and the necessity to be happy (about the same thing). He insisted that we make sense only if we accept affirmatively the "truth" that reality ultimately makes no sense. On a television appearance honoring his ninety-second birthday, Russell declared that "The secret of happiness is to face the fact that the world is horrible." Mrs. Alan Wood, wife of the biographer of Russell, once expressed her opinion that it is unjust for a young person not to have a second chance for happiness after having lost his life in a war. To this, Russell responded: "But the universe *is* unjust. . . . The secret of happiness is to face the fact that the world is horrible, horrible, *horrible*. . . . You must feel it deeply and not brush it aside. . . . You must feel it right here"—hitting his breast—"and then you can start being happy again."[5]

There is a blatant logical and emotional contradiction inherent in this deeply gloomy happiness and deeply happy gloom—hopeless hope—which I shall treat of at length further ahead. But I must agree with Russell's observation that the existence of the physical universe is sustained by atomic action. Today, this fact is commonplace knowledge amongst scientifically educated peoples. Albeit, I see nothing accomplished in the name of good sense to insist that this atomic action is inherently absurd. What it is that makes something make sense, or makes it absurd, is the same thing whether we are speaking scientifically or otherwise. Any phenomenon is absurd that lacks a rationale, that does not lend itself to explainability through factuality and logical reason. The assumption can hardly be taken as scientific that the world's atomic action is generated out of nothing by chance. For as a matter of fact, there is not one iota of evidence that something can be produced by nothing; altogether the contrary, the very idea of it is logically impossible. On the one hand, this type of atheist presumes to deal strictly in demonstrable facts and logical reason. On the other hand, he insists that there ultimately is no rational Scheme of Things whatever, meaning, that there can be no reasons, and no purposes, whereby we can account intelligibly for the production of the universe's energy. The idea that this energy (atomic activity) is generated out of nothing for no reason, and for no purpose, and by no logical cause is not an appeal to science; rather, it is only an intellectual retrogression to magic—and magic of the worst kind. It is a reversion to escapism, to that kind of horseplay with logic that is possible only in the minds of the naive, or else in the arbitrary mentality of those who would take every advantage of a logical world order insofar as possible without having to be bound by the absolute truths and ideals that inform it with God's reason and love.

Granted the idea that something can be created out of nothing, and by nothing, is absurd, What have we to gain by trying to build a philosophy of life on a radically anti-rational concept of reality that would make the accomplishment of a logically coherent viewpoint of the world totally impossible? Such a hopeless endeavor not only would bog us down in intellectual nihilism, but would ground us in demonic moral despair, or else in that hypocritical attitude that can neither truly affirm the ultimate sacredness of life nor truly renounce it. Wherever I turn on the university campus I hear some persons espouse this doctrine of the ultimate absurdity of life, in theory. But under no circumstances will anyone allow me to treat him as though his existence and his rights is nothing but a mere accident or an absurdity. If the metaphysical theory of these professors (and students) was correct, then certainly, there would be no ideals that either could or should command me to treat them decently. Pray tell, how could any intrinsic value in life, or any binding ideals determining how we ought to reason and behave, ever possibly be derived from an absurd accident that is by definition unreasoning and meaningless? How can an objective ideal determining what purposes and meanings we *ought* to choose to live by be derived from a total void of meaning and purpose?

To make sense, any action has to have a rationale. From the standpoint of atheism, the atomic action that sustains the existence of the universe (and all life within it) has no rationale because it is generated out of nothing, is *for* nothing, and is justified by nothing. Some existentialist atheists (such as Sartre and Camus) put an out-and-out *emphasis* on the absurdity of existence, and do not even pretend to find a support for their despair in the sciences. Others (such as Julian Huxley, Bertrand Russell, and Jacques Monod) claim to find in the sciences the justification for their despair, taking it as a scientific "fact" that the world's energy is inherently impersonal and comes out of nothing.

34

"I acknowledge," said an atheist friend of mine, "that there is no logical sense in saying that reality is absurd; however, I have to face the fact that the concept of a God is unempirical, and I must be governed by the facts. It is an obvious fact that the atomic energy in the universe is generated spontaneously. But there is no observable factuality whatever about a so-called God. Consequently, I regard him scientifically as a myth."[6]

Here again, we see an example of pseudo-science in modern intellectual life. My friend is fond of quoting traditional atheism's famous axiom of "spontaneous generation." It is apparent that these words must sound very scientific to some persons. The words are totally lacking in substance, however, if by "scientific" we mean capable of holding up under logical and factual analysis. It certainly is *not* a "demonstrable fact" that the atomic activity in the world is "generated by nothing." For the linguistic pseudo-sophistication of "spontaneous generation," I could readily substitute the terms hocus pocus, or abracadabra. But in this case, I should readily admit that I was dealing in fantasy or magic, not in demonstrable facts or in logic. What I am concerned with in this book is a demonstration of the existence of God in the broadest empirical sense, which is to say, with an argumentation that *makes sense*, by insisting on a *rationale* for the existence of atomic energy, and by respecting the rules of logic. If the reader will bear reiteration, we do not make sense by insisting that atomic energy ultimately does not make sense. *An intelligible philosophy of physics is impossible unless it rests on the foundation of a logical metaphysics, or theory of ultimate reality.* In other words, we have to presuppose that reality ultimately makes sense, or else there is no possible way to logically justify even studying it or talking about it.

In philosophy or physics, there is no getting around the necessity for logic. To be logical, we must presuppose that the ultimate structure of reality is basically logical. Which can hardly be the case if the universe's atomic activity is uncaused and devoid of a logical purpose.

To bring the issue into clarity, I think it is essential to compare the two basic assumptions about atomic energy (in atheism and theism), and then decide which one makes the most sense. In the first view, the atomic action in the universe is generated out of nothing. It is produced happenstance, which means, without a reason, purpose, or logical cause. It therefore has no rationale and is logically absurd. Also, it is aesthetically and morally absurd because it is blind, unfeeling, and devoid of care. None of the atomic action in the universe is *for* anything, for when it produces life at all it does so accidentally, or unintentionally, with no respect for need, beauty, or values. In fact, the universe's energy is inherently indifferent and insensitive to all of our aspirations and ideals. It eventually makes a mockery of all our needs, rides over our most cherished schemes, and reduces us to the same meaningless nothingness out of which it originally created us for no purpose whatever. It creates us absurdly. Then, in the end, it disconnects us from all that we ever did, said, felt or knew. It forever dispossesses us of all the beauties, meanings, and values we have discovered in our lives.

To be sure, there are different versions of atheism, just as there are different versions of theism. Many modern atheists would resent anyone attributing to them a belief in the "spontaneous generation" of the world's energy as I have heretofore described it. Many would say that this view was once widely held, but that it is now passé. Many are doubtful of the assumption that the world's energy is created *ex nihilo*, or indeed, that it ever was created at all. Such atheists would insist that the laws of thermodynamics imply only the transformations of energy into different forms (e.g., electrical energy into heat energy, or heat energy into light energy, etc.). The first law of thermodynamics (the law of the conservation of energy) implies that the energy content of the world is constant, which means that it need never have had an origin in time. As one atheist recently put it to my classes:

There is no problem of explaining how the world's energy was created. The world simply was never created at all. It has just always existed, and evidently always will. The energy is not generated either spontaneously or otherwise, for it simply has always been present in some form or the other. If one allows that energy is the same as action, then when we speak of potential energy we are speaking of potential action. Some people may use the terms "spontaneous generation" to describe the transformation of potential action into literal action. Nonetheless, the intrinsic energy has to have been there originally in a dormant or repressed state; i.e., it has to have been there in some form; it could not have been "generated out of nothing," if we are to assign validity to the first law of thermodynamics—the law of the conservation of energy, which states that energy can neither be created nor destroyed.

Only a day later, another atheist of a different persuasion had the following remarks to offer my class:

The concept of spontaneous generation really is nothing new. Some early Greeks espoused the idea that life is generated spontaneously out of inert matter, and today this interpretation of the origin of life is standard teaching in biology textbooks treating of evolution. Moreover, the theory, in physics, that energy and matter are generated spontaneously out of nothing also is old hat. Today the theory enjoys a sophisticated scientific fortification in the writings of Hoyle, Gold, Bondi, and others. There is not a more beautiful, or simple, cosmogonic system in existence than that of Hoyle. His is called the Steady-State theory of the universe, and it is expressed most intelligibly, indeed just charmingly, in his small volume entitled *The Nature of the Universe*. In this work, Hoyle demonstrates that energy and matter have to be continuously created anew, as old energy and matter go out of existence when they move to great distances away from their source of creation. Hoyle describes the creation of new energy as purely *ex nihilo*. His critics have charged him with ingeniously pushing a theory of no substance. They say he hasn't produced a mite of proof, in the way of experimental evidence leading beyond mere speculation. But then, neither have the protagonists of the Big Bang theory (which states that the world sprang from a primeval glob of hydrogen gas) produced a mite of evidence either. The assumed original state of the Big Bang, and the manner in which it allegedly produced the present cosmic order, is totally immune to our observations. At least, Hoyle has shown that if these hydrogen atoms had existed without a beginning, then they would have devolved totally out of existence long ago. Hoyle has been charged with violating a most fundamental physical law, i.e., the law of the conservation of energy. But the people who made this charge clearly have ignored, or have never read, page 130 of his book. Matter and energy are created at the same rate that they are destroyed. The creation of the world out of nothing therefore jibes perfectly with the "first law."

In 1951, when I was twenty-four years of age, I read Fred Hoyle's book and was fascinated by his ideas and pristine writing style. It is a certain fact that Hoyle espoused a philosophy of creation *ex nihilo*. However, I found nothing in his book to indicate that he believed energy and matter are destroyed. Rather, it appears to me he maintained that matter goes beyond our observation as the universe is forced to expand by the pressures exerted from the creation of new energy inside each galaxy. That is, it becomes lost from our view but is not destroyed.[7] But be that as it may, what I think is important is this: even at that novice stage in my philosophical development I was fortunately not gullible to the ludicrous bad logic of his basic assumption—that something can be created out of nothing, by nothing, and for nothing. For two decades, I watched the popularity of this theory sweep the scientific world, accepted by many scientists who ordinarily speak proudly of their rigorous dedication to thinking with *logic*. The assumption of creation *ex nihilo, pro nihilo* is a logical abomination. Even today, long after the Steady-State theory has lost much of its favor, I find many students appealing to it as a source of support for their anti-Christian philosophy of creation without a Creator.

I have no wish to quibble with the fine distinctions of the atheists over their discrepancies about the duration, or origin, of the universe's energy in time. My point simply quite precisely is this: *all* atheists, whether or not they believe that the universe's energy is generated out of nothing in time, share in common the assumption that *the existence of this energy is natively destitute of a rationale.* That is, *it is inherently barren of reason and purpose.* The existence of the universe is a mere accident, and the origin of man's life within it is only a fluke.

As George Gaylord Simpson (Harvard biologist) put it: "Man is the result of a purposeless and materialistic process that did not have him in mind. He was not planned. He is a state of matter."[8]

This is atheism.

Now, in the second view (theistic), the atomic action in the universe is generated by God, the Cosmic Actor, who has a reason and purpose for generating the action. This viewpoint serves to answer the question, *Why* is the atomic action there? God's reason and purpose in generating this action is to create a universe with living beings in it with whom He can share the experience of love, value, and beauty. Logically, none of these things could ever exist unless God contains their essences in his primordial nature, with which He acts creatively. With his infinite capacity to know and to understand, God can explain *how* it is possible for Himself to exist, to create, and to love. In his mind, He has the capacity to *explain* how existence is possible, and how creative action is possible. Thus, the atomic action in the universe is literally God Acting; it has a rationale; the atomic energy in the world is God's energy. Let us take as an illustration, our sun. I agree with my atheist colleagues that, in the last analysis, the sun as a physical reality is constituted of atomic action. But this action is generated by God, the Supreme Person who is perfectly logical in his scheming and acting, but is also perfectly moral and beautiful. The sun is a manifestation of God's creative power and care. And why? Because God is the ultimate Sensible Being. God is the ultimate source of the generation of values, the conservation of the values of reason, beauty, truth, and love. The sun is a revelation of God's creative action, motivated by his logical, moral, and aesthetic aspiration to propagate, sustain, and enrich life in his Cosmic Order. The laws of nature do not exist happenstance, derived from nothing "by chance," and for no reason or purpose. The laws of nature are an expression of the rational and loving will of God. In their unspeakably majestic and perfectly logical precision, they are nothing less than God Acting. The laws of nature are God Acting to guarantee a dominance of order over disorder, goodness over evil, and beauty over ugliness in the universe He creates.

This viewpoint makes sense because it gives atomic action, the existence of the universe, and the laws of nature a rationale. It makes logical, aesthetic, and moral sense. This is theism.[9]

That a loving, careful, creative, sensitive, reasonable, and productive person who cherishes life should be created by a blind accident and then be reduced to nothing forever by uncaring blind forces—this is a categorically senseless thought.

"I agree to that," said one of my existentialist students. "It is admittedly absurd that a life should come from nothing, and then return to nothing. But then, life is absurd. Your case for God rests solely on the assumption that reality should be basically logical. There is, in fact, tremendous evidence against this. Didn't you read Camus? Didn't you read *The Plague*? Didn't you read Camus' *The Myth of Sisyphus*? Aren't you overlooking all the *senselessness* in the world? You talk about order and unity in the universe, but what about all the disorder, disunity, and the evidence of illogical behavior in the humanity God supposedly created? What about

the needless suffering of the innocent? What about all the pointless failures, frustrations, disappointments, deprivations, bloodshed,
tears, and death? How can you accord all the ugly facts of reality
with your assumption that God is good and logical?"

I find this to be the most common question of agnostic and
atheist colleagues who teach in the university, as well as amongst
students. To this question, I shall set forth a detailed answer in
the chapter on Evil. Presently, let me return to the atheistic dogma
of chance.

If something exists out of absolute necessity (i.e., cannot fail
to exist), then by definition its existence cannot possibly be contingent upon chance. On the other hand, if the existence of some
thing is brought into being in the course of time, then it has to
be *caused*, or else its being is absurd. This is not only a logical
necessity but is an indisputable empirical fact. Many atheist philosophers define a pure chance event as one that is uncaused. But
I issue a challenge to any man alive to show a single instance of
something ever happening without it being caused to happen.
When not defined in this manner, "chance" for most atheists simply is never defined clearly at all.

"But you are overlooking a plain fact," said a student in one of
my classes. "Is it not a known fact that when you flip a coin, the
way it falls is determined by chance?"

"Not so," I said. "According to your definition of chance as an
event uncaused, that would be a contradiction in terms. You used
the word 'determined.' If an event is determined, it must be determined by something (a cause), or it is inconceivable that it could
be determined at all. In fact, the way a flipped coin falls is determined (caused) by a variety of factors; to wit, the law of gravity,
the force of the molecules of gas striking the coin in space (wind-
age), the force with which it is tossed, the manner in which it is
manipulated by the fingers, etc. I once had a friend in Mexico
who possessed extraordinarily sensitive digital nerves. He had practiced for years on how to flip a coin to make it fall as he desired.
He could win an average of nineteen tosses out of twenty, when
betting. "*Amigo*," said he, "chance has nothing to do with my
winning. *I* cause the coin to fall the way it does, in addition to
the laws and forces of nature that influence its trajectory and
motion."

Care in Atomic Action

Sometimes chance is defined as an event occurring without a purpose, i.e., without anyone intending for it to happen. For example, when I recently slipped on ice on the sidewalk and banged my bottom. But in this instance chance means an accident in a legitimate logical sense; it does not mean an event occurring uncaused. There is no incidence in history of an uncaused event. Obviously, a person's inadvertently falling on an icy sidewalk is caused by the fact that the slippery ice makes him lose his balance; whereupon, gravity pulls him down. But even when accidents occur there ultimately must be a reason and purpose *why*, and a logical explanation of *how*, accidents can transpire in the world. *It is not an accident that accidents can happen.* Even an accident must in *some sense* conform to, or be at least an indirect result of, purpose in the Cosmic Scheme of Things. Or to put it differently, logic demands that even accidentality must ultimately have a rationale in the world. There must be a sensible reason why there must be room in the world for the possibility (and indeed, inevitability) that accidents might occur. Even an accident of the most terrible nature must make *some* sense. Otherwise, the victim of it can see no reason whatever behind it, and will be hard put to sustain his sanity and hope in life. A person may become the subject of a truly harsh and traumatic accident, or of too many minor ones in a row. In such cases, if he can see no rationale whatever in accidentality, his emotional organization and will to live may be severely taxed. But here again, I wish to postpone a detailed treatment of this subject until the chapter on Evil.

Presently, I look inside myself and outward towards the world around me. Both inward and outward I see overwhelming evidence of reason and purpose in the abiding structure of myself and the world. I shall now enumerate and analyze some of the basic elements in this abiding structure that cannot possibly be pegged on chance. I hope to show how the simplest facts of history, psychiatry, mathematics, electronics, and genetics refute the atheistic reduction of reality to chance and absurdity. I hope to provide a reasonable proof of Care in the world ground.

3

Care in the Cosmic Order

For the world was built in order
And the atoms march in tune;
Rhyme the pipe, and Time the warder,
The sun obeys them and the moon.

Ralph Waldo Emerson

LOOKING INWARD, I find in myself some abiding knowledge, capacities, and characteristics that do not change. For example, when I awaken in the morning I can readily identify myself, which means, I can use my mental power to recognize who and what I am. I do not mistake myself for another person, nor confuse myself with the subjects and objects around me "out there." I know that in some ways I am caught up in change; I participate in change; I see, and in some ways help to effect, changes that take place inside myself and out there in the world. My moods, plans, ideas, and perceptions in some ways change more or less constantly. However, there are things within me and also things about the world around me that do not change.

There are some abiding characteristics both inward and outward that are not changing now, but will change in the future. But fortunately, there also are some *essences* both within me and without that are not changing now and can never conceivably change in the future. If no such essences existed, we could make no valid judgments at all about what is essentially true and what is not, and what is essentially right and what is not.

42

Care in the Cosmic Order

Without change, we could never grow. Nor could we ever improve the world in any way. To improve ourselves and the world is to in some way change ourselves and the world; it is to remove something from, or add something to, the scene of reality. This is of course impossible without some alterations of reality, or change.

Albeit, there must be something in the world besides change. The pragmatists tell us that the essence of reality is change, that everything in the world is constantly changing, excluding nothing. If this were true nothing could remain what it is, with a definite and fixed nature, unchangingly so, long enough even to be identified as such, or long enough even to have a nature or be what it is. Because of their dogma of the omnipresence of change, the pragmatists insist that *being* is a "semantical illusion," a meaningless word.[1] According to this school of thought, there simply are no beings and essences in reality ever. Reality is constituted exclusively of *activity* that ultimately is governed by nothing but chance. Pragmatism (a professional philosophical ideology) insists that "everything is relative," meaning, in effect, that nothing is ever definite, certain, or absolute.

No logical person can ever take this viewpoint seriously. Nor indeed can the pragmatist himself take it seriously in practice, for Is not he himself, by implication of his own dogmas, insisting that such a viewpoint has no compelling validity whatever? The pragmatist himself insists that no viewpoint is ever essentially, or definitely and certainly, true. All viewpoints are fallible, and no viewpoint is secure. In this case, how can pragmatism itself hold water?

Without change, no one could ever possibly act to enrich or to expand his identity. But if nothing ever abided or transcended change, then nobody could ever identify himself in the first place, nor anything around him. Because it is *being* and *essences* that make identity possible, the very possibility of identity is denied by relativistic theory. If there were no beings and essences, then there could never be anything to be identified. If there were no essences, then nothing could ever be what it is, and be in essence different from other things. Hence, there could be no certain identification, no differentiation, and no distinction of one being from another; and consequently, knowledge would be altogether impossible.

If we do not start a philosophy recognizing and honoring certain beings and essences, then there simply is nothing to start with at all, and consequently, no place to go.

An intelligible philosophy must presuppose that there are essences in reality. All subjects and objects, either concrete or abstract, are made up of essences or they are nothing whatever. Exactly what makes it possible for essences to ingress into, and out of, subjects and objects is a mystery no finite mind can ever explain. We have to leave the explanation of this process to God, in order to believe that life is ultimately intelligible, that it can be fully understood and explained. But we do not ourselves have to be able to explain essences in order to know *that* there are essences.

By definition, an *essence* is a quality whose being is definite, certain, and necessary. The essences of the world are the ultimate, primordial materials out of which things are made, or can be made. They have to have existed always and cannot fail to be, simply because, logically, they cannot be derived from nothing, and cannot be reduced to nothing. Which is to say, that which is essential is that which is not contingent upon accidentality or chance. Logically, we either start with this, or else we end up betraying logic altogether in a radical intellectual anarchy that denies that anything is essential. If there were no absolute or essential truths, then the whole enterprise of thinking would be a gross futility that could lead to no knowledge of any kind, nor to anything worth knowing.

What are some of these essential truths? What are some of the elements in the structure of reality that are demonstrably not accidental or reducible to chance? What are the things that are absolutely indispensable to a rational world order in which living beings can come onto the scene and experience identity and integrity? How, and why, do these things show evidence of Care?

First, there is the absolute truth that past facts remain past facts. Once something has happened, nothing can ever possibly change the fact that it did happen. Indeed, that the truth about the past could ever possibly change, or be undone, is logically and empirically above all question. In my book *The Autonomous Man*, I mentioned the law of cumulative time as essential to an intelligible world order.[2] However, I did not elaborate on its meaning, which is precisely this: *It cannot be an accident that past facts remain past facts*. There is a reason why this is true, and the reason pervades absolutely the entire Cosmic System to guarantee Care. The pith of God is Creative Care. God cares absolutely to sustain a System that always makes possible the production and sustenance of more and more care. Without care, no system could be meaningful; in fact, the very existence of it would be pointless, and could not even be conceived. Yet, the absolutes or essentials in the Divine System cannot be *contingent* upon God's will, for this would be logically a contradiction in terms. That which is essential must be inherent in the *nature* of God's will, as part of his power and knowledge. It is this alone that can explain how in his absolute goodness and rational love God can provide a guarantee of the conservation of the sacred values in the world for those who will cooperate with him. The goodness and rationality in God's will is an essential part of his Being; God's Care is never capricious or whimsical, never amenable to dissolution.

Past facts cannot just chance to remain past facts. The truth that past facts remain facts is not just a capricious datum in passing. The law of cumulative time is an absolute truth that is replete with meaning and Care, without which the whole System would be totally impossible. This law is pregnant with God's absolutely rational reason and loving purpose.

What is the reason and purpose that informs this truth? The reason is the *need* for living beings to exist and to experience positive identity and integrity. The purpose is to make possible the fulfillment of this need. Our identity depends categorically upon past facts enduring in truth. Before any person can identify himself, he must first endure for some time as an agent, endowed with the abiding capacity to perform the act of distinguishing between himself and other persons and things. This means that he must have a *past*; his existence has to prevail over the changes of time to give him occasions to interact with himself and others.

Personal identity depends upon three things: (1) one must exist with a definite and fixed nature long enough to be certainly what he is, and must possess a capacity to intuitively recognize what he is; (2) one must experience some things as having happened to him in the past, and some things which he himself has caused to happen; or in other words, he must have had experiences accrue in his psyche in time; (3) one must be able to remember his experiences, to hold onto his awareness of the truth about what his experiences have been like. Otherwise, without a memory (abiding awareness) of what he has been and done in the past, there is no conceivable way he could identify himself at all. Identifying is not an impersonal event that occurs accidentally in a vacuum. Identification is an *act* performed by an agent who needs and purports to relate meaningfully with himself and others. One has to have experiences of relating with himself and others, and of distinguishing between himself and others. Identity is always grounded in the need and quest for meaning. It is senseless to think that a person would act to identify himself unless he was searching to discover or expand his self-meaning. Also, identity is always grounded in a care for self-destiny; a person has to distinguish between what he is and what he can and should become but has yet to be. All such experiences take time. The individual accumulates his experiences in a succession in time. Any succession of experiences would be meaningless for identity unless a person could hold onto his awareness of them as abiding and connected truths that transcend time. If we extracted from a person his memory, or capacity to hold onto the truths about his past, then he could not identify himself in any way. If I awakened tomorrow morning unable to remember a single experience in my past, then I would not know who or what I am. Thus obviously, our experiences have to occur in a world order within an abiding superstructure of connecting reason and purpose before identity is possible. In a world of pure accidentality and chance, identity is inconceivable. In such a world there would be no reason whatever why anybody could or should exist. There would be no foundation for identity, no way in which one could find meaning and value in either himself or others.

The depth of a person's identity is dependent upon his integrity and dignity. In essence, this means the individual's ability and disposition to relate with himself truthfully and constructively. Integrity and dignity consist of one's power to act with wholeness of being, to act efficiently to fulfill his real life needs. This power may be hampered by ignorance, self-deception, and any form of self-alienation. One's integrity and dignity can be only as great as his ability and disposition to face and cope rationally with the truths about himself and his needs.

Now, there is a major prerequisite for identity that is entirely overlooked by every form of atheist philosophy, namely: any individual's wholeness of being is categorically dependent upon reasonableness in the structure of reality, and upon one's cooperation with that structure. To sustain his integrity and dignity, an individual must keep his picture of his past clear. First, he must make logical connections between his present and past experiences. Then, he must cope rationally with the truth about those experiences, which would be impossible unless he was an abiding agent endowed with the need and capacity to hold onto his experiences and integrate them in time. Identity would be impossible if the truth about what one has done in the past, and about what has happened in the world, was inconstant because it was pegged on nothing but chance. Because of their dogma of the omnipresence of change, the pragmatists insist that there can be no definite truth whatever about the past. Fortunately, philosophers can tend to such unrealistic assumptions only in pretentious theory; in practice, it is impossible for a person to sustain his sanity without honoring some truths about what he had done and experienced in the past. If pragmatism were true, there could be no such thing as a lie, a misrepresentation of what actually happened, or a deception about what one should have done. I can think of no more convenient a theory, for one who would escape from all accountability for the acts he has committed.

However much we might wish to change the past, because we have bungled and done terrible things, we can thank God that it cannot really be done, for if it could no truths would be binding, which would make integrity and dignity impossible. If the past was not certain, then there could be nothing certain to hold onto. Security would be impossible, for there could never be any settled ground on which to stand. We are the beneficiaries of this absolutely necessary truth, that the past cannot change. If one could change this fact, then he could render the whole of reality nonsensical, and therein escape from any obligation to make sense. If one could undo the law of cumulative time, he could undo all truth, responsibility, and trust. He could indeed stifle the wisdom of God.

The ideal purpose of the science of psychiatry is to provide the insights and techniques to liberate human beings intellectually and emotionally. But unequivocally, such liberation is impossible for an individual who is in no way willing to be bound by truth. Liberation from ignorance and mental sickness means the willingness to be bound by the essential truths of enlightenment and the responsibilities of good health. For example, the rational man feels bound by a need and duty to be reasonable. A good man feels bound by the need and duty to care constructively for himself and others. Anarchy or nihilism could liberate no one because it could sustain in no one a compelling sense of urgency about what is true and right. After all, if one will neither affirm nor deny any definite falsehoods or truths, then to what possible cause or purpose could he feel definitely and certainly bound or committed? Anarchy inevitably makes even its own protagonists the victims of their dogma of having no binding rules. In plain truth, the game of life cannot be played by human beings without rules, in view of the fact that all of us are sometimes selfish, arbitrary, and brutal. No one can feel bound to respect the rights and needs of others, nor to demand respect for his own, without appealing to some binding truths about human nature and needs. Nor can he do it without appealing to some objectively valid moral ideals that apply to all of us alike. Inevitably, the anarchist appeals to such ideals when his own well-being and happiness is at stake. His hypocrisy lies in his unwillingness to be bound by the same ideals with which he would arbitrarily bind others under the same circumstances. The anarchist cannot be trusted. He cannot trust other anarchists; in fact, he cannot even trust himself. Only the individual with logical reason and emotional integrity can deeply trust himself.

By an objective definition, *integrity* means that inner unity in the self that can be sustained only by a steadfast allegiance to one's real life needs and duties. No school of psychotherapy can contribute constructively to a man's mental health if it would presume to liberate him without binding him. *The science of psychiatry can be no more valid than the theory of ultimate reality it presupposes.* Which means, any theory is doomed to failure unless it recognizes those intellectual and moral absolutes that bind the individual with the responsibility to care uncompromisingly for his own well-being and that of his neighbors. When all is said and done, there can be no abiding source of inspiration for such care if one sees the ultimate world ground as devoid of love and reason. When caught in a crisis, no one is likely to hope if he can see no real basis for hope. Inevitably, atheistic psychiatry breaks down because it offers the victim of soul-shaking traumas no light at the end of his tunnel. Let us face this: there is light only in care, and this means the kind of psychotherapeutic care that creates faith in the ultimacy and permanency of Care at the very heart of reality. No psychiatry can offer this hope that takes the individual out of his context with the Infinite and Eternal Care. No psychiatry will work that would reduce the ultimate reality to careless accidentality and chance.

Now, in what else can we see evidence of Divine Care?
There plainly is evidence for it in the simplest truths of the science of mathematics—for anyone who is interested enough in such evidence 'to give it a chance. Let me first bear on the fact that mathematicians do not deal in principle with accidents, but with necessary truths. If all truths ultimately were only matters of accidentality or chance, then no manner of mathematical reasoning would be necessarily any more correct, or incorrect, than any other manner of reasoning. No discipline can be labeled a science that deals only in arbitrary judgments. The only way around arbitrariness in the intellectual life is to discover necessary truths that bind all of us alike. Unquestionably, mathematics is a precision science concerned with the discovery and understanding of objective absolutes that apply impartially to everyone the same.[3] For example, in a counting system it cannot be an accident that one plus one equals two. Of course, there are many different systems of mathematics, each of which is constituted of different terms, so that those terms that are absolute in one system are not necessarily absolute in another; indeed, many of the terms of a distinct system may not even be found in another. For example, the axioms and theorems of Euclidean geometry can be used to understand and solve the problems of two-dimensional space, but these same axioms cannot be applied to non-Euclidean geometry. Albeit, any system, in order to even *be* a system, must contain some terms that have a fixed meaning, and the relations between those terms must be constant and logically consistent. The truths of mathematics cannot be reduced to mere personal preference and taste. Nor can they be reduced to anything so relative as mere personal *opinion*. As a science, mathematics is not concerned with subjective opinions or personal biases, but rather with objective facts. It is concerned with laws that are essential to an intelligible world order. Which means, the *truths* of mathematics have to be rigorously logical, not merely the changing chimera of this and that individual's fantasies in passing.

The fact that one plus one equals two in a counting system is in no way dependent upon chance. In a counting system one plus one could not accidentally equal two at one moment, then change to equal three the next moment, and never add up to any necessary number at all. If this were the case, no mathematical equations or propositions could ever be definitely and certainly reliable. Where would this leave us, except in a world in which the psyche could find no solid truths on which to stand secure? Predictability is absolutely essential to a person's security. To remain sane, we have to find some fixity in the structure of reality around us. Also, we have to find some stable and reliable truths within. Otherwise, there would be no realities or truths we could certainly rely upon or confide in. Absolute mathematical truths are one of the fixtures in the world order that make this predictability possible, and in fact certain.

If the university registrar telephones me, saying, "Next semester you will have 75 students in your first class, 110 in your second class, 80 in your third class, and 63 in your fourth class," I will know what to make of this, or what working conditions to anticipate and prepare for, because the meaning of "75," "first," etc., is mathematically and psychologically fixed, assuring the kind of predictability in human affairs that makes sanity possible. Clearly, without this we would be hopelessly confused and bewildered by the use of any kind of mathematical language whatever.

As such, pure mathematics is concerned with discovering and understanding absolute truths in the abstract. Of course, mathematics deals with objects and the necessary relations between those objects. But there are in reality two different kinds of objects, namely, concrete objects that occupy space (i.e., are characterized by tangible attributes such as height, width, depth, size, form, and density, etc.); and, abstract objects that cannot be localized in space, but simply are omnipresent and subsist throughout time. Abstract objects are present everywhere all the time, which is to say, there is no place and time in which they are not true and reliable. In a world predicated on accidentality and chance, such truths would of course be impossible. The relativists often agree with this observation; but unfortunately (they tell us) we simply have to learn to live with the fact that nothing can last; nothing can survive the changes of time; nothing can be ultimately reliable.

Care in the Cosmic Order

Not only would mathematical relativism rape logic, but it would make a mockery of common sense in being sheerly impractical. To illustrate, let me take a simple term in a calculating system: the number one. In the abstract, oneness is an essence, an eternal truth that is reliably present anywhere in the universe at any time. There is no place where it is not true that in a counting system one plus one equals two. There never has been, there is not now, and there can never conceivably be a time and place in which this absolute truth could be falsified or undone. There has never been a time in the past when there was no oneness in reality, and no twoness, threeness, etc. Nor can such a time ever possibly come. Mathematically, oneness is oneness whether we are talking about one apple, one electron, one human, or one what have you. As an abstraction, oneness is an abiding essence that subsists absolutely throughout all space and time. And logically, it can in no way be contingent upon any particular manifestation of it in some concrete object, such as one pebble, or one chair. Before I ever existed as one concrete creature, the logical possibility that I could someday come into existence subsisted throughout an infinite past. In other words, there was never a time in the past when it was not logically possible that at some time in the future Dean Turner could come into being. This logical possibility always was *one* reality, informing the Cosmic Scheme of Things universally and absolutely. This *oneness* was there before I ever knew about it, and before any other human being ever knew about it. That this one possibility could someday be transformed into one concrete actuality—here I am, living proof of that fact.

Speaking of facts, any truth whatever must in some sense be absolute and universal. For instance, it is now true in Greeley that I am living in Greeley. But it is also true in New York and San Francisco now that I am living in Greeley. In fact, there is no imaginable place in the entire universe now where it is not true that I am living in Greeley. The fact that I am living in Greeley is now true on the moon, on Mars, and on any conceivable planet in the universe where the question might be asked, "Where is Dean Turner living now?" The answer to that question now is everywhere the same. The only way anyone could reject this truth would be to reject the concept of *nowness*, which is a practical impossibility, no matter what zany theory one might dream up to deny the reality of simultaneity in the universe.[4] The same point must be made for the past. Once something has happened, the fact that it did happen becomes omnipresent and immutable. For example, there never will be a time in the future, nor a place anywhere in the universe, where it will not be true that a human being named Dean Turner once existed on a planet named Earth. This fact is universal and absolute. It plainly is apodictic.

We do not invent absoluteness and universality. We invent, or create, our own acts and particular things; but the truth about those acts and things, once we have created them, is universal and eternal by virtue of the essential Cosmic Scheme of Things which we are not the creators of at all. We invent our own contingent and dependent truths, but the basic and necessary truths inscribed in ultimate reality we discover. For example, we invent the particular symbols with which we talk about mathematical truths. And these symbols are strictly relative to one's unique time and place in history. In English, people say "one plus one equals two." While in Spanish, people say *"uno y uno son dos."* But the mathematical truth which is symbolized by these different symbols is precisely the same, and is not invented by man, but discovered. This truth is in no way determined to be what it is by any man's subjective opinion, taste, or will.

In one of my classes a student declared,

Mathematical truths cannot be absolute. It is obvious that they are relative to the inventive imagination of the individual, and to the accidents of his culture. What was deemed true in some past times is not considered true anywhere in the world today. So-called mathematical truth is always tied in with objects and ideas, and history proves that these things change from time to time and place to place.

This student is himself missing what is most obvious about mathematical truth. Objective mathematical truths (as contrasted with mere subjective opinions) must be necessarily and inherently true, or else they are in no logical sense true at all. An objective truth is one that transcends the opinions in passing of this and that particular biased or ignorant subject. If the subject has a true opinion in his head, then it is because his opinion corresponds with the objective truth, which has to be something more than mere fantasy or the subjective perception of a biased individual. Objective mathematical truths are grounded in logic, and as such cannot change. What in fact does sometimes change is our perception and understanding of these truths. Of course, any individual's perception and understanding of these truths is relative to his individual capacity to learn, his opportunity to learn, and his disposition to learn. What is obvious is that our learning and understanding of mathematical truths is dependent upon a variety of factors in each individual's life. But as something objective and binding, mathematical truth *per se* is in no way dependent upon our perception of it. Mathematical *oneness per se* was never invented by a human being. If oneness *per se* did not precede and transcend a human being's perception of it, then before I existed the one logical possibility that I someday could come into existence simply could not have been real, which is logically a contradiction.

Mathematical realities subsist in the world independently of our perception of them. These realities apply to all creatures alike, although human beings apparently are the only animals who conceptualize them symbolically or verbally. Although she is of course very limited mentally, even a mother hen knows the significance of oneness, twoness, etc. She lifts her head and sees that *one* of her chicks is missing, whereupon she takes action to retrieve it. The mother hen apprehends the reality of oneness through her native common-sense intuition. If *two* chicks are missing, then she will recognize that *two* are missing.

Generally, we grasp the reality of oneness very simply, as well as other numbers. However, it is a vast misfortune that in our schools we are taught the basic terms of mathematics simply as bare *data* to memorize and manipulate, while no one ever broaches the subject of the ultimate personal meaning in such data. Children are taught that in a counting system one plus one equals two, but they never are taught the ultimate reason *why*. We are taught that nine times nine always amounts to eighty-one, but are never asked the question, Why? Five into twenty always goes four times, but *why*? On his deathbed, the average person may take a fleeting glance across his past, and wonder what is the significance *now* of the first grade lesson he learned, that one plus one equals two. It is an educational tragedy that as he faces the personal crisis of dying the average man can find no help, no personal meaning or value whatever, in all the mathematical data he has memorized and learned to manipulate as an "impersonal skill." Are we not normally taught that "numbers simply are numbers," and mathematical laws "simply are mathematical laws"? Are we not conditioned to think of calculating as nothing but the manipulation of dry informational data and axioms? Are we not effectually taught that these data and axioms have value only when someone needs to use them as means to some personal end? "Mathematics is valuable only because of its usefulness as a tool to help man solve his practical problems."[5]

Of course, no one can doubt that mathematics can help us solve some of our practical problems in life. However, I find it very lamentable that so few individuals see any "usefulness" in mathematical truth when they are facing death, or pondering God, or the crisis of the conservation of values. In its philistinish method of teaching mathematics, modern secular education has betrayed the human spirit. It is a gross mistake to treat the vital truths in the structure of reality only as data. It is a spiritual error to treat that data in such a way as to ignore the *personal meaning* that is inherent in it, or to treat it only as an extrinsic value. Unless they are informed with personal meaning, fixed in a cosmic scheme of Care, the truths of mathematics can help no one sustain his will to live when he is in spiritual agony or facing death. Neither can they help one feel a deep thankfulness for things being structured the way they are.

One plus one equals two.

This is not just a happenstance datum. Neither is it "only a mere abstraction," ultimately unconnected with our reason for being alive. Altogether the contrary, this bare "datum" is an absolutely invaluable *truth*, representing a cosmic distention of the divine reason and purpose in God's care for himself and his creatures.

I remember when I was a child, my first arithmetic teacher taught me that one plus one equals two. But until my dying day I shall never forget that Mrs. Mary Allen (who taught the first grade for sixty years in Stratford, Texas) did not try to put into my head only the dry informational data of a discipline that ultimately would have no personal meaning in my life. Mrs. Allen taught all her children that arithmetic comes from God. Now, I remember wondering, How? But at least, she kept my child's mind from looking upon arithmetical facts as chimerical things that just float around invisibly in the universe for no reason or purpose. I do remember the questions in my childhood which some of my teachers answered that today's secular instructors never even bring to mind. For example, Why does three times three always equal nine?

Why does two into ten *always* go five? Why does the sun always rise in the east? Why does my dog always give birth to puppies? Why does she never give birth to little monkeys, or tadpoles, or little elephants? Why does the onion plant in Mommy's garden always produce onions? Why doesn't it sometimes produce peaches, or cats, or dollar bills? Why do the trees continue to grow as trees? Why do they never turn into automobiles or horses? Why do Mommy's morning glory seeds always grow into morning glories? Why do they never grow into impatiens or blackeyed susans? Why does the robin's egg always hatch out a little robin, and not a tiny mouse?

"Oh, I don't know," said one of my nihilist colleagues, "there are no absolutes. Maybe tomorrow we will see a tiny donkey hatch out of a robin's egg."

"Like maybe tomorrow," I answered, "we will see you digest your bread by smacking it into your eye."

"Now you are trying to be clever," said he.

"And you are being pretentious," I answered.

"But I believe in an open world, where anything can happen. You deal in absolutes, which inevitably stifle freedom. We must keep the imagination free. Any absolutes are a hobble on the possibilities of thought."

"What is getting in the way of your thought," I retorted, "is plain facts and logic. I, too, am for freeing the imagination. But we cannot really free the imagination by running away from essential truths. You maintain that anything can happen, that all things are possible, that there should be no kind of limitations or binds. But if that is really the case, then why do you hold so dogmatically that God does not exist? If anything can happen, then why can't the human spirit survive the grave? Why can't there be sacred values that permanently endure? If you really want to honor all possibilities, then what necessity is there for your despair? Why can't there be a permanent basis for hope?"

"Because," said he, "your so-called essential truths would do nothing but bind the creative spirit."

But I must insist, no world can be intelligible without some laws, limitations, and binds. If there is to be any rhyme or reason in the world, some things have to be unmistakably possible, and some things apodictically *im*possible. If nothing was impossible, then it would be possible for the apple in my stomach to turn into a snake that would proceed to devour me and the whole universe. But to sustain my sanity, I must be able to rely upon the fact that such a thing is empirically impossible, that it is a notion no educated person can really take seriously. If all things were possible, then it would be possible that my beloved wife, son and daughter never existed, which I can hardly take seriously and still go on loving them. If all things were possible, then it would be possible that absolutely nothing is possible, which is reasoning simply *reductio ad absurdum*. In a world containing no fixed possibilities and impossibilities, there could be no definite truths and falsehoods that we could rely upon as truths and falsehoods, and hence, nothing certainly predictable to guarantee even a modicum of security and sanity.

The fact that one plus one equals two in a counting system is not a trivial fortuity appearing happenstance on the cosmic scene for no reason. This "simple datum" is nothing less than a *divine truth* informed with the inviolable reason and purpose of God. My atheist friends insist that this is simply a "bald fact" being present in the world for nothing, for no reason. But I submit to the contrary, it must be a truth laden with personal meaning, because it is there for a purpose. Indeed, for such an important and indispensable truth to be there for nothing would be the height of absurdity. Must not any thinking person ask, Is there not some discernible reason manifest in so important a truth? Throughout this book I take the position that there must be, and the reason manifest in this "simple" truth is this: there is an absolute need for oneness in the world, as well as for twoness, threeness, fourness, *ad infinitum*. If there was no need for oneness, then *eo ipso*, the existence of oneness would be needless, which is to say, pointless or without meaning. Without need there could be no basis for care. As I mentioned earlier, all care that makes sense is *for* something, namely, the fulfillment of some real life need. Otherwise, any care would be needless, or for nothing, which would be a contradiction if ever one existed. The concepts of need and care are unintelligible unless they go together. No philosophy of human nature and destiny can possibly do justice to man's need that does not postulate care as the ultimate reality. Undeniably, there could be no chance of fulfilling man's need for the conservation of values in a world where needs and values themselves were mere accidents.

Care in the Cosmic Order

Thus, to make sense out of even the simplest mathematical truth, we must look for a rationale informing it to meet our needs in life.

In actuality, that one plus one equals two is a truth replete with value for any person in any kind of a life crisis, if someone will but help him to see it, and if he will but care to see. In this simple truth, one can find a logical prerequisite for all of life's meanings, and a logical ingredient to intelligent care. Without oneness and twoness, there could never be two persons, each one of whom could care for the other one. In the trials of living and dying, a person with awareness can see in this "simple truth" a logically ineradicable principle of hope. Instead of an accident, oneness is an essence pregnant with vital meaning for mind and life; it is a truth informed with the perfect rationality of God which is manifest in his Cosmic Scheme of Care. Take the opposite assumption, that oneness is simply an inherently meaningless datum, just there *de trop*. If this were the case, what sense would it make? Or consider that oneness were not an absolute, and might never have been a truth at all. Where would this leave us, except with consummate nothingness? It is a plain truth that without oneness there simply could never be one single thing in reality; there could never be one entity or being, not one essence of any kind. Without oneness there could be no reality at all, neither concrete nor abstract. There could never be one subject, nor one object, not even one possibility. I can think of nothing more meaningless and contradictory than a world without oneness, in which there could never be one definite meaning of any kind. Without oneness, there could never be one beauty, one joy, one accomplishment, one hope. In fact, if there was no essence of oneness, then there could never be even one accident, nor one incidence of chance. It is curious the depth to which the human mind can plunge into irrationality, to escape binding truths. These days, philosophers who absolutize accidentality and chance, and who will allow nothing else to be real, are as common as ants. But if their theoretical world without essences was real, then the essence of oneness could never be; hence, not even one accident could ever possibly occur. When a philosopher denies essences he logically denies everything *in toto*, leaving no real possibility for philosophy of any kind. Oneness has to be inscribed in the cosmic scheme of things *in principle*; otherwise, that any one subject or object could exist or ever come into being would be *in principle* impossible.[6]

Commitment to Care

Divine Care is an expression of perfectly rational reason and loving purpose in action. To see the purpose and reason informing this simple truth, that there is oneness, and that one plus one equals two, we need only to ask, What would reality be like if this truth was extracted from the Cosmic Scheme of Things? And the answer to that question is obvious: without this truth, the whole System would come tumbling down; in fact, the world would vanish, as would the whole of reality with each one of its parts. Most lamentable of all, there could be no love, because without oneness not one person or creature could ever exist to love another. One plus one equals two. This means that one person (I) plus one other person (you) equal two persons (we) who can exist, respect, and love one another. Plus indeed one other Person (God) in whose Absolute Care our love can always find hope, no matter how terrorizing or trying the circumstances in our lives may be.

Thus, this "simple" arithmetical fact is not a meaningless chance datum that is valuable only to someone who arbitrarily sees value in it in passing. Rather, it is an absolute logical necessity upon which *all* value is predicated; for obviously, without oneness, not one value of any kind could ever possibly exist. And this being the case, I submit that we should come to appreciate this "simple datum" for what it really is, namely, a truth that is inexpressibly profound and of nothing less than infinite and eternal importance and beauty. Of course we have to teach our children the "secular" fact that one plus one equals two. But I propose that an arithmetic or math class can and should be an inobtrusive course in sacred and moral values.

What could it hurt to point out, in passing, what the *vital meaning* of this "plain fact" is for our lives and destiny? In modern secular courses for preparing teachers to teach, the methods recommended for instructing pupils in math are virtually a study in the nihilization of personal meaning. Today, math instructors concentrate almost exclusively on how to successfully fill their students' heads with axioms and theorems, and the rules and techniques of logical inference. The math instructor who even occasionally would focus his students' attention on the *personal meaning* inherent in these axioms is practically non-existent.* In truth, this simplest

*Here, I am reminded of Brigham Young's instruction in 1876 to Karl G. Maeser, founder of the academy which became Brigham Young University: "I want you to remember that you ought not to teach even the alphabet or the multiplication tables without the spirit of God" (BYU catalog).

mathematical axiom (that one plus one equals two) discloses that vital reason and purpose which man needs to recognize in the world-ground if he is to sustain his self-meaning and hope in life.

Now, let me bring the reader's attention to the physics of electrons. What are some simple aspects of this scientific discipline that challenge accidentality and show evidence of *Care* in the structure of reality?

To begin, there are numerous abiding characteristics of the electron that cannot be intelligently accounted for by the notion of chance. For example, the electric charge of this superlatively tiny "particle" is negative as long as it exists. If this charge was nothing but an accident, or was conditioned by nothing but "chance," then one logically could expect it to periodically vary, i.e., change to a positive charge, or to no charge at all. After all, it is the nihilist school of philosophers which claims that there is no reason why any particle should carry a given charge. Nor for that matter, is there any *reason* why any particular particle should exist in the first place.

Without some constant characteristics in the electron (and indeed, also in other particles), a precision physics of electrons would be neither theoretically nor practically possible. The nature and behavior of the electron could never conceivably be studied, nor successfully predicted, if it did not have some stable attributes and a definite conformity to law. In addition to carrying a negative charge, this particle always spins in a manner strictly obedient to law which makes it calculable to a truly minute degree of accuracy. This spin is called "angular momentum," and is found invariably in all electrons, no matter what related conditions are given. Also constant in the nature of the electron is its "rest mass." Still another constant is the fact that the electron is always in motion, and always possesses energy. The evidence is overwhelming that *all* electrons are governed by law; which is to say, no electron ever exists or functions in a nihilistic state of total non-amenability to some principles of invariance. Any electron will invariably conform to some principles and laws that govern how it will behave when it interacts with other particles, etc. For example, any electron that collides with a positron will suddenly form an atom that has been labeled "positronium," which is quite like a hydrogen atom, except with a positron instead of a proton. However, within an infinitesimally small moment of time this atom will be transformed into gamma rays. As entities, the colliding electron and positron undergo "annihilation," as the process is called; and the result is the production of a new form of energy that is always equivalent to the sum of the masses of the two particles, minus the binding energy of positronium. The new energy issues forth as a pair of gamma rays going out in opposite directions.

It is not my purpose to get technical in this book. My purpose simply is to bear on a fact of signal importance, namely, that the character and behavior of an electron (as well as any other particle in the universe) makes the precision sciences of physics and chemistry possible because it conforms rigorously to principle or law. I could cite numerous laws as examples, but there is no need here. Suffice it to say, countless experiments have borne out evidence beyond reasonable challenge that the structure of the physical world is by nature symmetrical. Indeed, it *has to be* symmetrical (logically ordered) in order that the physical sciences can be possible.[7]

There can be no reasonable doubt about the law of constancy of the electrical charge in the universe. When an electron is destroyed upon collision with a positron, the positron is always simultaneously destroyed (called "pair annihilation"). Thus, when a negative charge is eliminated, so also is a positive charge eliminated, to maintain an essential electrical constancy in the world. There is a similar process of a converse nature that is called "pair production." In this case, a high energy gamma ray is annihilated to produce an electron-positron pair, contributing to electrical constancy in the world. The constancy of the electrical charge of the universe is no longer scientifically in question. The only question that is at issue now is the philosophical one: Can this law of the electrical constancy of the universe (and innumerable others that make the world hold together logically) be predicated intelligibly on so indefinite and meaningless an idea as "chance"?

The principles of invariance constitute the pillars of all modern physical sciences. Without consistent lawfulness in the operations of nature, the predictability upon which all sciences are based would be impossible in both theory and practice. An experiment conducted with specific materials, and under specific conditions, when repeated under the same specifics will always produce the same results anywhere in the universe. When the materials, conditions, and circumstances of different experiments are precisely the same (which is a situation made possible only by logical absolutes and essences in a cosmic order), the results have to be invariably the same, or else experimentation itself would be hopelessly unachievable and contrary to logical reason.

In modern physics, there has been considerable controversy about invariance or lawfulness in the behavior of a particle in isolation, or on the sub-atomic level. There is unanimous agreement about the behavior of particles in atoms, and about the statistical predictability of their behavior in large numbers on the macroscopic level of observation. With regard to the electron, Heisenberg's principle of indeterminancy states that there are ultimate limits to our ability to determine accurately the position and momentum of an electron in space. The obstacle to accomplishing absolute accuracy arises from the fact that we have to use short-wavelength radiation to locate a particle in space, and in the very process of doing this we disturb the momentum of the particle, which consequently disturbs accuracy in measurement. According to Heisenberg's principle, it is impossible to determine the exact position and momentum of even one electron. And because of the lack of consummate accuracy now, we cannot deal in certainty about its position in space yesterday and tomorrow. But this is no significant practical problem, since we can, in fact, estimate with a high degree of probability the positions and momenta of the particle by means of its wave function. There are some philosophers who would use the principle of uncertainty to argue against the reality of causal laws in nature. But many physicists regard this as naive, and see no point in using the finitude in our powers of perception and measurement as an excuse to reject causality in the world. Heisenberg's principle has in no way undermined our capacity to work with objective validity in statistical laws. As compared with the size of a planet orbiting in space (whose position can be determined with extreme accuracy for practical purposes), an electron is virtually infinitesimally small. Hence, it is to be expected that man's instruments for probing into the locality and momentum of so tiny a particle in diminutive space-time would be awkward and blunt.

Our inability to probe, measure, and describe the submicroscopic phenomena of nature with the absolute accuracy of God can in no way refute the reality of law. In point of fact, when in a certain process the essential conditions are calculated as accurately as the uncertainty factors permit, then the probabilities of all succeeding conditions can be determined precisely by exact laws. The principle of indeterminacy is itself precisely stated, and is an exact expression of law. Regarding the uncertainty in the momentum, we know that it equals Planck's constant times the uncertainty in the wave number. We know that the uncertainty in position times the uncertainty in momentum approximately equals Planck's constant. Thus obviously, we can use the lawfulness of nature to precisely formulate what the limits are to our ability to measure and observe.

Because of the limited predictability of the behavior of electrons in space, some philosophers have taken to describing these particles as "free" and "undetermined." Heisenberg's principle of uncertainty has proven popular to some philosophers who would use it to argue for the reality of freedom of choice. Some talk as though they believe electrons are "free" to choose where they will go and how they will behave, at least submicroscopically, or when isolated from other particles. Some speak of the "submicroscopic chaos" in diminutive space-time where man's eye cannot probe.

I certainly am in favor of freedom of choice where it enables an individual to fulfill his needs without violating the rights of others. However, I can see no plausibility whatever in the notion that electrons are little psyches who experience a need to make free choices. There is not a tidbit of evidence that they are little thinking and feeling agents with a concern for self-direction. And as to the notion of chaos in their behavior, it makes no more logical sense than would chaos on the macroscopic level of reality where we can observe and measure objects with our eyes and hands. Of course, it is true that we can never know all that can possibly be known about an atomic event, however tiny or grandiose that event might be. In enlightened modesty, we have to acknowledge that we cannot explain how it is possible for an electron to exist in the first place. In fact, we can only defer to God to explain being *per se*. How it is possible for anything at all to exist, no human being can even begin to explain. But we do not ourselves have to be able to explain being *per se* in order to know that there are beings, and to know that being must ultimately be explainable, by God, in order to make sense. In the physical sciences, we inevitably raise questions that cannot be answered by the data of "brute physics" alone; whereupon, we have to turn from physics to metaphysics, in order to find answers to our questions. As for explaining the existence of the universe, the best the finite human mind can do is demand, and find, a *rationale* for the phenomena we observe, which we simply could never accomplish in a world ultimately constituted only of chaotic energy governed by no reason. Heisenberg's principle does not establish the ultimacy of chaos in the world, although he believed that it does and devoted himself dogmatically to propagating that conclusion as a "fact" for physics. I will treat of his view in detail later, in Chapter 9.

From the standpoint of logic, the principles of invariance informing the operations of physical nature cannot be a mere accident. That the laws of nature could operate uniformly throughout our universe's space and time, without exception and on the basis of chance alone, cannot be rationally conceived. It is in the first place logically impossible, for logic forbids that any event occur uncaused; and to make sense, the cause must be informed with a reason and purpose. But even if we forgot logic, and appealed only to "chance," then where could we really stand? "We could stand only on thin air," said a gambler I know who is an expert on odds. "No sensible gambler would put a penny on getting invariance from chance. It just cannot be found in the cards. Or, if it could be in the cards at all, then you would have to find it in an infinite deck. Which means, you would be drawing against infinite odds. In plain truth, the notion of invariance is logically incompatible with the notion of chance. Invariance and chance are as irreconcilable as right and wrong."

Returning to the electron, What is the reason and purpose informing the existence of this particle? To find it, we have to ask ourselves, What would happen if all electrons in the universe suddenly ceased to exist? Or in other words, What purpose is served by electrons being in the world? The answer to this question not only is certain, but is positively direful. Without electrons to attract protons, there would be only repulsion; which means, without opposite electrical charges in the world, no particles could cohere to form the atoms and molecules of normal matter. Without the building blocks of bodies to be cemented together, not a single bit of normal matter or tissue could exist. And conversely, suppose that only negatively charged particles existed, and there were no protons (positively charged particles) in the world. In this case, the results would be equally as useless or meaningless. For both electrons and protons are essential to the construction of all normal matter. Without protons, no atom could have a nucleus; and without electrons, no nucleus could have particles orbiting around it in space to give matter cohesion and carriage. Thus, it is evident that the reason why electrons and protons exist is to provide rudimentary building blocks and mortar for matter, for which there is a need in the world. If there was not an essential need for matter, then the existence of any matter would be essentially needless, and hence meaningless and inane. The atomic and subatomic activity of electrons and protons is not generated by nothing; it is generated by God, who has in his mind a reason and purpose for generating such action. This means quite literally that an electron and a proton is a product of God Acting. And the same can be said for a neutron, a graviton, or any other particle or manifestation of physical energy.

Earlier, I argued that no atomic activity can make sense without a rationale, which only God can provide. Logically, one cannot start with an objectively meaningless fact or phenomenon, and then infer objective meaning from it. An objective rationale cannot follow "raw data," or come after the fact. To make objective sense, any datum has to contain meaning *within* it; it has to be a representation or manifestation of meaning; it has to be informed with reason and purpose any time it exists, whether or not we human beings perceive it or are conscious of the meaning in it. The atheistic idea that the universe in and of itself is meaningless is a categorically absurd and useless assumption. Neither logically nor empirically can anyone start with gross meaninglessness, then somehow derive meaning from a total lack of meaning.

There has to have always been meaning in reality. There has to have always been reason and purpose. Meaning cannot be derived from absolute meaninglessness, but only from larger or prior meaning. Reason cannot be derived from absolute *un*reason, but only from larger or prior reason. Nor can purpose be conceivably derived from purposelessness, any more than a full meal can be consumed from an empty plate by nobody.[8]

God did not endow us with brains only to be happy with our using them to ignore or defy his purpose in the world. God's purpose manifest in the electron and proton is to make the existence and clinging together of atomic particles possible, in order that there can be matter, and that we can have bodies. The spirit by itself is of intrinsic value, to be sure. But a spirit with a body can experience values in life otherwise inaccessible to the spirit without a body. After all, a space with bodies in it possesses an aesthetic richness that no one could enjoy if there were no corporeal beauties in it to behold. Things otherwise equal, there is more to a spirit with a healthy and beautiful body than there is to the spirit alone. Without matter in the world, there could be no planets with embodied spirits to live on them. There could be no mountains to climb, no trails to hike, no forests to walk in, no awesome reconnoitering of the galaxies. Without bodies, there could be no visual experience of three dimensional space; in fact, not even of two dimensional space, for we learn to think of "height," "width," and "depth" only through our visual and tactile apprehension of bodies in space. In short, without matter, there could be no extension, no occupation whatever of space. If she possessed no body, how could I behold the sublime beauty of my woman's face? How could I admire her lithe limbs, and hold her charming hands? How could I hold her in my arms?

There is an indisputable need for beauty in any world. There is a need for living beings who can experience the richest possible variety of aesthetic values, both spiritual and physical. This need is God's *reason* for generating the atomic action that makes a dynamic physical life in the world possible. God's *purpose* is to honor that reason, to act creatively and lovingly to transform this possibility into a concrete actuality for the benefit of himself and his creatures.

4

Care in the Cell

I will praise thee; for I am fearfully and wonderfully made: marvellous are thy works.

Psalm 139:14, King James Bible

"THE MAIN REASON I cannot connect life with God," said an agnostic guest lecturer in my class, "is the fact that the sciences have proven there is no connection necessary." This lecturer proceeded to argue that

in the beginning of the earth's history there was no life. But as time passed, simple amino acids essential to the evolution of life began to be formed in the earth's atmosphere as lightning bolts and cosmic rays accidentally struck gaseous atoms of hydrogen, water vapor, ammonia, and methane. Evidence shows that the original organic compounds were produced in the sky. As the earth cooled, rains brought these airborne acids of protein down to simmering bodies of water and marshes where proper chemical conditions brewed globules of organic substance. Eventually, self-replicating molecules of nucleic acid were formed in these waters. Through infinite chemical accidents, occurring over countless eons of time, nature's blind experimentations with dead matter finally chanced to produce combinations of molecules and energy complex enough to create life. There never was, in fact, any necessity for a God, for the situation of lifelessness in the world could be saved by chance and time. The key component in life's origin and evolution was time. It simply took billions of years for enough chance reactions of matter

66

and energy to occur to produce that complex organization of chemicals we now label "life." But we have to be scientifically honest. On the long range basis of accounting backward in time, we have evidence to prove that this molecular complexity we call "life" is unmistakably the result of virtually innumerable accidents; it could never have been the result of any purpose.

This friendly lecturer's account of life's origin is rather widely accepted today, at least in many academic circles. However, most of the biologists and geneticists whom I know personally, do believe in God.

All atheistic accounts of the origin of life appeal ultimately to the magic of time. Atheists generally admit it is inconceivable that chance could suddenly produce complex beings with purpose out of purposeless dead matter. But I find it interesting, the kind of game that such philosophers play with semantics and logic. They define time as such as an objectively or inherently meaningless and purposeless process in the world; then, they ordain it with the magical capacity to do what logically can never possibly be done, namely, to derive life and purpose from forces that by definition are totally lifeless and purposeless. We cannot, in fact, meaningfully separate life from purpose. Empirically speaking, life and purpose are the same; for unmistakably, life is always a manifestation of purpose, and vice versa. A living being is a being acting purposefully, or else is a manifestation of purpose. Life without purpose clearly would be purposeless, and hence could make no sense whatever. In point of fact, where there is no purpose there is no evidence whatever of life, and vice-versa.

What would be the characteristics of life in a being totally uninformed with purpose? If we take all the interest, concern, and resolution out of a truly living being, then what evidence is there of life left within it? I am not suggesting that a vegetable or a plant is necessarily a living *agent*. But it must at least be the creative expression of the purpose of some living agent, if we are to account for its existence in a way that has meaning and makes sense. To make sense, the concepts of life and purpose have to be essentially the same, or at least must always go necessarily together.

It is essential to examine an alternative to atheism to see if there is not another account of life's origin that makes inherently more sense. Atheists and theists alike agree that the *biological* mark of life is the fantastically high degree of organization and coordination of parts and functions in even the simplest instance of an organism. For example, a person can study under a microscope a bacterium so tiny that it would take one hundred thousand of them aggregated in a straight line to measure a single inch. Yet, each of these wee creatures is so complicated in its structure and function that biologists strain themselves daily in search of answers to hundreds of questions regarding the nature of its life. Even a comparatively very large cell, such as the human female reproductive egg (the ovum), is so small that it takes one hundred and twenty five of them to measure an inch, which means each cell is just barely perceptible to the human eye. When one looks at the evidence of order in this little cell, and of logical intelligence in the coordination of its activities, one can describe its design and functioning as nothing less than astonishing, to speak indeed modestly.

Earlier, I asserted that there can be no logical alternative to God; and also, there can be no careful alternative to the kind of care in philosophy and science that is essential to meeting man's needs. When pressed to carry his argument to its inevitable conclusions, the atheist must accept absurdity as the ultimate reality in the world —which can hardly appeal to the rational mind, any more than the ultimacy of carelessness in the universe can appeal to the careful heart. I earlier mentioned that some atheists admit to this absurdity openly, such as Albert Camus in his *Myth of Sisyphus*, and Jean Paul Sartre in his *Nausea*. What else can they do, considering their insistence that primordial reality is nothingness and *unreason*? But of course, it is inevitable that such philosophers fail to make sense, for the simple reason that no rational case can be made for the proposition that reality is irrational. Sartre and Camus advocate absurdity emotionally, but with no more rational reason than the tantrum of a spoiled child. I cannot hope to communicate with any philosopher who would insist systematically that there is no essential system or order in the world. Without rational order, there could be no conceivable system; and hence, no systematic case could be made for or against any philosophical proposition or point of view whatever.

In a previous chapter, I appealed to invariance as evidence of rational order in physics and chemistry, etc. Now, I shall turn to the evidence of order in the sciences of biology and genetics, and attempt to account for that order by appealing to God. Incontestably, there is one crucial question which atheists can never answer;

indeed, as atheists, they can only conclude that the question is itself absurd because (as they see it) there can be no logical answer to it. And that question simply is this: If God did not order the universe, then *how* could it ever have been ordered?

By accident? By chance?

In previous chapters, I reiterated the point that it is logically impossible to derive systematic order from mere accidentality. In plain fact, there is never any evidence of systematic organization where there is not an organizer, or of orderly action where there is not an orderer, or of a meaningful integration of data without an intelligent agent to perform the act of integrating that data. Meaningful unity implies a unifier, just as meaningful design always implies a designer. To be plausible, the atheist would have to show how the universe could *possibly* have been ordered without God. Herein, I want to show more evidence of order in the universe, and then account for it with a rationale. My rationale is of course incomplete, for I do not possess God's power to explain. But it is at least a partial rationale that answers the important question, Why was the universe created at all? Which I submit offers more for the fulfillment of our intellectual and emotional needs than can be done by the atheist dogma that reality ultimately has no rationale whatever.

What are some instances of invariance in genetics? How could the science of genetics be possible without invariance? For the same reasons that physics and chemistry are radically dependent upon invariance, the science of genetics could not possibly be based intelligibly on mere happenstance events or chance. We can study and understand the structure of a cell only because all cells do have something in common in their structure, and *for a reason*. All cells have some definite and predictable aspects in common in their structure, content, and function. Otherwise, how could a science of genetics be possible? We know that all living cells have membranes surrounding their inner contents. And what is the reason and practical purpose for developing and sustaining a membrane around the contents of the cell? Obviously, the reason is the need to protect the life of the cell. The membrane is an outer wall which literally makes the cell a safe room in which to hold its essential contents intact. The *purpose* of the membrane is to fulfill that need. Here are some other instances of invariance in nature that make possible a science of living organisms:

(1) All cell membranes are porous. A porous film allows food matter to come into the cell, and waste matter to be excreted. The reason for this is obvious: the membrane is *designed* to keep out particles of matter that cannot, or should not, be taken in by the cell. It is designed to let in particles of genuine food content which the cell can assimilate to meet its needs.

(2) All cells need energy to sustain life. Hence, all cells must feed, must have a way of seeking and obtaining food matter, and then digesting it in proper proportions to maintain a dynamic chemical equilibrium within. All cells must take in food to meet the need for homeostasis, for a proper electro-chemical order to sustain life.

(3) All healthy cells have the ability to react to outside or cosmic forces. This is called "irritability," without which the cell could not adapt constructively to its environment. Without this, the cell could not respond to external stimuli in such ways as to survive. It is obvious that the cell's structure and functioning is *for survival*, which is indicative of a teleological direction in nature. The cell is a body, a vehicle created and maintained for the *use, need,* and *purpose* of a living being.

(4) Cells normally contain powerhouses to produce energy needed to sustain life. Scientific research has demonstrated that a cell normally contains between fifty and five thousand of these little power generating stations which have been labeled "mitochondria." The mitochondria produce enzymes that convert tiny batches of food matter into energy, without which the cell could not function and reproduce. Under very high magnification, these little power stations can be observed as fantastically impressive examples of engineering design. There is no possible way to argue logically that the mitochondria could have come into the cell "merely by chance," since it is obvious that they are there to serve a need. Seen in their splendid structure and functional role, it is clearly evident that they are built into the cell for a reason and purpose.

Any mitochondrion must perform the task of synthesizing high-energy compounds. Some of these are employed towards the synthesis of protein molecules needed to sustain the cell. To break down these compounds, the mitochondria must provide many enzymes, and must produce the right ones at precisely the right times in precisely the right way to do their job. There are thousands of enzymes found in a living cell, and each is a highly complex molecule designed to perform a certain task for maintaining a healthy condition. Since there are thousands of different proteins needed in the cell's protoplasm, there must be an incredibly complex system capable of synthesizing every protein needed. The synthesis of even a comparatively simple protein molecule involves a progressive succession of chemical steps, each of which is dependent upon a unique and precisely proper enzyme at the right time.

Actually, the cell must perform a great variety of very complex syntheses, other than the syntheses of thousands of different kinds of protein molecules. For example, it must synthesize the nucleic acid molecules, those of carbohydrates, and lipids, etc. In any living cell, there are untold thousands of unique chemical processes occurring to meet the cell's need for dynamic chemical change. Every one of these chemical reactions has to be precisely controlled and coordinated with the others by a master plan to keep the cell alive. If we consider the engineering knowledge required to perform a single one of these chemical syntheses in a man-made laboratory, we can see how awesomely, unbelievably complex must be the overall system for maintaining the life of a cell. For example, the task of oxidizing a simple sugar molecule is so complex that it can demand more than two dozen laboratory steps, each of which requires a different and proper enzyme to catalyze a chemical reaction. If in our imagination we multiply this hundreds of thousands of times, we can get a vague notion of the Divine Creative Genius required to conceptualize and act out the creation of life, for just a single cell. In a chemistry laboratory, we need complex equipment and elaborate procedures to perform just a single one of these complicated syntheses that are performed innumerable times as a matter of course by a tiny, invisible cell.

I cannot but wonder about some of my colleagues and students who talk loosely of molecular biologists someday creating a human being in a laboratory, starting with lifeless chemicals, and with some supposed blueprint drawn up by ingenious biochemists. The hopelessness of such unrealistic fantasies is betrayed by a simple fact, namely, that men cannot labor with the very best of chemical apparatuses and ever create even a single cell. Even the simplest living organism is always *more* than just an amassing of molecules with distinct properties, and always *more* than just hundreds of millions of chemical reactions taking place in a tiny being. Life veritably has more to it than chemistry. And even if men knew all that there is to know about the chemical intricacies of designing a cell, they still would not know how to project *life* into it.

(5) All living organisms contain manufacturing plants for producing proteins. No cell can live without proteins, and these are produced by little factories in the cell called "ribosomes." Biochemists have now proved that they are originally produced in the nucleus of the cell, and then are carried into the cytoplasm where they either float freely or cling to the micro-tunnels which constitute the cell's system for transporting its materials. In the human body there are of course many thousands of different kinds of cells. There are the specialized cells of various tissues and organs, and the cells of bones, skin, muscles, nerves, etc. *All* of these cells require proteins to subsist. These proteins (thousands of them) are manufactured in countless factories within the cell, and then are either used by the cell for its own maintenance, or else are exported out of the cell to be used by other cells of the body. These needed factories are so tiny that it would take about one million of them connected together in a line to make one inch. Yet, their efficiency in manufacturing is truly a marvel to behold.

(6) All cells possess a system for internal communications. This system is so highly organized and ordered that one could describe it adequately only with the most superlative of adjectives. I have heard biologists liken a tiny cell to a giant "industrial complex." One expert in my class termed the communications system in the tiniest cell an "unbelievable study in practical efficiency and accuracy, found only in the very best industrial complex management." In fact, he cited reasons why a cell has more intricate communications problems to solve than even the biggest industrial complex, and declared: "There is no possible way to plausibly account for the efficiency in the structure and functioning of even the *simplest* organism without appealing to a teleological principle." I agree with both of his remarks, except to note that they really are understatements. In any industrial complex with a well regulated management of trained personnel, one can find considerable method and conception in the conduct of business affairs. A good system generally will operate in a basically ordered way, as people orient themselves to prescribed roles, authorizations, commissions, regulations, decrees, and clearly defined divisions of labor, etc. But even in the best of such systems we seldom can find the rigor of organization and discipline equivalent to that found in the conduct

of life in a single cell. For all his genius and effort, man rarely builds a machine that converts and produces energy as efficiently as a cell. As compared with ordinary devices invented by man, a tiny cell functions with a truly awesome efficiency and economy. A single mitochondrion in a cell works about six times more efficiently than a steam locomotive. It converts more than half of its raw materials into needed energy, while the locomotive can convert only about eight percent.

For the conduct of its electrical energy, the cell has a built-in circuitry system made up of arrangements of component parts that dazzle the imagination. As I mentioned earlier, each cell has between fifty and five thousand mitochondria, and each mitochondrion has about fifteen thousand electron chains (i.e., chains of molecules that electrons can flow along or be transported on). The dynamic energy state of any cell is always directly dependent upon the mitochondria functioning as they should to meet the cell's needs. But despite their pivotal role in the power production system, these many tiny generating plants are themselves controlled by the cell's "headquarters" or "brain."

Every cell has a "brain" (nucleus) which controls its communications system, manufacturing system, transportation system, and power generating system with far greater accuracy than any industrial management ever controls its business affairs. Certainly, a writer is charged with responsibility when he makes statements such as this. But let us look at some genetic facts, to see what engineering genius informs the cell's life with intelligent reason and purpose. Unquestionably, there is more engineering genius evident in the design of a human female egg cell (ovum) than can be found in most computer machines constructed by man.

The communications system in a cell centers in its nucleus. The nucleus has a thick and strong membrane around it that is designed to afford it maximum protection. Such protection is essential, considering the fact that the nucleus contains within itself all of the coded information that is needed for the management of the cell's sustenance and reproduction of its kind. It is senseless to think that this membrane has been created "by chance," i.e., for no reason or purpose. There is no possible way to plausibly derive teleological effects from non-teleological causes. To find a reason and purpose for building a vehicle to serve life needs *after* it is built is clearly to ignore the logical in the very concept of the teleological.

73

To see evidence for this, let us study the nucleus of the female egg cell of a human being. When fertilized by a male germ cell (spermatozoon), this very small female egg (ovum) begins to reproduce itself by a stunningly logical process of self-division. Into each new cell it produces, it passes on its own genetic code that will govern the behavior of that cell, plus the behavior of all cells that are in turn produced by that cell, ad infinitum, throughout the entire evolutionary development and lifetime of the embryo, foetus, and human body. To me, it seems nothing less than a truly thaumaturgical accomplishment, that a human being evolves from a single microbic being, the female reproductive cell, which has been penetrated by the head of a male germ cell. The head of the male germ cell carries the male genes. When it penetrates the ovum, it contributes its own genetic code that will govern half of the development of the new human being's bodily traits. The fertilized female egg cell carries within it forty-six chromosomes (determiners of heredity) that will direct the production of new cells until it has produced a whole new human being. Half of these forty-six chromosomes come into the ovum when it is penetrated by the spermatozoon's head, or nucleus. That is, half of any human being's heredity is determined by the twenty-three chromosomes of his mother, and half by the twenty-three chromosomes of his father. The male reproductive cell has a head, a middle body, and a tail. Only the head, or nucleus, penetrates the female egg. When the sperm penetrates the membrane of the ovum, its middle body and tail break off and are left outside. What is more, the ovum will then take discriminatory action to prevent being penetrated by other sperms. When the chromosomes of the male cell unite with those of the female cell, fertilization is then complete, as a result of their fusion. The ovum then begins to reproduce itself by cellular division. This process of division continues through an incredibly intricate and complex series of logical steps (and I hasten to add, *teleo*logical steps), until it finally produces a human being who is at full maturation constituted of about sixty trillion cells. Each of these sixty trillion cells will contain a nucleus bearing *identically* the *same* genetic code of the original mother cell. It taxes my capacity to understand, how anybody could seriously attribute so remarkable an engineering feat to mere chance.

Any human being has literally untold thousands of inherited traits. The development of all of these traits has been directed by the "coded information" contained in the nucleus of that single fertilized egg cell of the mother. In this nucleus are chromosomes containing enough coded information that, if written out in a human vocabulary, would fill all of the volumes in my substantial home library. Each of these chromosomes is a long thread of joined phosphates, sugars, and nitrogen bases which, when taken together, are referred to as deoxyribonucleic acid, or DNA, for short. Actually, each chromosome is a huge molecule shaped in the form of a double helix, with many thousands of rungs on its ladder. Each chromosome can "reproduce itself" exactly and indefinitely insofar as needed for creating new life. Every cell in the human body contains the same number of chromosomes, the same quantity and quality of coded data for passing on its heritage. Each rung in the chromosome contains separate steps, or components that make up the units of molecular matter that influence heredity. Which of course, is what explains why a human mother will give birth to a little human baby, instead of to a baby donkey, kitten, or puppy.

Each unit of hereditary material is called a gene, and there are many hundreds of genes in a single chromosome in the nucleus. Genes are sections, or chunks, of the DNA molecule. Genes are bits of DNA, each one of which is unique in its chemical character. There are more than eight million ways in which the twenty-three chromosomes of the mother can possibly combine with the chromosomes of the father. And in view of the fact that each chromosome can possess many hundreds of genes, the chance that two fully identical individuals from different eggs could be born out of such a large number of possibilities is literally unspeakably small. The mathematical probability against it could be spelled out as one followed by over nine thousand zeros. In fact, there is only about one probability in seventy trillion that two such children with the same mother could be born with strictly complementary chromosomes.

What this means teleologically is that nature is governed by a Cosmic Director, who cherishes variety in his creative kingdom. Were it not for such a broad scope of possibilities built into the Basic Plan of nature, all of us would look alike, which would be an aesthetic catastrophe. But we cannot infer from these staggering probabilities against absolutely identical individuals that reality is pegged ultimately on chance. Wholly the opposite conclusion is directed by logic, for chance can in no way give a *reason* for variety. Only a reasoning Creator can give a reason for this, and that reason should be apparent to anyone who appreciates the intrinsic value of variety, or richness, in the beauties of nature. Variety cannot be left to chance, anymore than we can use chance to explain order in the development of a single organism or species. If no teleology was involved; if there was no intelligent conception, or planning, in the development of life, then how could we explain the fact that the eyes settle in their place in the head? If all were left to chance, then why would not one eyeball crop out on the left hip, and one on the ball of the right foot? In the evolution of the embryo and foetus, how can mere chance explain why the genes operate in the proper times and places, to guide the development of an integrated and ordered organism? My atheist colleagues tell me that this development is guided by mechanisms, which are developed by chance. It is inconceivable to me that the telescope at Mount Palomar could have evolved into being by chance. Not in kingdom come could such a thing ever imaginably happen. The creation of this telescope is unthinkable except as the result of a desire to implement a purpose. That all of its parts could have come into being happenstance, then accidentally fit themselves properly together, is a notion that not even a simpleton could ever entertain. The human eye is an immeasurably more complex physical and chemical object than this telescope. Is it not, then, a bit outlandish that some philosophers would bamboozle us into thinking it has developed by chance?

As I stated earlier, no living body can sustain itself without proteins. There are many thousands of them in living cells, and all of them are produced by exact and definite orders directing the activities of the entire cellular complex from the DNA in the nucleus. Recently, research in molecular biology has produced evidence for a very important fact, namely, that the DNA molecules delegate their authority to subordinate messengers which carry their authority out into the management of the whole cell's affairs. DNA molecules are double stranded. That is, they are made up of connected chains of atomic components that are chemically bonded together. Somehow, the DNA molecule produces a single-chained molecule that has been labeled RNA. This is short for ribonucleic acid, which is considerably like DNA, but with discernibly different molecular construction. There are two types of RNA. One is designated the "messenger" molecule, because it carries the *plan* for protein construction to the cell's manufacturing plants, which are labeled "ribosomes." The other RNA is a smaller molecule, called "transfer," because it transfers, or conveys, amino acids (raw building materials) to the cell's factories where they can be used in the construction of proteins that are ordered by the "messengers."

None of this can be logically attributed to chance. For again, chance by definition can never give a reason for the design of anything. Is it not evident, that there must be a logical reasoning process directing the activities going on in the cell? There are virtually innumerable mechanical, chemical, and electrical activities going on simultaneously in any cell at a given time. And in the human body as a whole, at any given time, there are more simultaneous activities in progress than anyone could ever even pretend to calculate accurately with the most powerful computer machines that we can imagine. It is no wonder, then, that even the atheists, who deny design in the world, must use words like "cunning," "ingenious architecture," "marvelous engineering," and "master plan" to describe these creative feats in nature. This is quite ironic, considering the fact that none of them will give credit to any designer, engineer, architect, or planner. One can hardly appeal to "cunning" in the building of a molecule of DNA, after denying that there is a real builder with cunning in his mind. For certainly, cunning is found only in a mind, never in any mere object or non-mental forces. In essence, the atheists are asking us to believe that the universe was built without a builder, and that there was never any conception or understanding involved. I have overwhelming difficulty grasping this atheist notion of the creation of the marvel of life without purpose. How could I accept this, when it is obvious that my automobile, my wristwatch, my ball point pen, and indeed, even the zipper on my pants could never conceivably have been produced without a designer and builder with understanding and purpose? How could a single cell (the ovum), barely visible to the human eye, without conception and understanding, *know* how to produce a creature such as I, who have a brain, a most intricate variety of neurophysiological systems, with a face, limbs, hands, fingers, toes, and sensitive organs of perception that enable me to see, hear, smell, taste, and feel? Not to mention the fact that I, who came from that cell, can think, remember, imagine, and choose. *How* could the ovum, described by the atheists as a microbic organism as dumb as it is tiny, ever have created me without the slightest notion of what it was doing? Its activities guided by no conception and purpose, How could it conceivably process the astronomical number of cooperative steps essential to the creation of a human being? How could it *blindly* produce a liver, pancreas, thyroid, pituitary, and endless other glands and organs that must *cooperate* intelligently in order to keep my body alive?

We are told that the RNA molecules bear hundreds of thousands of "instructions" to maintain life in the cell.

Whose instructions? Instructions to fulfill what plan? Whoever heard of meaningful instructions without any instructor? The activities of the ovum must ultimately be guided by God, through his understanding and purpose; or else, what "directing" or "instructing" is being done at all? The phenomenal exploit of producing exact instructions, at precisely the right times, and in precisely the proper proportions to develop and sustain a smoothly functioning human body day after day, and year after year, clearly demands an intelligent conception and direction that transcends the power of the human mind to comprehend. Atheistic biochemists speak loosely of the "self-replicating" units of the DNA molecule, while all along insisting that there is no "self" involved in directing the replication. In point of fact, there is no conceivable way to show mathematically how so demanding an enterprise could be managed effectively by the occurrence of gross numbers of "sheer accidents." On the one hand, French biochemist Jacques Monod argues that the development of the human organism is purely a matter of chance. But on the other hand, he argues that our existence and behavior is completely determined by laws of quantum mechanics. In plain truth, even a superficial familiarity with the facts proves his point of view to be contradictory and simplistic, as I shall show later in Chapters 8 and 9. It is obvious to anyone but a humbug philosopher that a human being has a *mind*. Quantum mechanics and the laws of thermodynamics simply can never explain the existence and functioning of mind. One need not be a scholar to know this. On the contrary, one is likely to find the denial of mind only amongst ivory-tower academicians.

The idea of "self-replication" of the genes by chance has been thoroughly refuted. Equally ill fated is the notion that their replication is determined by the laws of thermodynamics and quantum mechanics. Professor Eugene P. Wigner has addressed himself to this question with professional expertise as a mathematician, in his brilliant article, "The Probability of the Existence of a Self-Reproducing Unit."[1] Wigner lays no claim to any absolute proof; nevertheless, he shows unmistakably that according to the principles of quantum mechanics the probability is *nil* that the genes in the chromosomes could replicate themselves without guidance. For living cells can sustain and reproduce themselves only by taking nourishment from their environment and making it a part of their own structure or a part of their daughter cells. But while this is taking place, quantum changes in the chemistry of the cell make it impossible to *guarantee* that the cell will continue to replicate itself accurately. And consequently, the laws of quantum mechanics cannot be used to explain how DNA molecules can continue to accurately replicate themselves to perpetuate life. The presence of innumerable unpredictable quantum events in the molecules of living matter would make the continuation of their exact reproduction altogether uncertain, or at least, virtually infinitely improbable.

I find that most physicists acknowledge this to be a fact. However, there are some who apparently will strain themselves to any length to hold onto their materialism. For example, J. Bronowski, the philosopher of science, who would replace the omniscience of God with the omniscience of the physicist.[2] Bronowski responds to Wigner's argument by saying it proves only that the replication of the cell, according to quantum mechanics, is *uncertain.* And then he tells us that, if one is a genuine physicist, one never presumes to deal in certainty in the first place. But Bronowski misses Wigner's point altogether, which is simply an indisputable fact, namely, that while perfection in copying the DNA molecule may not be essential to the perpetuation of life, nothing less than miraculous accuracy *is* required—to beat the quantum odds against it.

Like Monod, Bronowski would reduce the whole complex phenomena of life to nothing but a few principles of physics that would deny any qualitative distinction between living subjects and mere physical objects. As he sees it, a living being is nothing but the aggregate of inert and swirling particles in a physical body. Between animate and inanimate matter, physics must allow no ultimate qualitative distinction whatever. As though with the omniscience of God, Bronowski declares that there is no mystery whatever in the process of life, that what the physicist cannot explain today he surely will be able to explain completely in time. For the informed physicist, there can be nothing at all mysterious about evolution, and there is nothing to be explained.[3]

While he does admit that dead matter and living matter are "different," he does not bother to describe or to define that difference. Moreover, he insists that dead objects and living beings are governed entirely by the same "rules," i.e., the laws of physics, and chance.

Professor Wigner demonstrates clearly that the origin and reproduction of life in the world cannot be explained by physics alone, but calls for an appeal to "biotonic laws." The notion of continued, exact replication of DNA molecules by mere chance is mathematically absurd. All evidence indicates that the so-called "self-replication" of the DNA by "spontaneous generation" is a myth. It is obvious that the DNA is "tailored," in a way that mere physics can never possibly explain. Although the "biotonic laws" that govern the development and reproduction of the cell are mysterious, it is evident that they must exist, since the living organism violates the second law of thermodynamics and standard quantum theory. There simply can be no accounting for the evolution and sustenance of life without biotonic laws, even though we cannot formulate them clearly. Also, there is no possible way to account for *consciousness*, the reality of man's *freedom of choice*, and the power of the mind to affect states in the body, in terms of mere physical laws. Wigner draws on biochemical facts, and employs a logical process of mathematical reasoning, to demonstrate that the replication of the DNA molecule by physical laws and chance is a scientific fable. I cannot believe that the biotonic laws he refers to can ever be clearly formulated. Yet, they must be recognized as a manifestation of the intelligent conception of God in action in nature. Otherwise, there is nothing left to appeal to but chance, which is an outrage to reason.

"I can agree with you," said an atheist colleague, "that the appeal to chance is not really intelligible. But then, neither is the idea of a God intelligible, in any strictly scientific sense of the term. You have yet to explain to me *how* a God could exist, or *how* He could create the universe and life. If you will explain to me how He can exist, then I will believe in him."

This is not a realistic line of reasoning. And in fact it is also not fair. The young atheist is willing to accept the notion of a happenstance world, while admitting that it is not at all intelligible. Clearly, he would demand more in my philosophy than he would demand of his own. I have an obligation to explain how God could exist and create the world, before he could live with his intellectual conscience in believing it. Yet, he has no obligation whatever to explain how the world could be created by nothing, before feeling disposed to believe it. This is a common disposition amongst vehement sceptics. They seem to be sceptical of everything except their own scepticism. They place themselves in a privileged position of intellectual immunity, where people who differ with them have to explain everything, and they have to explain nothing.

I define God as the Infinite Mind. He possesses the intelligence to explain what we know ought to be explained, but which we ourselves lack the mental power to explain. The appeal to God is an appeal to ultimate intelligibility in the world ground. The world must make sense. In order for it to make sense, its existence must have a rationale. That is, its existence must be informed with reason and purpose. Belief in God is a refusal to yield to that idea of absurdity that, when taken seriously, leads to despair, and offers nothing of positive value to meet our real life needs. How can I explain God's existence when I cannot explain even my own existence? If I could explain how even an electron could exist, or indeed, how it is possible for anything at all to exist, then I could explain being *per se*, and I myself would be God. I do not have to be able to explain how God can exist, in order to see logical reasons why his existence is a necessity. Plainly, I believe it is God who can explain us and the world; it is not we who can explain him. Even the atheist appeals sideways to ultimate intelligibility, in his persistent demands for an explanation, before he will believe. But his inconsistency is blatant and deceptive.

Biologists and biochemists can only *describe* the structure and functional patterns found in living organisms. They cannot explain how it is possible for the ultimate raw materials to exist out of which such organisms can be made. We label these raw materials "electrons," "protons," "atoms," "molecules," etc. One thing is certain, an intelligible philosophy of life must presuppose that the existence of these particles and batches of matter must have a rationale, which means a reason and purpose, as I have repeatedly stressed. Our belief in God offers an explanation in part for the biological phenomena we study, simply by answering the vital question, Why? Why the cell is structured as it is, and why it functions as it does, can be answered by clearly stating the demands of reason and purpose that are met by that very structure and function. God makes his creative purpose manifest to us in the world and life He creates. Admittedly, we cannot offer a whole rationale for life, because we cannot answer that simple, yet staggeringly profound question, How?

The appeal to God is an act of faith that there is an ultimate answer to that question. It is an act of faith in the ultimate intelligibility of reality. Which is not mere wishful thinking, but is an empirical necessity. Logical reason demands that any question that can be intelligently asked can somehow be intelligently answered, by someone. In the case of questions we have enough intelligence to ask but not answer, that someone is God. Positive religion is an appeal to a Supreme Intelligence, who we suppose in faith can provide complete answers to questions we have the mental power to ask, but lack the inherent mental power to ever satisfactorily answer. Our power of reason is not great enough to provide this answer, but it is great enough to understand the need for faith that an answer does exist in the superior mind of God. It is precisely this faith that is an empirical necessity, in the broadest meaning of the words. For it is this faith, and it alone, that will always enable us to circumvent emotional and intellectual despair. Besides, if one can buy the atheist's answer that there can never be a satisfactory answer, then surely he can appeal to God, if he will but *care*. For as I mentioned earlier, if one can account for the existence of the world by chance alone, then there is no imaginable reason why God cannot also chance to exist. If the existence of the world does not need an explanation, then neither does the existence of God.

It is obvious that the crucial difference between the atheist heart and the believing heart is not purely academic in its nature. The ultimate difference is one of care. No person can know the joy and beauty of loving God, nor the burden and dignity of a sense of responsibility to God, if he does not care for Him.

In their descriptions of organisms, atheist geneticists generally use the very terms that believers use, but without seeing the real significance and spiritual demands of those terms. For instance, they often speak of "design," and use the word with a plainly teleological connotation. One agnostic author states that the mitochondria "are designed in such a way as to make possible the production of needed energy for the cell." He also states that "the world system is designed to create and sustain life. The system provides photosynthesis for the life of plants, which expire oxygen that is essential for the life of animals, who in turn expire carbon dioxide that is essential for the life of plants." Yet, in the same book the author argues that there is no purpose whatever in the design informing these phenomena, and that there is no real system in nature. All world phenomena, and all life phenomena, are merely the result of "natural accidents," with no design ever intended.

Now of course, we do find instances of chance design in life, but always on the most limited scale, and always *following* some teleological designing. For example, during the last shedding season I combed a little mound of hair from my dog's coat, and then left it piled behind the gate of my backyard fence. Later that afternoon, I happened to see a bird fly down, pick it up, and carry it onto the notch between two branches of a nearby tree. The bird found the soft little batch of doghair just what she needed as a nest for her babes. Apparently, few things could be more appropriately "designed" for that purpose. However, I observed that the mother bird already had gathered little twigs as the basis for supporting something soft and keeping it in place, in accordance with her purpose. Such a limited example of "accidental design" can hardly be used as an argument to support the atheistic derivation of a whole universe from chance. To argue for atheism, one would have to show that the existence of the earth, the tree, the bird, her babes, the dog, and everything involved in this instance came from an entirely unmotivated and indefinite series of accidental events. What is yet more difficult, one would have to show that the very materials all of these things are made of would themselves have to exist for no reason and purpose.

An atheist guest speaker in my class once repeatedly described the activities in the cell as "directed" by the DNA molecules in the nucleus. But how can we talk sensibly about the direction of such activities, after doing away with any logical notion of a director, or of a logical source for directives? For surely, no one can have a really meaningful notion of "directing," without thinking of a directive that is sent out by some director. This speaker stated that "the cell's whole conglomerate of activities is supervised precisely by its central management's plan, which is executed by the RNA, i.e., the messengers who carry instructions to the cell's subordinate laborers who obey the DNA's directing code to a letter." Similar language can be found in almost any literature on genetics written by agnostics. When I question such writers on the semantical appropriateness of such terms, they invariably answer: "Well, you should bear in mind that we are speaking figuratively, not literally. Anyone who suggests that there really is purpose governing the atomic particles acting in the cell cannot be taken seriously."

But if this is the case, then what need is there to use the language of purpose to define those activities which the speaker himself insists are in no way informed with purpose? I submit, such language is used by all geneticists, however agnostic their theory might be, because in their practical minds they do, in fact, intuit that no activity can really make sense that is not *for* something; which means (and the atheist misses this meaning), that any chemical or electrical activity must ultimately be generated and governed by some act*or* who is acting for a reason and purpose. Out of respect for the rules of semantics, one should avoid using language that conveys an impression the speaker himself never intends to convey. Logically, one should not appeal to that which he himself categorically denies is possible. How can a person speak meaningfully of molecules "directing" their own activity if the molecules themselves are defined as lifeless and mindless bits of matter in motion for no reason? Both logically and psychologically, the term "directing" always implies a subject director. How, pray tell, can purposeless chance ever do any directing? Is this not obviously a contradiction in terms? It is my understanding of the atheist that, by his own definition, whatever happens by chance or accident happens without any direction whatever. The notion of directing without a director is a distinct contradiction in meanings. I do not know of a single instance in nature of meaningful directing without a director. The very notion of directing without a purpose is meaningless. When the executive of an industrial complex sends out a directive to his subordinates, one can see a meaningful instance of directing. For in this case, an actor performs the act of directing for a reason and purpose, which is manifest in any appropriately worded message that he might send out. Virtually all literature on the DNA and RNA molecules employs terms such as "coded information," "instructions," "directions," and "messages." As I indicated earlier, the label scientists use to refer to one type of RNA molecule is "messenger–RNA." In reality, the notion of messenger–RNA not carrying a directive informed with a reason and purpose is wholly unintelligible.

One very popular text on the cell declares that scientists are now laboring hopefully to solve the mystery of *how* the DNA molecules "direct" the activities of life. Far be it from me to stifle their dreams.

Care in the Cell

But I cannot help predicting that any dreamer who would find the solution to life's mystery in the purposeless behavior of dead matter is exerting his mind inevitably to no avail.

To find intelligible meaning in directing, one must look for the director who is doing the directing, and seek to find the reason and purpose in his mind. In the case of DNA molecules, if they really are informed with no reason and purpose, then they hardly can direct themselves or anything else. The real question involved here is not how purposeless matter can direct itself. Obviously, no particle of dead matter can have a self with which to direct itself to do anything. As I suggested in Chapter 2, when we speak of the behavior of atomic particles (no matter in how simple or complex combinations), we really are talking about atomic *action*. Certainly, in modern physics, the ultimate phenomenon we study is action. Molecular behavior means molecular action. How to explain this action after branding it intrinsically unexplainable can be only the pseudo-problem of despairful nihilists.

The intelligent question is, Who is the Actor who is generating this action? Who directs that atomic particles shall exist and governs their behavior? Who directs the molecular action in a cell? If I may repeat, this action logically cannot be generated out of nothing, just happenstance. It can make no objective sense at all if it is destitute of meaning and purpose. To find meaning in the notion of "directing" of the chemical activities in the cell, we have to look for a rationale in the director's mind.

In one of my classes, an atheist biologist stated:

It is virtually unbelievable how imaginative is the architecture of the DNA. Its coded information is so elaborate that I can not really comprehend it. One thing though is certain, this complex batch of matter possesses a distinct power never found in other chemical compounds: it can reproduce itself over and over, trillions of times. Today, science does not fully understand how to explain this marvel. But I have every confidence it someday shall.

Of course, what he says about the power of the DNA molecule is true, insofar as mere description of the molecular activity goes. But his confidence is misplaced, that scientists can understand this marvel with only a little more research in physics. How DNA molecules can be reproduced is a mystery science has no chance of ever understanding, as long as it mistakes descriptions of patterns of chemical activity as explanations of how these activities are made possible. A mere description of an act can never constitute an explanation of it. The day may come when submicroscopic analysis of the DNA's activities will be so sophisticated that it is truly minute. Nonetheless, this will not alter the fact that the DNA's structure and function is still mysterious, if we are thinking in terms of real explanation. Nothing less than an appeal to God can account intelligibly for the nature and behavior of this remarkable matter. We know that there are DNA molecules. We know a great deal about their component parts. And we know that duplications of them are passed on into newly created cells. We know that without this molecule there could be no transmission of hereditary traits, to insure that a robin's egg would hatch a robin rather than an ostrich. If there were no means whereby the reproduction of an individual or species was possible, there could be no generations of life producing more and more generations of kindred life. We know that there could be no creative evolution of animal kinds, and no variations in individual characteristics and life styles, if no mutations of the genes in the chromosomes were possible. But for reasons that I shall explain in the chapter on Evil, the very Cosmic Scheme of Things which guarantees that a creative evolution of life is possible cannot do so without also upholding the possibility that accidents might occur that can maim, frustrate, and even extinguish individuals and whole species of animals and plants. Certainly, there must be a discernible reason for all this if it is ultimately to make any sense.

We cannot hope to find more than a partial explanation for these chemical phenomena that are inherent in all biological life. This partial explanation can be found in a logical assessment of God's reason and purpose that is evident in the order and organization in these chemical activities. I previously argued that we find intelligibility in the world by finding an answer to the question, Why? Why is reality structured in such a way as to make it possible for DNA molecules to exist and function as they do? What is the reason and purpose evident in these chemical phenomena?

God's reason is his awareness of the need for the creation, propagation, and enrichment of a variety of life forms in his creative kingdom. That such a need exists, and always has existed, is an unquestionably objective fact that can be doubted only by a very despairful and depressed mind. Or to say the least, it can be doubted only by

Care in the Cell

a person who is inadequately conscious of the value of life. God's purpose is to honor this need. God's presence is real in the world, as He acts creatively, and progressively, to transform the possibilities for life into concrete actualities.

All this answers the question, Why?

The notion that God generates and governs the atomic activity in the world that makes possible the creation and sustenance of a biological basis for life gives that activity a rationale, and gives us a foundation for hope, gratitude, and rejoicing.

To be certain, a number of questions do arise concerning the manner in which God acts out his purpose in the world. I cannot doubt that there are biotonic laws operating in nature that are a direct manifestation of God's creative action. However, it would be a fallacy of great magnitude to remove entirely the element of chance in the evolution of life. The assumption that God exercises absolute dominion in the universe, that He controls every event that happens, or that nothing ever happens without his expressly willing it to happen, is as erroneous as the extreme idea that all events are reducible to chance. Atheistic biochemists naively argue that molecular biology can give us all of the information we need to understand the origin and sustenance of life. In Chapters 8 and 9, I shall address myself to the many contradictions in any viewpoint that simplistically reduces life to nothing but chance. However, an equally implausible extreme is taken by the theologians of omnipotence, who attribute to God's will the responsibility for every single event in the history of life. From their standpoint, when someone is killed in an accident, or dies of cancer, or is murdered or raped, it is because God in his unlimited almightiness personally wills it to happen, or else it could never happen at all. Such an extreme viewpoint is represented in any determinist, or predestinationist, who believes in God. I see in this viewpoint an injustice to God's rationality and love. Also, I see an especially curious ignorance of the meaning of freedom in both God's life and man's. Let me cite the reasons for this in the chapters that follow. Suffice it to say presently, no viewpoint on the nature of the world, or on man, can hold up under logical and factual analysis if it fails to recognize the role of both chance and divine action in the evolution of life.

"Chance" as defined by mathematicians is simply the likelihood or probability of the occurrence of an event. As thus defined, chance itself becomes a matter of statistical law, if we look at the occurrence of a given event in its context as a probable datum in a very broad or long range constellation of events. This is not the definition I have in mind when I argue that some things happen in the world independently of God's wanting them to happen, or of his acting expressly to make them happen.

As I define it, a true chance event is one that happens fortuitously, unpredictably, or as a matter of the strictest contingency. Which means, that not even God could ever have predicted it in advance, simply because the event was only a possibility, not a necessity or determinate fact. The most that God could possibly know about it in advance was that it really *might* happen, but also, that it really might *not* happen. If in God's mind there are no real mights and might-nots, then it follows logically that freedom and time are nothing but illusions. Also illusionary is the notion that life is an evolutionary process of things taking place in a creative advance. In order for the world to make sense, the Grand Design must in some respects guarantee a certain amount of freedom, contingency, and openness in the creative process of life. This means that the world must be structured in such a way as to guarantee a prevalence of order over disorder, or of harmony over chaos. As I stated earlier, no living being could ever possibly develop and sustain a positive identity (in fact, not even a negative one) in a world so chaotic that no predictability was possible. But at the same time, there must be a guarantee of room in the system for the possibility of a certain amount of disorder, unpredictability, and contingency in order that creatures can exist with freedom of the will to choose, rather than as mere dead machines. The cosmic system is not a machine, but rather an intelligent plan-in-action representing the purpose of a Divine Being who is himself creative and free. God bequeaths his freedom in varying degrees to his creatures.

The world must be basically ordered, but not absolutely ordered. In an absolute order no contingency could possibly be real. Every detail of reality would be a foregone conclusion, a totally determinate fact which nobody and no thing could ever conceivably change. In such a world there could be no issues, no uncertainties, and no alternative possibilities regarding what could be or not be, or what could happen or not happen. In an absolute order, the notion of "what might have been" would be as meaningless as the notion of what might happen but might not happen. An absolute order would be totally resistant to life. No freedom, creativity, or purpose could ever possibly function within it. For life *is* creativity and purpose, and creative purpose is the intention to change something on the scene of one's being, or on the scene of the world. Creativity is the introduction onto the stage of life of something new in the scenery, or of a novelty in the course of events in time. Creativity is the act of bringing something different into the world that did not previously exist (except as a possibility), or that previously was not a determinate fact. In an absolutely ordered world the indeterminate could never really be possible, since by definition, the indeterminate is that which has never been previously ordered, and may never be ordered. Where there is no real maybe-not, the idea of *maybe* reduces to what is already a determinate matter, in which case there can be no *maybe* about it.

To make sense, the world must be in part already constituted of determinate facts, with also some presently and previously determined possibilities and probabilities of what can, but may and may not, happen in the future. Unmistakably, the future, in order to be a real future, must be in some respects indeterminate and open. Insofar as the truth about the future is already determined, it is the truth in the here and now, and hence, allows no meaningful distinction between the future and the present. On the other hand, to make sense, the world must be partly indeterminate before any conceivable evolutionary life process can go on. Consequently, there must be room in the world for some events to take place by chance, accident, and as a result of decisions made by creatures in their freedom of volition.

By chance, I mean those events that happen which God has always known were logically possible in the world of his creation, but never were logically certain to happen. Logically, that which happens by chance is that which might not have happened, and which neither God nor anyone else ever expressly purported to happen. For example, my wife and I recently ran into a Black Angus cow on the highway in the darkness of night. By the time the unfortunate animal came clearly enough into my view that I realized she was there, it was too late to take effective action to avoid hitting her with my car. There were other cows in the other lane and on the shoulders and in the ditches of the road. It would be senseless to think this event was predetermined to happen in my life from the very beginning. As a matter of fact, earlier that evening my wife and I had discussed the alternative possibility of waiting until morning to begin the return trip home. But we made a free decision to drive home that night, whereas in reality we could just as readily have chosen to wait until the following day. Thus, the accident was contingent upon our decision to drive home that night, which was a free decision that need not have been made, and might not have been made. We simply could have exercised our freedom of choice to act on the other alternative instead. Moreover, once the decision was made, it was still a matter of chance that we encountered the cows and struck one of them on the road. Now I repeat, by chance I mean that *no one intended* for the event to occur. God did not intend for me to hit that hapless animal, and we certainly did not intend it to happen. And it goes without saying, the pitiable animal did not intend to get in our way and be killed. Thus, even God cannot know in advance all that is going to happen in the future, if the word "future" is to mean anything sensible at all.[4] In later chapters, I shall treat of what God can predict with certainty about the future. But the fact that something can be predicted accurately means logically that it is already an historical fact (determinate truth) in the here and now; i.e., God can predict with certainty that the truth about what happened yesterday will always be the truth, and He can predict with certainty that something is going to happen only if it is already a determinate fact that it is going to happen.

It stands to reason that in some respects the world could have been very different than it is today. It is obvious that some things have happened that need never have happened, and might never have happened. Also, many things never have happened at all that could and might have happened if chance and free will had never entered the scene. In the chapter on Evil, I shall allude to mutations in the genetic code of an organism that can result from accidents or chance occurrences. Unquestionably, the evolution of living organisms in this world must be partly explained by chance. But if I may repeat, this fact can make sense only if we can see a rationale in God's plan to guarantee some room in the universe for the possibility that accidents or chance events can and might occur. Between the illogical extremes of complete predestinationism and complete accidentalism, there can be only one sensible philosophy of reality, and that is a world order in which openness and contingency make possible the evolution of free beings who can assume responsibility for their acts. A feeling of responsibility can never exist in a robot. Nor can it exist in the mind of a person who feels he is the victim of a harmful chance event over which he has had no control whatever. The world must be what it is partly because God has expressly willed it to be that way. Yet, the world must be what it is to a certain extent because chance has made it that way, independently of God's directly or expressly willing it.

For example, a construction worker may accidentally slip off of a building. The law of gravity then makes him fall to the ground fifty stories below, and smashes him to death. In this case, God does not act to make the worker slip. But He does expressly act to sustain the law of gravity, in spite of the fact that he knows such accidents can occur and hurt his children. By allowing room for accidents and chance events in nature, God himself as well as his creatures can be the victim of them; for after all, any worthwhile concept of God must insist on his divine capacity to empathize and be sorrowed. Yet, his willingness to allow chance a role in nature, while knowing that harm and tragedy is made possible by it, must have a rationale acceptable to the caring heart, which I shall present in the chapter on Evil.

Many physicists and biochemists acknowledge that there is one fact which makes it logically impossible to attribute the evolution of life entirely to chance. The fact is commonly known that the energy system in a healthy organism is "negentropic." This means that in a living organism the principle of entropy is violated; it simply does not work, as it does in inorganic matter, or in non-living chemical systems in the world. Entropy is the measure of randomness, disorder, or chaos in a physical system resulting from the functioning of the second law of thermodynamics. The second law describes how the transformation of heat energy from one bit of matter to another is irreversible, and why there is a general tendency in any thermodynamic system for its energy to deteriorate or to reach a disintegrated, i.e., disordered, state. But so far as order is concerned, this tendency is unmistakably reversed in a healthy living organism, which is an *open* and different kind of physical system that cannot possibly be adequately accounted for by either the laws of physics or the notion of chance.

Let me quote a scientist's description of this deviation from the laws of physics in a living body:

A seemingly fundamental contrast between inanimate and living nature has been known for a long time. According to the second principle of thermodynamics, the general trend of (macro-) physical events is toward maximum entropy, i.e., more probable states, disappearance of differentiation, and states of maximum disorder. In contrast to the continual degradation of energy by irreversible processes, and in apparent violation of the second principle, living systems maintain themselves at a high level of order and in states of *fantastic improbability*, in spite of irreversible processes continuously going on. Even more, both in individual development and in evolution, living systems tend toward states of increasing order, organization, and improbability. In contrast to the principle of increasing entropy in physics, there appears to be a *negentropic* trend in living nature. . . .[5]

The foregoing is a statement from Professor Ludwig von Bertalanffy, in his essay entitled "Chance and Law." I would bring attention again to his statement that the development and sustenance of a living being, from the standpoint of mere physics, is a "fantastic improbability." And physicists do not make it any the more probable by simply labeling the living organism an "open thermodynamic system." In this interesting article, Bertalanffy goes on to describe as "inexplicable" the fact that "organic substances, nucleoproteins, or coacervates should have formed, against the second principle—systems not tending toward thermodynamic equilibrium but 'open systems' maintaining themselves at a distance from equilibrium in a most improbable state. This would be possible only in the presence of 'organizing forces' leading to the formation of such systems" (pp. 73–74, italics mine).

Bertalanffy's argument is convincing to most physicists, certainly to those who have addressed themselves in an informed manner to this topic in writing. But as could be expected, the devout materialist must find a way to sidestep this "fantastic improbability"—that a negentropic system (a living organism) could develop out of the general entropy of the universe. For example, J. Bronowski presumes to do it by merely labeling a conscious being an "open thermodynamic system." He argues that the second law does not apply to living systems in the surroundings in which they exist and function. The second law applies only in an isolated system, i.e., in a thermodynamic system which has no flow of energy into it or out of it; whereas, it is obvious that any living system is maintained by a net inflow of energy into it by recurrent acts of nourishment.[6]

Care in the Cell

That a living organism is an "open" system is of course a fact. Nonetheless, Bronowski misses the point—or evades it—that there is no conceivable way how a living system could ever have originated in the first place in a world that was, by his own insistence, universally dead before the origin of life in time on some planet. Once again, Bertalanffy's statement is that the origin of a negentropic system out of a system characterized by general entropy is "fantastically improbable." Evidently, this is just an expression of his intellectual modesty, which in the case of many scientists often is egregious. Bertalanffy apparently does not wish to be thought of as dogmatic, which would be the case if he denied outright that the origin of life out of a lifeless state is altogether inconceivable. Logically, the origin of life out of absolute lifelessness simply *is* impossible, and it is empirically inconceivable. Nothing is accomplished, or established, by the blind atheist dogma that this is just the way it happens. There is, in actual fact, not one fragment of evidence on record of any living organism ever having originated out of a lifeless state. The atheist biochemist Jacques Monod inadvertently admits that purpose can be derived only from bigger and more comprehensive purpose. Not realizing its implications against his basic philosophy, he tells us plainly in *Chance and Necessity* that "it is only a part of a more comprehensive project that each individual project, whatever it may be, has any meaning."[7] This observation is true, and one can only wonder why Monod is willing to betray it so flagrantly in his philosophy of man's purpose in the universe. Moreover, on page 142, he admits outright that we have no knowledge whatever of any life that did not originate out of prior life. His assumption that life originates out of nothing but dead particles is an article of atheist faith, grounded in no demonstrable factuality whatever. Bertalanffy's point is well taken. That a consistently negentropic state (a living organism) could be derived from a dead universe governed by entropy is, to say the very least, "fantastically improbable." I would classify the idea as impossible. That a consistent negentropy can be derived from general entropy—that is a contradiction in terms. What is even more naive is to overlook the reality of *consciousness* and *purpose* in a living organism (an animal), and to treat these mental phenomena as though they were nothing but physical functions of proteins.

What Bertalanffy calls "organizing forces," other biologists have labeled "integrative direction," "the principle of concrescence," etc.

In his book *General Biology and Philosophy of Organism*, Ralph Stayner Lillie proves that the evolution and sustenance of a living being would be impossible without an "integrative principle" affecting the physical processes going on in its developmental history.[8] It is unfortunate, however, that he appears satisfied in accounting for the evolution of life by appealing only to a "principle." Principles as such are logical abstractions that can never do anything, let alone guide and integrate the forces putting and holding a living body together. Philosophers who are unwilling to go farther than this can never account adequately for the creation of life in the world. To find a rationale, there is no alternative but to appeal to the Divine Creator who informs his action with this integrative principle in order to bring life into being and sustain it.

Principles alone cannot act. As I have maintained already, only an intelligent act*or* can act. And in the case of God, his action is always rationally and lovingly principled. Bertalanffy's "organizing forces" are meaningless unless he has in mind the Divine Organizer who creates or exerts such forces in the world. There is no reason to assume that blind forces spontaneously generated out of nothing could possibly organize a universe and bring living beings into existence within it. Certainly, there is no reason why blind forces either could or should act to implement some principle. After all, a principle has meaning only when it is present in the reason of some living being; otherwise, it has no conceivable meaning whatever. To find meaning in blind action without a reasoning actor is categorically unthinkable. In his essay, Bertalanffy does not appeal to God, but he does point to a simple error in Darwin's naive theory of selection *after chance*. The basic living organism develops into what it is by chance, according to Darwin, and then a "natural selection" process helps those to survive who are strongest. The plain truth is, no *living* being could ever conceivably originate in the first place without some purposeful selection process going on in the world.

The average man in the street knows little or nothing about the laws of thermodynamics. He is ignorant of entropy, Darwin's theory of selection, and Monod's and Bronowski's reduction of a human being down to nothing but an accidental machine. But in his native good judgment, he can sense that something is radically implausible about atheism in its basic assumption that there is ultimately no reason or love. Taking considerable pains, I once described the complexity of a DNA molecule to a custodian in the building where I teach. I then pointed out to him that atheist biochemists believe that these molecules come into being entirely by chance.

"But how can that be?" he asked. "The eyeglasses I have on my head are chemically simpler than this DNA molecule you describe. And so is my wife's brassiere and her cotton panties. Yet, I cannot imagine how these things could ever have been made by chance."

5

Care in Evil

Under the bludgeonings of chance
My head is bloody, but unbowed. . . .
I am the master of my fate:
I am the captain of my soul.

William Ernest Henley

"I COULD HAVE NO OBJECTIONS to your religious theory," say many sceptical students,

were it not for all the obviously senseless failures, disappointments, and sufferings in life. A study of the history of the animal kingdom reveals too many ugly facts for me to believe in a good God. Untold numbers of species have groped feverishly to survive, only to then be ruthlessly extinguished. There has been too much wasted energy, too much futile struggle, too much devasted hope. Right now in the jungles of life there is immeasurable carnage. The earth's oceans at this very moment contain billions of fish that are being chewed up and gulped down by bigger fish, who will later meet their retribution in the mouths of yet bigger fish, and so on, until eventually death will take them all. Millions of people are doomed to die of starvation. For many human beings and animals, life is brutal. You have been speaking of harmony and coordination in the life of the normal cell and body. But what about the evidence for biological chaos? What about the destructive warfare between species, diseases that kill off whole herds, and malignant cancer cells that obviously are not cooperating with the body whole but are acting to destroy it? All these facts are senseless and evil. They could never possibly exist in a world that had been created by your so-called rational and loving God.[1]

96

Care in Evil

I can appreciate these objections. My students were stating some unquestionable hard facts. Nonetheless, I cannot believe that anything constructive can be accomplished by drawing the inferences from these facts that my students, and many others like them, have drawn. In the preceding chapters, I asserted that there must be reasons for why and how such misfortunes must be inevitably possible; and these reasons, when interpreted in conjunction with all the known facts about animal nature and needs, can only mitigate against atheism, not against God. The young students' objections indicate a necessity to accomplish a more meaningful and logical theory of evil. Certainly, their own atheist theory of evil (that it will eventually win out entirely over good) is acceptable to neither a rational mind nor a caring heart.

Let me submit two definitions of evil before I theorize on the subject. First, evil is the occurrence of a misfortune; and specifically, a misfortune from which the victim in no way profits. Secondly, evil is wickedness; or, the free and knowing exercise of one's will to relate with oneself or others with motives that are morally bad. We all know that unfortunate events do occur, from which the victim may not learn or gain in wisdom. For example, I once knew a woman whose son was killed in a war. Instead of reacting to her son's death in a positive way, this woman wallowed in self-pity, steeped herself in liquor, and eventually became a torpid schizophrenic. Finally, she wasted away and died. Now, I am not making a moral judgment of her behavior, for I do not know the extent to which she possessed, or did not possess, a native insight into more constructive ways to emote and think. For all I know, it may be that she lacked the emotional and intellectual tools with which to respond to the situation in a more rational and mature way. But one fact is certain, there is a point beyond which gloom is strictly a useless emotion, and this woman died in it, having desisted in her will to live. In short, she did not react to the saddening death of her son with hope. Not only was her son's death an evil, but so was her reaction to it because she did not, or could not, react to it in such a way as to become a wiser or better person because of it.

Lacking insight into her inner wherewithal, I would not speculate on the extent of her moral responsibility for such behavior. The idea of moral responsibility implies a *choice* between responsible and irresponsible ways of acting. And the idea of a choice implies that one is emotionally and intellectually a free agent. Being a free agent

97

means that one has insight into the alternatives and the strength to act on the right one. Certainly, one cannot choose to do what one lacks the native strength to do. If one cannot perform an act because he lacks the power to perform it, or lacks knowledge of how to perform it, then he simply is not free to perform the act. On the other hand, when one knows what is the right thing to do, and has the power to do it, but chooses to do a wrong thing instead, then not only is his act evil because it causes needless harm and suffering, but he himself is morally evil because he is responsible for the evil act. This is what I mean when I speak of wickedness or iniquity: vicious or pernicious behavior which a person caused of his own free volition, which he had the power to avoid.

Whether we speak of pointless harm and suffering that is done haplessly, or done knowingly and deliberately, in either case we are speaking of evil. I cannot define an event, or an act, as evil if it serves the purpose of making growth possible for everyone who is affected by it. But it is obvious that not everybody affected by an event always responds to it constructively, i.e., becomes a better person as a result of it. Which is precisely what I mean by evil, as I use it in this book.

In my philosophy classes, sceptical students invariably object to the idea of God on the grounds that if He really existed, and if He really was good, then He would not allow these evils to happen in the world. For example, one man stated that he stopped believing in God when his little sister was stricken dead by a bolt of lightning. He said:

My little sister was innocent. She was not old enough to know anything about right and wrong. She could not possibly have done anything to deserve being struck dead by a bolt of lightning. If a good God really existed, He would never have allowed such an unjust thing to happen. If God did exist, and if He allowed it to happen, then He is a murderer because my little sister did not want to die, nor did any of us want her to die. Rather than believe in a killer God, I choose not to believe in a God at all. If God had the power to stop it from happening, but chose not to prevent it from happening, then it would be He who took my little sister's life—the selfsame God who allegedly admonishes us to respect life and choice, and says "Thou shalt not kill."

To this, an orthodox religious student in the class responded:

Do not make the same mistake that Job made in questioning God's actions. God took your little sister to Himself for reasons we do not know.

Care in Evil

Perhaps He knew that great misery was in store for her if she lived, which He wanted to spare her, and He granted her peace. The Bible says that The Lord giveth life and He taketh it away. Job stopped questioning God's wisdom, and you must do the same. You must have faith that God had a good reason for taking your little sister. You should acknowledge that we, like Job, cannot in our finiteness and sin always understand what God's reasons are. The Bible says that The Lord works in mysterious ways. Believe. Have faith. God will grant you that peace that "surpasseth understanding."

I cannot dogmatize that this scripture-quoting fundamentalist was in his viewpoint certainly wrong. For God being God, his ways must inevitably in some manner seem mysterious to us, when He performs feats that we lack the power to understand. However, I cannot believe that God ever acts irrationally, that is to say, illogically, and I think that there are logical reasons why the fundamentalist's viewpoint of God's taking the little girl's life is morally simplistic. Also, the atheist's viewpoint is logically untenable, because he is appealing to the ultimate necessity for goodness to dominate in the scheme of things, while at the same time arguing that there ultimately is no way out from evil.

The theory of evil in traditional theology is grounded in two illogical assumptions, namely, the omnipotence and omniscience of God. Traditional atheism suffers from essentially the same weakness, an inability (or indisposition) to work out a concept of God that is logically coherent. The atheist sees the contradictions that are inherent in the concepts of omnipotence and omniscience. He sees that if God possessed absolutely unlimited power and knowledge, then there is no reason why He could not perform any acts, even those things that the laws of logic forbid can ever be done. Which is to say, an omnipotent and omniscient God could create a world in which we could know all the joys of life, but without having to suffer any pains, frustrations, disappointments, tragedy, or dying. An omnipotent God could have created a world in which we would experience all of the joys that we have known in this one, but without any of the suffering.

I do not think that any logical person can believe in God's omnipotence. I must share the criticism of the atheist that if God could have created a world in which no evil was possible, yet in which we could know all manner of joys and self-fulfillment with no necessity whatever for suffering, then there is no conceivable reason

99

why He should not, or would not, have done it. After all, Do we not believe in God because of his benevolence, or intrinsically good will? A God who would force suffering on his creatures where there was no need to suffer in order to grow wise would be a Sadist worthy only of condemnation, not of worship. Needless suffering is never justifiable, the fact that God "works in mysterious ways" notwithstanding. I agree that God often works in mysterious ways. But this only means that we often lack the ability to understand his power and knowledge; it does not mean that He uses his power and knowledge to violate the laws of logic, or to act illogically. If the laws of logic do not bind God, then they are not binding at all. If the laws of logic are intrinsically or necessarily true, then *ipso facto*, they are necessarily as true for God as they are for man, and God cannot violate them with impunity any more than can man. In other words, if something is logically impossible, then it is impossible, period, even for God. For example, God cannot be absolutely good in his will and at the same time be absolutely evil, for this is a logical impossibility, and we could gain nothing in substance by attributing to God the quality of such irrational power. God could not kill himself and make it true that He never existed in the first place. Such an act is not logically possible, and even those theologians most fanatically devoted to the concept of omnipotence cannot take seriously the notion that God could really do such a thing.

God cannot do that which is inherently undoable; for if He could, then there simply could not be anything inherently undoable. If God could do that which is inherently impossible, then there simply could be no real impossibilities, and hence, no absolute truths or ideals (or falsehoods) even for God. In short, if everything is possible for God, even that which logic forbids, then it follows that nothing is really impossible. And if everything is possible, then it is possible that there really are no necessary or absolute truths, and no valid ideals. But then, in the name of good judgment, where would this leave us?

Logically, it would leave us only with the god of nihilism, to which we would have no truly binding duties at all. God cannot exist and be absolutely non-existent at the same time. God has a nature, constituted primarily of essences or absolutes that cannot fail to be, or He is no God at all. A part of God's nature is his essential reasonableness. God loves, and his love is intrinsically good. But one reason why his love is intrinsically good is because it is intrinsically rational. This means, God is free from the degrading and weakening effects of self-contradiction. We gain nothing in our worship of God by throwing away logic as a criterion (*one* of the criteria) for building a rational understanding of his nature. God did not endow us with the capacity to reason logically, only to ask us to throw away logic in our reasoning about him. There is no conceivable reason why we should respect the laws of logic unless they are necessarily true, which means *in essence* true. If these laws are in essence true, then they are true for God, since He could be no more propitious in thinking illogically (contradicting himself) than could his children. To be absolutely binding, an ideal must bind even God; which means, not even God could violate the ideal and win, anymore than we could violate it and win. Valid laws of logic are absolutely necessary ideal principles for distinguishing between rational and irrational ways of reasoning and acting, right and wrong. We can no more afford to be illogical in our reasoning about God than we can afford to be illogical in our reasoning about math, business ethics, or anything else. God never invented the laws of logic. Rather, they are a part of his greatness. Their validity is not contingent on a caprice in his will, as though He could will them to be true one moment, and false the next. To be binding at all, these laws have to be *in essence* true; which means, they never were invented, but have always subsisted as an inherent part of God's eternal being.

I see no way to establish a cogent theory of evil unless we ground it in hard facts and in strictly logical reason. The fundamentalists contribute nothing to credible theology when they speak of the "foolishness of God." God is no fool, ever. Nobody can ever make a fool of him, and He will never make a fool of himself. In my judgment, what is foolish is the bad logic of theologians who speak reverentially of God's absolute wisdom on one hand, but then on the other hand ascribe to him the quality of "foolishness," as though they wish us to believe that God might act contrary to inherently sound principles of reason and value.

Theologians often speak of God's "foolishness" in his sacrifice to save man who is not worth saving. In part, this attitude arises from taking too literally certain scriptures in the Bible that properly should be interpreted with more imagination and judgment. To wit, Isaiah 64:6: "All our righteousnesses are as filthy rags." This scripture is taken by most fundamentalists to mean that in our sin (inherited from Adam) we are absolutely bad, even though we be saved through Jesus' sacrifice, from eternal damnation in the life hereafter. It would appear to me, one could make inherently more sense out of this scripture by interpreting it simply to mean that, no matter how good we are at times, we are at other times beset with bad motives, and at all times are lacking in the supreme right-eousness of God. Which is simply a comparison, and a statement of fact that God's righteousness is always superior to our own. But we can hardly take seriously the fundamentalist notion that there is no righteousness whatever in human character or behavior before one is "absolutely saved." The notion that all "non-saved" human beings are *nothing but* sinners would seem incredibly cynical, were it not for the fact that most ministers who espouse the idea in theory fortunately do not honor it with the same cynicism in practice. In-deed, if they did so, then they would have to cease preaching about the "intrinsic value of life," just as they would have to about good works and love.

I am a Christian because I find the philosophy of Jesus inherently plausible, which I could not do if I could see no goodness whatever in the natural sinner's mind and heart. Christianity was originally designed to improve the goodness of man (with all its faults and sins), not to deny that there is any natural goodness in the human heart at all. Granted, only God can measure all of the iniquity in human life; we should never use this fact as an excuse to deal in naive absolutes, such as the assumption that a human being is either absolutely good or bad, depending on whether he is "saved" or "lost." I am a Christian primarily because of the goodness in the unselfish and careful love of my mother, in whose ways I saw the value and realism in Jesus' love emulated by a human being in practice. Anyone who would describe the goodness in my mother's love as "filthy rags" and mean it literally would only reveal a total lack of feeling of the value of Christian love that it is possible for a human being to practice. I know about Jesus' love because a very careful person understood the meaning of it and passed it on to me through a truly responsible example. Today, I am the bene-ficiary of an equally great example of such care, in my wife in my home. In the end, it is this example of care that sells Christianity in the world, for nothing else can. Jesus did not believe in the omnip-otence of God, as theologians traditionally have defined that term.

Care in Evil

He taught that there are some things that cannot possibly be done, that not even God can do them. An outstanding instance of the limitation of God's power is his inability to *force* righteousness and love. Not even God can force someone to love him. There are some absolutes in the teachings of Jesus, and one of them is that love can never possibly be forced.[2] The only possible way to teach the value of unselfish love is by unselfish loving. Jesus is unmistakably lucid in His teaching of this fact. The Sadducees failed to teach love because they tried to do it by suffocating the spirit in a straightjacket of useless theological dogmas. No one can really show Christian care by merely preaching abstract canons. One can do it only by treating another person, as well as oneself, to the kind of goods that can fulfill his real life needs.

I learned of this care in the cradle and on my mother's lap. I felt the trueness, warmth, and joy of such care throughout my boyhood, as my family made me feel needed, wanted, appreciated, and loved as an end in myself, not just as a means to someone else's selfish ends. Jesus can not "save" anyone who does not care for Him. Jesus spoke of Himself as "the way." Which means to me, that the way to the good life is through practicing the kind of care that Jesus exemplified in the most momentous imaginable manner, to try to teach the value of care. Jesus rebelled against the Sadducean preoccupation with empty theological and moral abstractions. He focused his attention almost exclusively on the philosophy and act of caring, responsibly and sacrificially, that others might feel the presence of divine goodness in His careful life. For those who have the capacity to exercise this care, but refuse to care, all of Jesus' sacrifices were in vain. But there was nothing "foolish" in that care, regardless of how free we are to ignore it, deny it, or rebel against it.

The very hope of Christianity is that the careful heart might charm the careless heart.

But it is a fact of life that such care need not succeed, simply because of the reality of man's freedom of choice, whereby we can reject the responsibilities that burden the life of careful love. I am not suggesting that God lacks the power to coerce, or that He never has a will to coerce. There is no reason why He could not, or should not, use coercion to check evil after it goes beyond certain bounds. I am only saying that He does not, or cannot, use his power to coerce love. God's ultimate power lies in his love, in his rational goodness, in his capacity to inspire admiration. But that power is limited by the reality of man's freedom, which is a point Jesus' life establishes at great pain.

Ideally, any person should always respond reasonably to reason, and lovingly to love. But the fact is, anyone is free not to, for anyone may choose not to pay the price in trouble and suffering that responsible care often demands. There are two essential concepts in which I base my entire theory of evil. These are (1) the ultimate limitation to God's power, and (2) the necessity for the possibility of evil in the world in order to make freedom and goodness meaningful.

If we lived in a world in which no evil was possible, we could not exist as human beings with a sense of personhood and selfhood. At best, we could exist only with the hebetude of a vegetable, or as androids or robots. A person is able to sense that he is a person only because of his freedom of the will to choose. To feel like a person, one has to sense that he is a *self*. This means that he intuits within himself a capacity for self-determination, self-direction, and self-management. A human being is distinct from a cornstalk and a cow by virtue of his capacity to look inward, and to discover therein a capacity for self-examination, self-criticism, self-affirmation, self-rejection, self-deception, and self-alienation.

A human being is a subject. A piece of chalk is an object. An object merely exists. An object experiences nothing whatever; it experiences absolutely no *dis*satisfaction of any kind in just being what it is. By contrast, a person is a subject, which means, a being who cannot be contented in merely *being*, but who must act to *become* something better than what he is.

When a subject looks inward, he sees two selves: (1) the self which he thinks he *is*, and (2) the self which he thinks he can and *ought* to become, but has yet to be. In other words, a person cannot rest content in just being, but must *live*; which means precisely this: he must care about something which he thinks is important, and must act that care out. An object is an object because it is totally devoid of care. I do not mean that an object is not informed with care, or is not an object of care (for this is the position of the atheist who sees the objective universe as inherently devoid of care). I simply mean that an object is not an agent who can exercise or feel care. A subject is a subject owing to the fact that he not only exists, but has the capacity to know that he exists, and to find meaning in his being. What makes it possible for him to find meaning in his being is the fact that he is a spirit, i.e., a being who has need, the capacity to recognize that need, and to care to act to fulfill it. A subject is a being with care.

Valuable care is action to fulfill need. A human being is a spirit (in possession of a body) who has a need for identity. I do not deny that the other animals have a need for identity. I have no doubt that my cats and dog need to be recognized and cared for as ends in themselves. After all, they are not objects; they too have needs, and must act to fulfill their needs. But a human being has an inherent need for a unique kind of identity, namely, that of a person; and the fulfillment of this need can come only from the exercise of his freedom to choose between responsible and irresponsible modes of being and becoming.

When a person looks inward, he must seek something of value that he knows he must act to conserve or discover. The moment a person becomes self-complacent, then he ceases being a subject and becomes like an object. That is, he just exists but is not really *alive*. To find and sustain his authentic identity as a person, one must act to fulfill his unique personal needs. I shall treat these needs in some detail in Chapter 7, on Jesus. Presently, I wish to focus on the need for a sense of responsibility and dignity, since this ties in crucially with the problem of why there is evil in the world.

No human being can experience a sense of positive identity by looking inward and seeing nothing. He must see that it is important for him to be what he is, but equally important to act to become what he can and ought to be, to do justice to his needs. He always needs richer self-meaning, self-value, and self-beauty. There is no escaping the burden of being a subject. When a person can no longer accept within himself the pain of responsibility for being what he is, and for becoming what he ought to be, then he can only rebel against his own being. In which case, he will in effect reduce himself to an object-like being through death or insanity.

Looking inward, a person must see something important and beautiful that he has made of himself. To feel uniquely a person, one must feel that he is responsible for having become what he is, at least to some important extent. If he sees in himself only a replica of others, that he talks, thinks, acts, and feels like everybody else, then he will feel more like an object than a subject (an object of environmental conditioning), and will see little or no positive identity in himself. Being authentically human is having a sense of power as director of one's own being. One must feel that he has done with himself, for himself, and to himself some things only he could do through his own choice as a free agent. He must feel that he is what he is because he has decided to be that way, not just because he has been conditioned (as an object) to be what he is by environmental and hereditary forces over which he has had no free control.

To feel authentically human is to feel responsible. I am not suggesting that a human being is absolutely free, that he is nothing except what he makes of himself. This is the mistake of the existentialists, who rule out heredity and environment as casual factors in the determination of human behavior. The plain truth is, all three factors (heredity, environment, and freedom of choice) play a significant role in the development of a human being's identity. Unquestionably, a child with abnormal endowments, or gross defects inherited through no choice of his own, may have greater than normal problems in building a positive self-identity. The same can be said for the unfortunate child whose environment is abnormally threatening and unloving. But without a sense of choice as a free agent, a person could never acquire any sense of accountability for his own acts. There can be no practical argument against the concept of freedom of choice in man. Even my colleagues who espouse determinism (predestination) most dogmatically in theory, invariably in practice hold me "responsible" for my acts. I definitely can have no responsibility for my acts if they are not really my acts, i.e., if they are caused entirely by forces over which I have no free control.

In sum, a human being's sense of identity as a person can be no greater, nor more positive, than his sense of uniqueness in being what he is through his self-determination, by free choice. To have a positive identity, one has to feel responsible for being what he is, and feel glad that he is what he is. Moreover, he has to feel glad that he can act to achieve more self-value and self-beauty, to become a greater self.

Now, what does this have to do with evil and God?

Precisely this: in a world in which no evil was possible, no human being could exist. If we extract from a human being his sense of responsibility and dignity, we dehumanize and depersonalize him; we reduce him, in effect, down to a robot.

Care in Evil

What is it that makes a sense of responsibility possible? Exactly this: two alternative possibilities for action must be seen. One alternative must be an act to be performed because it is the most constructive thing to do. The other alternative is an act that *ought not* to be performed because it would be destructive, or at least less constructive. The key to responsibility is choice. A person develops a sense of responsibility by making decisions that result in positive benefits to himself and others.

The same can be said for a person's sense of dignity. One derives a sense of dignity from choosing to act on an alternative that he thinks is dignified, knowing that he could have acted on an undignified alternative instead. One derives his sense of responsibility and dignity from feeling that he has committed the right acts, knowing that his actions were directly assignable to his choice as a free agent. All of which would be inconceivable in a world in which no irresponsible or undignified thing could possibly be done.

The sense of personhood and selfhood which enables a human being to identify himself as such must be the central fact in a theory of evil. No theory of evil is viable that assuages evil, or assigns it ultimate dominance in the cosmic scheme. But we have to be realistic and logical, and there is both a factual and logical necessity to see that in the real world *there can be no personal identity where evil is impossible*. To support this thesis, let me cite the following facts:

(1) Atheists have argued that if a good God existed, he would have created a world in which no failure was possible. This is nonsense. A human being has a need to succeed in accomplishing worthwhile goals that he knows ought to be accomplished. But in reality, the idea of such accomplishment is meaningless without the possibility of failure. Where there is no possibility of failure, no human being can feel the responsibility to succeed. As I have argued already, there can be no human identity where there is no sense of responsibility. And there can be no sense of responsibility where there is no sense of challenge. Certainly, there can be no sense of challenge where there is no risk. Without the risk of failure, how could anyone feel the challenge and responsibility to succeed? That we might be human beings, God has created us with freedom of choice, and has structured the world in such a way that choice is meaningful for personal identity. God could keep the possibility of failure out of our lives only by program-

ming us to behave as robots, so that we would automatically and mechanically do what he wanted us to succeed in doing. But in that case, there would be no persons in the world. There would be only robots. Robots could not care. They could not know the meaning of love for one another, or love for God.

(2) Atheists have argued that a good God would have created us in such a fashion that we could not behave destructively or unreasonably. This too is nonsense. For again, in this case we could not exist with a sense of personhood or selfhood. A robot is not a self, and can in no way care to behave constructively. Where there is no risk of destructive or unreasonable behavior, no one can possibly experience a challenge and responsibility to behave constructively and reasonably. Where there is no risk of senseless behavior, who can possibly feel a need and responsibility to make sense of his life? If it were not possible to hurt ourselves and other persons, by ignoring and abusing our real life needs, then who could feel the challenge and duty to do justice to such needs? If I could not harm myself and others with senseless and useless hatred, then how could, and indeed why *should*, I feel a responsibility to love? If I could not bring disorder and chaos into the world, how could I feel a challenge and responsibility to create order and harmony? If I could not choose to reason irrationally, then what obligation could I feel to reason rationally?

(3) "But you are including only deliberate evils caused by human beings," said a sceptical student in one of my classes. "I cannot object to your connecting freedom of choice and the possibility of senseless behavior to personal identity and selfhood. But what about all the evils in the world caused by accidents, or by forces over which man has no control?"

Here again, the answer to this question centers upon the need for risk to make personal identity possible. If no accidents could possibly happen that injure or destroy, then no one could feel a need for caution, self-restraint, or carefulness in his actions. If no accidents were possible, then no one could feel a challenge or responsibility to avoid them, or to prevent them from happening. In which case, man's sense of responsibility for the human condition would be enormously diminished, if not completely destroyed. For example, if I am driving down the street of a community in my automobile, what is it that makes me feel responsible for my driving? Obviously, I feel responsible for my driving, or in control of it, only insofar as I am aware that I can accidentally hurt myself and others if I fail to exercise care to prevent it. By definition, an accident is an event that occurs which nobody deliberately causes or intends. Where there is no possibility of carelessness which can hurt oneself and others, no one can feel the need to practice circumspection, nor the challenge and responsibility to care. If God created a universe in which no carelessness was possible, in such a universe no one could experience a meaningful notion of care.

"I can go along with that too," said a student, "but what about accidents that have nothing to do with man's choice or control?"

Earlier, I alluded to a student's remark that his little sister had been killed by a bolt of lightning. The student rejected the idea of God on the grounds that if a good God really existed He would have prevented this from happening. I would describe the little girl's death as an accident, not a case of God killing her "because He had a good reason to take her" (quoting the fundamentalist intervarsity crusader). The pages of a gigantic tome could be filled citing instances of such accidents. But to make a point briefly, let me mention only a few. When I was a boy, I possessed an extraordinarily beautiful and loving dog as a pet. As time passed, he went blind, which was a misfortune none of us could prevent or control. Then one day, while crossing the street, he was killed accidentally by a car whose driver did not see him. I remember coping with resentment, asking, "Why did God allow it to happen?" My wife and I have a beloved friend who is a young woman in her middle twenties, of rarely great humor and beauty of spirit. But she weighs less than fifty pounds because she was born with a bone disease that prevented normal growth. All of us know persons who were born blind or deaf, or both. We know persons born with serious malformities that make life hard.

I cannot believe that God directly caused any of these things to occur. All such events are true accidents, which means, no one whosoever intends for them to happen or deliberately and knowingly causes them to happen. When God created the world, He did so fully conscious of the fact that accidents could happen, and indeed, inevitably would happen and cause suffering. God knew when He created the laws of nature that they could maim and kill his creatures. A lightning bolt is an expression of the laws of nature in action. God knows that if a creature is caught in lightning he can be hurt or killed by it. He knew when He created the earth with oceans on it that some of his children might be drowned in it if they were caught in it under unfortunate circumstances or conditions. But this makes God the cause of the accident only indirectly. It does not mean that He ever wants an accidental drowning to occur, or that He acts expressly to kill one of his children or creatures with a bolt of lightning.

Earlier, I alluded to a student's description of the carnage in the oceans and jungles. When he created the world, God did it in such a way as to guarantee that a great variety of living beings (both plants and animals) could and would evolve. He knew that conflicting interests would ensue between different animals with freedom of volition to act. He knew that hungry tigers could kill gazelles for meat to survive. He knew that carnivorous fish would eat other fish to live, then be eaten by yet others with the same urge to live. He knew that germs, like all animals, could not live without feeding, and could hurt and kill larger creatures, including man. But logically, we cannot believe that God had the power to create so vast a variety of creature types in his animal kingdom, and simultaneously prevent the feeding of life on life. From the standpoint of logic, we cannot define God as seeking the greatest possible production of joy, then impute to Him unnecessary evil in the world he created. Believing in the absolute goodness of God's will, I must also believe that He created life in this world under the most benevolent conditions possible.[3] To believe that God's purpose is to bring as much joy into his creative kingdom as possible is to believe that He did not have the power to create better conditions under which his earthly creatures could live. If He could have created on earth a kingdom of varied animal species, all of whom could have lived without feeding on one another, then surely He would have done it. One thing is certain, an animal kingdom such as we know on earth is infinitely better than no variety of animals at all. A vast kingdom of predacious animals is better than the much more limited number of herbivores who could live on plants alone. If all the world's carnivores suddenly craved only plants, then vegetation on earth would rapidly disappear. Only God can measure the extent of anxiety and pain suffered by animals pursuing and devouring one another, and seeking to escape pursuit. But in his universal awareness, God himself must experience all this anxiety and pain. In his knowledge and divine empathy, God himself must suffer all that his creatures suffer. He must be the supreme victim of his own creation. Yet, with this same awareness and empathy He experiences the sum total of pleasures and joys felt by all of his creatures, plus the unique joy of knowing that He is the ultimate source of it all.

Certainly, my little animal friends have minds, that are in some respects like my own and in some respects different. Obviously, my dog Lady-bo knows that she is alive; she knows that she has needs, and acts to fulfill her needs. Lady-bo does not conceptualize her awareness of reality in verbal symbols, although it is apparent that her barks have real meaning for her. Still, she obviously has a mind and experiences many adventures and joys in living the life of a dog. For example, she finds great joy in love and play. I can make no sense whatever out of the notion that her spirit might one day be reduced to nothing.

Often, persons and other creatures die from diseases caused by the parasitical feeding of germs. God could prevent this only by making the existence of germs impossible. And what would be the consequence of this? For one thing, the scope of his kingdom would be reduced immeasurably, since there are literally astronomically great numbers of these little creatures in existence. And they are so tiny that men usually have difficulty thinking of them as life-experiencing creatures in their smallness. Yet, it is quite obvious that they are alive, by any meaningful definition of that term. A being is alive if it has need, interest, and purpose. Otherwise, there is no conceivable reason why it would act. Any animal, however big or small, acts because it has something to act *for*. These little creatures must experience *some* value in being alive; or else, there is no reason whatever why they should act to sustain their lives. On however primitive or simple a level, they nonetheless must *feel* some value in acting, and experience some joy in fulfilling some need.

"But you are being terribly anthropomorphic," said an incredulous student. "There is no direct evidence whatever that a germ feels anything or experiences any value. It appears more obvious to me that a germ's behavior is governed entirely by chemical mechanisms. A bacterium is simply a tiny machine." This is, in fact, the most common point of view amongst students in general. Rarely do I find a student who believes that lower animals have spirits, that they have some experience of life. This is one of the great blemishes in Western culture, which is truly an enigma to people in the East. I find that many of my ministerial colleagues

111

are hunters who obviously *enjoy* "bagging" a deer. In this respect, traditional Christendom is the most philistinish religion on earth. How can these little animal creatures be machines? No machine, big or little, has any interest, motivation, or reason to *act to preserve itself*. One can apply a blowtorch to my automobile, and it will not move, precisely because it does not feel the heat. The same can be said if we apply heat to any other machine, however tiny it might be. But if we apply heat to any animal, including the tiniest bacterium, it will feel that its well-being is threatened, and will move to try to save its life. This movement away from threat can in no way be explained by physics. It can be explained only by animal psychology which deals with the living behavior of creatures, including the smallest.

If no germ life was possible, man could not exist with the kind of body he now owns. For a certain quantity of bacteria is essential to his digestive system to transform food particles into assimilable substances. Of course, these particular germs do not feed on tissue, and they are found in even greater abundance in herbivores than in carnivores. For example, they are found in far greater quantities inside the digestive system of a cow. As for tissue-feeding disease germs, most of them are consumed by antibodies before doing any serious damage or taking a higher life. Perhaps their existence is justified because the *experience of value* in their lives *in toto* is greater than the harm they do. Besides, a person's dying from a disease would be an intrinsic tragedy only if he had no soul and could not survive the grave.

Howbeit, I am presenting the above opinion only as conjecture, not as an apodictic truth. I see more value-experience in any good human being's life than in that of the whole germ kingdom *in toto*. Even so, it is obvious that much violence is done to the needs and rights of animals by the failure of people to see intrinsic value in their lives. What is more, the evolution of germ life cannot be accounted for entirely in terms of the express purpose or direct action of God. Chance does unmistakably enter into the evolution of creature types, to some extent. It may be that the origin of parasitical or tissue-feeding germs is a result of *chance*, which God knew full well was possible when he created the world, but did not directly act to make happen. Just as the genes in a human being's germ cells may be mutated by chance, there is no reason why chemical accidents could not alter the feeding habits of bacteria by mutating their genes. A good argument could be made that germs are a necessary part of the development of life as a whole.

We have conclusive evidence that chance plays a certain role in the evolution of human beings and their body characteristics. When someone is born with a deformity, it very often is the result of a genetic accident that has caused a mutation in a normal gene in the DNA. It is not uncommon that a normal mother and father will produce abnormal children. The abnormality may be something superficial, such as the absence of a toe, or something very problematical, such as a stunted limb or a hunched back. It may be an abnormal brain, or sickle cell anemia, or some other fatal hereditary disease. Sometimes the damage is done by an accident to the pregnant mother. But very often, the deformity is hereditary rather than merely congenital; i.e., it is caused by an abnormal gene, which is one that has been mutated accidentally by an X-ray, by some cosmic ray, or by heat, or by some chemical. DNA molecules can be reproduced trillions of times without flaw. But eventually an accident occurs: say, a cosmic ray strikes a gene in the DNA molecule, and alters the genetic code. This means plain and simple, the gene had been damaged by chance and can no longer function as it was originally designed to function. It does not mean that God specifically took action to make it happen, or that he wanted it to happen. I cannot feature God wanting one of his creatures to be born deformed. Cosmic rays operate in accordance with the laws of nature. As I asserted earlier, God has programmed these laws to function with a logical consistency that makes predictability and understanding possible for his creatures. He could prevent such accidents from occurring only by perpetually intervening, to build an impenetrable protective shell around every one of his creatures, to protect it from risk.

But we must ask, What would happen if God did exactly this? It is a known fact that most mutations are caused by chance, are harmful and disadvantageous to the organism, and constitute a real risk either to the individual or to his progeny. What would life be like in a world totally devoid of risk? One thing is indisputable, it would be dull, to say the least. There can be no sense of adventure where there is no risk. With no risk whatever, ennui would set in, and eventually the will to live would die down. In a world without risk, there certainly could be no care. For if a person's needs were guaranteed automatic fulfillment by God; or, if a man

113

could face no risk of failure in fulfilling his own needs, then he could have no cause to care. Above all, without risks man could have no problems. Where there is no risk whatever, there simply is no problem whatever. And with no problem whatever, who could find life interesting at all? When we start running out of problems, what do we do? We do, in fact, start inventing our own problems to make life interesting, to keep from dying of boredom. If I may reiterate here: with no risk of any kind there could be absolutely no sense of challenge or responsibility, and consequently, no identity as a human being or person.

"I cannot see your point," said an atheist student. "I cannot see why God, who you define as careful for the well-being and happiness of his children, would hesitate to intervene to prevent someone from being mutated by a cosmic ray that would produce a deformity. You have previously said that the laws of nature are God acting. If that is the case, then why couldn't God suspend the laws of nature in any situation that called for it to protect his creatures?"

There are virtually innumerable risks extant in the world, even though we are unconscious of the vast majority of them. To remove all of these risks, God would be so busy suspending the laws of nature that they simply could not effectively prevail to sustain a predictable world order. If I was moving in the direction of a cosmic ray that might mutate a gene if it struck me, in order to stop me God would have to either stop the cosmic ray (suspend his laws), or place an obstacle in my path, or else suspend my freedom of volition to decide for myself when, where, and why I would move. Recently, I saw a cat run over by a pickup-truck in the road. The cat was bee-lining towards a squirrel on the opposite side of the street, and forgot to check for the danger of traffic; hence, he failed to see the pickup coming. To prevent this from happening, God would have had to suspend either the will of the driver of the pickup-truck or the will of the cat. If He had intervened and stopped the driver from propelling his pickup, He could have saved the cat. But then, He would have had to suspend the volition of the cat to save the squirrel. If God suspended our freedom of volition anytime we exercised it to move in the direction of risk, then we would lose our freedom, period; or else, it would be so seriously diminished that we could not exist and function as human beings at all. Neither could a cat really exist and function as a cat. Nor a squirrel as a squirrel. On innumerable occasions I have seen squirrels come into my yard, unconscious of the fact that they were risking death in the claws and teeth of my cats.

Now, I am not contending that God never has the power to intervene; rather, I merely am trying to clarify a fact of prodigious importance that theologians generally have ignored or failed to understand, i.e., that the conditions for practicable intervention by God are limited by (1) His rationality, and (2) His unalterable moral dedication to holding us responsible, insofar as possible, for determining our own lives. I am not contending that God could never, or would never, intervene under any circumstances. Rather, I wish only to delineate some of those conditions that inevitably place restrictions on the power of a rational and moral God to intervene to alter men's decisions. God cannot honor our bewailing, self-indulgent pleas for His intervention when that intervention would diminish our sense of the need to manage our own lives responsibly. The free decisions that men make often have disastrous consequences; and certainly, God can see how injudicious many of our decisions are at the time we make them. Even so, He is powerless to prevent us from making unwise choices while at the same time upholding that very freedom of choice which makes us human. God cannot protect us from all harm without suspending our very humanity. We are foolish to believe that God could or would intervene arbitrarily, that because of his supposed omnipotence there must be no limitations whatever to his power to intervene.

Granted, this leaves us here with some further questions to treat —it would take a whole book to explicate the criteria determining when God can and cannot intervene. But one thing is dictated certainly by moral logic, and that is: because God's moral logic is consistent He cannot be erratic in his criteria for intervening; his power to intervene is governed by moral absolutes; He cannot play favorites, cannot whimsically change his criteria for intervention to placate the incompatible interests of selfish individuals. Because God's own care is perfectly rational and moral, He cannot intervene in any way that would diminish our sense of responsibility for what goes on in the world. For example, Why did God not intervene to prevent the Nazis from unjustly and ruthlessly killing millions of Jewish people? Answer: He could intervene to prevent such injustices only by suspending that very decision-making freedom that makes human responsibility possible. But this He cannot and will not do because He is responsible care, and He knows that He must do his utmost to encourage responsible care in Man. God cannot let us have it both ways—cannot let us be truly human while guaranteeing that there is no possible harmful consequences of our freedom.

I am not suggesting that God's tolerance of injustice is unlimited. Indeed the contrary, this is impossible because of the inherent goodness of his care. Yet it should be apparent (from the innumerable obvious examples of God's not intervening) that He deals with injustice by allowing the laws of moral retribution He has inscribed in nature to operate effectively on the long range (on a continuation of life in this world into the next). God upholds our freedom to make decisions. But He systematically upholds the laws of moral retribution, or restitution, guaranteeing that on the long range we shall have to face the moral consequences of our decisions.[4] God cannot save us from the dangers of freedom without destroying us as persons. But neither can He save us from the burden of accountability for the decisions we make in that freedom. To prevent all of the damage that we do to one another in our freedom, God would have to suspend our freedom anytime we might use it to do harm. As a result of such intervention we would be turned into robots, which would be more dehumanizing for Man than God's allowing us to remain human with all of the harm that we freely do. To prevent World War II from happening, God would have had to dehumanize us more than we were dehumanized by all the harm of the war itself. Nothing could be more dehumanizing to a man than to turn him into a robot.

Ordinarily, theologians argue that God is omnipotent, and that consequently He has carte blanche liberty to intervene under any conditions at any time (but simply chooses, for some indiscernible reason, often not to do it). My ministerial colleagues usually infer unlimited power of intervention from Jesus' counsel, "Ask, and ye shall receive." I take this counsel very seriously myself. In fact, I do not know how any person could relate personally with God without it. Without daily prayer, my relationship with God would not seem personal at all. I would be at a loss to describe how great is the value and meaning of prayer in my life. It is through prayer that a person's encounter with God is most personal and direct.

But it is one thing to infer omnipotence from the words "Ask, and ye shall receive," (Jesus showed no intimation whatever of intending omnipotence); it is quite another thing to interpret it as an indication of the unfailing generosity of spirit in God's responsible care. The scripture does not specify what we shall receive. Looking at this particular counsel of Jesus in the light of his teachings as a whole, I believe it is unmistakably evident that He did not intend for us to regard our God as a celestial shaman who can arbitrarily do anything for us at any time.

As a whole, Jesus' teachings place a great priority on the meaning of responsible care, both in God's life and in man's. It is inconceivable to me that God would ever intervene in any way that might lessen the yoke of our own responsibility to care. For without that yoke no man can be a human being, much less be a Christian in spirit.

The essence of God is Responsible Care. All acts of God, including any conceivable acts of intervention, are guided by Divine Care. This means indisputably that there must be a point beyond which intervention is morally impossible. The more God does for us the less we feel we have to do for ourselves. God knows that we have to care to fulfill our own needs (and His). He knows that if we stop caring we cease being human. God cannot intervene to do our caring for us. If He did that, then we would lose our own feeling of the need to care, which would defeat His own purpose as well as to dehumanize us.

Lo, this means suffering for both The Lord and his children.

Aside from these limitations, I can imagine no reason why God could not intervene where some situation might warrant it, either in the case of an individual or in the course of history as a whole. But the assumption that God is omnipotent is offensive to moral reason, and I find it odd that atheists have seen the fallacy in it very clearly, while most theologians have not. A God of unlimited power could have created a lasting utopia on earth such as orthodox theology promises only in a future life. But then, Is it not indeed queer that the atheists, seeing the irrationality of omnipotence, would prefer to have no God at all unless it be an omnipotent one who would make their lives always perfect?[5]

The atheist assumption that a good God would create only a utopian world is altogether naive. In a world where no suffering was possible, no one could conceivably know the full meaning of joy. In reality, we know what joy is because we can compare it with the sensation of joylessness or pain. We know what the sense of satisfaction means, because we can compare it with *dis*satisfaction, or pain. For example, no man can know the joy of eating a delicious meal, until first he has suffered from the pain of hunger, or the pain of an *un*satisfied need for food. In fact, the greater the pain of one's hunger, the more joy he can find in eating his food. No person can experience a joy in learning, until first he has been somehow pained by his ignorance, suffered the sensation of an *un*satisfied need for knowledge. No man reaches out to unite with a woman in love, until first he knows the pain of loneliness, of an *un*satisfied need or yearning for a woman's love. Then after he marries, his capacity to love responsibly can be no greater than his capacity, and disposition, to suffer for the sake of his woman's needs when a situation calls for it. The man who is unable, or unwilling, to suffer for the sake of his love will lose it.

In fact, we understand all of life's significant values by comparison. The very structure of reality is dipolar in its logic. Even God's knowledge must involve distinctions, which are inconceivable without the possibility of opposites. For example, in a world where no falsehoods were possible, no one could know the meaning of truth. In such a world, no one could ever say, "I appreciate the fact that you are telling the truth," simply because this would involve at least an implied distinction between truth and falsehood, which no one could experience without a notion of falsehood. Where no injustices were possible, we could never know the meaning of justice. The statement, "I appreciate the fact that you do justice to my needs," could never be made. If no unreasonableness was possible, we could never know the value of reasonableness in life. Who could fully appreciate reasonableness, if he could have no notion of what it is like to be treated unreasonably? If bad health was impossible, who would ever say, "I truly appreciate having good health"? If the experience of a misfortune was impossible, if no one could even imagine it or experience it vicariously, then who could ever comprehend or fully appreciate the meaning of good fortune? If a person were the beneficiary of nothing but pure goodness, how could he fully understand or appreciate it as such?

Thus, I necessarily conclude that the possibility of evil in the world is not a mere happenstance fact. If we could experience no possible evil, we could never fully comprehend or appreciate the meaning of goodness. God has ordered things in such a way that we have to face real risks, in order that we might experience adventure, excitement, challenge, responsibility, and the meaning of dignity in one's identity as a person. In the allegory of Adam and Eve in the garden, we find a perfect symbol of God's purpose for man on earth. God wishes us to become fully human. He wishes us to know the meaning of existence as a *spirit*, a free agent who can *understand* goodness. If we took this story literally, it would imply that God intended for Adam and Eve to remain forever fixated in the bliss of that little empty paradise. Literally, it would be the bliss of ignorance, of their inability to distinguish between good and evil, and of no necessity to choose. We cannot take literally the assumption that God forbade them to "eat of the fruit of the tree of *knowledge of good and evil*." For this would imply that God wanted them to never have such knowledge, to be unable to make distinctions. It would imply that He wanted them to remain like little happy animal pets, ignorant of right and wrong. But when taken as an allegory, the story is pregnant with religious truth value and meaning. It symbolizes that God wants each one of us to become fully human, which we cannot do without knowledge of good and evil, and a consciousness of responsibility for our freedom of choice. Not to mention the Fall, which is a symbol of what happens in every human being's life, that we use our freedom to abuse ourselves and God.

There is a reason and purpose for the possibility of ugliness in the world. This reason is God's need, and the need of his creatures, to experience and fully appreciate the meaning of beauty in the divine creation. God's purpose is to fulfill that need, which could never be done in a world in which no ugliness was possible. Ugliness exists not in things, but in attitudes and situations. For example, when a situation is trying, it is ugly for a person to give up all hope in life, while there is still room for hope. Cynicism is ugly. Irrational and pointless hostility is ugly. Lovelessness is ugly. But if we could never possibly experience any sensation of ugliness, not even an imaginary notion or vicarious feeling of it, then we could never fully appreciate the blessing of beauty. For the meaning of it would be no more distinct than the meaning of light in a world where there could be no darkness, shades, or hues. It is like our understanding of the meaning of "tallness," which we derive from our comparison of it with "shortness," and vice versa. In a world in which everything and everybody were exactly the same size, it would be meaningless to ask, "What size is this?" or "What size is that?"

Thus, the fact that evil things can happen in the world is no matter of mere chance. That accidents can happen, that suffering and tragedy is possible, that we must live with the challenge and responsibility of facing real risks, is a fact that has a rationale without which we could never know the meaning of being truly human.

As for why we must die, I think no wholly satisfactory answer is likely to be found to this question until *after* we have died. I love the earth so much that I am perfectly at home with the thought of spending an eternal life on it, with my loved ones. Yet, I feel equally as great a longing to explore all of the natural beauties of the universe, which if it is infinite would take an immortality of time. Of course, the atheist physicist would point out that entropy is running this universe down, and eventually there will be no conditions in it conducive to life. But these same physicists claim that this universe is finite in its order, both in space and in its duration in time. I think the evidence for this is substantial, but it certainly is no reason for despair. For if God could create one universe finite in space and time, there is no reason why He could not create an infinite number of similar universes progressively throughout endless time. Moreover, there is also no reason why He could not create universes in which the laws of physics and chemistry were different. It would be purely arbitrary to say that God could create only one kind of physical system, i.e., the universe characterized by the physical laws we are familiar with now. There is no theoretical reason why God could not create a physical system characterized by a set of different laws, whereby people could have bodies that would never grow old. But if He wants a variety of types of universes, and a variety of types of life, it stands to reason that no one but He himself, as The Infinite Being, could participate in all the different types at once. And logically, even He could not participate in future kingdoms except in his progressive creativity that takes time. Which is an idea that I shall treat of at further length in Chapter 7.

"But if it is possible to have a body that never grows old or wears out," asked a student, "then why didn't God create us with such a body in the first place, rather than subject us to the terror of dying and the agony of unwanted separation from our loved ones?"

This is the question of questions, that probably causes more agony than any other the human mind can ask. For one, I can find no answer to it that completely satisfies my needs. But this is often the case in philosophy, and we sometimes must concern ourselves with finding the most satisfactory answer available, rather than one that is completely satisfactory or perfect. Certainly, the atheist answer, that all life proves eventually to be futile, can satisfy no real need at all. If my answers are not wholly satisfactory, they are at least better than the atheist answer, which is nothing more than a useless submission to despair.

I am not altogether happy with the traditional answer of religionists, but it does have genuinely sensible meaning. Namely, that the type of conditions we have to live under in this world (the risk of being killed, or the eventuality of dying) does, as I have explained already, provide the groundwork for the development of genuine personal identity through the necessity for responsible care. No one can doubt that if one knows he may be killed, or may die, through carelessness, these conditions of risk are basically what is most conducive to the development of a strong sense of the necessity to exercise care. But once one has developed this sense to the point that he *cares for the sake of caring* (rather than cares with the negative motivation of fear of the harmful consequences of not caring), then it makes sense to assume that he is spiritually ready for a body that would not grow old, in a kingdom in which people could live more happily together because they had learned how to care positively for one another's needs, rather than out of fear of pain or dying. It is altogether reasonable to assume that after a person has developed a positive identity, and after he has learned to motivate his actions positively, he would no longer need to face so much risk of the harm of not caring in order to be motivated to care. He would care responsibly for the sake of caring responsibly, rather than for the sake of escaping the pain of irresponsible care.

I am dealing here with a fact that no realistic psychologist could deny. Only spiritually and morally mature persons are prone to care deeply for each other's needs for the sake of fulfilling those needs, rather than just for the sake of escaping the pain of careless neglect of those needs. And undeniably, nobody is born on this earth with

121

this kind of positive identity and moral disposition already developed in his soul. Thus, there is a certain hoary realism in the traditional notion that life on this earth is a kind of preparation of the spirit for life in another world. If another world is possible in which persons can care responsibly without having to be goaded and whetted to do so by the fear of risk of irresponsibility, then, *eo ipso*, in such a world one could experience the joy of being a person without the need for much risk, or at least without the need for the risk of dying.[6]

But there may be other reasons for the necessity of dying on this earth. For example, the world would eventually become overpopulated beyond all tolerance if we did not die. There is no reason to assume that God wants any of us to spend an eternity on this planet, even if it could last that long, which it cannot unless God intervenes to alter the laws of physics that otherwise guarantee its doom. If I may say so in passing, eternity is a lot of time. But to live any less than that is not enough, for those who know that there is intrinsic value in life. Anyone who is deeply and affirmatively alive knows that it is impossible to ever experience enough meaning, enough value, enough beauty. Anyone who deeply loves another person knows that there can never be enough love. The closer I get to my wife in love, the more sentient we become to the fact that we can never get close enough. Each time I discover new beauty in her, I ache more acutely in my awareness of how much there is in her to behold. Every day I discover in my little daughter new facets of personal charm that arouse in me a wonder, adding definitively to my sense of the richness of being alive. I can say exactly the same for my son. And what is very remarkable, my mother (who is eighty-eight years old) has the most sensitive capacity to wonder of any human being I ever met. As a person lives more deeply, he becomes more conscious of the need to live yet more deeply, more conscious of the fact that he can never live fully enough.

The sin of most modern philosophy is its refusal to think big.

Nowhere is this sin so prominent as on college and university campuses where proud pessimists are found in all quarters who are not even conscious of their depression. The purpose of education should be to free our imagination, to expand our vision of the possibilities of what we can become, accomplish, and possess in an open future with no end. Education that establishes in one's mind the notion of an eventual end to his life, the cutting off and terminating of his possibilities once and for all, is an exercise in dereliction because it is a betrayal and abandonment of need. We need no philosophy, no science, nor any other kind of intellectual discipline that would diminish our estimation of our possibilities in the future. In this universe, the laws of physics as we now understand them would doom all life to destruction in time. But there is no need whatever to believe that this is the only universe that exists or can possibly exist, or that the laws of nature known to us now are the only possible laws of nature. We must honor our imagination, that other universes characterized by some basic differences in the laws of nature are possible; or, to say the least, that there are some conditions accompanying and following our dying in this world that make possible the permanent conservation of the person and his identity. For a human being not to believe this when he feels a need for it is to act contrary to his own need. Though I have said it before, it certainly can bear repetition: *No person needs to be reduced to a non-person.* No person needs to believe that this is his fate. If I may reiterate a fact, a need is always *for* something—something of value—and there can be no conceivable value in death. By definition, death would be non-existence, and in non-existence no value could exist. To believe that this is one's fate is neurotic. But since the symptoms of this neurosis are metaphysical, rather than medical, most of its victims are not even conscious of the fact that they are sick and do not seek therapy.[7]

6

Care in Need

Vain is the word of a philosopher that does not heal any
suffering of man. For just as there is no profit in
medicine if it does not expel the diseases of the body,
so there is no profit in philosophy if it does not expel
the suffering of the mind.

Epicurus

AT THE ULTIMATE HEART of reality is need.
Without need, there would be no need for reality of any
kind. There would be no need for truths, beauties, values, or meanings. There would be no need for goodness, nor for the experience
of goodness in any form. An intelligible concept of need is a *sine
qua non* for a wholesome and practical philosophy of life. If there
were no need there could be no need for any kind of philosophy,
nor any kind of life.

Need is metaphysical. By this, I mean that we could never possibly exist without need. Any existence could make no sense without need simply because, in such case, there would be no need for
anything to exist. Much modern philosophy categorically fails to
make sense because it denies that there are any essential needs.
In its absolute anti-absolutism, any strictly relativistic philosophy
must collapse because it denies that there is any categorical necessity; i.e., it denies that there is any absolute or essential need of
any kind. All strict relativists defeat their own purposes, in effect,
by denying that there is any definite or certain need for anybody

124

to believe in the doctrine of relativism. In reality, no philosophy can make sense that does not start out with absolutes, and the absolutes must be inherently true. In fact, relativism itself starts out with absolutes, and indeed persists in them stubbornly. But this doctrine inevitably falls because it leaves itself no solid ground to stand on, and no reliable props. Relativism is logically incoherent and hypocritical because it deals in absolutes while pretending not to, and its own absolutes are false. Relativism absolutizes change, uncertainty, indefiniteness, and indeed relativity itself. For obviously, when a philosopher rejects all absolutes he is absolutizing relativity itself, which leaves him in a netherworld where he can make no definite statements of any kind about reality and then stand behind them seriously. In other words, he can never say anything and really mean it, because not even he himself can affirm that what he says is ever definitely and certainly true. Why hold stubbornly to a doctrine that will not affirm even its own validity or necessity?

One absolute need is for need itself. Need is essential to any intelligible world order. There is a categorical necessity for need. That is, need must inform the whole cosmic scheme of things, and inhere in all reality, one way or another. Now, I am not suggesting that all actions in the world are categorically necessary; for if I did this, I would be condoning and justifying even the most useless and pernicious acts, by implying that there is a need for such acts to occur. Many of our most destructive acts occur not because there is a necessity for us to commit them, but only because we choose to commit them, which means, the acts arise out of freedom of volition, rather than out of any categorical necessity. Certainly, we could choose to leave such acts unperformed, and as a result the world would be better off. I should have to insist, however, that the *possibility* of such acts is necessary, i.e., that there is a categorical necessity for freedom of choice, for reasons that I shall delineate in the following chapter. Without freedom of choice there could be no personal identity, nor understanding of the meaning of moral responsibility and goodness. In reality, there is and always has been a need for persons to exist. The world ground ultimately must be personal. The ultimate and eternal reality must be God, the Cosmic Person, who creates all finite persons and creatures out of himself, and basically out of need. There is an absolute need in reality for persons to exist, for the simple and obvious reason that any world with persons in it contains more value than could the same world with never any persons in it at all.

God has to have always existed in the past. The atheistic assumption that the world ground is ultimately impersonal, that in fact there ultimately is no world ground at all (except meaningless chance), can meet none of the essential criteria for a practical, need-oriented philosophy of life. Atheism assumes that persons are brought into existence in this universe accidentally by blind impersonal forces that represent no reason, purpose, or need whatever. From the standpoint of logic, anybody who can believe this surely can believe anything he wishes, for it is not logically possible that persons and personal effects can be brought into being by causes that are categorically impersonal in essence. What is more, even if this were possible one could not use it as an argument for atheism, or an argument against God. For if the existence of a finite person need have no personal cause, or, if a finite person need not be constituted of personal essences, then the same can be said about an Infinite Person, and there is no conceivable reason why God cannot exist.

One fact is indisputable: there is a *need* for God to exist, for the plain and unarguable reason that there could be no conceivable time when God's non-existence could be better than his existence.[1] The idea that an Infinite Mind exists, characterized by infinite understanding, reason, and creative love, is inherently better than the idea of a godless world that is only an absurd accident that inevitably fails to honor our needs. From the viewpoint of atheism, all reason, love, and creation is ultimately accidental, temporary, and doomed to destruction. Only a very unfortunate person characterized by a sick sense of values could say that such a predicament would be better than God. That there is a need for God can be understood by anyone who has tasted a profoundly joyful love for another person and felt the need to conserve the beauty and goodness of that love. Or at least, this understanding will exist in the mind of a practical person who is conscious of his real life needs and is willing to honor them with what he chooses to believe. Before any human being ever existed on this earth, there was in reality a *need* for human beings to be brought into existence, and for them to find meaning and joy in their love for life and one another. The intrinsic value of being a rational and loving person always needs to be conserved, and any person who is fully conscious of such value will feel that need. Even the atheist must acknowledge the need for the conservation of life's sacred values, once he ever experiences such values in full consciousness, and then chooses not to be demonic in his relationship with himself.

But systematic and dedicated atheism inevitably is demonic because it functions in opposition to one's real life needs. There is no possible way to argue that there are no intrinsic or sacred values in life. For if no such values existed, there could be no value in arguing for or against anything, period. Nor, after granting that intrinsic values in human life do exist, can anyone sincerely argue that there is no need for their permanent conservation. Anyone who argues that there is no need to conserve the value in being a person either has not yet discovered much value in himself or others; or else, he is the beneficiary of that very value but without adequate awareness of it, or without adequate appreciation of it. At any rate, once a person experiences such value with awareness, he must then affirm the need to conserve it, or else be demonic.

Atheism is not an empirical doctrine. It is not a philosophy of life resting on demonstrable facts and logical reason that necessitates despair over the conservation of life's sacred values. There is no possible way to demonstrate that God does not exist. Nor can anyone demonstrate that a person is a mere glob of brain chemicals doomed to eventual dissolution. Atheism is a negative religious *faith*, grounded not in unconfutable facts but only in prejudicial thinking or in an indisposition to believe in God. The fundamental assumptions of atheistic philosophy are in no way dictated by intellectual necessity. The doctrine enjoys the support of no facts whatever. On the contrary, it ignores many facts that no practical philosophy can ever afford to ignore.

For example, it ignores the research of the science of parapsychology, which has demonstrated that the immortality of the human soul (that the mind can transcend the body chemistry and survive the grave) is an unmistakably real possibility, and in fact, a high probability. That the human mind is not reducible to chemistry has been demonstrated by the feats it has performed in telepathy, clairvoyance, hypnosis, and telekinesis. There is no doubt that the mind interacts with its body, produces effects in its body, and is affected by its body. But the idea that the mind ultimately *is* the body, or is only the epiphenomena of the electrochemical activities in the brain, clearly is out of keeping with the discernible facts.

As a particular discipline, the science of chemistry deals exclusively with chemical facts, i.e., with chemical effects and chemical causes. Or to be more specific, it deals with data in the physical and atomic world characterized by attributes or qualities that we describe as substantial or material. Chemistry is the science of the composition, structure, properties, and reactions of matter, especially of atomic and molecular systems. In contemporary philosophy and psychology there are numerous doctrines that reduce a *person* to mere chemistry. Such doctrines deny that a human being is in any way a free agent, that he can exist and function in some ways independently of his body chemistry. Such doctrines insist that a person always behaves the way he does because he has been conditioned or compelled to behave that way by electrochemical forces in his body over which he has no free control.

This would mean that freedom of choice is an illusion, and that a person is 100 per cent a product of his body chemistry. It would mean that we are just very complex biochemical machines, and that is all we are. Words like "soul," "psyche," "mind," and "spirit" for these doctrines are semantical illusions if they are meant to signify a free agent who is not chemical in his nature. Such doctrines go by a variety of names, but in general are labeled as "behaviorism" or "determinism," meaning that our behavior is determined strictly by environmental influences and the laws of biochemistry. I find that the majority of teaching and practicing psychologists whom I know personally do adhere to this way of thinking.

A critical analysis of this point of view will reveal that it is grounded in oversimplification and an ignorance of some plain facts about the nature of a person. Of course, if I may repeat, the mind does interact with the body, affects it, and is affected by it. And indeed, this is a very great mystery, how the mind and body can affect one another. But we make no sense at all in talking about S/R (stimulus and response) after we have done away with the respond*er*, or the agent who responds. It is semantical nonsense to speak of stimulus *and* response, as though one were assigning to the two terms logically distinct meanings, and then annihilating that very distinction by equating the terms, as though they meant exactly the same thing. Logically, the impersonal stimuli (electro-chemical forces) coming into the brain from outside cannot respond meaningfully to themselves. If there is no responder, then *who* can be meaningfully stimulated, or *who* can meaningfully respond? The pronoun *who* refers to a spiritual agent, not to a glob of swirling atoms or to a multiplicity of impersonal forces operating in a lump of tissue. Philosophers crassly oversimplify when they reduce mind to nothing but gross chemical forces. Behaviorism can be taken seriously only by persons who intuit no real personal meaning in the word "self."

A person *has* a body, but he does not *have* a soul or self. Rather, he *is* a self, a spiritual agent, and he can neither logically nor psychologically equate his self with his body. I am not a body; I *have* a body; I *am* a person, a spiritual agent who can think, feel, remember, imagine, act, react, and choose. Now, to a certain extent my ability or opportunity to react to a stimulus coming into my brain depends upon that stimulus getting in, which sometimes it cannot if the brain is damaged, or saturated with alcohol, or narcotized with a drug, etc. If a stimulus is kept from getting into a person's brain tissue, such as a light stimulus in the deficient visual apparati of the blind, then one cannot respond to it. This is true because the spirit *is* housed in the brain, which is where the stimuli appear for a response. But it does not follow from this that the spirit *is* the brain. Behaviorists would have us believe that the mind and the brain are the same because certain physical stimuli can evoke certain memories, etc. But in point of plain fact, remembering is an *act* performed by the mind; memory is mental; it is constituted of *awareness* of one's past experiences and acts. I would readily grant that certain stimuli to the brain can evoke certain memories. But all this proves is that the mind is performing the intelligent act of remembering, by associating certain types of past experiences with certain types of past stimuli that accompanied those experiences; and certainly, one cannot infer from this that there is no distinction between mind and brain, or between the stimuli and the agent who responds to those stimuli.

The mind's association of certain memories with certain stimuli in the brain does not prove that the spirit *is* the brain. Much misunderstanding of the nature of memory has been caused by the famous recent experiments with "the chemistry of memory" at Baylor University. The press reports that I have read on these experiments have been almost uniformly naive. Very common have been such headlines as "Mice Memory Captured in Research Test Tube," "Memory is Merely a Matter of Molecules," etc.

In these experiments, Baylor scientists collected the brains of over 6,000 rats who had been conditioned to respond in given ways to given stimuli. Then they isolated chemicals from these brains and injected them into other laboratory rats who were not trained to respond in the same way to the same stimuli. The untrained animals then behaved as though they had been trained like the others. The so-called "memory material" was found to be a peptide, which is a chain of amino acids.

It is unfortunate that so many readers have been perturbed by reports on these experiments. There is no factual or logical reason to infer from them that "remembering is chemical," or that "mind is merely molecular." For in point of fact, nothing has been proved by these experiments except that common chemical stimuli in the brains of rats tend to be interpreted in a common way by the rats' minds. In other words, the minds of rats are not characterized by anything near the degree of freedom of the human psyche to *decide* how it will respond to given chemical stimuli in the brain. Even in the human mind there is never unlimited freedom of choice as to how to respond to any and all chemical stimuli in the brain. Our minds work partly spontaneously or freely, but also partly lawfully, as we too have a disposition to respond in common ways to certain types of chemical stimuli in our brains.

Baylor scientists acknowledged that "None of these substances are directly applicable to human learning and memory."[2] That memory (remembering) literally can be held in a test tube is an altogether gullible notion, for anyone who would take it seriously. For what was held in a test tube was simply a peptide, which is in fact only a chemical that has no memory of anything at all. Injected into untrained rats, a peptide provided the same *stimulus* that was present in the brains of the trained. But the *response* to that stimulus, whether in trained or untrained rats, obviously was mental, if we are to assume that there was something going on in the rats' *minds.* What is evident is that the untrained rats behaved in a way similar to the trained ones, in response to the same chemical stimuli present in their brains. But it does not follow from this that *remembering* is chemical. Real memory involves a *knowledge* of past events, and knowledge as such is never physical or chemical in its nature. Certainly, neither is the *past* physical. In a mere physical object, or chemical, there can be no remembering of anything whatever. That rats often tend to respond in common ways to common chemical stimuli in their brains is a demonstrable fact. But it is also a demonstrable fact that there are many exceptions, and that even a rat has some degree of mental autonomy, and is *not* merely a chemical machine. I myself worked with rats in the experimental phychology laboratory and found this to be an indisputable fact: even the most conditioned rats are known to be less than always predictable in their behavior, and mechanistic psychologists are notorious for their failure to observe deviant behavior in conditioned rats objectively.* The idea that the mental act of *remembering* is nothing but a mindless chemical called a peptide—this is too gullible a notion to merit further attention.

Today, it is a well known truth that a brain with a spirit in it who does not have a will to see can see nothing at all. This is a fact that has been observed over and over in the modern science of psychosomatic medicine. In extreme cases of fixed unwillingness to relate with the outside world (such as in acute catatonic schizophrenia), a person will respond to no external stimuli whatever; e.g., he will not even respond to a burning match with a flinch. Every psychiatrist knows about "conversion hysteria," of paralyzed limbs that will not respond to any stimuli (not even to pricking needles or extreme heat or cold) until the patient changes his mind and wills to respond. In addition to this, there is the overwhelming evidence gathered by parapsychologists that a human being sometimes in a mental act of immediacy can *intuit* events occurring thousands of miles away, without the use of sensory apparati, and with no physical or chemical media whatever involved. This is known as clairvoyance, or also as telepathy when communication with another person is accomplished without the benefit of any physical media. Rigorously controlled laboratory experiments have produced evidence beyond reasonable doubt that many persons often can see into the possible future, and indeed, predict some events totally beyond the space-time range of their biological senses. There is no possible way to explain seeing into the future in terms of the

---

*Anecdotally, the reader may recall the so-called Harvard law of animal behavior that "Under carefully controlled experimental conditions, a laboratory rat—will do as he damn pleases."

material data of mere chemistry and physics, which scientifically can be observed only in the present.

What is more, the same parapsychology laboratories have revealed the special talents of many individuals who can move objects, and break glasses, and influence the behavior of matter simply by concentrating on it and willing it. Some persons can control the throw of dice by concentrating on electrically rotated wire cages which produce so many uninterrupted series of sevens and elevens that it defies all explanation by "chance." This is known as telekinesis, or the power of the mind to control matter. There is a consensus of opinion amongst parapsychologists that these talents or preternatural psychical capacities actually lie latent within all of us, but as of now most of us have learned very little about how to recognize such power and successfully tap it. One thing has been established for certain: scepticism interferes radically with this ability, and there is a growing consensus that there is a close correlation between the possibility that a person can do such things and his faith that he can do them. We know, for example, that a person in a profound hypnotic trance can do many things that he cannot do in a conscious state when his power is diminished by his own inhibitions and doubts. Absolutely uninhibited in a hypnotic trance, any person can do more push-ups than he can do in a conscious state where he obstructs his own capacity with the debilitating effects of self-doubt. He can lift more weight, make his body more rigid and resistant to force, and exercise more control over his metabolism and nerves.[3]

However, we need not turn to ESP (extra-sensory perception) or the preternatural aspects in human behavior to find evidence for the spirit. A person needs only to look at the simplest facts about his ordinary natural *self*.[4] For example, the self can never find itself in anything external to or outside of itself. The self can find itself only in itself. No person can find his self in his foot, heart, liver, thumb, or brain. Nor can he find himself in any atomic particle or quantum, or in any atom or molecule, or in any biological tissue. Neither can he find himself in any chemical or chemical reaction, or in any combination of chemicals or chemical reactions. We can take a person's brain out of his skull and examine any part of its tissue under a microscope. But therein we can find no signs whatever of a self. Under a microscope we can find only biological tissue and its electrochemical components and activities; we can never find any love, hope, purpose, thought, feeling, imagination, memory, or choice. The brain is a complex organic object with such physical attributes as size, form, weight, texture, cells, and their atomic components. One can always find in the brain a variety of electrochemical activities, no single one of which he can ever find in his *self*.

The self is a subject, not an object.[5] The self has no tangible or physico-chemical properties of any kind to make it localizable, observable, or measurable in space. The brain *occupies* space. The self does not. The self is *in* space, but it does not displace it, and it has no substantial or palpable attributes such as size, shape, color, hardness, or weight. The self is not a material being, but rather, is a spiritual being whose essential qualities we can learn nothing about by studying mere physics or chemistry. In studying physics and chemistry we learn only about the phenomena of physics and chemistry; we learn nothing about the self. To learn about the self, the self has to study itself. I learn about the nature and needs of myself by studying myself and other selves. I learn about what it means to be a person by being a person, not by being that conglomeration of physical forces that sustain the existence of my body and brain. I am no more my brain than I am my automobile, for both are outside of myself, even though I am in much more intimate and lasting possession of my brain than my car, because the former is a much more needed vehicle for my purposes in this life. I study my brain. It does not study me. I talk about the electrochemical activities in my nervous system and body. They do not talk about me. All of the stimuli that come into my brain are physical—e.g., the light waves that come into my eyeballs and eventually are transmitted electronically to the brain, sound waves through my ears, and chemical forces (molecules) striking the nerve end organs in my skin. At just about any moment during a conscious state my brain is deluged with electrochemical data that come into it from the outside. I must unify and associate all of these data, read meaning into them, and interpret their significance for me and for others in the world. Certainly, the physical data coming into the brain cannot interpret their own significance, for this would be both logically and semantically impossible. These electrochemical activities in the brain constitute a *plurality* of phenomena, while only *one* singular irreducible being (an agent) could ever logically conceive of itself as a self, or say "I." My sense organs are biological

133

objects. I, a subject, reflect on them; they do not reflect on me. I reflect on my body; but also, I make myself the object of my own reflections. It is I who think of myself as a self and distinguish my self from my body. It is I who say *I*. The pronoun "I" refers to a self, a person, an irreducible spiritual *being*.[6] It is inconceivable that a bunch of swirling atoms or electrochemical activities (impersonal forces) could ever say "I" (except on a phonograph record where there is no self-identity at all).

A philosopher can hold to behaviorism only by ignoring the most important facts in human experience.[7] The phenomena of physics and chemistry in the body and the world are certainly important. Far be it from me to deny the needs that are served for God and his creatures by the physical realities that He has created in this world. But purely physical and chemical data would be meaningless if it were not for meaning in the world, and meaning as such is never merely physical or chemical. Meaning as such has no height, width, depth, wavelength, texture, or any other physical or chemical qualities. If there was no mind in the universe, these physical attributes would have no conceivable meaning whatever. For indeed, there would simply be no one for whom they could have any meaning. A philosopher can be a materialist only by overlooking those realities in the world that are in no way material. For example, *awareness*.

Awareness is psychological. It is found only by the self within the self. When a man holds a chemical in a test tube, that is exactly what he holds in his test tube. He does not hold a test tube full of meaning or awareness. The meaning of the chemical in the test tube lies in the purpose that its being there serves. Awareness cannot be observed or measured with physical or chemical devices. It can be observed only by intuition, that wondrous power found only by the mind within itself. Awareness has no conceivable chemical attributes whatever. The same can be said for reason, purpose, love, hope, truth, choice, value, insight, need, feeling, and will.

If the behaviorist wishes to argue this point, then surely he can offer us some evidence for his position. For example, let us take an instance of what I would define as a purely spiritual thing, namely, an *idea*. To be very specific, let us take the idea that justice is better than injustice. Now, if an idea is in essence physical or chemical, then precisely what are some of the physical or chemical properties of this idea, that justice is better than injustice? I challenge the behaviorist to show that his claim does have some foundation in fact. Since he claims that everything constituting a human being is in the last analysis chemical, then precisely *what* is chemical about this thought, or this idea, I have in my mind, that justice is better than injustice? If the behaviorist is right, then surely he can answer the following questions with definitive answers as a chemist: What is the valence of this idea, that justice is better than injustice? What is the idea's atomic weight? How could a chemist determine the molecular formula for the idea of justice? What is its specific gravity? Its density? Its mass? Its boiling point and freezing point? All atomic particles are always in motion, at some discernible rate of speed. How then could a chemist or physicist measure how fast this idea is moving? And does it have an axis? What indeed are the characteristics of its motion? Does it move in waves? What is its charge? Now of course, anything that is in essence chemical can be chemically classified. How would a chemist classify the idea of justice? Is it a gas, compound, or liquid? Is it a solid? Or is it a plasma? What is its intrinsic energy? What are some of its thermal qualities? For example, if this idea were held close to a burning match, would its photons move toward or away from the fire? What is its atomic number? How many of these ideas would it take to knock an electron out of its orb? What are some of its reactive characteristics? For instance, how would the idea of justice react if it were dropped into a vial of hydrochloric acid? If I moved justice close to a magnet, would it gravitate toward the positive or negative pole? And what about injustice? Would it gravitate toward the opposite pole?

Now clearly, enough said. Thoughts, feelings, ideas, decisions can never possibly be classified as physical or chemical for the simple reason that they are spiritual realities totally insusceptible to any kind of material classification. A body is physical, but the person using that body is spiritual, and the attempt to reduce a spirit to something merely physical or chemical is a philosophical blunder of the greatest magnitude.

Any psychiatrist will verify that when a person decides he no longer has any desire or need for his body, then his body will die. When the person inhabiting the brain of a Homo-sapiens organism loses his will to live in that organism, then that organism will degenerate for certain; or to say the very least, it can be kept "alive" only by artificial means. I have known many men who retired in excellent health from their lifelong jobs because they were super-annuated with no choice in the matter. Whereupon, they promptly lost their motivation to live because it had been previously focused very predominately in their daily work. These men felt that they no longer had anything which they could do with their bodies; hence, they felt no meaningful relationship with their bodies and no reason to tend to them carefully.

In one of my classes, an atheist guest speaker stated that he could believe in the immortality of the mind if he could just succeed in believing in the existence of a mind at all. As he put it, all of the evidence of human behavior in the laboratory proves that the so called "mind" is nothing but the neurophysiological processes present in the brain. But I must submit, if there is no evidence for the existence of minds, then there is no evidence for anything whatever. For it should be obvious that the evaluation of evidence is a mental process, that indeed, if the act of evaluation is not mental, then what is material about it? Also, it should be obvious that thought is a mental effect producible only by a mind, and findable only by a mind within itself. Undeniably, no chemist can find any thought in any chemical, or chemical reaction, or in any chemical property of any kind. The world's most ingenious chemists can never put chemicals together in such a way as to produce a thinking agent. Or, those who claim that it can be done—let them do it and then talk about it. In their laboratories, biochemists study the biological vehicle for life: the body. But the will to live that inhabits this physico-chemical vehicle is a mystery that no chemist, however brilliant, will ever be able to penetrate with mere physics or chemistry. It takes a mind to recognize a mind. Indeed, it takes a mind to recognize a body or any physical forces whatever. Recognition is not a material being or activity, but rather, is an act performed by a mind. If the fact of mind cannot be discovered by intuition within the mind itself, then it cannot be discovered at all. The mind is a dynamic spiritual agent capable of performing many different kinds of acts of mentation. Mentation simply is never a chemical phenomenon, and does not lend itself to chemical analysis. For it should be obvious that analysis itself is an act of mentation and is not a material phenomenon of any kind. We analyze the facts of chemistry. The facts of chemistry analyze nothing whatever.

The possibility of the mind's immortality lies inherent in the fact that it is in essence non-material. The *relationship* of the mind with the brain is of course dependent upon the structure and quality of the brain and the stimuli that enter it. But this relationship is also overwhelmingly dependent upon the mind's *will* to use the brain. And there is ample evidence in parapsychology that the mind can function with varying degrees of autonomy as an agent, i.e., independently of the electrochemical activities in the brain. This means that the mind's existence is not dependent upon the brain, but rather, upon the spiritual essences which constitute it. If one can see this fact clearly, that the *self* is not material, then he can see the unmistakable logical and empirical possibility of the permanent conservation of his personal identity in his immortal spirit and memory.

As I mentioned earlier, despair is useless, in fact harmful, when it acts inimically to one's real life needs. Of course there are intelligent and necessary forms of despair, such as when one despairs of fulfilling immoral desires, or of adhering to unreasonable notions, or of persisting in inane or destructive behavior. There are times when one should give up; and this means giving up behavior that does unnecessary violence to our real life needs. In the luxury of our freedom of choice we do not always enjoy the benefits of choice; but rather at times, we are caught up in the agony of choosing, and sometimes we are the tragic victims of our very own choices. For example, in our freedom we may choose to despair when there is no real necessity for despair. We may even despair diabolically and perversely. We may uselessly malign and depress ourselves, and make others the victims of our own self-mistreatment. A man not only can be vicious to others, but can be vicious to himself in frustrating, abusing, and denying his own real needs. What makes freedom even more of a burden is the fact that a human being can mistreat himself with seemingly no consciousness whatever of the fact that he is doing himself harm.

In the dynamics of freedom, a person can use his own mind to deceive and misguide himself, and to repress his awareness of his own real needs. Because he is a free agent a man can choose how he will relate with himself; and in this freedom he may distort his understanding of his own motives, desires, and self-relations. He may choose to act contrary to his own better judgment. He may dissemble, corrupt himself, and make a mockery of his own dignity. Worst of all, if he is a learned and polished individual, he may do it in ways that are socially esteemed and clever. In fact, I have found no despair quite so gifted as that of the learned university philosophy professors who are hoaxed by their own intellectual snares. Many bait their students with semantical chicanery and logical sleight of hand. But what is most interesting is the proud manner in which they masquerade how they inveigle and swindle even their own spirits. We see the most august examples of such artifices in some Nobel Prize writers who monger despair as though it were something precious and sacred. For instance, Camus, Sartre, and Russell.[8] Personally, I can feel more respect for Judas Iscariot who despaired out and out, than I can feel for the befoolers who would dress up despair as something intellectually sophisticated and emotionally urbane. Atheists of this sort hide from the ugliness of their own doctrine, which is in theory an affirmation of the ultimacy of meaninglessness and death.

By its very premises, atheism in principle makes a mockery of all of our life needs by insisting that we nurture them ultimately in vain. In fact, the doctrine maintains that after all is said and done there can be no real need whatever. The respected atheists preach in eloquent language that there is no basis for hope, that in the end there is only nothingness and death. In the time of reckoning, all of the needs of the human heart will be stifled, and all its yearning crushed. But then, in the same breath these pundits beseech us to care responsibly for one another, as though the enterprise of care could discover some values that can and ought to be permanently conserved. They speak of their "humanism," of man's need to care truly and sincerely for himself and his fellows. Then they put rouge and a smile on the sepulchral face of hopelessness, to pass it off as something noble and beautiful in the human spirit.

I do not wish to give the impression that I look upon all atheists as hypocrites and dissemblers. I am convinced that some of my friends are atheists because they have been emotionally conditioned and intellectually indoctrinated in negative philosophy. Moreover, I have known some persons whose experience of life has been so deprived of reason and love that it is understandable why we say nothing meaningful to them when we speak of the divine reason and love of God. Unquestionably, there are unfortunate persons in the world who have been so terribly mistreated by life that we could not readily expect them to understand the intrinsic value of responsible and loving care. Surely, no one can understand such care who has never had meaningful access to it. It is a plain truth that a human being learns nothing about the divine reason and love of God until he is first treated reasonably and lovingly by some person who cares for him on this earth. Albeit, I can see nothing to gain by approaching such persons with the attitude that all human care and effort proves eventually to be an utter waste.

Because professional atheism is grounded in a faithful commitment, it is unquestionably a religion. But it is a cheap religion because its despair is unnecessary, since it settles for drastically less than that which is unquestionably possible. This is precisely what immoral despair is: settling for less than that degree of need fulfillment that is conceivably possible. A person is simply arrogant, not to mention self-defeating, to sweep the cosmos with his human sight and declare categorically that all of his life needs are doomed ultimately to be thwarted. From the standpoint of atheism, the ultimate reality is needlessness and carelessness. Or, if some atheist did grant that there is ultimate need, then his very concept of need would be irrational since, by his own words, he is insisting that the need is ultimately for nothing because there is no truth and value that the need is for. I fail to see how anyone could take such a philosophy seriously and find any genuine inspiration or encouragement in it. When its fundamental premises and logical implications are taken emotionally to heart, atheism can be only a leaden philosophy, poisonous when ingested.

While earning my doctorate, I had the disillusioning firsthand experience of seeing how impractical are so many professors whose philosophy of life is not oriented around need. Hour after hour, I sat in classes listening to professors talk in theoretical obscurities totally unrelated to the realities of care. The dominant impracticality of most modern philosophers is their general lack of understanding of need, and their lack of devotion to need. In fact, I found the theories of most of my professors of philosophy and psychology to be so incompatible with real need that one could use them to rationalize the most irrational and hideous imaginable kinds of human behavior. My professors of course would not intend their theories to be thus used. But in their relativism, most of my graduate school teachers insisted theoretically that no needs of any kind are really essential, that no need can exist except in the perception or imagination of an individual who entertains it. With this kind of teaching, professors do nothing to deepen their students' understanding of their own real needs, nor of the nature of the human condition at large. For in the world of actual fact, if a person has a need, then he has the need whether he perceives it or not, or acknowledges it or not, or cares about it or not. At the beginning, I asserted that need is metaphysical, that where a need exists it is real independently of whether we are aware of it or care about it.

For example, every person alive has a need for more wisdom and understanding, regardless of how ignorant he may be of this need, or of how self-complacent he may have become in his ignorance. A person may be afflicted with a malignant cancer and have no awareness whatever of it because the more painful symptoms of it have not yet set in. Or, he may experience pain but have no understanding at all of the factual causes of it in his body. But certainly, his lack of awareness of the need to know about the cancer does not undo the reality and relevance of the need as a fact. The fact of the cancer being there can make the crucial difference between the person dying or remaining alive. Obviously, he needs to learn about the cancer in his body even if he is totally unaware of the need. The need is an objective fact. The subject's lack of awareness of the need does not in truth cancel out the reality of the need or its relevance to his life. Every human being needs to see something of value in himself and in others even if his experiences of life become so unfortunate or distorted that he loses all awareness of this need. Need exists in and of itself, as an objective fact. For example, before any artist can contribute to the beauties of the world he must first become conscious of the need for more beauty. But any subject's awareness, or lack of awareness, of his real needs may make the crucial difference of whether his needs will be neglected, abused, or fulfilled. The need is metaphysical, but the awareness of it is psychological, and no philosophy of education can be realistic that is not conscious of the difference. Any educational philosophy is adjusted to reality only if it is need-oriented both in theory and in practice. The purpose of education is to make us conscious of our essential life needs. A person is educated only insofar as he can distinguish between desires grounded in a true understanding of need and desires that are not. Of course, the educated man must be insightful into effective means and methods of fulfilling these needs.

In a realistic philosophy of care we cannot separate the idea of need from the idea of value. Today, there are many nihilistic schools of philosophy and psychology that deny there are any absolute or essential values. Philosophers usually have two basic terms for speaking of values. One: something has *intrinsic* value if it is valuable in and of itself, or if it should be sought as an end in itself, rather than simply as a means to some arbitrary end. Two: something has *extrinsic* value if it is not worth seeking as an end in itself, but is useful as a tool to accomplishing some personal goal.

Relativistic schools of philosophy and psychology deny that any intrinsic values are possible. There is never anything in existence that is *inherently* valuable, or *in essence* valuable, or valuable *by nature*. In other words there is nothing in the world, either concrete or abstract, potential or actual, that is *necessarily* valuable. From the viewpoint of the relativists, a thing has value only if someone reads value into it or arbitrarily places value on it. There is no thing of any kind that is necessarily valuable for anybody at any time. When pressed to take a certain stand on a value judgment in principle, the relativist will never take any position except the position of never taking any definite or certain position, since, he claims, no value judgment can ever be necessarily true.

I fail to see how there can be any justification for any moral judgment if there are no essential truths or objective facts in which a judgment can be grounded. No idea of need can make sense unless it presupposes that there are intrinsic values. For as I have stated already, a need is always for something, and How can there be any real need if there is nothing of real value that a person ever has a definite and essential need *for*? If there is no thing that is inherently good, i.e., valuable in and of itself, then How can we say that somebody has a real need for it? Why do I have a need for something if it is not necessarily valuable? For example, Why do I have a need for positive self-worth if there is nothing necessarily good about self-worth? Without intrinsic values, self-contempt would under any circumstances be equally as good as self-respect. And if this were the case, Why *should* parents and teachers treat their children in such ways as to help them develop respect and confidence in themselves?

In point of plain fact, there could never be even any *ex*trinsic values to life if there were no intrinsic values at all. For example, it should be obvious that positive health is an intrinsic value. Positive health is something worth seeking as an end in itself. It is something that everybody needs, that no living being can afford to be without. No person ever has to justify his desire for positive health simply because it is an intrinsic value, i.e., is by nature good, in

141

and of itself. Certainly, the individual may have to justify the means he employs to accomplish and sustain good health. For instance, he does not have the right to good health if he will not recognize and honor this same need in others, or if he violates this need in others by treating them only as means to his selfish ends. Any person is better off with positive health than he is without it, even though there are distorted minds who neurotically torture themselves with sickness because they do not relate with themselves in terms of intrinsic values.

In a grocery store, I use money as a means to buy food to maintain my good health, which is an intrinsic value. In eating food I fulfill my need for two intrinsic values: (1) the experience of harmless joy, and (2) the experience of positive health. Every human being has a need to experience joy in life and a need to be healthy. Surely, no rational man would ever recommend bad health and joylessness as things worth cultivating as ends in themselves. Nor would he define money as an intrinsic value in life. We have no need for money as an end in itself, but only as a means for the achieving of good ends. Yet, in a grocery store money cannot exist even as an *ex*trinsic value unless it has the *intrinsic truth* value of being in a man's hand when he goes to pay for his groceries. *Being* is an intrinsic *truth* value, since without it there could be no truth or value of any kind. A psychotic cannot buy groceries by imagining that there is money in his hand before the cashier. A grocery store cashier simply will not hand out groceries for illusions. The purchaser must *in truth* have real money in his hand, or he will get no groceries, but only an astonished look and refusal from the store's manager.

In my experience as a teacher I have worked in ten grade schools, high schools, colleges and universities. From observation of many teachers, I have concluded that the dominant shortcoming of our secular educational system is its failure to teach people to think and act in terms of life's intrinsic needs and values. Consequently, in my teacher-training classes I now put a strong emphasis on the necessity for teachers to help children and adolescents learn to recognize and honor their own real life needs. This can be done effectively only if they also learn to recognize and honor the essential needs of the people around them. It is unfortunate that children and adolescents, and indeed also adult students in the universities and colleges, too often learn to direct their lives by criteria that are false. There are three false criteria for judging human behavior that I find unwholesome in the character and thinking of most teachers. And in fact, I find it also true in the case of most ministers and parents.

These false criteria are: (1) custom, (2) personal power, and (3) personal preference and taste.

Unmistakably, the fact that something is customarily done or not done cannot make it right or wrong. Nor can the fact that someone has the power to impose his values on others, or to do something and get by with it politically and socially, necessarily make his action right. Power is good only when it is used as a means to achieve some intrinsically justifiable end. Only a neurotic egotist would wish to cultivate power as an end in itself, or to use it immorally to violate the needs and rights of others. The most commonly used false criterion for judging is personal preference and taste. Sometimes a student will ask, "Teacher, why do we have to do this?" And the teacher will answer, "Because I prefer for you to do it, that's why." In such case, the teacher is using his individual preference and taste as a determinant of the needs and rights of others, which is always a grossly unsatisfactory answer to a thinking student's question.

Or the teacher may answer, "We are doing it because that's the way it always has been done," which is an empty appeal to custom or tradition without a rationale. No thinking person will accept custom *per se* as a justification for an act (especially an act of imposition of one's values on others) any more than he will accept some other individual's unique taste as the dictator of his own. Many teachers, like parents, and indeed business and political bosses, often appeal merely to power. I once heard a high school student ask his teacher, "Why do I have to memorize all of these poems? Can't we just read them and discuss them, and give our reactions to them?" Only to hear the teacher reply, "You will memorize them because I am telling you to memorize them, that's why. And if you don't do it, then I will lower the boom on your head!" Obviously, in this case the teacher did not understand the student's right to a rationale for the imposed assignment, and to his need for a satisfactory answer to a sincere question. Before that course was over, the teacher and students had become systematic enemies.

No person can ever justify his behavior by appealing to custom, power, or taste. There are good and bad customs, and some customs are categorically ignorant of the individual's real life needs and rights. It was contrary to Adolf Hitler's personal preference and taste to allow Jewish people to exist in the world. He attempted to justify his actions to extinguish them (he was directly responsible for the murder of between six and eight million) by appealing to the customary distaste for Jews in Germany, and to the German people's gullible sanction of his authoritarian and ruthless use of power. Clearly, if we are going to object to these false criteria in judging human acts, then we must substitute in their place some objectively valid principles regarding man's needs and rights, or else be every bit as arbitrary as the arbitrariness that we condemn in others. Unless there are some essential truths and facts about human nature and needs, all judgments about right and wrong must be purely arbitrary, and a rational philosophy of life is categorically impossible.

What are the essential or intrinsic values of life? What are the things that *all* children, in any culture or generation, have the need to learn and *ought* to have the opportunity to learn? Regardless of his nationality, race, and social and economic class, what are the things that *no* human being can afford to be ignorant of, despite the peculiar mores, fashions, fads, and cultural forces in his particular environment?

Some of the major intrinsic values of life are positive health, emotional and intellectual integrity, reasonableness, openness to growth, compassion, unselfish love, unselfish joy, the experience of beauty, constructive creativity, constructive hope, and constructive faith. Anything that necessarily fulfills intrinsic life needs is of intrinsic value. My cats define purring as an intrinsic value (it represents joy). My little five year old son (Taos), and my little daughter (Summer), obviously define the joy of warm affection as an intrinsic value—which they feel, and I feel, when I hold them in my arms. Whatever enhances the depth of one's communion with other persons and creatures (as indeed also, with the plant life around one) is valuable in essence. When I studied educational philosophy and psychology, my teachers largely wasted my time by focusing my attention almost exclusively on the processes and laws of learning and other academic abstractions. Of course, I readily affirm the value in understanding such processes and laws when they can be used to effectively enhance the quality of care in the practical conduct of our lives. But such courses often are a waste of time because they scarcely touch on the essential needs in man and the animal and plant life surrounding him. Even my teachers devoted to Abraham Maslow, who is most noted as the educational psychologist of need, were basically superficial in their understanding and dedication to need. In fact, Maslow's own list of vital life needs is inadequate, as is his concept of moral freedom.[9]

It is no wonder so many students have protested such courses. Despite the claim of educators to have done it already, I believe there is an urgent call to revitalize the whole teacher-training enterprise in the education colleges. And this can be done only by bringing minds to bear on life's intrinsic needs and values. Technologically, we are progressing so rapidly that many people are confounded. But this only increases the danger we constitute to one another if we do not learn to use our newly discovered powers with more constructive kinds of care. Beginning in the grade schools, teachers must spend more time talking with their pupils about life's essential needs and values. It certainly can be done with the simplest language by imaginative teachers. It can be done with creative sociodramas, where children make up their own plays and act them out spontaneously with their own language. For example, I know an excellent second grade teacher who leads her children frequently into creative dramatics in the classroom, for purposes of teaching them the logic of human rights. Recently, I observed her children dramatize the harmfulness of racial prejudice and discrimination in a series of creative plays. In each play, some white children wore black masks and learned through vicarious experience something about what it feels like to be ostracized, rejected, and needlessly restricted in their freedom simply because of the color differences in skin. Children are very imaginative, and can learn enormously through projecting themselves into situations even where their sharing of the experiences of others is purely vicarious. In addition to this, the children learn simply by being in the presence of a teacher who is a living example of the values she wishes her children to cherish.

I think a great help could come from administrators selecting more meaningful readers as learning texts for children. Unmistakably, most texts for teaching reading are totally devoid of significant life situations from which children can learn something about intrinsic needs and values. They are indeed incredibly bland. Billy sees Spot. Spot sees the ball. Billy runs for Spot. Spot runs for the ball. Such readers are a study in innocuous banality. Even if they do an acceptably good job of teaching children how to read, they teach *nothing but* the skill of reading, while better readers could at the same time teach the children something they need to know about life (such as was done, and is done, by the McGuffey Readers).

This can and must be done even more so on the higher levels of education, where the exiguity of care-oriented instructors is hardly open to doubt. Most high school instructors are conscious of the taboo administrators generally place on using the classroom to broach the very sensitive and controversial topics of life. And because they are conformists, most teachers do not wish to become involved in a hassle with anti-intellectual school board members and administrators. Consequently, they carefully avoid ever discussing those subjects in life that the students really need and want to talk about the most—sexual morality, religion, right and wrong, and human nature and destiny. Most teachers would under no circumstances ever broach the subject of God, nor encourage it if a student brought it up. I have conducted my own research on this question, of the generally diluted and delicate intellectual atmosphere in the typical high school teacher's class. Issuing queries to thousands of high school graduates, I have found that most of them believe they were "gypped" of a really meaningful education in the public schools.

What is their most often cited reason for this? The fact that teachers too often act out the role of mere instructors, with no concern further than feeding dry informational data into their students' heads, in order that they can make an "A" or a "B" on their exams.

Said one student bitterly:

My teachers never wanted to talk about the things I needed to discuss the most. Moreover, whenever they did occasionally discuss the really important problems in life, they would invariably talk about them only in the abstract and in the third person singular, so as not to get involved by revealing their own personal insides. For example, they would talk only about alcoho*lism*, but never about their own bouts with drinking. They would talk only about psychological problems in the abstract, such as "identity," etc. Never would they discuss their own personal experiences of loneliness, friendlessness, temptations to insanity, and their own stupid mistakes and sins. I felt almost all of my teachers were "keeping their distance," as though they felt a need to hide their insides,

146

or else they were afraid to really get close to me as a person. Students are not utter fools. Most can readily distinguish between mere cordiality and real friendliness. A teacher is cordial if he observes the regular social amenities and mores of courtesy in addressing you as a human being. But he is really friendly only if he treats you like he finds your presence a genuine joy and wants to cultivate a closer association with you as a beloved person. Most teachers cultivate a general inhibitedness, in this respect. But worst of all, they would address themselves usually only to the banal, trivial, and obvious. Of course, we would discuss current events, but these were always things of merely temporary importance in passing. We seemed to never discuss the crucial, vital, perennial questions of the human spirit and the universe.

I regard this dramatic statement as having altogether too much foundation in fact. It is an unfortunate truth that students and teachers usually talk the least about the things they need to discuss the most—a fact demonstrated by how deep an impression is made on students by the one or two authentically caring teachers they may have had.

In the following chapter, I want to isolate these needs in particular. I especially want to discuss the necessity of a need-oriented theology or philosophy of religion, and the meaning of need in the divine life of God. I believe that, heretofore, most theologians have been amiss in their very definition of the divine. And consequently, they have bogged down in concepts of redemption and salvation that have not effected any significant improvement in the quality of our personal care.

7

Care in Jesus of Nazareth

It is impossible to deny that the Christian God is first
and foremost the God of sacrificial love, and sacrifice
always implies tragedy. . . . To deny tragedy in the Divine
life is only possible at the cost of denying Christ, His
cross and crucifixion, the sacrifice of the Son of God.

Nicholas Berdyaev

THERE ARE TWO ESSENTIAL TYPES of intrinsic value.
One is a *potentiality*, or a logical possibility inherent in the
cosmic scheme of things at large. For example, before any human
being ever comes into existence, there already exists the logical
possibility that he can, and might, someday come into existence.
It is logically unarguable that without such a possibility informing
the scheme of things there could never be any human being at all.
Since any human being is constituted basically of essences, these
essences must have always existed in reality, and God's power to
bring them into a union to create a new living human is itself
essentially good. I have already argued the logical inconceivability
of creation without essences and a creative agent.

The relativistic or pragmatic doctrine that there are no beings
and essences is nothing less than farcical. The idea that in reality
there is nothing except action or change is so unrealistic it is silly.
How can there be any cause for action, or any meaning to action,
if there is nothing to act on and no actor to perform the act? An
intelligible concept of creation entails three essential realities: (1)
the existence of essences or primordial materials out of which

148

things can be created (since no thing can be created out of nothing); (2) the existence of an agent who can manipulate these things, or act on them, to bring them into new combinations and unions for new effects; and (3) the logical possibility that the actor can act creatively on these essences that exist. In fine, there must always have existed a Creator; there must always have been the logical possibility for him to act; and within the domain of his being and order there must always have been the primordial creative essences for him to work with or act on.

The day will never come when someone will demonstrate how things can be created out of nothing, by nothing, and for nothing. The claim of the nihilists that this is what happens clearly violates every known fact of life. No scientist has ever been able to produce any real effects by experimenting with nothing, and for no reason and purpose.

"But I was taught in my course in physics," said one of my students, "that mass or fixed being can be converted to energy or action. Since being and action are two different concepts, you cannot derive action from mere being or an actor; so, action simply has to come from nothing."

My response to this objection was: "Can you really take seriously the notion that something can come from nothing? Can you show logically how either being or action can come from nothing? Is this really conceivable? If it is really possible, then indeed how?" By definition, an actor cannot be a merely static being; rather, he must be a dynamic agent, that is, a being who not only is but who also acts. Or in other words, he must contain inherent within himself the essence of the capacity to initiate action. The nature of the actor (a subject) is both to be and to act, to be and to become. I do not pretend to be able to explain that essence. As I stated earlier, I cannot explain how it is possible for me to exist. And likewise, I cannot explain how it is possible for me to act. But I certainly do know that I exist, and that I am able to initiate my own acts. Obviously, no one else commits my acts for me. I categorically will assume no responsibility whatever for acts that I do not cause, in part or whole.

Neither theoretically nor practically can moral responsibility be assigned only to an act. Responsibility has to be assigned to the agent who initiated the act, or who freely played some role in causing it. For otherwise, if the act is initiated by nothing, then there is nothing to whom responsibility for the act can be assigned, which means that there simply is no responsibility at all. This is an idea no one can take seriously and still feel accountable for his acts. My learned colleagues, who pretend to take it seriously, in fact do hold me responsible as the agent who commits my acts. If someone I am seriously trying to communicate with denies that there are any essential truths, values, or needs; or, if he denies that he exists as an agent responsible for his acts, then I can see no point at all in any further effort at conversation. For why should I try to communicate if there were no essential truths to be communicated? And why should I recognize a person who will not recognize me or even himself? If he will theoretically not recognize the reality of his own being, he is hardly in a position to demand of me that I recognize his existence and rights in practice.

The second kind of intrinsic value is an *actuality*. A person who is sick will be unable to see any sense in becoming healthy unless he feels a need to be healthy. Also, he must sense within himself and in his situation a potentiality for health that he can transform into an actuality or concrete fact in his daily life. All human beings think about the world in terms of two aspects: (1) the way things really are (concrete actuality), and (2) the way things can and ought to be or become (the ideal). No human being in any culture will always accept things as being exactly right the way they are. In fact, not even the lower animals do this; for they too are acting, which means they are trying to transform some potentiality into an actuality, to fulfill some need or desire. No creature in the entire animal kingdom is ever absolutely contented for long. All living beings act, and all action is committed to transform some possibility into some actuality.

Regardless of their cultural differences, all human beings always have to act to remain alive. We have to act in order to enjoy the sensation that life makes sense because it is marked by purpose. Purpose is the intention to do something which one feels he can or ought to do, but has yet to do. Be it good or bad, all action is informed with some purpose. Just to be is not enough; for this is, as I asserted earlier, the lot of the object, and even the object must be informed with some purpose in order to make sense. But the subject is alive, and to sustain his sense of being alive he must act. In the case of a human being, because he is a free agent, he must inevitably cope with the question of the justifiability or unjustifiability of his acts. All of us think in these terms in practice, regardless of what nihilistic dogmas some individuals may espouse in theory. Even the psychopath, who is classically defined as never thinking in terms of right and wrong, does in fact do so because he uses the words *ought* and *should* as much as a normal human being. The inordinate selfishness of the psychopath does not undo the fact that he too thinks in terms of the way he is treated, versus the way he feels he ought to be treated. In human life there is no getting around the inevitable bind of the ought. Even the psychopath, like the anarchist and nihilist, has ideals which he holds over the heads of others.

Semantically and logically, the word "ought" is meaningless if what the relativists and behaviorists have to tell us is true. Both doctrines systematically deny that there are any essential moral needs and values. Yet as much as anyone else, they talk about what ought to be and ought not to be. Now, if there is no intrinsically true reason why I ought to behave in a given way, then on what grounds can they claim that I ought to behave that way, except on the basis of their personal taste or subjective bias? Personal taste and subjective bias can constitute no compellingly plausible case for any point of view of any kind. And if there is no essential need for me to act in a given way, then why should I act that way? According to behaviorism, there is no freedom of choice involved in any act. Any act is just as necessary as any other act, since nobody ever acts except in the way that he has to act, because he is driven by the laws of physics and chemistry to act that way. In other words, everything that happens has to happen since it is made to happen by the laws of nature and cannot possibly be prevented. If one takes this notion seriously, then he has to conclude that the word *ought* is essentially meaningless since there is never a meaningful distinction between what a person does do and what he ought to do.

Why ought a person to have behaved differently than he did behave if, in fact, it was impossible for him to have behaved in another manner instead? If everything in the world *has* to be the way it is, then how is this any different from the way it ought to be? Logically, when something happens out of sheer necessity there can be no alternative way that it can possibly happen. The behaviorists go in a perpetual circle, speaking of "engineering" better behavior, or the kind of behavior that ought to be found in human society. B. F. Skinner and his school plead with us to cooperate with them in accomplishing a better world and environment. But they do this only after insisting that we are nothing but conditioned products of our environment. Skinner is unconscious of this logical and moral contradiction of his viewpoint, as is obvious in his best-selling book, *Beyond Freedom and Dignity*.[1] To plead for man to exercise more control over his environment, while simultaneously defining man as having no choice, should appear an obvious contradiction. According to Skinner, whatever influence man has on his environment is determined strictly and entirely by his environment; hence, it is useless to talk about ecological decisions we *ought* to have made in the past or ought to make in the future:

In one of my classes a behaviorist psychologist solemnly declared:

The old notions of freedom of choice, sin and virtue, and so-called responsible and irresponsible ways of behaving are only wrecking havoc in human life. We ought to dispense with such foolish terms in human language. Concepts like sin and virtue, right and wrong, and moral and immoral can only turn people into self-righteous judgmentalists or guilt-ridden neurotics. These naive distinctions can have no legitimate place in mature human relations where they tend only to diminish sympathy and compassion. They have only made people punitive and condemnatory towards one another, rather than understanding and helpful. Teachers must do everything in their power to condition children to stop thinking in such terms. There is no way to measure the harm that has been done by such needless and stupid criteria for judging human actions.

While listening to this speaker (whose exact words were recorded on tape in the class), I jotted down the following questions in my notebook: If all behavior is necessary, then why was there no need for people to think in such terms? Why ought people not to think in such terms under conditions which make it the only possible way to think? What is "needless" and "stupid" about an individual thinking in a given way if he cannot help but think that way? Who can call a man "foolish" if he does something because he has to do it, is driven to do it by forces over which he has no control, and cannot possibly help doing it because he has no choice in the matter?

Care in Jesus of Nazareth

It is of course true that human beings often are condemnatory and punitive when they ought not to be. But the behaviorists are not the first to recognize this fact. In the whole history of human thought, nobody was ever more insightful into this fact than Jesus of Nazareth, who made the most momentous imaginable effort to try to teach us how to judge one another rationally and with true compassion. However, He was never so foolish as to treat sin and virtue as semantical illusions. Jesus was trying to perfectly exemplify the intrinsic needs and values in human life, and to inspire us to feel an inviolable sense of personal responsibility for our acts. If the behaviorists sincerely believe that moral responsibility and irresponsibility are semantical illusions, then they have only begun to see the havoc that will come if people in general cease thinking in such terms. If the behaviorist theory of human nature is correct, then no human being could ever possibly have avoided doing what he did. Which means that no matter how destructive or senseless a person's act is, he can always excuse it or rationalize it by saying, "I had to do it. I could not help doing it. So don't blame me. There was nothing wrong in doing it."

The notion that no human behavior is ever blameworthy would mean logically that all human acts are justifiable or right. It would mean that there is no such thing as hypocrisy, for hypocrisy is defined as the individual doing what he himself feels he ought not to do and can avoid doing. Certainly, a person's body chemistry can never make him a hypocrite. One is hardly a hypocrite in doing what he cannot help doing. The fundamental premise in behaviorist ethical theory is that no human being ever acts decently or indecently, compassionately or uncompassionately, rightly or wrongly, but rather, only instinctively or mechanically like a machine. It hardly behooves one to distinguish between compassionate and uncompassionate acts in a chemical machine. What is wrong with "uncompassionate" behavior if it is equally as justifiable as the opposite way of behaving because it cannot possibly be avoided? My behaviorist colleagues often chastise the "hypocrisy" they see in Christian theory and practice. Only God knows how right they are, how vast a mind it would take to count all the hypocritical acts we believers have committed in our daily lives. But then, it should be pointed out, in passing, that the essence of real Christianity is not human hypocrisy and never was; but rather, is the divine teaching and character of Jesus in whom the admonition is well known that only the guiltless should cast the first stone.

We can hardly diminish hypocrisy in the world by denying that hypocrisy is possible. Nor can we diminish injustice in the world by theoretically justifying all human acts. The behaviorist notion that injustice is a semantical illusion not only is theoretically contradictory, but is practically insane. We can teach children how to do justice to human needs only by teaching them unmistakably what these needs are; and then, by holding them definitely responsible for their acts when we know that they know what they can and ought to do. In effect, the behaviorist ethic claims that we can teach people to behave more responsibly by teaching them that there is no such a thing as irresponsible or blameworthy behavior. This doctrine cannot be taken seriously even by university eggheads without doing real damage. Any would-be escapist could find it a perfect opportunity to absolve his conscience in committing the most vicious imaginable act without the slightest feeling of misgiving or compunction. For he could always declare, "You are wrong to judge me. Everyone does only what he has to do."

To bring more responsible behavior into our lives, we must isolate the objective facts about human nature and needs. Then, we must teach these to our children (as indeed, to one another) and demand conformity of recognition and action towards these facts and needs. This cannot be done without cultivating in each individual a sense of personal responsibility for the acts that he commits in his freedom. For the unmistakable truth is, no rational person is going to feel that he either could or should be responsible either to himself or others unless he can generate his own acts. If we want to abase his sensitivity to the quality of his acts, all we have to do is convince a person that his acts are not really his own at all, since he is nothing but a complex batch of chemical reactions or a product of social conditioning. How can a person feel responsible if he takes seriously the notion that he has no control over what goes on inside himself and in the world?

In the philosophy of Jesus, nothing was more eminent than the precepts of freedom, responsibility, and the spiritual essence of a person. Jesus did not deal in phony absolutes, and He demonstrated an astonishingly sharp insight into the burden and complexity of making valid moral judgments. In fact, He showed an incomparably clear consciousness of how easy it is for us to hurt one another when we indulge in simplistic and precipitous moral judgments. Jesus rebelled strenuously against proud and self-righteous carelessness in judging the motives and acts of one's fellow man. He despised the rude habits of the Sadducees, whose puffed-up moralizing respected not the needs of a fellow human being, but only the tyranny of blind and vacuous theological abstractions. In the time of Jesus, religious authorities were generally even more conformist and unreasoning than the prelates and priests of today. Jesus differed with them not only in his claim to be the Messiah, but in an intense rejection of their preoccupation with the minutiae of theological and moral dogma. He unmistakably looked upon most prelatism as a form of vanity.[2] He saw it as bearing all the trappings of mindless conformity and as a devotion to empty dogmatic abstractions that do nothing to enhance the quality of man's relations with himself and God. The relevancy of Jesus is timeless, as the practice of religion then was as cheap in general as it is today, often aground in bogus theological know-it-all-ness and shallow and pretentious care. Jesus was not crucified because He was lacking in charisma or in the ability to make clear his points. Altogether the contrary, He was murdered on the Cross because it was all too obvious that He saw perfectly through the sham theology and pretentious morality of pompous men of power who preached righteousness sternly but felt no really decent care.

But Jesus did not turn to relativism when He saw the harm done by conformity to false absolutes in life. Knowing true absolutes, He could see the harm done by false absolutes, and that a false absolute can be confuted and corrected only by a true one. The absolutes in the teachings of Jesus are all grounded in the intrinsic needs and values of life. Jesus did not espouse his absolutes as mere doctrinal abstractions to be professed in theory. Rather, He felt their reality to the core of his being. He informed his every thought and action with them, *de die in diem*. Matchlessly and perfectly, Jesus cared for the fulfillment of every human being's needs in life.

These needs, however, have been treated only superficially by most ministers from behind their pulpits. Today, as in the time of Jesus, most religious zeal is for the propagation and disputation of doctrinal abstractions, rather than for the fulfillment of man's and God's concrete needs. What is worse, most theologians do not regard man's needs as intrinsic at all, but only as contingent upon the will of God in whose omnipotence and immutability there is no unfulfilled need whatever. Beyond any doubt, the most crucial error in religious theory and practice today is the notion that God himself is above need.

In one of my graduate classes, a Barthian fundamentalist declared:

We have to understand that God is of the realm of the supernatural. God transcends all that we experience and know, for in his divinity He is categorically of another quality. In our sin, we cannot touch him or be near him, except through the gratuitous intermediation of Christ. Because man is estranged by the Fall, in his alienation he can know nothing by his own wits about God. Man has made the natural order demonic. The whole kingdom of the natural has been perverted, and in it man is now qualitatively completely other. Yet today, liberal theologians in their sin of pride are wont to make as though by their own resources they can understand God. The intellectuals with their demonic wit would undo the meaning of Christ, by achieving their own independent redemption and salvation. In the liberal seminaries of today, no sin is more evident than the anthropomorphism of the would-be independent truth makers who assign human qualities and frailties unto the Almighty. In their finitude they would reduce God to the finite. In their suffering from sin they would afflict on God the suffering from sin. In their need caused by the Fall they would have God fall with them, by shackling Him with their own need. In the purity of innocence, Adam and Eve in the Garden of Eden knew only the beatific conditions of the paradise in which God had placed them, in an unsullied state of needlessness in life. Not until they disobeyed God and fell from his grace did they ever once experience a single sensation of want or need. As surely as the sun rises in the east, the cause of our need is sin. Before the Fall, there was no need. And yet, our liberal seminaries ostensibly devoted to spreading the Word of God each generation are becoming more infiltrated with pseudo-apologists who would attribute need to God. No need has come from God. All need has come from sin. Unfulfilled need is a mark of imperfection, not a mark of the divine. To attribute such need to God is to attribute an imperfection to Him, which is an act of blasphemy that cannot be hidden by any amount of eloquence of words.

I was the primary object of this lofty charge of blasphemy. If the attribution of need to God is blasphemous, then I do qualify as a blasphemer. For I totally fail to understand how anyone can construct an intelligible philosophy of morality and religion unless he recognizes that some needs are essential to life, including the life of God. Nowhere in a logical analysis of the concept of need, and nowhere in the Johannine and Synoptic Gospels can I find any indication of the existence of a need-less God. In fact, these scriptures are replete with intimations of God's need, especially in the teachings of Jesus. One has only to consult a concordance to find scriptural sources of how need-oriented are the religions of Judaism and Christianity.

In Matthew 6:8, Jesus alludes to God's experience of need in the Sermon on the Mount. He declares, "Your Father knows what things you have need of before you ask him." Now, how can God understand our needs if he himself has no experience of need? Judaic–Christian religion teaches that God is a perfect empathizer, that He feels what we feel through his understanding and sharing, or it teaches nothing whatever. The very essence of the spirit of Jesus was his immaculate empathy, his ability to feel the needs of another person with that depth of exactness and understanding that constitutes divine care. We can hardly say that God is sympathetic to our need if we deny that He himself experiences need. God is God because He experiences the bite of our need even more sensitively than we do ourselves. He shares our needs; our needs are his needs; and He is God because He is absolutely devoted to the fulfillment of our needs. Moreover, He is divine in his care because He is absolutely devoted to the fulfillment of his own need, which is to transform the possibility for more beauty and joy in the world into a concrete actuality through his creative action.

To deny that there is need in God is to say that there is no need for Him to exist and to act, which is patently incompatible with the character and teachings of Jesus. In a variety of scriptures, Jesus indicates unmistakably that we can either please or displease God. We can glorify God with creative faith, good works and love. Or, we can frustrate and thwart God's own purpose in the world by neglecting our possibilities to create beauty and goodness in our relations with each other and with Him. When we choose to act destructively and perniciously, we hurt God just as surely as we hurt one another. The reason why we can hurt God is because He cares and feels. When we care destructively, or do not care at all, God feels and knows that the quality of life in the world is different than what it needs to be and ought to be. We are, in a certain sense, the leading instruments of God's care in the world. He knows that there is always a need for more joy and beauty in the world. And because He cares absolutely with all his being, He is vulnerable to our freedom, which we can exercise to oppose his will, to bring insipidity or corruption into a life where there should be aesthetic and moral splendor.

Christianity is intrinsically a plausible religion because Jesus exemplified perfect care. This means that He had an awareness of the intrinsic needs in life and devoted himself indefectibly to their fulfillment in himself and others. Knowing that we are free agents, Jesus understood and acted on the necessity to exemplify responsible care in a perfect way. In fact, He declared categorically: "I am the way," meaning, as I interpret it, that He was showing us by his perfect example the kind of care that we ourselves must practice if we are ever to enhance the quality of life for ourselves and God. Jesus scorned vain and dissembling words, where people pretend to care and brag about caring, but do not in fact feel or act out any positive care at all. Christ Jesus is anathema to any form of superficiality or pretension to care. He even called himself an "offense," knowing how resentful people would feel toward the burden of his demands. No one ever felt more acutely than Jesus how we use our freedom to desecrate God's purpose in the world. Who has seen more clearly than He the extent of joy and beauty there could be in the world if only we would use our freedom to care more responsibly? Jesus himself exemplified this care, which reminds anyone who confronts Him honestly that it is not only a joy but is a Cross to bear. The offense of Jesus lies in his appeal to us to care as He cared. People in general are not offended by the sight of divine care in Jesus. We are offended only when He exhorts us to practice an equally responsible care. Said He, with no tongue in his cheek: "Be ye therefore perfect, even as your Father which is in heaven is perfect."[3]

This, beyond any doubt, is the source of the offense of the Christian religion. How often do we take kindly to someone suggesting that our care is shallow and mean? How much less burdensome it is to dissemble than to carry a Cross. Jesus' sacrifice on the Cross symbolizes the price in pain and frustration that anyone might have to pay who really cares. What makes Christianity inherently plausible is not only the joy it promises, but the pain of care that

it demands in return. As Elton Trueblood has so beautifully remarked, this religion is plausible not just because of the thought
that Jesus is like God, but because of the thought that God is like
Jesus.[4] God is perfect care. Thus, the source of the offense in this
religion is the very source of its plausibility. What makes God God
is the price that He has to pay, and is willing to pay, for being
God. By giving his children freedom, He has opened his heart to
not only the possibility of responsible, loving worship, but to the
pain of rejection and mockery.

This is the difference between Christianity and other religions.
What Christianity has to offer that other religions do not is Jesus
the Crucified, who offers God to man, but only for a price: acceptance of His yoke. Jesus is imposing. Those who would find
only a promise of joy in him know him not. Jesus presented himself as "the way." But as He himself described it, this is not the
way of those who worship a utopian god of ease. Rather, it is the
"straight and narrow way which leadeth unto life, and few there
be that find it."

The antinomians have missed the very entelechy in Christ's
morality. Through careless and wishful thinking they have reduced
him to a "savior," through whose grace man can be lifted up to a
heavenly bliss by faith alone. In his "original sin" (they tell us)
man's righteousness is as "filthy rags," and he can do nothing to
deserve the salvation from sin that God bestows upon him purely
as a gift of grace. They tell us that through a vow of faith and the
taking of sacraments, man can through the commitment of Christ
be saved from eternally useless suffering in a bottomless pit of
hell-fire.

What is essentially wrong with the antinomian interpretation of
Jesus' suffering is that it takes the meaning of that suffering in
spirit out of one's own life. I believe that Jesus exemplified the
divine life, hoping that by doing it we could see the significance
of it, and then would choose to take up the Cross with Him. Indeed, He did very pointedly declare that "he that doth not take
his cross and follow me is not worthy of me" (Matthew 10:38).
Antinomianism is an escapist philosophy because it reduces God's
sacrifice to "foolishness," and denies the necessity for man to suffer
with God. As a student once asked in my class, "Who can be saved
from being a damned liar as long as he continues to tell damned

lies?" If I read Jesus correctly, a man can be saved from sin (any sin) only when he *cares* enough to stop sinning that he does actually stop.

Antinomians interpret the kingdom of heaven as a "beatific city" in which the "saved" soul can live painlessly, with no problems of any kind. He will have it "absolutely made," as people say; he will have to suffer nought, and will have to pay no price whatever for the joys of living in a utopia.

I do not get the slightest notion that Jesus would wish the kingdom of heaven to be interpreted in this way. For He did very clearly equate good faith with good works, and insisted that the measure of one's saving faith is the genuineness and depth of his care manifest in good works. That Jesus can "save" someone from being a liar who does not care enough for truth to tell it and face the pain and problems of telling it; or, that He can save someone from cynicism, lovelessness, and bitter hatred who does not care enough to overcome these faults by his own choice, plainly is a notion in violation of everything that Jesus did and said.

That He equated salvation with the quality of one's care is evident in his impassioned rejection of careless faith, and in his entreaties for responsible action from any believer. Said He:

Not every one that saith unto me, Lord, Lord, shall enter into the kingdom of heaven, but he that *doeth the will of my Father* which is in heaven. . . . Ye are the salt of the earth, but if the salt have lost his savour, wherewith shall it be salted? It is thenceforth good for nothing, but to be cast out, and to be trodden under foot of men.[5]

Surely this implies that we are the instruments of God, to bring beauty and goodness into the world. If we do not care, or if we care wrongly, then even God is the victim of our freedom carelessly used. Or as I stated previously, our freedom is God's fate. Jesus' dissatisfaction with ordinary care shows plainly in his implorations on the Mount. He declared:

Ye have heard that it hath been said, Thou shalt love thy neighbour, and hate thine enemy. But I say unto you, love your enemies, bless them that curse you, do good to them that hate you, and pray for them which despitefully use you, and persecute you, that ye may be the children of your Father which is in heaven. For he maketh his sun to rise on the evil and on the good, and sendeth rain on the just and on the unjust. For if ye love them which love you, what reward have ye?

160

Do not even the publicans the same? And if ye salute your brethren only, what do ye more than others? Do not even the publicans so? . . . For I say unto you, that except your righteousness shall exceed the righteousness of the scribes and Pharisees, ye shall in no case enter into the kingdom of heaven.[6]

Jesus alludes to the kingdom of heaven on varied occasions. From all of his uses of this phrase, I gather that He equates being in heaven with being spiritually in a state of responsible care. Always, in his parables He suggests that being in heaven means being in a divine state. But what is the divine? I cannot look at the teachings of Jesus and define the divine in classical terms at all. Traditional theologians have defined the divine as being strictly supernatural or categorically outside the understanding of man's sinful and imperfect mind. That is, divinity is perfection which man, due to his imperfection arising from the Fall, can never even begin to comprehend. Man in his fallen state is the embodiment of imperfection, and God in his transcendental infinitude is absolutely perfect. What does perfection mean, to the classical theist? It means that God is omnipotent, omniscient, immutable, and absolutely self-fulfilled and happy. God is perfectly complete, and in need of nothing. He already is all that He could ever possibly be. He already knows all that could ever possibly be known. For indeed (they say), if there was something that God could come to know in the future but does not yet know, then He would be marked by ignorance, which is an imperfection that we would be blasphemous to attribute to God.

I see no evidence in the Scriptures, nor any reasons discovered in logical analysis, to believe that Jesus attributed any of these mythological traits to God. On the contrary, the idea that God is omniscient was first developed philosophically by Philo Judaeus, an Hellenic Jew. The notion of omniscience is expressed unmistakably by King David in Psalms 139, verse 16.[7] Moreover, the idea of absolute predestination (effectively negating the reality of man's freedom of choice) is logically implicit in David's thought. David expressly believed in man's freedom of choice; and consequently, he could not have been conscious of the contradiction in his view. He took the idea of God's absolute foreknowledge for granted, but also took for granted the notion that we are free agents responsible for our acts, i.e., that the direction in which history moves is partly determined freely by *us*—in many ways that are not pleasing to God. Whatever his admirable traits might have been, King David was nonetheless an *ad hoc* philosopher if ever one lived. He was not God speaking; he was a fallible man speaking, and was not always given to carefully examining his own views.

The origin of the notion of omnipotence (as absolutely unlimited power) is altogether obscure and is nowhere ascribed to God in either the Old Testament or the New. There are numerous scriptural references to God as "all powerful," and "Almighty," but never in such way as to suggest, or imply, that there are no impossibilities for God. Immutability and absolute self-fulfillment are theoretical characteristics found in the concept of God as the Unmoved Mover, conceived by the Greek philosopher Aristotle over three hundred years before the advent of Jesus. These concepts of God were introduced into Christian philosophy by theologians who translated Aristotle and Philo long after the time of Jesus, and are nowhere to be found in the mouth of Jesus himself. Jesus did not say directly, and did not remotely imply, that God is a *static* being without need. Nor did He in any way attribute omniscience to God. He does allude to God being "all knowing" but in such a way as to include only the past and the present, and only that part of the future that is already predetermined. Not once did Jesus indicate that God's life is complete. Nor did He once suggest that God is absolutely self-fulfilled and happy. And nowhere is there a scripture to show that He denied that God has an open future. Absolutely the opposite is the truth. Jesus indicated that God's future, like ours, is always partly open, indeterminate, and dependent upon free choices that we have yet to make. To a certain extent, God's future is literally unknowable because it can be predicated only on free choices that have yet to be made. For logically defined, a free choice is one that has in no way ever been previously determined; and hence, until the very time when the choice is made, it can be nothing more than a possibility, and not a determinate and knowable actuality.

Let us settle this question, logically and once and for all, by taking up a particular concrete case of freedom of choice. Let us say that one John Doe is contemplating a murder. He does not *have* to commit the murder. Because of John's freedom of choice, the murder is a possible act that he can either perform or leave unperformed. Since John has not yet decided whether to kill or not to kill his potential victim, God himself must wonder how he is going to decide. God *cares*. Clearly, the existential reality of freedom and the reality of time to God is what makes it possible for him (or anyone else) to care. How could God *care* about John's decision if history were already complete, and if the murder, or decision not to commit the murder, was already an historical fact? The classical theists deny that time is real for God. But Jesus said nothing to give one a cause to believe such a thing. Quite the contrary, he portrayed his Father in heaven as deeply engrossed in history at every moment of every day, *concerned* about our future as his own.

If one were to take seriously the concept of God's omniscience, then logically, he would have to drop the notions of freedom and care. For obviously, God cannot care about what is going to happen if it has already as much as happened. Nor can He be concerned about the course of events if there are no open alternatives that make concern meaningful. A rational man will inevitably ask, How can God be concerned about the future if He does not really have a future? Consider the following confutation of the notion of God's omniscience:

(1) If it is true that John is free to decide to commit the murder, this means that he *might* do it; and consequently, God cannot know for certain that he will *not* do it.

(2) On the other hand, if it is true that John is free to decide *not* to commit the murder, this means that he *might not* do it; and consequently, God cannot know for certain that he will.

(3) Thus in conclusion, the only thing that God can know logically for certain is what the alternative possibilities are, i.e., that John *may* commit the murder, but also *may not*.

The reality of this existential uncertainty in time is what makes the matter a real moral concern to God. The reality of any freedom at all, and the unknowns of the future inherent in that freedom, must apply to God as well as to man, if we are to look upon God as a *living* God who is the examplar of care. And this is precisely what Jesus did: He suffered supremely as the exemplar of responsible and loving care. The prophecy of Jesus that he would be betrayed by Peter and Judas did not instance a belief of Jesus in the omniscience of God. Rather, it indicates an extraordinary insightfulness into the character of these two men. No man is ever *absolutely* free or self-determined. And obviously, men sometimes are bound by psychological or emotional character sets which are the results of past conditioning, even if one in his earlier freedom has conditioned himself to be what he now is. Apparently, both of these disciples could be predicted to commit betrayal because they were governed by an emotional set towards betrayal, which Jesus could sense clearly in his uncanny sensitivity to their compulsive character and behavior. Either Judas and Peter in their weakness lacked the strength and psychological freedom to avoid betrayal, in which case Jesus could predict it infallibly; or else, they were free to decide not to betray him, in which case his prophecy of betrayal could not be infallible. One thing is certain: Jesus nowhere in the scriptures attributes omniscience to himself. What is more, in the pursuit of his objectives He likens his own problems and motives to those of God. At every turn, Jesus brought his philosophy to bear on the reality of freedom, the burden of responsibility, and the anxiety inherent in one's freedom to determine an indeterminate future. Otherwise, why would the Bible speak hyperbolically of Jesus' "sweating blood" in the Garden of Gethsemane? This anxiety is morally meaningless if He had no choice in the matter, or if time is a mere illusion.

The reality of freedom in God, and the openness of the future for God, is essential to any concept of him as a loving Person. If history were complete for God, or if He already knew all that could ever possibly be known, then it is logically inconceivable that He could be *alive*, or that He could *care*, in any meaningful sense of these terms. For certainly, an omniscient and omnipotent God could not conceivably be anxious about anything. In his exhaustive knowledge, He could experience no curiosity, wonder, mystery, adventure, surprise, or awe. If all of his needs were absolutely fulfilled already, then He could not act for any sensible reason simply because there could be no need to act. It is inconceivable that an omniscient God could experience any responsibility or love. How could God be responsible to guide the basic course of history if history already was complete? What could there be for him to do or change if all had been done already? If everything that God ever needed or wanted to accomplish has been accomplished already, then who could argue that He is acting *now* with purpose? As the classical theists interpret it, time is unreal as an objective truth; i.e., time is a reality only as an illusion in the finite mind. But if this were the case, then how could theologians speak of God as a God of love? Love is a disposition to *do* something for the beloved person or creature; it is a desire to bring more beauty and joy into the life of the beloved than he has known heretofore. Any dynamic and creative love is always at the present moment future-oriented; i.e., it is aware of the need for more time. How can love be real; how can God or his creatures love someone if time is unreal?

God himself needs time to create. It is logically impossible for God to transform all possibilities into actualities at once. For example, God can grow thousands of trees on one given spot on the earth, but only one at a time. Before a mother can become pregnant a fourth time, she first has to be pregnant the third time, and before that the second, etc. Any progressive series of events takes time. The traditional notion that God is creative simply cannot accord with the notion that his being is timeless.[8] God cannot simultaneously be both creative and immutable. Immutability is absolute changelessness, and creativity is unimaginable without change (without change, nothing new whatever could appear on the scene). Theologians would get around this by having us look at time from two different angles of perception. From God's angle of perception, time is unreal. But from man's angle, time is real. Thus, they would have us believe that the proposition that "time is real" is simultaneously both true and false. But clearly, this violates the simplest rule of logic, that the same proposition cannot be inherently and simultaneously both true and false. Because God's life is dynamic and creative, He is time-bound on a cosmic scale, moving into an open future, facing as many unknowns as there are instances of real freedom of choice in himself and his creatures. The biblical allegory that God created the world in six days obviously indicates that God experiences time, that He must complete one creative act before starting a second.

The Father of Jesus is a creative God of action. He is a God of need and care.

Jesus never defined the divine in any academic terms. I do not wish to put words in his mouth, but from the context of all of his actions and teachings as shown in the Gospels, it appears quite certain that He equated divinity with intrinsic value and need. Intrinsic needs and values are divine. For example, the need for beauty is divine, and beauty itself is divine. For without the need, who could find real value in the thing needed? Jesus was divine because He not only needed the intrinsic values of life, but laid hold of them in all of his thoughts and actions, out of an impeccable and indomitable dedication to doing God's will. Jesus understood what the intrinsic values of life are, and freely chose to inform all of his thoughts and actions with them, *sans pareil*. In his brief life, He demonstrated the divine goodness a person can bring into life if he will only choose to do it.

Jesus did not see the perfection of God as omnipotence and omniscience. Rather, He saw God's perfection in the absolute goodness of his will. God knows perfectly what the intrinsic needs and values of life are; and, at any moment, He is exhausting his present possibilities to bring into the world all that joy and beauty which He knows is needed. God's divinity lies in his understanding and responsible care. Also, it lies in his power, without which He could do nothing for either himself or others. But his power is limited by his own nature, by the inherent goodness of his nature, by the primordial categories within his being. His power is also limited by the laws of logic, the law of cumulative time, and other laws that inhere in his nature. Also, his power is limited in some ways by his own past decisions and acts, as well as by our own past decisions and acts. Power *per se* is not an intrinsic value; power can be used for either good or bad ends, and hence it is good only when it is used for good ends. There is nothing in God's nature that is not intrinsically good. Bald power *per se* is not divine, not worthy of worship, and we do not compliment God by attributing power to him that might be irrational, evil, or stultifying. Affirming that God is omnipotent is affirming that He has total, absolutely unlimited dominion over man and the world. But this leads inevitably to the conclusion that man has no freedom of choice, that we are manipulated entirely as the objects of God's all-powerful will. Accepting the idea of omnipotence as divine, Martin Luther saw no alternative but to renounce as an illusion the classical notion that man is free. In his essay *The Bondage of the Will*, the reader can find Luther's reduction of man to an android. The inconsistency with Luther's own career is striking.[9]

God's power is also limited by the time barrier that is inherent in the divine creative process. This time barrier is manifested unmistakably in both the Old and New Testaments, where the word "eternity" plainly is used to signify not a state of timelessness, but rather an endless process of time. The Bible treats God as being infinite in his creative power, but not absolute. That is, God's power is not absolutely unlimited. However, the fact that there are impossibilities for God does not mean that his possibilities are exhaustible. There is literally no end to the possibilities of what God can become and accomplish in his creative life in future time. In God, the Infinite Creator, the possibilities of creative goodness are inexhaustible. Even the science of mathematics attests to this.[10]

Much misunderstanding about God's power has arisen from a naive interpretation of Jesus' remark that "all things are possible with God" (Mark 10:27). To glean full meaning from a scripture, a person has to interpret it in the light of its contextual setting and in the light of rational analysis. To logically distinguish between what is possible and what is impossible, we have to have some criteria that are objectively reliable, and these must be primarily the laws of logic. Logic is the science of possibility and necessity. Theologians who dispense with logic in their thinking about God's power inevitably end up with blind dogmas which no logical mind can accept. Viewed in the light of Jesus' teaching in their entirety (as we know them), and in the light of logical interpretation, Mark 10:27 can be taken to mean only that God can do all that which is possible for him to do; there are things which we cannot possibly do but He can; and there are things that cannot be done at all, even by God.

By throwing out logic, traditional theologians would turn Jesus into a figure of fantasy and absurdity. Jesus was, in fact, a uniquely exemplary practitioner of logical reason and, as a result of this, his epistemology has proven to be the most practical in the history of philosophy. It is only by illogical reasoning that we can evade facing those facts that are foundational to any sound theory of knowledge and morality. These facts are: (1) God has needs, (2) all living beings have needs, and (3) enlightened behavior is always oriented around an awareness of these needs. The epistemology of Jesus is suggested plainly in Matthew 7:15–20, where He insists that "By their fruits ye shall know them." Unmistakably, Jesus' theory of knowledge is based on *need*. It is by their fruits that we shall know who speaks the truth, and who are the "false prophets, which come to you in sheep's clothing, but inwardly are as ravening wolves." It is not by a person's show of erudition that we should know him, not by his high station in government or business, and not by his status in the world of learning. Rather, we know a person by the truth or falsehood of his beliefs, and this can be accurately determined only by the fruits of those beliefs when they are acted upon in practice. Or in short, the truth is that which most greatly leads to the fulfillment of need.

Realistic psychologists sometimes make lists of the vital life needs which they think all of us human beings share in common. In the Gospels, the life of Jesus clearly evinces an understanding of all of our needs. I shall list eighteen of them here, which I regard as crucial to any practical study of human nature. They are:

1. The need to be loved and to love.

2. The need for positive self-esteem.

3. The need for self-discipline, for a sense of accountability for one's decisions and acts.

4. The need for a sense of personal accomplishment (that one has done something, or produced some effects in the world that are of lasting importance).

5. The need for a basic sense of security, a feeling of well-being.

6. The need for emotional and intellectual integrity (an inner order, a unity of being).

7. The need for freedom of self-expression, self-realization, and growth.

8. The need for intrinsically valuable knowledge (those things that are always worth knowing).

9. The need for constructive creativity (to bring fresh effects into one's life and the world).

10. The need for the ability to communicate constructively, both with oneself and others.

11. The need for a communion with nature (that one finds intrinsic value in the world around him).

12. The need for a sense of priorities (for a knowledge of intrinsic values, whereby one can distinguish between what is important and what is trivial).

13. The need for faith that existence makes sense (that one's life in the world has a permanent rationale).

14. The need for faith in the conservation of values.

15. The need for beauty.

16. The need for hope.

17. The need for a compassionate and constructive sense of humor.

18. The need for unselfish happiness or joy (joy that regards the joy of others).

These needs are universal in the life of mankind. I do not foresee any significant improvement in the quality of education (in the school, church, or home) until a radical switch in emphasis takes place in what is deemed important for human beings to study. Because of his own professed desire to bring glory to God, the Christian cannot afford to tarry in trivial theological disputes at the expense of misunderstanding or neglect of these needs. The importance of these needs, and of efficacious techniques for fulfilling them in our daily lives, must find more place and time in the home, in the classroom, behind the pulpit, in the store and factory, and certainly in the town, state, and federal governments. It cannot be emphasized enough that nurses, doctors, lawyers, teachers, and people in *all* of the helping professions must come to understand these needs and devote themselves sincerely to meeting them in practice. During the last seven years I have conducted polls in all of my classes. I have discovered that over eighty percent of these students (close to ten thousand) look upon most doctors and lawyers as basically avaricious philistines insensitive to these needs in their patients and clients. I am afraid these polls cannot be ignored, if we are interested in the truth about the helping professions.

The accounts of his life show that Jesus was incomparably conscious of these needs in human nature. It is evident that He deeply experienced all of these needs in himself. In his little book *The Humor of Christ*, Elton Trueblood makes an invaluable contribution to Christian theology by showing that Jesus was in his manly nature most truly human.[11]

One problem that troubles some persons is the traditional portrayal of Christ as the ever sombre-faced reformer who never smiled, laughed, or joked. Jesus did in fact deal in sharp-tongued wit at times, and on occasion was sardonic and very hyperbolical. That his humorous utterances generally are mistaken by unimaginative interpreters to be something to be taken literally is undoubtedly the source of most misunderstanding about Jesus. His purely symbolical references to Satan, his allusions to hell-fire, and other scriptures make him appear a demonologist or sadist unless one sees the humor in his sardonicisms and hyperboles. Jesus frequently spoke in parables, allegories, and sometimes very dramati-

169

cally exaggerated language in order to make a ringing and memorable point. Many simplistic interpreters would make him a fool. They would have us take *seriously* the notion that God will burn many of his children in a pit of fire forever. Such a notion is categorically incompatible with a rational concept of love and mercy and a compassionate philosophy of justice. Jesus, the divine example of the careful heart, was no more sardonic about heathens than about the sadism of the traditional believer.

When properly understood, Christianity is not a religion of weakness and escape, but a religion of care. As Jesus himself constitutes it, Christianity is not an engulfment in spiritless dogmas. It is a need-oriented religion in action dealing with life's sacred goods.[12] Or to do justice to the words of the Master of Care, it is a religion of carrying the Cross. Those who will carry it for goodness and beauty for their own sake are in heaven already; they are in the kingdom of God regardless of how much they must strain and suffer. And those who will not carry this Cross are in hell, because they either care negatively or do not care at all. Caring about good, and being in good care, is being in heaven. But not caring about good, or being in bad care, is being in hell. And this is true no matter how snug and safe one might feel in his carelessness or bad care. It is hell not to care unselfishly and deeply, and not to feel deeply and unselfishly cared for by another.

As I interpret Jesus' words, the kingdom of heaven lies within the spirit, or else one has not entered it at all. Intrinsic values are divine, whether they are found in the spirit of a human being or in God. Unselfish love is divine. Reasonableness is divine. Constructive creativity is divine. Beauty is divine. Responsible care is divine. And the willingness to suffer for the sake of these things is divine. Insofar as any human being cares enough for the intrinsic values of life to seize them, and to hold them within his being —he has entered into the kingdom of heaven. In the kingdom of heaven (be it in this world or in any other) people live by life's intrinsic values. The purpose of the good life is to discover intrinsic values and to act carefully to conserve them permanently. Anything that is intrinsically good and beautiful should last forever. The destruction of anything of intrinsic value would be an intrinsic evil. In his divine sense of the sacred, Jesus understood this perfectly and attested to the meaning of it with his sacrificial love, death, and resurrection. Without a guarantee of the possibility of the permanent conservation of all that which is sacred, ultimate reality could be only evil. Only God's existence can constitute this guarantee, assuming man's responsible cooperation with His will. Jesus' life manifested the ultimate rational nature of reality; He illustrated it in His Resurrection, in His Promise of everlasting life for whoever truly cares. Jesus exemplified God's Perfect Care to save all that which is sacred. The uniqueness of Jesus' contribution to history lies expressly in this fact.

A person can deny the necessity for conserving life's sacred values only by denying that there are values that are sacred. One can deny that there are sacred values only by denying that there are intrinsic values. But then, in effect, Is one not denying that even his own life, or any of his own words or acts ever have any essential or necessary value? No person can feel that it is essential to act (either to discover a value or to conserve a value) if, at the same time he acts, he feels that nothing whatever is of essential value. If nothing whatever is in essence valuable, then there is no essential reason why anybody ever ought to act. Earlier in this work, I stated that the denial of intrinsic values can lead only to intellectual, emotional, and moral nihilism—to the destruction of all life motivation for anyone who really takes it seriously. No one can take atheism seriously and still sustain his will to live. To say that there ultimately is no reason to act (i.e., no value that is in essence worth discovering, accomplishing, or preserving) is to say what there is essentially no reason to say, which is a *reductio ad absurdum* and an utter waste of time. It is sorrowful that so many philosophers win accolades today while reducing all values to mere subjective will and taste. To be philosophically sound, more is needed than just cerebral brilliance or arbitrary conation. One has to be able to feel that something in life is sacred (e.g., unselfish love) and, in that feeling, to experience an *aching* to conserve the value of what one feels. In the denial of intrinsic values, a person only shows affective insensibility and axiological despair. Nothing whatever of essential value can be accomplished by theoretically disestablishing all essential values.

"The fool has said, 'There is no immortal life.' "

Now why is it foolish to say such a thing? Because, in essence, foolishness is saying, or doing, what there can be no essential value whatever in saying or doing. If life is in essence valuable, then it is essential to act to find some way to conserve it; i.e., it is essential to stand, both in theory and in practice, for the conservation of that value. Only the experience of some intrinsic value can make a person feel that it is intrinsically better to be alive than not to exist at all. To fully recognize an intrinsic value is to recognize the need to conserve it forever. What makes a person essentially valuable now is not that he can be used as a means to someone else's end; rather, it is precisely that there is something in essence good in him that can and ought to be permanently conserved. No personal values can be conserved unless persons can be conserved. If there is no reason to live forever, then there is no reason to live for another day or hour. For what reason should anyone believe that he will live forever? For exactly the same reason that he should believe that he will live for another minute or second. If there were no intrinsic values in life, if it were not intrinsically better to find joy and beauty in being alive than to experience no value at all, then there would be nothing essential about acting to conserve any life, just as nothing of essential value would be lost in destroying any life. The fool acts to preserve his life (obviously); but he contradicts his actions with his own words. If he means that life is not worth continued conserving, his words belie his acts. Or if he means that life is worth conserving but there is no possible way to conserve it, then he is affirming what there can be no possible value in affirming; he is saying what there can be no possible rational motive for saying. A parrot or tape player might sound the words, "There is no way to save life," yet it would not be a sensible communication, but only a mechanism at work. For a *person* to say such words is foolish because the very words defeat any motivation for saying them.

Tell me one good reason why a person should live for another minute; then for that same reason I will say that he should live forever—to find some value or to hold onto some value. It makes no sense to affirm that life *should* last forever, and in the same breath insist that it cannot. The fool declares, "All things will pass away." Regardless of what value he may be holding at any moment, he is feeling—if he takes his philosophy seriously—"And this, too, shall pass away." If he *feels* that the thing valued is valuable enough to hold onto pemanently, then he can only be depressed by his concomitant feeling that he *cannot* hold onto it, that a blind and insensitive universe will cruelly destroy it forever. Or to avoid being depressed by his own pessimism, he must repress from his mind his conscious awareness of the thought that he and all his loved ones will be forever undone. He must constantly put out of his mind his sense of the long range futility of his acts. Otherwise, looking at his loved ones he can only feel: "How beautiful and good you are, and how infinitely better it is for us to be alive and know the joy of loving one another than not to exist at all—but one day we shall lose it all; we shall be nothing but stinking corpses." And close behind must come the fatal thoughts: "Since we are finally to become nothing we amount in essence to nothing now, you and me, and everyone. And if we allow ourselves to see this clearly, that all of us are as nothing, then there can be no joy. And if there is no joy, then why bother to act lovingly, to continue our love, or to be anything or do anything?"

Such thoughts do not need to be articulated, or to be held in clear consciousness, to do their poison. One can see here the close connection between morality and eternal life, how easily one can be motivated to take another life (even one's own) when one sees nothing of essential and lasting value in it. We can see what Paul meant when he said: "If the dead rise not, then let us eat and drink, for tomorrow we die."[13] However, one is hardly likely to find many atheists who would agree with this. I have, in fact, more often found it vigorously denied, e.g., by the words of Corliss Lamont in his vehement *Illusion of Immortality*:

It is said that the denial of immortality leads to a philosophy of "Eat, drink, and be merry, for tomorrow we die." We hope that men will always be merry; but there is no reason why at the same time they should not be intelligent, courageous, and devoted to the welfare of society. If this earthly existence is our one and only chance to have a good time, it is also our one and only chance to lead the good life. . . . There will be no second chance. . . . This is our only chance. . . . The knowledge that immortality is an illusion frees us from any sort of preoccupation with the subject of death.[14]

Lamont's book is certainly the most famous negative work ever written on the subject of immortality. It contains many poems, rhetorical flowers from great atheists, and evinces as great an effort as any ever made to establish a philosophical point that is totally futile and valueless. There is no little irony in his claim to be "freed from any sort of preoccupation with the subject of death."

173

No logically and emotionally consistent person can make this claim and then proceed to preoccupy himself with writing on the subject for three hundred pages—and thereafter write and speak on it again and again. Lamont's flowers are proffered in vain, for there simply is no conceivable way to hide from the fact that *the extermination of an intrinsic value is an intrinsic evil*. No one seeing intrinsic beauty or goodness in a beloved person can claim to be "merry" while believing in the ultimate destruction of that person. And how can one be "devoted to the welfare of society" by insisting that every individual making up that society will be ruthlessly destroyed? An appropriate co-title of Lamont's book would be *The Futility of Loving and Living*. A work of considerable literary erudition, it nonetheless proves to be a prodigious effort in vain. For the careful reader cannot help but see that Lamont (1) denies the existence of a *spirit* or *soul*, (2) denies the reality of freedom of choice, and (3) does away theoretically with any individual's responsibility for his acts. Thus it is understandable that he would deny that there is any intrinsic value in life. The irony of his whole work is that he continues to talk as though he sees as much value in life as those of us who actually *feel* its value and the necessity to preserve it. There is no reason why I should be anything less than candid: I have never met a professional atheist who revealed a capacity to *feel* the sacredness of a human being's life. Or if they have this feeling, they demonically fail to honor it with a philosophy that is compatible with it in theory. In the case of Lamont, his work well stands as a prototype of atheism's axiological hypocrisy. Beseeching us to care, he denies that there is anything intrinsically worth caring about. In fact, he belabors the point that there are no values in life *worth* permanently conserving. He intends his "whole book . . . precisely to show that to believe in immortality is to *trample reason under foot*."[15]* He calls on Albert Einstein to buttress his view, labeling him "that most brilliant of contemporary minds."[16] Einstein once abrasively declared that he could not believe "the individual survives the death of his body, although feeble souls harbor such thoughts through fear or ridiculous egotism."[17]

No one need be impressed by such an *argumentum ad idolum*. But it does remind me of a philosophy conference where I once

*The reader may find interesting empirical evidence for survival beyond the grave in Raymond A. Moody's book *Life After Life* (Atlanta: Mockingbird Books, 1975).

saw an atheist rap the table with his knuckles and declare, "I here and now categorically deny that any God exists! People create all gods in their imagination out of fear and conceit. The only cure for the longing after a God is to grow up emotionally!"

The person who said this surely was in no mental or moral position to charge the religious believer with fear and conceit. Every atheist I have ever known has attempted to rationalize his pessimism by calling it realism or courage. One atheist once declared to me, "You have not the courage to face the fact of death, so you invent this God to nurture a greedy and egotistical desire to live forever." The simple truth is that the desire to live forever is no more evidence of greed or egotism than is the desire to live for another moment. Modern psychotherapy holds quite the contrary, that a lack of desire to continue living indefinitely is only evidence of moral and social sickness. Not seeing any values worth continuing to live for is a sign of axiological morbidity, and any psychoterapeutic practices not oriented around *positive values* are worse than useless; they are inevitably harmful. No other mental condition is quite so morally morbid as that of the person who makes a cynical mockery of life while pretending to affirm it. Any man who cherishes life with his whole heart, and mind, can never fall to the spiritual pikerism of ascribing belief in the finality of death to moral courage.

Nothing is gained by the common atheist appeal to "social immortality," i.e., that the human race is immortal while individual persons are being continuously destroyed. As modern astrophysics and ecology have it, the conditions that make possible the sustenance of earthly life cannot always continue without interruption. And what, then, will be left of human value? Without God, nothing whatever. There can be no disputing this simplest fact: the denial that there is intrinsic value in a human being's life can lead only to moral nihilism; the denial of the conservation of that value through the immortal life of the individual can lead only to depression or to playing a game of self-deception to avoid the pain of awareness of one's own depression. To feel the beauty and goodness of life but not to be depressed by the thought of losing it is an emotional contrariety which one can be unconscious of only by repression. There can be no joy in the thought that all joy will be lost, that all effort to hold onto joy will prove in vain. France's esteemed atheist Albert Camus asserted canonically that there ultimately is no reason for happiness; reality is "insane," and human existence is "absurd." In fact (said he) in a world where happiness is not naturally meant to be, the decision to be happy is itself "absurd." Appealing to man's native capacity for rebellion —out of purely arbitrary volition—Camus charged man to be happy in spite of there being no reason to be happy, there being no more intrinsic value in happiness than in a suicidal renunciation of life. Camus apotheosized "The Absurd Man," calling his dogged will to live "the happiness of resignation" (see his *Myth of Sisyphus* and *The Stranger*). But Copenhagen's "Great Dane," Søren Kierkegaard (in *The Sickness Unto Death*), saw through it and labeled it simply for what it is: morbid despair grounded in the spiritual schizophrenia of negative faith. In despair one negates through negative faith the very thing one needs to affirm in order to be most truly at home with his existence as a person. And what constructive motivation can there possibly be for this? Absolutely none. No conceivable real life need can ever be fulfilled by it; nothing of real value ever can be gained.

For years I have been a counselor of persons with emotional and spiritual problems. Sorrowfully, I know that a few have killed themselves suicidally out of axiological despair. There is essentially nothing wrong with renouncing or abandoning life if the fundamental presuppositions of atheism are true. For after all, if life has no intrinsic value then it is inherently not worth living and any decision to sustain oneself can be made only as a part of the natural madness. Or if the atheist does affirm that there is intrinsic value in life, then he is clinging to a philosophy that is in essence unacceptable to the careful heart and rational mind. Nothing can be gained by tarrying in a state of axiological schizophrenia. Atheism is in essence despairful (self-defeating), although the only atheists I have ever known to really acknowledge it were those who committed suicide to be consistent. There are many forms of spiritual sickness, but the supreme schizophrenia is that of the philosopher who can neither truly affirm nor truly renounce the sacredness of life. I have known many atheists (under the label of secular humanism) who have indeed insisted that life is sacred. But then, they have accepted in their minds and hearts the ultimate meaningless destruction of what they themselves define as sacred. This is the supreme contradiction, the equal of which cannot be found in the annals of abnormal psychology. But it has become quite common; I see it daily on the campus: professors talking and acting as though there *are* values essentially worth conserving—while tendentiously insisting that, in the end, it all adds up precisely to *nothing*.

However brilliantly atheism might express itself, there can be no escaping the fact that it is affectively contradictory and deficient. To be a sincere atheist in one's heart is to see no intrinsic value in life; it is to fail to realize what is at stake in the life of love; it is simply to fail to care. It is impossible that any human being can love his mother as I do mine, or see the value in his wife and children that I see in mine, and accept any philosophy that would condone or espouse their eventual destruction. Once I heard my mother conversing with a sceptic who asked her, "Why do you believe in survival beyond the grave? Why do you believe in the immortality of the individual person?" My mother responded, "I believe, because I would need an immortality of time to make all the friends I want to make. I would need an eternity to learn all the things I want to learn, to do all the things I want to do. I would need forever to find all the ways I want to find just to show my children how much I love them." Unmoved by this (as though he saw my mother only as a poetic sentimentalist), the sceptic said, "But wanting it to be that way doesn't make it so, and you must admit that your belief is rooted only in wishful thinking, not in any demonstrable facts." Whereupon my mother answered, "I'll tell you some certain *facts*: I *do* wish for the preservation of my loved ones with all my being, and the day your own survival beyond the grave, and the survival of your loved ones—that you may continue to know the joy of loving life and one another—*means* enough to *you*, then you too will believe in it, with or without any evidence to prove it."

Therein is the crux of the issue. A philosopher after the cast of Lamont would describe my mother's care as something merely "super-greedy."[18] His view simply betrays the lamentable absence of any profound sense of the sacredness of life. For after all is said and done, people will stand both in theory and in practice for only what they *care enough* to stand for. I began this book remarking that rational and fruitful care can never stand against itself. Nobody really *feeling* that life has sacred value can accept any philosophy that does not stand for the conservation of that value, without self-contradiction and senseless melancholia.

177

Commitment to Care

Seeing so much of this around me makes me feel sad. It makes me ache with awareness of the goodness of my own fortune. It makes me wonder, how different it might all be, if everyone had known the warmth and beauty of my mother's love, the education I experienced at her knee. But sorrow over the despair of others is not without its educational value for me. It makes me understand more clearly than ever the meaning of the Cross, the yoke in the Care of Jesus. I now see in Him the imperative that we learn to feel nothing less than the infinite and eternal importance of every human being's life. Until we do just that, we shall continue to commit the same old sins, and inflict on one another the same needless harm and suffering, that we have done throughout the whole of human history. If morality and philosophy of values ever are to come together on a certainty, it has to be this: how we treat one another depends directly on how much value we see in one another, and to see anything less than infinite and eternal value in any person's life is less than enough. Jesus set for all history an example without precedent of divine reverence for life. He was (He is) the crowning peak of true manliness, of an ever uplifting vision of man's nature and destiny *before God*. In all time to come He will be a beacon light for the careful heart, the rational mind. He cared with all his being. He felt the sacredness of life with peerless rationality, rightness, and grace.

Out of His Care, The Lord gave to us freely and totally the value of Himself—that we "should not perish but have everlasting life."

Part II

Some Supporting Arguments

8

Chance and Necessity Reviewed

Modern man has tried the suspense of believing nothing, and because suspense is soon unbearable, he has ended by believing almost anything.

George Arthur Buttrick

IN PREVIOUS CHAPTERS, I indicated that in Part II I would treat of further basic fallacies in materialistic or atheistic biology. As I already have shown with quotations from leading protagonists of atheism, their doctrine ascribes the origin of life to chance, i.e., to undirected and meaningless forces operating in a universe that exists without aim. As I have mentioned earlier, the most prominent representative of this viewpoint today is Jacques Monod, winner of a Nobel Prize for his research and contributions in biochemistry. Monod is most widely known in France, but even in English-speaking countries he is considered by many atheists to be the bellwether of truly "objective" or "scientific" philosophy. And clearly, the airs of his lordly style in *Chance and Necessity* show that he does regard his position as the only "authentic" one for educated persons with open minds.[1] However, his influence is most likely to be short-lived, in view of the fact that his spirit and style is generally quite heavy. Consequently, I think it would be wise to critique the agnostic philosophy of a more influential philosopher, namely, the famous English sceptic, David Hume. Hume

181

is esteemed as the classical objectionist to teleological philosophy in professional or learned circles. I shall examine his views on chance, and criticize them in detail, in Chapter 9.

Most atheists, including Monod, acknowledge the fact that there are laws of nature. But they do not, and cannot, mean the same thing by the word "law" that is meant by a person who believes in the existence of God. The atheist ultimately cannot distinguish between that which happens haphazardly and that which happens lawfully, i.e., happens for a necessary reason or purpose. For the atheist, the laws of nature themselves ultimately are pegged on nothing but chance, which is the equivalent of saying that they are not the expression of any reason or purpose, but exist inexplicably or without any rationale. If the atheist is consistent, he can give no reason (other than his perceptual habit) to explain why the sun will not, or should not, rise tomorrow in the west instead of in the east. For after all, since the sun always has been rising in the east just happenstance, i.e., without any reason for so doing, there can be no logical reason why it should not rise tomorrow in the west instead of in the east. The fact that in the past the sun always has risen happenstance in the east constitutes no rationale whatever for why it should not suddenly rise from some other direction, or not rise at all. Atheistically speaking, there is no rationale of any kind for it existing or moving in any particular way in the first place. Of course, an atheist would say that the sun is made to rise in the east by the laws of nature. But this can scarcely give anyone a reliable rationale for a prediction, if the laws of nature are there for no reason. If the laws of nature that make the sun rise in the east are there for no reason, then there can be no reason for them to be the same tomorrow.

A mere *description* of the sun's and earth's "happenstance" pattern of activity does not constitute a rationale for that pattern. Atheistically defined, the sun's activity and the earth's relationship to the sun is totally blind and devoid of any reasoned cause. No mere description of that activity can give it a direction when, by definition, the activity is in the first place not directed toward any end whatever. The description of purposeless activity as "predictable" cannot give it a purpose, nor inform it with a reason why it should conform to prediction. Activity that is totally devoid of reason and purpose is inherently unintelligible. No amount of labeling and describing can make it make sense.

Chance and Necessity Reviewed

In previous chapters, I have shown how it is impossible to make sense out of objective data that are not informed with some reason and purpose. Yet, scientists abound these days whose definition of their own professional purpose (science) is not only unrealistic and naively narrow, but is downright illogical and hypocritical. That common school of philosophy of science known as "positivism" ("scientism") tells us that the only legitimate personal care of the scientist *qua* scientist is to divest himself entirely of any personal care. Or, the only legitimate purpose the objective scientist can ever have is to refuse to deal in purpose at all. On page 21 (of *Chance and Necessity*), Monod defines scientific objectivity as "the systematic denial that 'true' knowledge can be got at by interpreting phenomena in terms of final causes—that is to say, of 'purpose.'" Throughout this very muddled book, Monod carefully attempts to prove that any care in the universe is strictly a chemical accident. What is more, care as such can mean nothing to the true scientist. The objective scientist can address himself only to observing, measuring, predicting, and describing the patterns of data as they occur in the world. As a technician with purely personal motives, a person may well try to use and control these data. For whatever purpose he wishes to use the knowledge of the scientist, the technician is the beneficiary of the purely disinterested and detached inquiry into objective truth by the scientist. As such, the professional scientist can never look for a rationale behind scientific data, or informing that data, to find some reason for the existence of the world. In short, to ask the question *why* the data occur in the patterns they do, and to seek to discover in the patterns a reason and purpose to answer this question, is to turn from physics to metaphysics, which Monod regards as scientifically naive and dishonest. Yet, the plain truth is, this scientist himself deals continuously in metaphysics, in the same book in which he presumes to deal purely in physics. He himself treats of the question, Why is the universe structured in the way it is? And what is his answer? It is the completely despairful and indefensible answer that there can never be a satisfactory answer. To Monod, all that exists, exists merely happenstance, and all that happens, happens merely happenstance. The universe is caused by nothing, explained by nothing, and exists for nothing.

Admittedly there is purpose (care) in the universe, but it is brought into existence accidentally by blind atoms that are here

183

for no reason. As Monod understands it, the original and ultimate reality in the universe is absolute carelessness. Blind, impersonal atomic forces somehow carelessly give birth to beings who care. A total and universal *un*reason accidentally produces beings who reason. A universal dearth of purpose accidentally produces purpose. And in saying these things, Monod would have us believe that he is presenting the hard facts of an objective scientist, not the subjectivity of his despairful personal opinion. He sees the ultimate "objective" truth of the universe as "chance," which is the alpha and omega of all that there is. The primordial reality is death and darkness. It is the ultimate total dominion of *un*reason over reason, of carelessness over care, of blindness over vision. Monod states expressly in his book that only blind meaninglessness in the universe can ever produce vision and meaning. There are laws of physics and chemistry, laws of logic, and laws of mathematics, but the presence of these phenomena in the universe is purely desultory and random. Says he: life is produced merely by chance "caught on the wing, preserved, reproduced by the machinery of invariance and thus converted into order, rule, necessity. A *totally* blind process can by definition lead to anything; it can even lead to vision itself." And note, the italicization of "totally" is from Monod himself (p. 98).

Monod admits that life is constituted of care. Care is a characteristic that is never observed in inanimate objects (he believes). Yet, he would have us believe that life is nothing but a "chemical machine" (p. 45), produced purely at random as incalculable numbers of tiny inanimate objects accidentally swarm together to form very complex collocations of molecular matter. A human being is nothing more than a fantastically complex compilation of blindly interacting chemicals. Purpose is only a fitful epiphenomenon of crowded proteins and nucleic acids, which in turn are only products of fortuitous collocations of atoms. The existence of the atoms in the first place is a pointless and unaccountable fluke, and the entire physical process (in either animate or inanimate beings) is simply a sequence of adventitious happenings devoid of a rationale. Yet, what scientist could possibly deny the presence of purpose in the biosphere? No one can, except in the manner that Monod does it, by simply defining purpose as something purely chemical or physical in its nature. When a philosopher's position is inherently fuzzy, it is always clever to use fancy language to hide that fact. For the common word "purpose," Monod substitutes the term "teleonomic functioning," which he then defines as precisely the sum total of electro-chemical activities going on in an organism at any given time. For Monod, a person is just a cybernetic engine, exactly the sum of the chemical properties in his body, and nothing more. There are many scientists of equal rank with Monod (as rank is determined by scholarly acclaim) who think that his reduction of a *person* to mere physics is extremely simplistic, to say the least.[2] But this has not deterred some narrow reviewers from presenting Monod's opinion to the public as the final word in modern objective philosophy. For example, Christopher Lehmann-Haupt in *The New York Times* reviewed *Chance and Necessity* as the delivery of "hard proof" that a human being owes his existence "to nothing but a roll of some cosmological set of dice."[3] In point of fact, Monod presents no proof of any kind, but merely mistakes his own subjective metaphysics as facts of physics. That a person is nothing but a fact of physics is no fact of physics at all.

As I have shown in the chapters on Need and Evil, the viewpoint that a person is more than merely the sum of the chemical parts of his body is based on facts and logical reasoning that materialistic philosophers systematically ignore. Rather than cope with these facts scientifically, Monod simply chooses to mention the viewpoint in passing as a stubborn obstacle to scientific objectivity, and is satisfied to slur it with contumelious adjectives. On page 79, he describes any vitalist (spiritualistic) type of thinker as "foolish" and "wrongheaded" for being so naive as to "quarrel" with materialism. Any scientist seeing more in a person than chemicals is "at odds with objective knowledge" (p. 171). All who see a person as a *spirit* just "face away from truth, and are strangers and fundamentally *hostile* to science" (italics his own, p. 171). Those who disagree with Monod are hypocritically "pleased to make use" of science, taking every advantage of it; but otherwise, for its objectivity they do not or will not "care." Their "divorce" from objectivity is "so great" that it cannot but offend any scientist or philosopher with even "a little intelligence." As believers in a mind or soul, they are caught up in a "lie so flagrant that it afflicts and rends the conscience of anyone provided with some element of culture." For the position I am espousing in this book, Monod has abusive language indeed. He describes it as a "disgusting farrago of Judeo–Christian religiosity," an offense to "all those among mankind who bear or will come to bear the responsibility for the way in which society and culture shall evolve" (pp. 171–172).

After stripping the objective scientist of any right to care, Monod himself then admonishes us for not caring about his doctrine that theoretically would annihilate any obligation whatever to care. It is ironic how often this atheist appeals to freedom of choice, moral responsibility, and care for the intrinsic values of life, while all along espousing a reductionistic doctrine of man's nature that theoretically would make such things categorically impossible. For example, he insists that judgments of science and judgments of value must always be essentially incompatible and divorced for "objectivity." In fact, "science outrages values. . . . Science is no judge of them and *must* ignore them. . . ." Science "*subverts* every one of the mythical or philosophical ontogenies upon which the animist or soul-psychology tradition . . . has made all ethics rest: values, duties, rights, prohibitions."[4]

After his nihilist metaphysics, the passionate plea for moral responsibility in the last chapter of Monod's book could become a classic study in fallacies for freshmen students of logic. For after denying any possible objective basis for moral value judgments, freedom of choice, the existence of a responsible agent, and any rights and duties, he then tries desperately to reconstruct the world he thinks he has succeeded in completely putting down. First, he treats the idea of *care* informing the objective data of the world as a retreat into subjectivity and lies. It is dealing in magic, it is unobjective, for the scientist to seek in his data some clues revealing the rationale for the structure of the world. True objectivity must consist of confining one's philosophical position strictly to what can be conclusively proven in the science of physics. In the first place, Monod does not accomplish this objective in his own philosophizing, for it is simply impossible. In the second place, we should be naive indeed to accept so narrow and dehumanizing an idea, that physical science alone is an adequate foundation on which to build a moral and religious philosophy of life. In the name of objectivity, Monod overlooks the most important objective truth of all, namely, the fact that nature in *all* its reality is a question that always goes beyond mere bald data that can be demonstrated in the sciences. Here is a certain objective fact: we always have had, and always shall have, a need for more knowledge and understanding than we can reap from the physical sciences alone.

The atheists are not alone in their assumption that order can be produced by chance. Even some religious scientists and philosophers believe that chance is a possible explanation for the existence of order in the world. In fact, the most famous illustration of the possibility of accidental order is that of the great English mystic-physicist, Arthur S. Eddington. In *The Nature of the Physical World*, Eddington declared that an army of monkeys banging on thousands of typewriters might eventually produce, by sheer accidentality, all of the literary works in the British Museum. Eddington tried to demonstrate that "chance might imitate organization"; in fact, he went so far as to say that organization (order) is not necessarily the antithesis of chance because, on the broad scale of events, "There is safety in numbers."[5] But from a first hand reading of Eddington, it is obvious that both atheist and religious philosophers often have misunderstood and misquoted him, for he clearly discusses his belief in God and his objection to reducing man to nothing but mere considerations of physics and chemistry. Not only was Eddington an unusually brilliant physicist and mathematician, but his writings clearly establish him as a self-declared mystic with an affirmation of the existence of a Supreme Being. His classic example of how order "might" be derived from chance has been exaggerated out of all proportion by those who would use it as a rationalization for atheism and despair. It is unfortunate that people have so often quoted him out of context, and misrepresented his philosophy of physics and life. Consequently, I should like to present his classical illustration of how order "might" arise from chance, and then put the meaning of it in its proper perspective, to show that it cannot be used as a rational argument for atheism, or against the design argument for God.

Eddington states that we can divide a container into two compartments with a partition that separates one half from the other half. Then we can put, say, roughly a quadrillion molecules into one compartment, and none in the other. Then, we can remove the dividing partition in order that the molecules of gas will be free to flow into the other half of the container. Thereupon, the molecules will spread into the whole container and should

remain so ever afterwards. The molecules will not return to one half of the vessel; the spreading cannot be undone—*unless other material is introduced* into the problem *to serve as a scapegoat for the disorganization and carry off the random element elsewhere.* . . . Now each molecule is wandering round the vessel with no preference for one part rather than the other. On the average it spends half its time in one compartment and half in the other. There is a faint possibility that at one moment all the molecules might in this way happen to be visiting the one half of the vessel. You will easily calculate that if n is the number of molecules (roughly a [British] quadrillion) the chance of this happening is $(1/2)^n$. The reason why we ignore this chance may be seen by a rather classical illustration. If I let my fingers wander idly over the keys of a typewriter it *might* happen that my screed made an intelligible sentence. If an army of monkeys were strumming on typewriters they *might* write all the books in the British Museum. The chance of their doing so is decidedly more favourable than the chance of the molecules returning to one half of the vessel. . . . In one sense the chance of the molecules returning to one half of the vessel is too absurdly small to think about. . . . The adverse chance here mentioned is a preposterous number which (written in the usual decimal notation) would fill all the books in the world many times over.[6]

All that Eddington is stating here is that *contingent* order is theoretically derivable from chance. But certainly, he never states, nor implies, that there is no *intrinsic* order in the Cosmic Scheme of Things, and he does not equate intrinsic order with chance. The difference between Eddington and Monod is striking. Eddington is simply expressing his intellectual broadmindedness in acknowledging theoretically what "might" happen. But agnostic readers fail to note his italicized emphasis on this delimiting term "might." We have to remember that Eddington describes such a chance as "too absurdly small" or "preposterous . . . to think about." Yet theoretically we do have to think about it, he insisted; but we do not have to be taken in by it—as would an "absurd" and "preposterous" gambler betting all his money (or in the case of Monod, betting his whole existence) on the credulous assumption that all the order in the universe, and in our lives, is only a product of blind chance.

Chance and Necessity Reviewed

Eddington does not suggest that we use his monkey illustration as a foundation for building a philosophy of life. But Monod would have us stake our whole human struggle and hope on a wild gamble against unutterably great odds. If it is true that the one chance against molecules moving entirely into one half of a small vessel would require a number filling many times all of the books in the world, then unarguably, the chance that all the order in the universe could be derived from blind accidentality is effectively *nil*. In fact, such a chance is so remote that no philosophically sane person could possibly accept it as a credible explanation of the structure of the world that we live in.

I find it curious that a man such as Monod—who places an extreme value on the cautious, critical, sceptical approach to reaching conclusions based solely on high probabilities—would bet all his money on a proposition that he himself describes as having only an incalculably poor chance. Actually, neither Eddington nor Monod present any evidence that the *universal* presence of laws could be based purely on chance. And even more important, Monod simply ignores the fact that the laws of physics transcend all the known changes of time. The qualitative similarity of phenomena and relationships in systems simultaneously existing throughout the universe is a major aspect of the teleological argument for God. And it certainly is odd that Monod chooses to ignore those *universal qualities* that give organization, unity, and symmetry to nature. The pillar stone in the design argument for God is generally ignored by atheists, and it is a fact categorically inexplicable by chance: the laws of physics not only hold consistently throughout all known space; but what is of most crucial importance for the philosopher, they hold *consistently* throughout all known changes of time. The regularity and prevalence of nature's laws throughout innumerable successions in time can be accounted for by nothing, unless we appeal to teleology in the very structure of reality. For the number of these changes in time is absolutely inconceivably great—googolplexes times googolplexes, to say the least. In fact, the process of time in which our universe exists may never have had a beginning, and the number of successions of lawful events may be infinite. Unless we appeal to a Cosmic Law Maker, there is no possible way to account logically for this radical conservation of natural law throughout time. That events can happen by chance (i.e., unintended) in very limited physical situ-

189

ations is of course unarguable. But that thousands of fixed laws can operate uniformly throughout all known space, and abide totally unaffected by interminable changes in time, solely by chance —this is categorically unthinkable. It is no wonder that an overwhelming majority of human beings can sense that something is basically absurd in the atheist philosophy.

When a philosopher is so devoted to despair that he chooses to ignore numberless odds against the validity of his position, then one can only conclude that his attitude is purely *subjective*—not "objective," as Monod would like us to believe. All available objective evidence shows unmistakably that the notion that our universe is ordered so majestically by mere chance is nonsensical. A close examination will show that Eddington's example of accidental order is empirically unsound because it begs the question for anyone who would use it to rationalize atheism. True enough, there is a theoretical *mathematical* possibility that an army of monkeys could accidentally produce all the sentences of all the books in the British Museum. But we would be very ingenuous not to recognize that this "absurdly small" chance is a mere mathematical abstraction. That Eddington's monkeys could accidentally arrange all of these sentences together in exact order, on papers which they had accidentally put into their typewriters, then accidentally number all the pages correctly and properly bind and finish the books (not to mention place all of them in their properly classified positions in the British Museum)—this is an absolutely implausible notion to a rational and objective mind. In Eddington's illustration, the existence and presence of the typewriters is taken for granted as given. Also the typewriter ribbons, endless reams of paper, erasers and other things essential to successful typing are taken for granted as given. Precisely what makes the atheist argument burlesque is that such things can never possibly be plausibly taken for granted as given. To argue from Eddington's illustration for atheism, one would have to show that the monkeys were strumming on typewriters that were produced accidentally, that the typewriter ribbons and reams of paper were products of sheer accidentality, and likewise for everything else involved. Which is precisely what Monod does—he reduces *the whole of reality, with each and every one of its parts and their specific relations,* ultimately to chance. He even defines *mind* as nothing but the random behavior of intricately organized combinations of proteins (p. 17 and elsewhere).

Not once in his entire book does it occur to Monod that a human being has a *mind*, that *seeing* is a visual sensation, and that sensations are mental. Curiously, he is unable to distinguish between the electronic data on a television tube and the *image* of it in the mind of the person who is watching the tube. A television set does not see anything; neither does an eye, nor a brain. The electronic data on the face of the tube do not see themselves. Neither are the electronic data in the brain seen by themselves. The image is a gestalt produced by the mind to read meaning into the data that otherwise would be meaningless unto themselves. Without a person in the room to watch the television screen, there is no vision in the room. Without a mind in the brain to interpret the physical data in the brain, there is no vision in the brain. A brain without a mind in it can see nothing at all.

A quadrillion molecules in a small vessel in a laboratory constitute only an infinitesimal fraction of the known number of molecules existing in the universe. The currently estimated size of our universe is approximately a British tredecillion (10^{78}) atoms, or the number one followed by seventy-eight zeros. Here, it is imperative to mention a pivotal fact that Eddington went out of his way to point out: the chance is damningly small that all the molecules of the container could move into one half of it purely at random; but if this once did happen—which would constitute an anti-entropy type of state—then there is no conceivable mathematical possibility that such a state could *sustain* itself purely by chance. As Eddington pointed out, the second law of thermodynamics would make the continued sustenance of such a state impossible by chance, and it could be sustained only by someone putting the dividing partition back in its place to prevent random disorganization from occurring. In other words, there would have to be a *controlling agent* to sustain the order. What is more, this instance of "organization by chance" contains nothing remotely near the degree of complexity of order characterizing the chemical structure of a living cell. In the cubicle of gas, the molecules are in motion apart from each other in space, with nothing whatever in their relations that is characteristic of life. In a living cell, the molecules are *connected* in a continuously *controlled* and *sustained* manner to meet the cell's purposes and needs. To deduce from Eddington's limited hypothetical situation of accidental order that all atomic and molecular order in the world is a product of mere chance—this is an arrant violation of physical law, as well as a rape of common-sense reason. It is not only a question of foolish gambling against categorically unthinkable odds. It is a question of the *credibility* of an argument that ignores all the relevant variables in Eddington's monkey illustration. Some variables ignored are: the reality of the *conception, understanding* and *purpose* informing the design of the typewriters, the reams of paper, the inked ribbons, the classification and shelving system in the British Museum—not to mention the fact that the monkeys responsible for the accidental literary production would be acting for some purpose. Only just yesterday, a guest lecturer said to my students: "*All* order ultimately is a product of chance." The philosophical axiom for such speculation surely must be: "an absolute minimum of evidence and an absolute maximum of improbability."

Albeit, Jacques Monod presents this kind of speculation as though it were required by known facts, rather than as a bad gamble, and he prevails upon us to accept his wisdom. The question arises: How would wisdom be possible, for a philosophy of spiritual and moral values, if we seriously took up housekeeping with despairful Monod? In his last chapter, "The Kingdom and the Darkness," he presents the heavy and tedious assumptions of his philosophy of ethics based on chance. I must list them thoroughly and carefully in order to effectively critique them. They are:

1. Objectivity is the factual data of the world separated from all purpose, meaning, and evaluation (p. 21).

2. Objectivity is the "*conditio sine qua non* of true knowledge" (p. 174).

3. "Knowledge in itself is exclusive of all value judgment" (p. 174).

4. "Ethics, in essence *nonobjective*, is forever barred from the sphere of knowledge" (p. 174).

5. Science is the pursuit of objective information, and must systematically avoid considerations of meaning, purpose and value. "Science outrages values. . . . Science is no judge of them and *must* ignore them. . . ." (p. 172).

6. "The postulate of objectivity . . . prohibits any confusion of value judgments with judgments arrived at through knowledge" (p. 175).

7. No philosophy can be *"authentic,* unless . . . it makes explicit and preserves the distinction between the two categories" of objective knowledge and ethical values (p. 175).

8. *"Inauthentic* discourse, where the two categories are jumbled, can lead only to the most pernicious nonsense, to perhaps unwitting but nonetheless criminal lies" (p. 175).

9. *"The very definition of 'true' knowledge reposes in the final analysis upon an ethical postulate"* (p. 173).

10. "In an objective system" of philosophy, "any mingling of knowledge with values is unlawful, *forbidden"* (p. 176).

11. "True knowledge is ignorant of values" (p. 176).

12. "True knowledge is ignorant of values, but it cannot be grounded elsewhere than upon a value judgment, or rather upon an *axiomatic* value. It is obvious that the positing of the principle of objectivity as the condition of true knowledge *constitutes an ethical choice and not a judgment arrived at from knowledge, since, according to the postulate's own terms, there cannot have been any 'true' knowledge prior to this arbitral choice"* (p. 176).

13. "Thus, assenting to the principle of objectivity one announces one's adherence to the basic statement of an ethical system, one asserts *the ethic of knowledge"* (p. 176).

14. *"Hence it is from the ethical choice of a primary value that knowledge starts.* The ethic of knowledge thereby differs radically from animist [religious or vitalist] ethics, which all claim to be based upon the 'knowledge' of immanent laws, religious or 'natural,' which are supposed to assert themselves over man. The ethic of knowledge does not obtrude itself upon man; *on the contrary, it is he who prescribes it to himself,* making of it the *axiomatic* condition of authenticity for all discourse and all action" (pp. 176–177).

15. "No system of values can be said to constitute a true ethic unless it proposes an ideal reaching beyond the individual and transcending the self to the point even of justifying self-sacrifice, if need be" (p. 178).

16. The authentic approach to ethics "sets forth a transcendent value, true knowledge, and invites" a person "not to use it self-servingly but henceforth to enter into its service from deliberate and conscious choice" (p. 178).

17. "Where then shall we find the source of truth and the moral inspiration for a really *scientific* socialist humanism, if not in the

sources of science itself, in the ethic upon which knowledge is founded, and which by free choice makes knowledge the supreme value—the measure and warrant for all other values?" (p. 180).

In the same chapter in which he presents the above postulates of his ethic, Monod describes religious philosophers who disagree with him as victims of "deceitful servitudes" (p. 180). Also he declares that we are propagators of "criminal lies." He borders on eloquence (a rarity in his writing) in his description of man's need to despair. "Man knows at last that he is alone in the universe's unfeeling immensity, out of which he emerged only by chance. His destiny is nowhere spelled out, nor is his duty. The kingdom above or the darkness below: it is for him to choose." Man's life is nothing but "an anxious quest in a frozen universe of solitude." Only when man chooses to be "authentic," will he "wake to his total solitude, his fundamental isolation. Now does he at last realize that, like a gypsy, he lives on the boundary of an alien world. A world that is deaf to his music, just as indifferent to his hopes as it is to his suffering or his crimes" (pp. 180, 170, 172–173).

Monod's work in the Pasteur Research Institute in Paris does evince his dedication to accomplishing something valuable and unselfish for man. But we would be witless to allow this to blind us to the blatant contradictions in his theoretical philosophy of morality and despair. For unmistakably, he renounces the notion that man is accountable to any transcendental or objective ideals, or that he has any *duties*, in any meaningful sense of the word. From the aforementioned postulates in his "ethic," the following contradictions stand out like a giant wart on a person's nose:

1. Monod reduces everything to blind chance, then speaks of man's "freedom of conscious choice." Such a notion of choice is meaningless, after he defines a human being as nothing but a chemical machine. It is a contradiction in terms to insist that a person is nothing but a product of blind chance, and at the same time say he makes conscious choices. The idea that conscious choices are made by chance, or by a machine, is absurd.

2. Monod states categorically that the objective universe is devoid of ideals. But then, he appeals to ideals that transcend the individual, as though there could be some ethical *truth* about how an individual *ought* to behave. It is illogical to make any kind of appeal to transcendental moral truth after insisting that a "primary value" is nothing but an "arbitral choice."

3. It is ridiculous to say that "true knowledge is ignorant of values," and in the same breath say that he has chosen "the ethic of true knowledge." He tells us that ethics is "in essence *nonobjective* . . . forever barred from the sphere of knowledge." But then, he asks us to believe that *his* ethic is "objective," that it is based in "true knowledge." Which is even more nonsensical after he reduces objectivity itself to something only arbitrarily axiomatic because it is reducible to nothing but an "arbitral choice." Plainly he tells us: "The positing of the principle of objectivity . . . *constitutes an ethical choice and not a judgment arrived at from knowledge.* . . ." How can he insist that *"the very definition of true knowledge* reposes in the final analysis upon an ethical postulate," and simultaneously insist that "Ethics . . . is forever barred from the sphere of knowledge"? He starts out demanding a total divorce of objective truth from ethical values. He ends up insisting that neither objective truth nor ethical values are immanent in nature in any manner, except in the arbitrariness of the individual's choice. Plainly, he declares that the "ethic of true knowledge" is in no way objective, that it "does not obtrude itself upon man," but *"on the contrary, it is he who prescribes it to himself"* by a purely "arbitral choice."

Philosophical criticism is supposed to be polite, but Monod's incomparable arbitrariness, coupled with his imperious sarcasm, certainly tempts one to retort sardonically. But keeping it impersonal, What can he possibly mean by "objectivity" after declaring that it "does not obtrude itself upon man"? Man's duty, he tells us, "is nowhere spelled out" (p. 180). Which means, there is no *objective reason* why the individual should define his duty in any one way rather than in some other. Then, he peremptorily dismisses all of us as nitwits who do not define duty as he defines it. First, he forbids any claim of ethics to true knowledge. Then, he prohibits the mingling of science with ethics. Finally, he proclaims himself the inventor of a scientific ethic based on true knowledge. Actually, he ends in sheer ethical nihilism in disguise.

Monod is guilty of the most sophomoric fallacies in reasoning about the issues he addresses. Each of his major mistakes is inevitable to anyone trying to theorize on the basis of atheistic premises. For example:

(1) He denies that there is any validity to the principle of intelligibility. As I have stated repeatedly, this principle asserts

categorically that for any phenomenon or event to make objective sense it must be informed with a rationale. In denying this (by simply systematically assuming God's non-existence *ad hominem*), Monod falls inescapably into the trap of confusing mere description for explanation. We do not and cannot explain a thing merely by describing it. Monod chooses purely arbitrarily to *describe* the evolution and behavior of life as occurring solely by chance. But thus describing it does not necessarily make it the truth.

(2) He acknowledges that there is a "flagrant epistemological contradiction" (his own words) in the assumption that purposelessness can somehow explain purpose, i.e., that purpose in the world could have been brought into existence by causes that were the expression of no purpose at all (pp. 21–22). But then, motivated as he is to stand as an atheist, he tries to subjugate the objectionability of the contradiction by describing it as just the way things factually happen to be. As a matter of fact, however, it is both logically and empirically impossible to derive purpose from a prior state of absolute purposelessness. In Chapter 9, which expounds a rational epistemology for quantum mechanics and microbiology, I shall develop a demonstration of this fact in detail. In Chapter I of his book, Monod recognizes this fact and admits to it plainly. However, he promises to "resolve" the contradiction with an argument that supposedly is to follow in subsequent chapters. He does not promise to undo the reality of the contradiction. Rather, he promises to show that it simply must be accepted if we are to have a philosophy of life squaring with his "principle of objectivity"—which he assumes, purely *ad hoc*, is validly defined. This is how he would presume to "resolve" the contradiction. But instead of actually resolving it, he unwittingly proceeds only to show how philosophy must inevitably flounder when it attempts to build on the rationalization of an absurdity. Instead of giving logical reasons why we should accept a logical contradiction as the truth (which, of course, would only logically compound the contradiction), Monod just dogmatically *describes* purpose as evolving out of purposelessness, after he defines purpose in a way that is boorishly unrealistic. Defining purpose as nothing more than the behavior of proteins is unsurpassably witless.

(3) He pits his "principle of objectivity" against the principle of intelligibility, and therein creates a false dichotomy between factuality and logic that can serve no conceivable real need. As I

have shown earlier, Monod defines the "principle of objectivity" as all positivists define it (p. 21), i.e., in a manner that interprets all objective data in the world as being inherently uninformed with reason and purpose. He then repeatedly states that this principle requires that we refuse ever to deal in meanings, purposes, and values as long as we presume to be objective. My response to this is: no one in the real world can ever possibly *live* by this definition, and Monod is himself a studious demonstration of that fact. For while insisting that the objective person will *not project his definitions onto the world*, Monod does it, unconsciously, in every line in his book. It should be obvious to any alert reader that Monod is projecting his own theoretical metaphysical constructs onto the world to make it conform to his subjective picture of it. His description of his own picture of the world as purely objective betrays no little guile. There can be no intelligibility in renouncing the principle of intelligibility in the name of another principle whose author acknowledges to contain a "profound epistemological contradiction" (p. 22). Again, objectivity to the positivist means refusing to seek a rationale informing the objective data we deal with in the name of science and truth. But to accept this would be only to pile absurdities upon absurdities. For palpably, there can be no objective rationale for presuming to deal in phenomena defined as inherently barren of an objective rationale. There can be no rational purpose for presuming not to deal in purpose. There can be no meaning in presuming not to deal in meaning. There can be no value in presuming not to deal in values. Monod is himself conscious of these facts, which is why he has to admit that positivism contains a brazen contradiction. Nonetheless, he goes on to *describe* the world as objectively meaningless, objectively purposeless, and in-and-of-itself valueless. Except perhaps in Camus and Sartre, I think I have never seen two hundred pages more saturated with starkly clashing presumptions and disclaimers. Monod labors strenuously, that we may see the objective value of seeing the objective world as valueless, the objective meaning of seeing the objective world as meaningless, and the objective purpose of reading the objective world as purposeless. All this is distinctly difficult to believe. How can any rational person not feel embarrassed for Monod? For while he presumes not to deal in meanings, he should have to admit that his thinking and writing is logically meaningless. Nothing whatever is really explained by his description of reality as inherently inexplicable. No prowess of mind is shown in arguing that reality ultimately is mindless. This has to be one of the most irrational books ever written. It would be hard to find in any one volume more non-sequiturs, paralogisms, and obfuscations.

The further he goes, the more embarrassing Monod's situation becomes. In the beginning of his book he appeals to the laws of nature as though they are real outside of his mind. Also, he appeals to the laws of logic as though they have objective ontological status in the world. Yet all along, he assumes that these laws abide in the universe strictly out of no necessity or reason. And in the end, he clearly denies that there are any objective realities at all (pp. 176–177). He plays equally as unruly with the principles of sound language usage. He describes atomic particles, and any conglomerations of them in molecules, as mindless. He describes their combining into living cells purely by chance. But then, he also describes them as having "quite literally, a microscopic discriminativeness (if not 'cognitive') faculty" whereby they are able to "recognize" each other and unite chemically for the sake of their "teleonomic functioning" [purpose] (p. 46). Only a philosopher bent on standing on an absurdity can so blatantly violate that most essential of semantical rules, *videlicet*: avoid the use of self-vitiating terms. Indiscriminate discriminativeness, uncognitive cognitiveness, unrecognizing recognition, blind vision (p. 98), etc.

Monod devotes much effort to showing that "invariance precedes teleonomy." In plain language, he means by this that a living machine exists first and any purpose for its existence follows only afterwards. That is, there is no purpose for the rudimentary biological machinery of life to exist in the world. The existence of the world itself, and the chemical laws, mechanisms, and potentiality of chance events to bring life about—*have categorically no rationale*. But Monod does not present a single evidential datum to substantiate this belief. The semantico-logical implausibility of his position is betrayed constantly by his unavoidable use of the language of a teleologist from beginning to end.

Monod's strong subjective bias against the idea of God is unconcealed. He attributes *all* belief in God to egocentric anthropomorphism and irresponsible wishful thinking. Man in his vainglory has craved a divine inheritance, to be the center of the universe. He is in principle only a meaningless accident, but he has wanted the universe to exist purposefully *for him*. But here, any thinking person might ask about Monod, Is he not himself taking that position that is most completely anthropomorphic in its nature? For most people do, in fact, believe that reality is ultimately centered in God, not man. But once Monod has done away with God, and any objective duties and values that would lay a binding claim upon his life, then what is there to keep him from acting the role of a god himself? If God did not exist, then why couldn't any man justifiably consider himself to be the center of reality? If God did not exist, then *ipso facto* we would have no accountability to Him, and no necessity or motivation whatever to look *up*. This would make anyone the center of the universe who cared to consider himself as such. Instead of looking up to a Being higher than oneself, a person could look only to himself, or to someone else taking the place of God (another fallible individual, or an institution, a system, etc.). Monod states that no individual has any accountability to anything or anybody external to himself, other than what he *chooses*. It is he himself who insists that "science subverts . . . all ethics . . . duties, rights, prohibitions" (p. 172). Thus in effect, he makes himself ethically the center of the universe, subject to no objective ideal restraints of any kind. He, and he alone, by a subjective "arbitral choice" can determine what is valuable, what is right, and what his duties are. Nothing in objective reality can justifiably prohibit him from doing anything he wants to do.

How can any person become metaphysically, psychologically, or ethically more anthropomorphic than this?

Western mankind traditionally has believed that there is a covenant between God and his children, between ultimate purpose and man's purpose, between nature and each of its living creatures. Only God's existence can provide a tie between the individual and the world in which he otherwise would live as a lonely alien. Monod says that we fabricate this idea of God, and the idealized notion of a covenant, only to avoid facing the "unfathomable gulf" between man's egotistical purpose and the ultimate purposelessness of the world. We invent an illusory Cosmic Scheme of Things, trying to escape from our ultimate solitude and doom. Mocking belief in God as immaturity, Monod declares that we must "break this tie because the postulate of objectivity requires it" (p. 31). Believing in God is "abandoning the postulate of objectivity"; and objectivity requires that we abandon the quest for a rational understanding of the existence of the world and our lives within it.

A summary analysis of Monod's position may be stated thus: he does not start with objective data and logically infer the necessity of atheism from them; rather, he starts *ad hominem* with atheism, and then defines objectivity in a completely arbitrary manner to support it. It is apparent throughout his entire work that his atheism is voluntaristic and passionate. He appears to be happy at the notions that God does not exist. In fact, his vituperative anti-theist language suggests that he probably would be angered if suddenly he discovered accidentally that God does exist. Any practical person, concerned with dealing rationally with *values* and *meanings*, must reject this "principle of objectivity" as a pseudo-postulate; for quite simply, taking all meaning, purpose, and value out of science and ethics is not real objectivity—it is an axiological crime.

I am reminded of Evan Esar's quip that such an atheist "cannot find God for the same reason that a thief cannot find a policeman."[7]

Once a philosopher chemicalizes the human spirit; once he denies the reality of mind and reduces biological explanation merely to physics, we can expect that thereforward contradictions will issue forth perpetually.

Fortunately, we can be grateful to Monod, insofar as humanity might be the beneficiary of his talent for practically useful biochemical research that might lead to the conquest of diseases. But it is indeed bad fortune when some person takes such an irrational and despairful philosophical theory seriously in practice, lets it depress his spirit, and then wastes away or takes his life in despair. Monod insists that, as we face the realities of "objective" knowledge today, "what we see opening before us . . . is an abyss of darkness" (p. 170). Curiously, he would have us believe that he really faces this abyss, but that he is *joyful* in his "authenticity."

9

Hume and Contemporary Physicists

To suppose universal laws of nature capable of being apprehended by the mind and yet having no reason for their special forms, but standing inexplicable and irrational, is hardly a justifiable position. Uniformities are precisely the sort of facts that need to be accounted for. That a pitched coin should sometimes turn up heads and sometimes tails calls for no particular explanation; but if it shows heads every time, we wish to know how this result has been brought about. Law is *par excellence* the thing that wants a reason.

Charles Sanders Peirce

ALTHOUGH HE IS NOT of our time, the Scottish philosopher David Hume (1711–1776) even today is probably the most widely respected antagonist of the teleological argument for God. In the *Dialogues Concerning Natural Religion* he sets forth a variety of clever arguments through his imaginary characters. And certainly, we can give him credit for one important accomplishment: he did succeed in logically refuting the idea that the world we live in could have been designed by an omnipotent and omniscient God. But then, it has never been my concern to defend such a theological construction in this book, but on the contrary, to treat of a concept of God that a logical man with a respect for facts can believe in with his whole being. Like Kant, Hume only succeeded in showing the necessity to revise the concept of God— although this was not his intention as a sceptic. The omnipotent and omniscient God has been totally confuted, and in the minds of logical thinkers done away with once and for all. Yet, Hume's scepticism actually contributed nothing to the construction of a logical world-view of his own.[1] For the alternative that he would substitute for God—blind chance—enjoys no more logical support

201

than the notions of omnipotence and omniscience. In this space, I must confine myself to only one of his concepts, namely, that the universe's order is derivable from chance—since this is the core of his whole philosophical position, and since all his other agnostic points have been thoroughly refuted.

In Part VIII of the *Dialogues*, Hume's character Philo asks, Why cannot the universe's order be purely a product of the chance motions of eternal matter?[2] And arguing for this position, he states: "Motion in many instances . . . begins in matter, without any known voluntary agent. . . . The beginning of motion in matter itself is as conceivable *apriori* as its communication from mind and intelligence." With this in mind, Philo proposes a "new" hypothesis for the origin and structure of the world as we know it. He describes it as a "hypothesis . . . that is not absolutely absurd and improbable." Philo then tells us that all matter and motion can exist just pointlessly and must, from the standpoint of each discrete physical entity and event, be purely lawless and chaotic. But then, he goes on to tell us that all of the accidental motions of purposeless matter in the universe "in less than infinite transpositions, must produce . . . economy or order; and by its very nature, that order, when once established, supports itself, for many ages, if not to eternity. . . . For this is actually the case with the present world" (pp. 182–183).

Earlier, I alluded to Eddington's famous claim that "in a chance situation there is security in time." Similarly, Hume's Philo believes that lawless physical activities must "in a great, but finite succession [of changes in time] . . . fall at last into the present or some such order."[3] Chaos must prevail until "finite, though innumerable revolutions [of dead matter] produce at last some forms, whose parts and organs are so adjusted as to support the forms amidst a continued succession of matter." To give his hypothesis some appearance of sophistication, Hume attempts to describe the evolution of law out of lawlessness in detail. Says he:

No particular order or position ever continues a moment unaltered. . . . Every possible situation is produced, and instantly destroyed. . . . Thus the universe goes on for many ages in a continued succession of chaos and disorder. But is it not possible that it may settle at last . . . so as to preserve a uniformity of appearance, amidst the continual motion and fluctuation of its parts? . . . May we not hope for such a position, or rather be assured of it, from the eternal revolutions of unguided matter, and may not this account for all the appearing wisdom and contrivance which is in the universe? (pp. 184–185).

Like all his predecessors and disciples, Hume makes no plausible case for this theory, for he presents no objective evidence and no logical rationale for it at all.[4] In fact, he does what all atheists and agnostics inevitably must do in order to try to make sense out of an ultimately purposeless world—claim to close down the house of teleology while sneaking into it through the back door. Note Philo's use of teleological language when he speaks of the "wisdom" and "contrivance" that is obviously in the structure of the universe. He plainly admits that his assumption is only slightly less than absurd. Which is precisely what we should expect of *any* theory that, by its own admission, has nothing more substantial to rely upon than blind chance. Hume does attempt to explain order in the present world of space-time by appealing to order that is the result of innumerable successions of events in time. But there is no logical reason whatever to assume that a world that is originally *devoid* of any intrinsic or necessary order should ever produce any accidental order, let alone a progressive order, or an order that is sustained indefinitely across innumerable successions of time. Hume's position is exactly like that of Monod. It is nothing more than an incredibly presumptuous gamble. For even he himself as much as admits that his agnosticism is desperate. Otherwise, why should he depreciate the plausibility of his own theory by describing it as "not absolutely absurd and improbable"? (p. 183).

Hume argues that there are no laws governing the behavior of matter at any time. In essence, the universe is totally devoid of government; it is purely an accident that it is at the present time incredibly highly ordered. But if we were to take this notion seriously, then we should be unable to account for the fact the same laws that operate throughout the known world today (1978) are precisely the same as those operating in 1968, 1958, 1948, and so on, into the past indefinitely.

There is one striking empirical fact that Hume, like all sceptics, must ignore, and that is this: that *the greater the order, and the longer the duration of that order in time, then the less plausibly it can be accounted for by chance.* I have granted that some instances of accidental order in extremely limited space-time situa-

203

tions can of course exist. But the notion that *universal* and *abiding* order can be pegged merely on chance, while chance itself is defined as containing no causal nature whatever that is essentially conducive to order—this is obviously a violation of the simplest rules of semantics and logic. The desperate attempt to get around bad logic with an appeal to the magic of time is plainly a trick. It is a resort to that kind of logical sleight of hand that is unimpressive, to say the least, and must not be allowed to pass off under the guise of intellectual "objectivity," "authenticity," or any other forms of semantical deception.

Hume states that there is no *apriori reason* why the existence and motion of matter should be informed with purpose or reason. It is curious that the contradiction in this position is never obvious to the atheist. I am tempted to believe that the inability to see it is not due to a natural blind spot in the mind of the sceptic. Rather, it must be due to the spirit of scepticism itself, i.e., the will of the sceptic to cling to anything, however absurd, in order to rationalize his escape from accountability to some absolute truths, ideals, and duties. After reducing all necessity to blind accidentality, Hume is in no position to resort to the notion of the *apriori* to support any of his arguments. For if the ultimate reality is nothing but meaningless chance, devoid of any necessary or essential truth and reason, then logically there can be no meaning whatever to the notion of the *apriori*, i.e., that which is *universally* and *necessarily* valid *reason*.

How contradictory can the human mind become? Hume insists that there is no reason to explain the movement towards order in the world. But then, he himself proceeds to give a reason to explain the evolution of that order, *post hoc*. After insisting that there has been no reason involved, then why use reasoning to explain that which he himself insists there can be no reason to explain? Giving *un*reason as a reason is giving no reason at all. Plainly, for Hume the reason for order in the world is *un*reason, (i.e., chance). But the simple truth is that *un*reason can never provide a reason for anything; *un*reason can explain nothing; and consequently, it can never be used as a tool for constructing an intelligible philosophy of life. Hume tries to explain what he himself in principle insists can never be explained; thus, he wastes our time. His explanation is that ultimately there can be no explanation for anything—and he goes to great pains to explain this!

Hume and Contemporary Physicists

Hume argues that all effects must exist independently of causes, and that even if there were discernible causes then there need be no reason or purpose informing these causes. The plain truth is that even if Hume's assumptions were true (that all effects are uncaused, or all causes are unreasoned), a world of such effects and causes would be essentially unintelligible, and could never be known and understood. Hume gets us nowhere, except into waters of absurdity over our heads.

Monod is in no less embarrassing a position when he calls himself a "captive of logic" (p. 27 in *Chance and Necessity*). It is of course anyone's freedom to so flatter himself, but it is hardly a way to make a case for a point of view after one has denied that there is any categorical necessity whatever. The laws of logic cannot just *chance* to be definitely binding. The notion that laws of logic can prevail in a world categorically uninformed with logical reason or purpose is itself a logical contradiction. A logical man cannot use purpose and reason to argue that there is no categorically necessary purpose and reason. There is no possible way to start with absolute chance and then derive categorical necessity from it. Without categorical necessity, the notion of binding laws of logic, or *apriori* truths, is altogether meaningless. Hume argues that there is no *apriori reason* why the existence of matter and motion must have some reason. This is like stopping up one's nose to gain access to purer air. The use of reason to ultimately undermine or deny reason is a paralogism unbecoming even a freshman.

Humean metaphysics overlooks many salient facts which we find when we study the structure of reality objectively. I refer to those categorical facts that cannot possibly be accounted for by any notion of accidentality. Neither can they be seriously ignored without needlessly damaging the human psyche or will to live. These are the facts that I have alluded to throughout this book, and in summary, they are:

1. The reality of universals in the world (*apriori* truths, as well as empirical constants that are omnipresent in life, etc.).

2. The inviolable law of cumulative time.

3. The reality of categorical necessity (such as in *relations* in logic, mathematics, relations between need and value, relations between logical necessity and factual necessity, etc.).[5]

4. The reality of ever-abiding categories, such as *being, possibility, actuality, abstraction, concretion, process, relations*, etc.—

without which no world of any kind could be at all conceivable.

5. The reality of harmonious accomodation of parts to the whole (e.g., in living organisms, as well as in the ordered structure of parts in the atom, the ordered interplanetary relations with their predictable orbits, etc.).

6. The laws of nature and their uninterrupted duration through uncountable changes in time.

7. The basically aesthetic structure of reality (that the universe is everywhere informed with some intrinsic values and beauties). I should not attempt to argue this with logical abstractions, for this kind of understanding can be grasped only through the intuition—through a person's capacity to *feel* beauty, or to apprehend it *ab intra*, even though it be objective or existing in the world outside a man's head.[6]

8. The reality of advanced life forms in the world.

There is a unanimous agreement amongst molecular biologists that mutations occur in the DNA molecule by chance. Moreover, there is unquestionable evidence that the overwhelming majority of mutations are harmful to the organism and its progeny. Some mutations have no noticeable effect, for either better or worse. A few are even advantageous. But undeniably, the influence of most chance mutations is mutilative, which means that the notion of *progressive* evolution solely by chance is logically a fool's gamble. Without biotonic laws operating in nature to counteract the destructive, or obstructive, effects of chance mutations, there is no logical reason to assume that human beings could ever have evolved in the first place. The argument of the atheist, of course, is that the good done by a rarely advantageous mutation can counterbalance and outweigh the harm done by the overwhelming majority which are harmful. Darwin used a similar argument and called it "the survival of the fittest" by "natural selection." By chance, some creature-types survive and progress, while most are undone by the ravages of accidental change. This is the popular view amongst biologists in general, despite the fact that, mathematically, chance cannot explain the origin of life in the first place, nor the maintenance or reproduction of life, nor account for the fact of general evolutionary progress. This is obvious, since the evidence against overall progress by mere chance is damning (over 95 per cent of genetic mutations being detrimental). But be this as it may, the habit of many scientists of reducing the philosophical issues of life to questions of mere mathematics of chance is naive because of:

9. The reality of *mind*, of *consciousness* in the living organism, and of the autonomy of the human *spirit*.[7]

The existence of the mind, with its obvious capacity to purposefully order its own thoughts, to initiate its own activities, and to assume responsibility for its free choices—this spiritual reality cannot conceivably be derived from a mere mathematical abstraction called "chance." While neither Hume nor Monod would acknowledge this fact in theory, they nonetheless would always insist that their adversaries honor it in practice, which constitutes a practical refutation of their own professed convictions. I cannot imagine Monod (or a person like Hume) ever allowing me to treat him as though he were a mere machine, or a mere object of chance. Every atheist I have ever known would demand that people recognize and honor his right to personal autonomy and to freedom of choice. This matter of *"human rights" is not a question of chance, nor of physics or chemistry, nor of how machines are constructed.* In practice, the atheist inevitably holds other persons accountable to certain transcendental moral ideals that can never logically be grounded in mere blind chance.

Today, the most scientifically "in" group of metaphysical nihilists is the so-called Copenhagen school of physical indeterminists. This school of physics would build its whole interpretation of the cosmic order on one simple principle, namely, Werner Heisenberg's "principle of indeterminacy," which I spoke of in an earlier chapter. Many physicists simply take this principle for no more than what it actually is, a lawful statement of the fact that we cannot, from the standpoint of *current* methodology and knowledge of the physical world, measure with absolute accuracy the position and velocity of a particle at the same time. There is no logical or empirical reason to assume that the principle implies anything more than this. Any physicist with scientific objectivity and humility must acknowledge that Heisenberg's principle is grounded in the data of the physical world only as we now know it. The principles of quantum mechanics may not apply with absoluteness and finality to physical entities and laws beneath the quantum level that may possibly be discovered in the future.

Nonetheless, the Copenhagen group and its protagonists believe that they have introduced a shocking new concept of physics, where indeterminism in nature is the final and absolute fact in physical reality. Accordingly, they view the statistical laws of quantum mechanics as the ultimate limits to possible knowledge in physics. Traditionally, philosophers and scientists have believed that order in the macroscopic world has its roots in a causal lawfulness on the microscopic level. The "new physics" rejects this, and regards the ultimate reality as sheer indeterminism, or absolute purposelessness and causelessness. Which is to say, there is no reason why any particular particle ever moves the way it does or is located where it is. In short, the behavior of any particle is uncaused. For example, the behavior of an electron at any given time and place cannot be perfectly predicted because it is capricious, indeterminate, and not affected by any lawful force or agent. This is not to say that the electron is not affected by other particles or forces, but simply that its existence and behavior has no rationale. Nor has any quantum a rationale.

The two men responsible for the beginning of this radical interpretation were Werner Heisenberg (a German) and the great Danish physicist, Niels Bohr. Both were clearly conscious of the necessity to re-think physics if their metaphysical dogma of ultimate capriciousness were true. However, both seemed to be naively unconscious of the contradictions for a rational philosophy of life if their definition of indeterminacy were carried to its logical conclusions. It is not my purpose in this book to treat of their contradictions in any fine or technical detail. This would necessitate a whole volume dealing with both the physical and metaphysical aspects of the issue. Suffice it to point out here, the indeterminist dogma has been systematically exposed in a number of works by recondite scientists. For example, it has been done brilliantly by David Bohm, an American physicist now living in England. It cannot be my purpose to detail his arguments here. But I am moved to praise his book, *Causality and Chance in Modern Physics*, for its extraordinary erudition and sophistication. Bohm must be credited for repudiating the so-called Copenhagen school with razor-sharp logic and a remarkable grasp of the facts of physics.[8]

It appears that there are few physicists who can independently reason their way around the weaknesses in the theory of stark lawlessness in submicroscopic physics. Moreover, many physicists accept the theory reluctantly and with much difficulty, because they can sense that in the last analysis it simply cannot make sense.

That anyone would espouse absolute lawlessness as the ultimate ground of world order is evidence of how men otherwise quite learned can be prodigiously naive. No other person has addressed himself to the errors in this theory quite as effectively as Bohm. I refer the reader to his book for an exceedingly astute statement of a more rational philosophy of quantum mechanics. Bohm presents the arguments of the indeterminists lucidly and with complete fairness. But then, he demonstrates how their theory leads inevitably to the quicksand of complete relativism, is grounded in circular reasoning, and is based in nothing more substantial than a mere *ad hominem* assumption.

Probably the most respected of the strict indeterminists was the late J. von Neumann. Born in Budapest, he spent the greater part of his career in America, and is most often cited for his famous "theorem," which claimed to establish that there can be no entities beneath the quantum level of atomic action. Also, he insisted that there can be no laws operating in nature beneath the quantum level of physical reality, or that, even if entities and laws did exist at a deeper level they could never possibly be experimentally studied, observed, measured, or known. In fact, von Neumann and his followers concluded that Heisenberg's principle established once and for all an absolute limitation to our ability to know and measure the physical world on the microscopic level. Beyond current theory of quantum mechanics, nothing can ever possibly be known about causality or physical entities and measurements smaller than the quantum. Now, classical physics would reject any theory threatening the law of the continuity of motion. But strict indeterminism has gone so far as to renounce this law, along with causality.

The indeterminists have admitted that this viewpoint leads to ultimate irrationality. No less an intellectual than the distinguished Niels Bohr tells us that, because of Heisenberg's principle, he felt forced to conclude that there is an "irrational trait" in the process of the movement of a quantum of energy from one system to another. This "irrational trait" consists of the capricious, uncaused nature of the behavior of a quantum. As Bohr himself pointed out, this means that there can never possibly be a rational way to analyze or understand the details of this process of transfer of quanta. And what is more, strict indeterminism inevitably concludes that *an atom can have no properties whatever except those that are observed.* When Bohr was asked, With what does quantum mechanics really deal?, he answered that it deals with nothing except the statistical relationships found in the observable and measurable data of the macroscopic world. Beyond this, he believed that nothing can ever possibly be known for certain about physical reality.

Thus, in one sudden stroke, the indeterminists presumed to do away with causality and the objective reality of individual microobjects too small to be directly observed. David Bohm's book reduces this suicidal theory to precisely what it is, *id est*, an exercise in bad logic, very bad science, and very very bad metaphysics. As he shows very clearly, the whole theory rests entirely on that restrictive philosophy of science called "positivism," or "operationalism," which admonishes us never to use any methodology except that in current vogue, and never to think in terms of any entities except those that are already known to exist. What this amounts to, Bohm says, is a blockage of inquiry, or a needless termination of progress in scientific discovery and understanding. Bohm reminds us of the history of science, which proves that discoveries of new methods and new entities could never have been possible if all scientists had tied their hands with such a stingy-spirited philosophy of science as positivism. Ordinarily, this term connotes looking forward to better things in the future. Ironically, the way professional philosophers use the term—to refer to a highly unimaginative school of philosophy of science—it has hardly anything positive about it. For example, Ernst Mach, the Austrian physicist and philosopher, insisted throughout his life that atoms do not exist because we cannot see them. To Mach, the atom was merely a "mental artifice" or symbol, and the atomic theory was merely a "mathematical model."

Current quantum theory would have us believe that physical research has exhausted all *possibilities* for the discovery of entities below the quantum level, because any method of dealing with such entities, and with presumed laws governing their behavior, is from the standpoint of present-day methodology totally inconceivable. Bohm exposes this fatalistic dogma systematically by showing that the history of science, as well as the facts of physics, necessitate postulating the existence of *infinite* aspects in nature— whereby it is always a mistake to assume that we have exhausted the possibilities of improving and extending scientific methods and understanding. It is sheer anti-science to assume that we shall never be able to detect entities which we do not now know how to discover beneath the quantum level. It is unwise to assume that any present theory of atomic reality is exhaustive, all-comprehensive, and methodologically exclusive. Bohr's argument for ultimate "irrationality" in physics clearly betrays a bias toward the irrational; for unmistakably, it is grounded in nothing except a blind, experimentally unverifiable assumption about what we supposedly can never know. This is difficult to comprehend, considering the fact that it was Bohr himself who originated the "principle of the inexhaustibility of nature's aspects," which logically mitigates against his assumption that von Neumann's theorem establishes a final barrier against discoveries deeper than quantum data.

The Copenhagen school ignores another singularly important fact, namely, the reality of the causal efficacy of *consciousness* in the world. I can influence the atomic or electrochemical activities in my brain simply by exercising my *will*. Now how this is done, I should never presume to explain. But that I do it is an unarguable truth in need of no proof—since it is generally a waste of time to try to establish the obvious. According to standard quantum theory, all physical energy comes in quanta. Which means, before I can influence physical action on the macroscopic level, I first must influence it on the level of quanta. For example, I intend to raise my hand and lift off my hat. The intention is not physical; an intention has no physical or chemical attributes of any kind. But I then somehow initiate the physical action of moving my arm with my will, and this action starts physically at the level of quanta in my brain. Such a feat of course transcends the capacity of any physicist or neurophysiologist to explain. I leave it to God to explain this power of mind over matter—but it is obvious that I, a free spiritual agent, can do it, and that settles the matter once and for all, except perhaps for some ivory-tower philosophers who have lost their capacity to apprehend the obvious. Even the clever British philosopher Gilbert Ryle, who sarcastically belittles the notion that there is such a thing as a mind, obviously uses his mind (?) to influence his body and environment, and to make hopelessly confused arguments against the existence of his own mind.[9]

If I can exercise my will to influence the positions and transfers of the quanta in my brain and nervous system, then it stands to reason that God can be performing the same kind of feat. To make sense at all, the existence and behavior of atomic particles and quanta must ultimately be an expression of God's rational and loving will. One need not be an expert on psychosomatic medicine, or be a professional parapsychologist, to realize this. He need only have common-sense intuition of the fact that mind can influence matter. And in order for it to make sense, the existence and function of any matter must be informed with the reason and purpose of mind, with the design of ultimately meeting some need.

The existence of a quantum must be sustained by the creative action of God. To make sense, it must be amenable to influence or control not only by laws of physics, but also by the ultimate laws of psychology working in God's mind and in the minds of his creatures. That is, the behavior of a quantum can be influenced by God's will or by the will of his creatures. Some people may believe that this violates the principles of physics; but certainly, they cannot say this if they are familiar with the technical and logical problems of modern quantum theory. Nowhere is the necessity to understand this fact implied more clearly than in Hans Reichenbach's technical analysis of physical theory in *Philosophic Foundations of Quantum Mechanics*. Although he does not suggest the influence of mind in determining the behavior of quanta, he does demonstrate that *the behavior of quanta cannot in principle be accounted for entirely by any physical law*.[10] Thus, the only rational solution to the conflict between absolute determinism and absolute *in*determinism in physics is to suppose that the behavior of quanta is caused in part by physical law and in part by the will of creatures. But again, for us to view physical law as something rational, we must bear in mind that it is a manifestation of the creative will of God governing his world. Heretofore, physicists such as Bohr (strict *in*determinist) and Einstein (strict determinist) have speculated that thought is an emergent product of quantum physics.[11] Now, to make sense out of the physical world and our creative influence within it, it is clearly necessary to turn this around, and to presume that causation runs from mind to matter. Or in other words, causation runs from *purpose* to its creative products. The laws of physics are an imposition of God's will on the world. Man, in his freedom, can within the limits of his power impose his will on the world.

It is generally supposed in quantum physics that the law of conservation of momentum does not fully hold on the quantal level of reality. It is likewise considered that the principle of the conservation of energy may not fully hold. But these suppositions logically create a dilemma only for physicists who insist on being either absolute mechanists or absolute indeterminists. There is no need for this harrowing problem to persist; we need only remember the fact, grounded in commonsense observation, that minds influence matter. Certainly, this fact can help us to understand that neither a mechanistic nor totally indeterministic explanation can suffice to account for everything that happens in the physical world.

I find an implied corroboration of this point in a desperate measure resorted to by some physicists to preserve the principle of the conservation of energy in the quantal realm. Just how serious this situation is may be judged from the following excerpt from a recent physics text—even if the reader is unable to follow the technical symbolization:

The entity which possesses the quantum of energy (and the corresponding momentum) is the zero mass wavepacket which we know as the photon. Thus we may regard an electromagnetic field as a *photon gas*. To proceed a step further, the electromagnetic interaction between two charges is propagated by means of the exchange of *virtual* photons between the two charges. These photons are called virtual because their emission and reabsorption would constitute a violation of the conservation of energy were it not for the fact that they cannot be *detected*.

The uncertainty principle permits a discrepancy in the energy of an amount $\triangle E$ provided that this non-conservation lasts for a time interval no greater than something of the order of $h/\triangle E$. Thus, a charged particle can continually emit photons of energy $\triangle E$ and reabsorb them without violating the conservation of energy since the whole process is *undetectable*.[12]

As with some adulterers, undetectability is taken as permission to break the law. This type of reasoning satisfies certain theoretically interesting equations, but it can hardly be taken seriously as constituting real knowledge. Let us not blame this diligent author, however, for failing to say what cannot logically be said or thought. Rather, let us break away from the inherent and stultifying limitations of the profession of physics when it is opposed to rational metaphysics. Specifically, let us suppose that the principle of the conservation of energy, as well as the conservation of momentum, is indeed sometimes violated at the quantal level of reality, and that minds can be a factor in this violation—that is, that minds can directly influence matter.

To put it simply, I can influence the momenta and directions of the quanta in my brain by exercising my will to control my body. And on the larger scene, God's will can influence the momentum and direction of any quantum in the entire universe. This should not be difficult to affirm considering the fact that, without God, there is no possible way to account rationally for the existence of a quantum in the first place. This is not to suggest that God's control of a quantum is ever capricious. Indeed just the opposite. It is only by an appeal to God's lawful and rational influence in the world that we can escape ultimate irrationality in physics. If it should prove that there is a yet deeper level of knowable physical reality below the quantal level, that discovery would be nothing to the present point, which is that at any level of reality science must allow room for a rational explanation of what occurs.

"Sheer obscurantism," I may expect to hear. "You find in the half developed state of quantum mechanics an excuse to populate the world with every kind of scientifically meaningless entity, e.g., a 'soul.' Science will one day supersede such curious superstitions."

We need not be spiritually browbeaten, however, by the arbitrariness of scientists who do not hold themselves consistently accountable to their own logical ground rules. Many such scientists reject the notion that it is God who generates, degenerates, and controls the behavior of particles—on the grounds that we can never *detect* His doing it. Yet how curious that it does not bother these same scientists to suppose that particles are "transitory," i.e., created out of nothing and then reduced back to nothing. According to widely accepted quantum field theory, "Transitory violations of energy conservation permit particles to be formed out of nothing and vanish again."[13]

In point of plain fact, no scientist has ever *observed* the creation of something out of nothing or the reduction of something into nothing. How can a logical man accept this notion with no difficulty—the creation of energy out of nothing, by nothing, and for nothing—yet have difficulty accepting the creation of energy by a Creator for a logical reason?

Unfortunately, scientists have persuaded even much of the public that only science can discover or understand genuine knowledge. Many, indeed, have fallen for Bertrand Russell's agnostic

214

dictum that "Whatever knowledge is attainable, must be attained by scientific methods; and what science cannot discover, mankind cannot know."[14] But the reader will by now, I trust, see that not all knowledge is scientific knowledge in the sense of depending on measurement and experiment with various kinds of laboratory hardware. The arrogance of too many scientists, including even the most famous, often blinds them to their own unconscious and irrational presuppositions, some of which we have been considering throughout this book. They refuse to see, even when their errors lead them into blind alleys for fifty years.

It is time that true philosophy reopen the clogged wells of knowledge upon which our very being depends. Is it obscurantism to show that the universe is intelligible in a way that science, by itself, has failed to show? What science cannot learn, philosophy may and must. Otherwise, we live as victims of needless and disastrous self-limitation, keeping our understanding from going as far as it can go in the search for intelligibility in the world.

Philosophers can never accomplish an intelligible accounting for the existence and behavior of living organisms as long as they regard biology as only a mere handmaiden to positivistic physics. Any attempt to explain life by raw physics without turning to a rational metaphysics inevitably will flounder in a hopeless circle that encloses one theoretical contradiction after the other. Probably the most well-known example of an attempt to break out of this circle is the work of Walter Elsasser, a theoretical physicist, who wrote *The Physical Foundation of Biology,* a book which made him famous in academic circles.[15]

In Chapter 3 of this book, Elsasser builds up the reader's hope for a way out of the old mechanistic biology. He argues that the storage of information in the germ cells and brain, and the phenomena of memory, cannot possibly be accounted for by a totally deterministic physics. This argument certainly is a tremendous contribution to a breakaway from the fatalism of the mechanistic interpretation of man's nature. What is more, in Chapter 4, he argues that mere statistical laws of quantum mechanics also cannot account for the storage of information and the general behavior of an organism that is alive. Elsasser insists that "biotonic laws" work in the organism to distinguish its behavior from that of a merely inanimate physical system. Also, he insists that these laws are not incompatible with the laws of physics, but simply supplement them, work in conjunction with them, and coexist with them in a way that is never found in any inanimate system. Then, he argues that "the ultimate explanation of the coexistence of biotonic with physical laws . . . cannot under any circumstances be based on the sole fact that quantum mechanics as opposed to classical mechanics introduces certain statistical features into the description of events at the microscopic, atomic level" of a living system (p. 147). Thus also, he insists that there is no possible way to deduce the organization and behavior of a living organism from a totally *inde*terministic physics.

Logically, this should have led Elsasser to see clearly that the behavior of a person, or creature, cannot be adequately accounted for by either extreme in modern physical theory; that is, life can be explained neither by the laws of strict determinism nor by the "statistical laws" of strict *in*determinism. In fact, Elsasser did obviously see the futility of trying to account for the existence and behavior of life by mere laws of traditional physics. Yet for all his noble effort, he himself failed to break out of the vicious circle of traditional scientism in the discipline of biology. Unfortunately, he accomplished little toward the construction of a rational understanding of life—for he rejected vitalism out of hand, which maintains that the organization and behavior of a living organism ultimately can be guided and explained only by the reason and purpose of a creative *spiritual agent*. Elsasser did describe the biotonic laws as "withdrawn from direct observation" (p. 156). And plainly, he stated: "The structure and behavior of organisms cannot be derived deductively from a few simple axioms or principles, as is the ideal of physics" (p. 218). But while this is of course true, it can lead us nowhere until we turn from raw physics to a metaphysics of reason and purpose manifest through the creative action of *God* in the world, and through the creative actions of his creatures.

Elsasser shared the bias of most of his contemporaries in biology and physics against vitalism, which is the philosophy that the ultimate essence of life is spirit. Consequently he was unable, despite his great reconditeness and effort, to accomplish a breakthrough in the modern discipline of biology. This breakthrough is long overdue, and it can consist only of the *care* of scientists and philosophers to find the ultimate explanation for life in *Care*.

Hume and Contemporary Physicists

Let me reflect briefly on another influential protagonist of the indeterminist school—Max Born, whose thoughts in the Waynflete Lectures are published in a book entitled *Natural Philosophy of Cause and Chance*. I choose this work because it is an exemplary display of those errors in reasoning common to physicists who subscribe to the lawlessness view. Born asks, "Can our desire of understanding, our wish to explain things, be satisfied by a theory which is frankly and shamelessly statistical and indeterministic? Can we be content with accepting *chance*, not cause, as the *supreme law* of the physical world?"[16] Born then answers his own question that, yes, causality does exist, but is itself merely a phenomenon of chance. "Causality in my definition is the postulate that one physical situation depends on the other, and causal research means the discovery of such dependence" (pp. 101–102). We have to bear in mind, however, that by "dependence" Born obviously means nothing more than that certain events, which chance to affect each other in space-time, are caught up in purely accidental relations that are amenable to predictability in terms of statistical laws of probability. In his roundabout way, Born is proclaiming that all "laws" in the physical world are in the last analysis really not laws at all in the traditional sense of the word; that is, laws do not *govern* or *guide* the physical activities of the world. Rather, laws are merely descriptive norms which enable us to predict with high probability the patterns of events occurring by chance in an essentially lawless world.

Speaking of the unknowability of the objective world, Born says: "I think that the concept of reality is too much connected with emotions to allow a generally acceptable definition." He goes on to say that "we are aware of objects with invariant properties," but that these invariants are nothing except that "which our minds construct in a perfectly unconscious way." After Born addresses himself to the matter in detail, it becomes obvious that the indeterminist reduces objective reality to nothing more than that which exists in the perception of the observing physicist.[17] For example, "particles are real" only insofar as they "represent invariants of observation." Contrasting the particle theory of matter with the wave theory, he declares that whether the particles or waves are something "real" or merely a "fiction to describe and predict phenomena in a convenient way is a matter of taste" (pp. 103–105).

From the standpoint of the physicists' *present* inability to *know* which theory is true (due to the absence of any form of conclusive evidence at hand), one certainly ought to grant that each theorist is entitled to his personal preference or "taste." Says Born: "I personally like to regard a probability wave, even in 3N-dimensional space, as a real thing, certainly as more than a tool for mathematical calculations" (pp. 105–106). But is this purely *ad hominem* way of philosophizing not essentially a waste of the reader's time, considering his simultaneous dogma that neither the particle nor wave theory can be anything more than merely the subject's tool for mathematical calculating? For Born insists that physical reality can be nothing more than the patterns of perception that occur frequently in physicists' minds. For him, "*reality* is understood to mean" nothing but "the sum of observational invariants," and he "cannot see any other reasonable interpretation of this word in physics" (italics mine, p. 125).

Born is deferential to Einstein, in allowing that a greater physicist than himself has rejected his theory of ultimate lawlessness in the world. Albeit, he feels that Einstein failed to look at indeterminism with an open mind, and that he was impractical in his insistence on complementarity between the objective world of physics and the enlightened physicist's observations of it. Says he: "Einstein's principle of the existence of an objective real world is . . . rather academic" (p. 123).

But then lo and behold, on the following page he tells us of his faith that "the predictions of statistical calculations are more than an exercise of the brain," and that "they can be trusted in the *real* world" (italics mine, p. 124). Now if nothing can be known about the real world, or if all assumptions about it are merely "academic," then how can anyone trust that his theories will enable him to ever truly predict what will happen in it?

One of Born's objections to Einstein's absolute determinism was its theoretical denial of freedom of the will to choose. Einstein did reject freedom as a myth, and made a mockery of it with sarcasm.[18] But as could be expected, in going from one extreme to the opposite (from Einstein's absolute determinism to Heisenberg's absolute *in*determinism), Born ends up trapping himself in an equally vicious circle. Insisting on the individual's freedom of choice and responsibility for his actions, he walks into that trap ineluctably awaiting any theoretician who would presume to live in a meaningful world based on nothing but sheer lawlessness. Now that modern physics has discovered this fundamental truth, he tells us —that ultimate reality is lawless—there can be no turning back. "Though I am very much aware of the shortcomings of quantum mechanics, I think that its indeterministic foundations will be permanent. . . . There remains now only to show how the ordinary, apparently deterministic laws of physics can be obtained from these foundations" (pp. 126, 109).[19]

Born's intuition is good in sensing the logical contradiction between absolute determinism and freedom. But his disclaimer regarding the "shortcomings" of indeterminism is not at all convincing, for he seems to show no awareness whatever of either the physical or metaphysical trappings of this dogma. What is more, no one to this day has shown how the *laws* of physics could ever possibly "be obtained from these foundations." Scientifically and logically, the Copenhagen school has provided no more satisfaction than merely to postulate its dogma that ultimate reality is lawless. It should be no surprise that the assumption is supported by no real evidence, considering the fact that it is logically impossible and involves a flagrant contradiction in terms. There is no imaginable reason, either factual or logical, to explain how, or why, determinate laws could ever be obtained from absolute indeterminism or lawlessness. The dogma that law is "somehow" obtained from absolute lawlessness, and is "somehow" explained by a *causeless* abstraction called "chance"—this is a barefaced impudence to logic. The very existence of a binding logic is dependent upon an intrinsic and absolute order in a lawful scheme of things that transcends all chance.

Absolute indeterminism would lead logically to metaphysical, scientific, and moral relativism—which we need in the intellectual and moral community today about as much as we need a breakout in leprosy. It is long past time to stop playing the relativist game, where philosophers try to pass off antirational and nihilistic concepts as truths that people need to understand. What possible thing of value can ever be gained by assuming that ultimate reality is irrational and lawless? To say that ultimate reality is lawless or irrational is to say that it has no rationale. But if I may repeat a point thematic throughout this book, *no rationale can be given for the assumption that the world ultimately has no rationale*. The fact that we cannot at this time simultaneously predict with absolute certainty the velocity and position of an electron is no reason whatever to assume that there is no reason or purpose informing its existence and motion. Furthermore, even if we *never* find a physical methodology that enables us to do it, that is still no reason to conclude that there is no reason informing the existence and behavior of atomic particles. To hold to this dogma seriously is to commit intellectual harakiri. While it passes off as a scientific theorem, it is really nothing more than a negative metaphysical assumption grounded in faith. In fact, the most often cited reason for this dogma is simply that its protagonists know nothing else to conclude. Sometimes physicists—even the greatest ones—are endowed with a poor mind for metaphysics and can give no positive or rational reasons whatever for the conclusions they reach about the nature of reality.

Einstein's and Planck's absolute determinism fails because it would make a world with free moral agents impossible. But absolute *in*determinism fails for precisely the same reason. It is unimaginable that a rational person, characterized by a sense of permanent importance in his existence and acts, could ever come into being in a world constituted intrinsically of chaos or lawlessness. In such a world, it is impossible that a person could ever find the kind of intelligibility that he needs to fulfill his intellectual and moral quest. The overall position of the atheist is inherently and hopelessly negative. No case can be made for atheism, simply because it can never be meaningfully or rationally stated.

Freedom cannot be derived from lawlessness. Neither can a valid ideal. Nor a meaningful or responsible thought. Nor love, nor hope.

But we need not aggressively try to malign the atheist for all his subjective negatives. That would in the first place be incompassionate, and in the second place it would accomplish probably no communication with the atheist himself if he is a devoted professional. But as I asserted already, the professional atheist inevitably traps himself logically by appealing to that which he denies. It is essential that someone point this out for purposes of rational understanding—to try to prevent further victims. Notice, for example, that in J. Bronowski's reduction of evolution strictly to chance he ends up appealing to that "*stability* which *lay hidden* in the primitive building blocks of cosmic hydrogen."[20] Ignoring the issue of how these atoms could have gotten there in the first place, he

Hume and Contemporary Physicists

proposes chance exclusively as the explanation for order and life. But then, he states plainly at the end of his argument that time could never conceivably have brought order out of disorder unless there were a cosmic system "full of *preferred* configurations and hidden stabilities, even at the most basic and inanimate level of atomic structure" (p. 244, italics mine).

In these cryptic appeals to ultimate order, Bronowski can take advantage of God's reason and love, but without having to assume any accountability to it or feel in any way bound by it. What can he mean by "preferred configurations" in the atomic activities of the world? If he does not mean to be taken teleologically, then it is pointless and contradictory for him to use such language. But if he does wish us to take him seriously, then it is obvious that he is unconsciously appealing to ultimate purpose in a Cosmic Scheme of Things, even though he consciously denies it. For without purpose, the term "preferred" plainly is meaningless.

10

Einstein, Simultaneity, and Scientific Orthodoxy*

You blind guides! You strain after a gnat
and swallow a camel.

Matthew 23:24

1. A Hidden Premise

In Chapter 3, I alluded to "zany" theories of time that deny the reality of an omnipresent moment in the universe. By this, I meant specifically the late Albert Einstein's Theory of Relativity. Arguments pro and con about the validity of this theory have been going on sporadically ever since its first publication in 1905. Of course, it has been a dominant theory in physics for over fifty years. The German mathematician Hermann Weyl stated in 1922 that "*We are to discard our belief in the objective meaning of simultaneity; it was the great achievement of Einstein in the field of the theory of knowledge that he banished this dogma from our minds,* and this is what leads us to rank his name with that of Copernicus."[1] In 1949, Henry Margenau, American physicist, stated that relativity theory was so well confirmed by experience that its denial was all but unthinkable.[2] Herein, I shall comment at length on why such optimism is not at all justified.

*With minor changes this essay is also published in a separate paperback edition under the title *The Einstein Myth*, by Institute for Space-Time Studies, Box 7123, University Station, Provo, Utah 84602.

Einstein, Simultaneity, and Scientific Orthodoxy

Needless to say, no one could discredit the validity of Einstein's early contributions to quantum theory and the photoelectric effect. Neither could anyone doubt his powerful and persistent creative imagination, or his wide mathematical ability. Today, Einstein is perhaps best known for his denial of absolute simultaneity for any events throughout the universe. This denial is a feature of his Special Theory of Relativity, which is his early theory, restricted to physical situations involving no accelerations or gravity. He later developed a more expansive theory which he labeled the General Theory of Relativity. As to the Special Theory, it is certainly time to expose the *myth* that there is no universal simultaneity or nowness in the world. Herein, I shall show how much one may justifiably find fault with relativity, as indeed many before me have done. It is not easy for most people to identify the source of the trouble, and it is yet harder to construct an alternate theory which does the same needful work as Einstein's postulates. In what follows, I ask the reader to remember that I am attacking a *theory*. That is, *I am not attacking the experiments which are supposed to back up relativity*. I shall show that the *same* experiments which have been presumed to back up Einstein actually are more appropriately understood as backing up another, little known theory, primarily associated with the name of the late Herbert E. Ives, an accomplished American physicist.

In 1905, Einstein in effect asked for, and in time received, the general acceptance of a paradox or contradiction. To put it in plain language: if you are in a car on the highway and are passing another car going in the same direction, you will pass it more slowly than you would pass it if it were coming toward you from the opposite direction. But a light ray will in fact (according to the relativists) pass you at the same rate of speed no matter whether it is moving in the same direction as yourself or in the opposite direction. And (they say) this would hold true even if you were traveling almost as fast as light itself! The German philosopher Aloys Wenzl stated the problem in this manner:

If light spreads out—independently of the motion of its source—equally in all directions, if it is a reality—whether wave or corpuscle is at this point of no concern—which moves, then it cannot proceed with objectively equal velocity with reference to [a stationary] observer A, on the one hand, and with reference to an independently moving observer B.[3]

Fortunately, the contradiction can be stated in simple, concrete language. If you, the reader, are traveling at 50 miles per hour in your car, and if I start chasing you at 10 miles per hour, then I reduce your speed with respect to me to 40 miles per hour. If I increase my speed to 50 miles per hour, then from that point onward your car has no speed at all with respect to me, and you do not get any farther away from me. If I increase my speed to 55 miles per hour, then after a while I can catch up with you, pass you, and if you do not alter your speed, then you will get farther and farther behind me. But now, this would not be the case at all if I were chasing a photon (a particle of light) and were continuously increasing my speed while the speed of light remained constant at 186,283 miles per second. Even if I increased my speed to 186,282 miles per second, I nevertheless could never get even one fraction of distance closer to the light particle. In short, no matter how fast one chases a particle of light—be it 20 miles per hour or 186,282 miles per second—*the distance between oneself and the light continues to increase* at precisely the same rate as before: 186,283 miles per second. Thus beyond the suggestion of a doubt, according to the theory of relativity, the behavior of light flagrantly contradicts the simplest arithmetic principles logically essential to explaining the distance relations of objects in space according to their respective positions and velocities.

Einstein's special theory is based, as he himself said, on a "free-will . . . definition of simultaneity" which he acknowledged to be a purely arbitrary, or unobservable and unverifiable, stipulation.[4] With all due respect to Einstein, he committed one of the most deplorable, galling contradictions of all time. To accept such a contradiction, one simply has to believe that nature is perversely illogical. The contradiction in Einstein's special theory has been noticed often enough. Harald Nordenson, Swedish industrialist and philosopher of science, makes clear in his valuable book *Relativity, Time, and Reality* that Einstein's contradiction is at bottom that of "the indiscriminate use of the word 'time' in two different meanings which makes his theory untenable from a logical point of view."[5] The first 67 pages of Nordenson's book contain an excellent exposition of this contradiction and its ramifications.[6]

Wenzl (who was quoted above) acknowledged the contradiction but, like many others, resigned himself to it when he declared that we simply have to stomach it because "objective matters of fact seem . . . to provide the foundation for [it]."[7] But fortunately, objective matters of fact prove just the opposite, and those few individuals who have doggedly doubted relativity, and all along refused to accept a contradiction as the truth, can now be proud of never having surrendered their better judgment.

No one has exposed the arbitrariness, the circularity, the sleight of hand in Einstein's relativistic concept of simultaneity more lucidly, or logically with more finesse, than the American philosopher Arthur O. Lovejoy, in his article "The Dialectical Argument against Absolute Simultaneity."[8] Calendar-wise, this 1930 article appears to be out of date. But its relevance could not be more contemporary, for it unassailably establishes the reality of absolute simultaneity once and for all. In his usual systematic way, Lovejoy builds up to the delivery of a lethal blow against relativity. The object of his main attack is Einstein's thought-experiment with lightning flashes on the railway embankment, together with his arbitrary definition of simultaneity, from the early part of his book *Relativity*. Here are Lovejoy's own words:

A proposition asserting the simultaneity of two events is, obviously, an assertion concerning the magnitude of the time-interval between them—namely, that the interval is equal to zero. . . .

It was apparently, as we have seen, in order to avoid circularity in his definition that Einstein chose the alternative of making it a "free" or arbitrary definition. Let us now ask whether he has in fact completely succeeded in avoiding circularity. Does he not presuppose certain meanings of both "simultaneity" and "time of an event," "in order to arrive at" his own definitions of those terms; and—what is more curious—are not these tacitly presupposed meanings at variance with those in the formulation of which he employs them? These questions, I think, must be answered in the affirmative. For though he *makes* the time of transit of the light-rays over the paths A-M and B-M *equal* by "stipulation," i.e., by pure definition, the stipulation relates only to the equality and not to the notion of "time of transit" itself. That we already know what is meant by saying that a duration elapses during the transit of light over one or the other path, he seems quietly to assume; but in doing so, he also assumes that we are already familiar with concepts which would ordinarily be expressed by the distinction between "simultaneity" and "non-simultaneity." To put the matter in another way: in "stipulating" that the times of transit of light from A to M and from B to M shall by definition be equal, Einstein is applying the quantitative predicate of equality to something which, in order to be capable of having that predicate, must be assumed to possess number or magnitude, and this something is, explicitly, "time." He is, therefore, "begging" the idea of time-interval —before defining simultaneity. But the idea of time-interval—and still more obviously, that of motion during a time-interval—contains that of succession, in which is implicit the distinction between successiveness and non-successiveness, i.e., simultaneity, of events. And this distinction is not that between simultaneity and successiveness at a place; if it were, it would be inapplicable to the concept of motion, i.e., of successive occupancy of a series of increasingly distant places. It appears impossible for Einstein to formulate his definition of simultaneity-at-a-distance without first accepting both the meaningfulness and the truth of the law of the finite velocity of light, which itself presupposes that the meaning of simultaneity and non-simultaneity-at-a-distance is already known. His so-called "definition" of time is in terms of relative motion, which, plainly, already contains the idea of time and of the two characteristic types of temporal relation.

It seems evident, finally, that Einstein himself does not adhere to the relativistic conclusion which he has deduced in this questionable way from his definition, and that he can not do so without vitiating the rest of his argument. For, after he has ascribed to each moving system a "time" of its own, in which events simultaneous on any other such systems are of differing date, he continues to speak of periods of time during which the two systems are in motion with respect to each other, and during which, also, some determinable number of events is occurring on each. *While* such and such things are happening on S [spatial reference frame or spaceship], we are told, such and such other things are happening on S' [relatively moving frame or spaceship]. Now this sort of proposition can have no meaning if there is no *common* duration with a common measure, to which the motion of both systems with respect to one another, and the two series of events, are referred. You can not say that while S moves to the right S' moves to the left, if there are in reality simply two distinct "whiles," one definable solely with reference to S and the other solely with reference to S', for in that case, you will have isolated the two systems so completely from one another that the relation called "motion" can no longer be conceived to subsist between them. There must, in short, be a common "while" between any two systems of which relative motion is asserted. But if there is a community of "whiles" there must also be a community of "whens," unless motion, change, and time-lapse are assumed to be discontinuous. All changes in relative position or otherwise, asserted with respect to S, must be in one-to-one correspondence with *some* events in S'; otherwise there would be intervals during which there was motion and time-lapse for one system, but not for the other—which would be a contradiction, since the motion is reciprocal and therefore never predicable of the one at any instant when it is not predicable of the other. . . . Distance, or spatial separation along a common axis, is a symmetrical relation; and a change in this relation between the two cannot occur in the case of one of them unless it at the same time occurs in the case of the other. One body cannot start to become nearer to the other unless the other at the same instant starts to become nearer to it; if the latter is denied, it is *thereby* denied that any relative motion between them has begun. . . .

The assumption of this common time is not less necessary even if (in accordance with another portion of the Special Theory) the "time" on S' is said to be "slower" or more "dilated," than that on S. This can only mean that, between two of the instants identical for both, fewer physical changes of a given kind—e.g., complete revolutions of the hands of a clock—occur on the one system than on the other. The very expression of the relativity of clock-times is impossible without the presupposition of an inclusive duration of which the measure is the same for both reference-bodies and is therefore independent of their relative motion. To say literally and exclusively that a given "reference-body has its own particular time" is simply to deny that it is in motion at all with respect to any actual external system.

This argument of Einstein's, then, seems to be one more example of a type of phenomenon familiar enough to the student of the history of philosophy; it is another case in which the very premise which is unheeded and even denied may, by the attentive ear, be heard the while softly murmuring, "When me they fly, I am the wings."

These passages are Lovejoy's conclusions briefly stated, without the detailed argument that more forcefully substantiates them.[9] Lovejoy used no mathematics in his writing. The errors he speaks to are logical errors and are already present before any mathematical operations become possible. No experiments using scientific laboratory hardware are needed to show the fallacies in Einstein's work. Lovejoy's is a highly rigorous and sophisticated solution to the problem of the nature of time. He was far ahead of his generation and unfortunately has received no credit for his genius in understanding the concept of nowness. He showed such clarity that his professional adversaries, if they knew of his argument, could not retort. In any case they did not.

One of Einstein's flagrant contradictions is that he insists that there can be synchronically running clocks within the *same* frame of spatial reference, that is, within a frame in which the clocks have a fixed spatial relationship to one another; yet, he also categorically denies that there can ever be any definite or absolute simultaneity in *any* spatial frame of reference at all. That is, he denies that the same clocks can *ever* be regarded as running synchronically. Says he:

We see thus that we cannot attribute *any* absolute meaning to the concept of simultaneity. Rather, two events which, considered from one system of reference, are simultaneous, can, considered from a system moving in relation to the former, not be considered as simultaneous.[10]

Harald Nordenson has focused this contradiction into another formidable criticism of relativity. With an uncommonly masterful grasp of the principles of physics, mathematics, and logic, Nordenson demonstrates rigorously that if the fundamentals in Einstein's theory were correct, then it would be impossible that there could ever be any synchronically running clocks, not only when they are billions of light-years' distance from each other, but even when they are located "adjacent" to each other in space. Had Einstein been more logical in applying his postulates—and less biased in his eagerness to defend their validity—he easily could have seen that, according to those postulates, there could never be any true simultaneity between clocks even a foot apart from one another. However close to each other they might be, no two clocks would be telling the *same* time, since the very notion of objective sameness of time (simultaneity or nowness) is excluded by Einstein's definition of it. Nordenson's demonstration of this fact is unerringly conclusive.[11] Nordenson is a member of the Swedish Academy of Science, which distributes Nobel Prizes in physics.

2. Return to Parmenides

In 1908, the Russian mathematician Hermann Minkowski declared, "Henceforth space by itself, and time by itself, are doomed to fade away into mere shadows, and only a kind of union of the two will preserve an independent reality."[12] Minkowski declared that time had been "deposed from its high seat" by Einstein. "One may expect," he asserted, "to find a corresponding violation of the concept of space appraised as another act of audacity on the part of higher mathematics. Nevertheless, this further step is indispensable for . . . true understanding."[13]

Einstein, Simultaneity, and Scientific Orthodoxy

It was Minkowski's fortune, or misfortune, to have found mathematical equations, or a "geometry," to delineate the disastrous logical consequences of Einstein's special theory for the status of space and time (although, of course, relativists do not think them disastrous at all). With the aid of Minkowski's reasonings, I shall show that if Einstein's absolute relativization of time were true, then the universe would be static, devoid of happenings, and consequently, there could be no objective meaning whatever to anyone's notion of time.

Minkowski made explicit the implication of relativity that space and time can no longer be said to have any meaning independently of each other. In order to describe physical events, a person (he said) is free to choose from any of an infinite number of uniformly and linearly moving spatial frames of reference. Each reference frame within this scope of choices goes at a different speed, and thus, has its own proper time and proper measuring system, as special relativity demands. This infinite manifold is the "four-dimensional space-time continuum," to use Einstein's term (or "metric space" or simply "space-time"). The use of any one of these frames of reference is as valid as the use of any other, for physical description. But Minkowski did find one thing to rely upon as "absolute," viz., that the "interval" between two specific events would always be the same, and this "interval" would be the square root of the difference between (a) the square of the distance that light would travel during the time interval apparently separating the events and (b) the square of the spatial interval apparently separating the events. That is, this difference would be constant for any pair of events and for any choice of spatial reference frames. According to Minkowski, this constant "interval" is the *only* reality that can be used to realistically describe spatial and temporal situations; and consequently, what we are accustomed to thinking of as "space" and "time" as independent realities are nothing but "mere shadows."

On this basis Minkowski erected his so-called "light cones" or "null cones" in space-time, whereby he classified all events with regard to their relation to any one given event—say, in relation to you (here and now). Minkowski divided "space-time" into a definite past, a definite future, and a wide ambiguous zone "in between" the past and the future.[14] In this in-between zone are found those events that are too distant in space to have an influence on you, or to be influenced by you (here and now)—even by light signal,

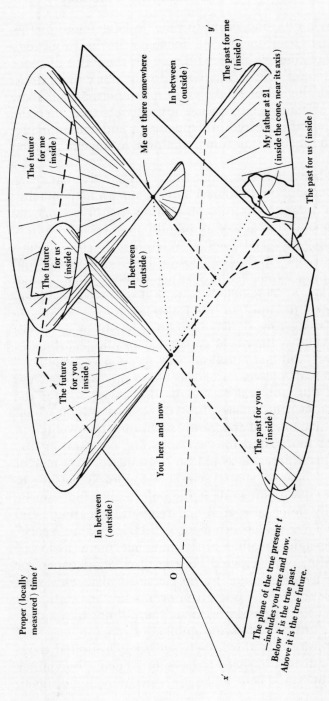

Above are two "null cones," shown as cut off. Each point in this diagram represents an event in space-time. In its extensions, the diagram has places for all possible events to be plotted according to measured time t' and measured spatial co-ordinates x' and y'. The z' co-ordinate is left out, since there is no way to show four dimensions in a single view. Each cone is drawn in relation to some given event which is at the apex of the cone. That is, the apex is located at the spatial and temporal co-ordinates of the given event. The conical surface includes all (and only) those points at a given slope from the apex. Any point on the conical surface is spatially as far from the apex as light would travel during the separation of the point in time from the apex. "The plane of the true present" was not mentioned by Minkowski but will be constructively treated of later.

which is the fastest causal influence presumed to be possible (as Henri Poincaré, *not* Einstein, was the first to suggest).[15] All events in this in-between zone can be correctly regarded as *either* simultaneous or *not* simultaneous with you (here and now), since you can always choose, or not choose, to describe the situation from the point of view of a spatial reference frame which makes the events "simultaneous" by Einstein's definition. But as Lovejoy has clearly demonstrated, this scheme can have nothing at all to do with true simultaneity. For Minkowski's notion of simultaneity is the same as Einstein's; that is, it is patently illogical and hence equally as chaffing. The contradiction is unmistakable: two events can *at once* be both simultaneous and not simultaneous. Thus, Einstein and Minkowski serve us the same gall. We are asked to believe that there is now existing an infinity of separate time systems that do not exist *now*.

By 1913, Einstein embraced Minkowski's mathematical formulations. But even such dubious time-distinctions as are claimed by Minkowski's null cones cannot logically be maintained on the basis of relativity theory itself. American philosophers Robert Weingard and Hilary Putnam have successfully argued that if the concept of time in Einstein's relativity is true, then there can be no objectively real time distinctions whatever. The whole of reality (which the man in the street divides into past, present, and future) must actually be tenseless, and the man in the street simply deals in illusions. That is to say, any event that is actually *past* for one observer is actually *present* for another and actually *future* for yet another. In other words, there simply can be no universal simultaneity in the cosmos; and, as Weingard and Putnam have shown logically, if we accept Einstein's relativity then we must also accept the assumption that all time distinctions are merely subjective illusions in the eyes of this or that biased observer. That is, every event whatsoever ("past" or "future") must logically collapse into the Ever-Ever Land of the Universal Present. Minkowski's null cones destroy the very time distinctions which they purport to make. They are self-destructive entities, which is something that Weingard and Putnam unfortunately failed to make explicit.[16]

Weingard's and Putnam's proof can be quickly outlined. Consider yourself (here and now) as being in my "in-between" temporal zone and vice versa. That is, you (here and now) are not decisively in either my future or past. Also, I (out there somewhere)

231

am not decisively in yours. Consider now a third space-time event, say, that of my father on his becoming twenty-one years of age. My father's twenty-first birthday is an event which is so placed in space-time that it is decisively in my past but (at your great distance) not decisively within yours, being rather in your in-between temporal zone instead. But if my father, at twenty-one, is not in your past, then neither is he in my past, since you, as a viewer of my father, are not in my past. *All* temporal relations are transitive, which they must be in any linear view of time, or else the very idea of time would lose all meaning. Because time is linear or transitive, it follows that if 2:30 is later than 2:20, and if 2:20 is later than 2:10, then 2:30 is also later than 2:10. In the present case, if I (out there somewhere) am not later than you (here and now), and you (here and now) are not later than my father at age twenty-one, then I am not now later than my father at age twenty-one. From this Minkowskian view, all these events are in an indefinite present. A full application of this procedure results in the exclusion of absolutely every event from one's past or future. This result can be evaded in only two ways: (1) either we must drop the idea of temporal relations as being transitive (i.e., be prepared to say that 2:10 is later than 2:30), or else (2) we must drop Einstein's and Minkowski's relativization of space and time. Relativistic physicists generally maintain that some temporal relations are transitive while some are not. Whether or not temporal relations are transitive depends on whether null cones are penetrated by a line connecting two space-time events. But relativists have failed to provide a rational criterion for making absolute distinctions between transitive and intransitive temporal relations. Their criterion in making such distinctions is purely subjective or arbitrary, since they themselves deny that there is such a thing as absolute simultaneity that can be known. The relativist's denial that some temporal relations are transitive is dictated by nothing except his desperate need to find some way to preserve the "integrity" of his theory after his out-and-out denial of absolute simultaneity logically destroys the very idea of the passage of time. Without transitivity of time, no consistent meaning whatever could be given to anything in physics except statics and static electricity. The truth is, Minkowski has inadvertently enabled us to see the blind, perverse folly of relativity more clearly than ever. As E. Cunningham observed long ago: "If all motional phenomena are looked at from this point of view [of

Minkowski] they become timeless phenomena in four-dimensional space. The whole history of a physical system is laid out as a change-less whole."[17]

So far, I have deferred to common usage in attributing the null cones to Minkowski. Actually, it was the French mathematician Henri Poincaré who discovered the basic mathematical insight essential to the concept of the null cones and who published it in 1906, over a year before Minkowski's basic article appeared. In two of his footnotes, Minkowski did refer to the whole of Poincaré's rambling forty-seven page article, but not in a sufficiently particular way to warn the reader of Poincaré's priority.[18] H. A. Lorentz attempted to remedy the resulting lapse of proper credit in 1921.[19]

How strange it is, that both Weingard and Putnam accept the theory of relativity after showing that it would reduce time to nothing more than an empty fantasy in our heads, totally devoid of any sensible meaning. Both seem unbothered by their own conclusions. And indeed how odd that they continue to deal in time distinctions after they themselves insist that the distinctions they make are meaningless because the universe is static.

History is unfortunately a study in how professional philosophers lose contact with reality and make a mockery of simple common-sense knowledge. With regard to time's arrow, the Greeks and ancient Indians (Asiatic) tried to turn it into cycles of pointless and depressive repetitions. Kant tried to make it only a subjective category—nothing more real than merely a mode in which we think. Then came Einstein, whose tamperings with the obvious would do away with time altogether, and indeed with any happenings at all as such. To push Einstein's reasoning to the limit, the universe would be static, with nothing at all *going on*, whatever the illusory appearances. The adoption of this position would be a return to the impossible world-view of the early Greek philosopher Parmenides.

As Einstein and his disciples have it, there are *now* things going on in other space-time frames of reference, say in galaxies moving in relation to us, that are in our past or future. But this is an obvious *reductio ad absurdum*, for anything that is going on at all (no matter where) is going on now, and consequently, is clearly not in the past or future but is in the *now*. To exist at all, a thing has to exist now, no matter where. The reality of the universal present cannot be undermined simply by switching frames of reference as to movement in space. Unless we can *simultaneously* refer to different

233

reference frames in space, it is unthinkable that we could ever put things together in such a way as to have an intelligible world-view.

Innumerable different things may be going on in different places. This makes it possible for us to have a notion of *where* things are happening. But as a matter of plain and indisputable fact, we can have no intelligible notion of *when* different things are going on except in the *now*. My learned relativist colleagues talk glibly of things now going on in the past and in the future. The contradiction is outrageous. Clearly, a past event cannot still be going on, for in that case it is in no meaningful sense a past event. Nor can a future event be going on already, for in that case it is a present event, and no meaningful distinction is allowed between the present and the future. Relativity theory *equates* the meaning of past, present, and future. At the same time, it presumes to meaningfully distinguish between them. Logically, I cannot think of a more unbearable result.

The unbearability of this result becomes even clearer when one considers that the law of contradiction cannot be stated generally without reference to time. That is, the law of contradiction states that a thing cannot be both A and not-A *at the same time*. For example, a man cannot be both learned and unlearned in the same respect at the same time. But while a young man may be unlearned, the same man may be learned after he has grown older. And consequently, the same entity can have contradictory attributes, but only at different times. Or more precisely, the law of contradiction pertains to everything which comes into being, or which changes, or which goes out of existence. Only such timeless entities as universals or essences can escape this net and thus allow of a nontemporal law of contradiction as to themselves. Also escaping this net are past events in their eternally continuing pastness, and possibilities insofar as they remain merely possibilities. The law of contradiction, stated with reference to time, is a *sine qua non* not only of logic, but also of the very possibility of meaningful discourse, whether that discourse be about time, relativity, or almost anything else. Thus, it is most awkward for Einstein's theory that it is incompatible with the law of contradiction. Einstein's blurring of all temporal distinctions in effect would rob the law of contradiction of its entire scope. If there were no "same time" at which contradictory attributes could not inhere in something, then the law of contradiction would lose all of its teeth. If a young man were unlearned at a given time in one frame of reference, then the time at his location as judged from some other frame of reference would be different and *equally valid*, according to relativity. And hence, since the time would then be essentially indeterminate even at the one place, there could be no law forbidding contradictory attributes of things.

But if one prefers to step out of time into Minkowski's Ever-Ever Land of the Universal Present, then the law of contradiction could hold very well. In fact, it would hold all too well. For it would forbid all change and succession. The young, unlearned man could not become a learned man, for that would constitute a contradiction of attributes at the "same time." Hence, I offer the relativist his only choice, if he is to adhere to his relativity. Either he must permit contradiction in the structure of anything and everything, or else he must forbid all change. And then, no matter how he chooses, the very possibility of meaningful talk becomes eliminated, once and for all.[20]

Among present-day philosophers of science most saliently denying a universal nowness, or a world-wide instant, is Milič Čapek, of Boston University. Čapek insists that the complete relativization of time and space does not undo the reality of time as a process of becoming, i.e., a process of linear movement from a definite past into the future. But in effect, he denies that a cosmic observer (God) exists who can know at once everything that is going on everywhere.[21]

One crucial fact that has been blatantly ignored by philosophers such as Čapek is this: a logically coherent philosophy of physics is impossible without universals, and *a universal truth is inconceivable without a universal instant.* For to say that there is a universal truth is to say that something is true *now everywhere.* Čapek and his relativist cohorts presume to make statements applying to the universe as a whole, or to *all* frames of reference, regardless of relative motions of galaxies, stars, etc. But their system turns out inevitably to be no logical system at all, since there are no truths in any moving space-time frames of reference (according to relativity) that at a *given moment* can apply to *all* relatively moving frames of reference alike.

The notion of nowness can have no clear meaning whatever unless there is an *apriori* time reigning independently of every system of reference or permeating all systems of reference alike; or in short, a common and universal moment. But this is precisely what Einstein rejects out of hand. The irony in his popular delusion (which has hoodwinked two whole generations of physicists around the world) is that he nonetheless consistently appeals to the classical notion of uniform time, i.e., *unconsciously presupposes it*, in every single attempt he makes to deny it. If we were to follow Einstein consistently, we would have to conclude that there is no truth in any physical location *now* that is also true in other places, for the simple reason that there is no nowness common to all systems in which a common truth can inhere. If there is no common nowness, then plainly there can be no truth that is common in all places now. Surely, Einstein's contradiction could hardly be more blatant: it is absolutely true now everywhere that there can be no *now* everywhere.

At this point I could cite from modern literature in physics innumerable examples of the unconscious appeal to *apriori* time by physicists who overtly deny it. Suffice it here to quote Hans Reichenbach, the German-American philosopher of science. Said he: "Time appears to be a completely macrocosmic phenomenon; it is born anew at every moment from the atomic chaos as a statistical relationship."[22] Reichenbach's appeal to *apriori* time is betrayed obviously by his use of the phrase "at every moment." How can time be born anew at every moment? Here, he clearly is presupposing objective time as a medium of any events being born anew. Time is a backdrop, an objective reference, for clearly he is telling us that at every moment a new moment arises; i.e., a moment is created *during* a moment, which is patently an appeal to *apriori* time.

It is unfortunate that physicists have for the last seventy years reacted to Einstein's space-time concepts with compartmentalized minds. Most physicists whom I know personally do believe in universal truths (a good use of the native intelligence with which God endowed them). Yet, they have fallen for Einstein's complete mockery of common-sense knowledge of the nature of space and time like a bunch of bowling pins in a strike. In pursuit of this extraordinary academic fad, they have overlooked the simplest facts, such as for example the impossibility of ever obtaining universal, or objective, time values if Einstein's notion of time (or lack of any logically defined notion of it) were true. Without universal time (a world-wide instant), it is inconceivable how there could be any objectively binding facts of history. History presupposes an absolute past, which presupposes an absolute present appearing between the past and the future. Einstein always predicted *in advance* what the outcome would be in experiments dealing with the movement of light to certain given points in space. Now, How could this ever possibly be done without some *apriori* meaning to time which he himself expressly denied? How peculiar that even the brightest of his disciples failed to see the contradiction in his frequent use of the *apriori* to try to deny any meaning to the *apriori*.

Without a cosmic clock (God's omnipresent awareness of the whole of reality at a universal moment) no cosmic system is logically conceivable. The hoaxters have had their day. But it is time for their powerful and irrational orthodoxy to come down. For all along they have been dealing in universals while espousing metaphysical dogmas about space and time that clearly would make all universals self-contradictory. As I have shown, the relativists end up denying that there are any meaningful time distinctions. But there is no reason why we should take their theory seriously, since the relativists themselves do not and cannot take it seriously in practice. All relativists do in fact use different tenses in their daily talk and in their laboratories. If they do not mean what they say, then why do they say it?

Without uniform time or a cosmic moment, the notion of any universally binding distinctions between past, present, and future would be logically and empirically inconceivable. Or to put it more simply, without a universal given moment there cannot at any given moment exist any universal truth whatever. And as a consequence, there could be no universally valid ideals for making binding moral distinctions, i.e., that are clearly applicable to *everyone everywhere* at a *given* time. Clearly, this would lead to complete moral relativism in the universe. The denial of a cosmic moment (a universally given time) would do completely away with any meaningful notion of a universally valid moral ideal that determines duty or responsibility for everyone everywhere. It is unfortunate that so many philosophers and scientists are taken in by Einstein's denial of uniform time, not at all realizing that when carried to its logical conclusions it would imply epistemological nihilism and a complete breakdown in universal ideals or binding morality. If there is to be no genuine future, then prudence and morality itself lose all meaning, since rational actions are always *aimed* at making something happen in the *future*, not precisely in the present moment, nor in the past. For if the desired effect sought by action were *present already*, then no action whatever would be needed to bring about the effect. In fact, I encounter several students in my classes every year who invoke Einstein's theory to justify their anti-moralism. Most physicists of a Judaic-Christian conviction have not the faintest notion of the fact that Einsteinian relativism is antithetical to their religion. This is unquestionable despite the disclaimer of professional relativists that their theory "is utterly noncommittal concerning the theses of ethical relativism."[23]

3. By Witches' Tricks

Relativists indulge in much illogical talk about the movement of light. Arthur Eddington pointed out that the theory of relativity is a "dodge," that it dodges the question of whether light travels. If the relativists say that light does not travel, then their talk about the *velocity* of light becomes meaningless and contradictory. On the other hand, if they admit that light does have a velocity, then they have no way, from the standpoint of their own postulates, to make the objective validity of light meaningful. Eddington claimed that it takes no time for light to travel from one point to another, that if one could travel at the speed of light, one could move along the orbit of the earth from 1 January of this year to 1 January of next year in no time at all.[24] In *Relativity and Common Sense*, Hermann Bondi also insisted that there is no passage of time for light.[25] I have found this same claim made in many different books on relativity. A light beam leaves Alfred, strikes a mirror, and then bounces back to Alfred without there being any passage of time whatever informing its motion. Because Alfred is moving much slower than the speed of light, his clock will show that it takes time for the light beam to leave him and come back to him—and time, Bondi claimed, is simply what is told by a clock. However, if Alfred could travel at the speed of light, his clock would not record any time at all; and hence, he could instantaneously be anywhere he wanted to be, and his world and life would be tenseless and timeless. Bondi remarked that a person has to surrender his common sense to believe this; yet, he recommended that we do just that because the evidence of physical experiment establishes it as a matter of fact.

What I see here is a typical example of how protagonists of relativity make a mockery of the most abecedarian principles of realistic semantics. One of these principles is that one should avoid using language that is self-contradictory and hence meaningless. It is meaningless to speak of the "velocity" of light and in the same breath imply that light is everywhere at once because it takes no time for it to move from one point to another. Relativity theory ends up making light omnipresent, for it is meaningless to say that it travels and at the same time say that it does not travel. If the reader will pardon my crude display of common sense, it is inconceivable that there can be any travel without time. For *after* light leaves point A, it *later* arrives at point B. *Before* it can return to point A, it must *first* reach point B and *then* reverse its motion in order to journey back to point A. To say that it takes no time to move from A to B, and then to move from B back to A, is to defile common-sense intuition beyond countenance. No one can *meaningfully* say that "Light travels at a rate of 186,283 miles per second," and in the same breath insist that "it takes no time for light to travel." Thus, in effect, relativity theory reduces the question of whether or not light travels purely to the subjectivity of this or that particular observer's biased perception and unreliable clock.

No, thank you, Mr. Bondi. You can surrender your common sense if you wish, and pretend that it is in behalf of a higher form of wisdom. I say pretend, because you would have us think that your position on this question is a matter of physical fact. But the plain fact is, no one ever has, and no one ever possibly can, *observe* that "there is no passage of time for light." There is no imaginable way to ever prove such a thing experimentally, for by the relativists' own terms, it is impossible for a real observer ever to travel at the speed of light. Bondi admits to the contradictions therein involved, yet he accepts the theory even so, as unfortunately so also did Eddington.

One reads with weariness the endless wrangles about Einstein's relativity, which are far too numerous to note here. One even gets the impression that some "philosophical" types actually enjoy perpetuating a dispute and do not wish to see the dispute solved. C. S. Peirce speaks of "overcultivated Oxford dons" for whom "any discovery that brought quietus to a vexed question would evidently [also] vex because it would end the fun of arguing around it and about it and over it."[26] In any case, it would be advantageous to a truth-seeker to have a criterion by which he could decide when to omit the perusal of certain writings on a complex problem. There is indeed such a criterion, or maxim, which is applicable to the present case. It simply is this: do not take seriously arguments which are based on a contradiction. For if you do, you will deny yourself much truth. Those who see and understand your contradiction may attempt to explain to you why and how your position is logically untenable. If you are bent upon avoiding having the contradiction in your position identified as such, then in order to rationalize or defend it you will have to resort to yet more contradictions and become quickly lost in a logical mirror-maze. This is exactly what happens to the dogmatic relativist. Those who pursue him into his maze to help him may themselves become weary and befuddled, while the relativist (thumbing his nose at logic) congratulates himself on having won again. The rational thinker is not given to dodging. But for the relativist, dodging is a cultivated art. Getting caught up in his maze of dodges can turn even an otherwise clear-headed person giddy. Relativity theory does inevitably turn anyone giddy who subscribes to it seriously, even though one may not be at all conscious of his giddy state. And why should this be? In order to adequately answer this question, I must unavoidably become somewhat technical henceforth in my writing. So, I hereby warn the lay reader that at times the contents of this section may become rather abstruse and heavy. Herein, I cannot allow myself the space needed to popularize the concepts discussed.

In the study of formal logic one learns that *from two contradictory propositions any proposition whatsoever can be derived* by processes which are themselves valid. A proposition is the substance of a declarative sentence or statement. For instance, let us suppose, for discussion's sake, that *both* of the following propositions are true:

Light takes time to travel.
Light does not take time to travel.

Now, let us call the first proposition p. Then let us call the latter proposition not-p, or $\sim p$. The symbolic logician summarizes the contradiction as $p \cdot \sim p$, where the dot stands for "and." Well, the logician observes, since p is true, then it is also true to say that either p is true or that some other random proposition called q is true or that they are both true. He summarizes this as $p \vee q$ (where "$\vee$" stands for "or" in the sense of "and/or" or "either or both").

The "other proposition" q can be *anything* you please, such as the proposition:

Light always travels in left-handed corkscrew patterns.

Label this proposition as q. If, as we are assured, p is true, then "p and/or q" ($p \lor q$) is, wrapped together, a true proposition (even though at this point one may not believe that q is true). But look again at the contradiction $p \cdot \sim p$, arrived at previously. From the latter half of that contradiction ($\sim p$) we see that p is not true, which is what $\sim p$ says. Yet, since we have just declared the combined proposition p and/or q to be true, then that leaves q as true by default, since $p \lor q$ means that either proposition p or proposition q (or both) must be true. Thus, it is necessarily established that light always travels in left-handed corkscrew patterns.

We observe that the logical steps taken (after the acceptance of the two initial contradictory propositions as true) are all valid. The final absurdity results from the initial absurdity of accepting a pair of contradictory propositions as true. In logic, such a pair, taken as a pair (as a contradiction), is always *false*.[27] Now, the Einsteinians are not so crudely direct as in the example just given. For if they were, then they would see their error. Rather, their multiple steps, reflected in their mirror-maze, conceal the truth from themselves. The truth is that one cannot start from the contradiction that light both travels and does not travel and expect to arrive at any true conclusion. Remember the oldest maxim of computer operators: Garbage in, garbage out.

The point here is so important that an illustration in terms of the still widely understood skill of arithmetic is worth while. Say, we start from the assertion that $1 + 1 = 3$ is true (a contradiction). Subtracting 1 from each side, we have $1 + 1 - 1 = 2$. That is, $1 = 2$. Again subtract 1 from each side and we have $0 = 1$, or $1 = 0$. Now multiply each side of this "equation" by any given number, such as 12. Thus $12 = 0$. But do the same with *any* number you please, and the result is that any and every number $= 0$; $100 = 0$; $5000 = 0$; $50 = 0$; *ad infinitum*. So, as we see, the contradiction $1 = 0$ is very prolific of other contradictions. But that is not all. Take any "equation" arrived at through the last step— for instance, $76 = 0$. Now add to both sides the same number, such as 2. Then $78 = 2$. Or add any other number instead, such as 10;

then 86 = 10. Or again, go back a step and choose another multiplier for 1 = 0, such as 100, then 100 = 0. Add 2 to both sides and get 102 = 2; or add 10 instead, and 110 = 10. From this point, a few thought-experiments by the reader will demonstrate to him that any and every number equals any and every number. All this results because we accepted 1 + 1 = 3 as true! One could have started with any arithmetical contradiction accepted as true and have arrived at the same conclusion. Thus, *a single contradiction can obliterate an entire theoretical structure.*

Doubtless this was the secret of the lively witch in Engelbert Humperdinck's charming (and theistic) opera *Hänsel und Gretel*: "Five and six, by witches' tricks, make seven and eight. . . . And nine is one, and ten is none, and much is nil, or what you will." Should one believe the relativists any more than to believe the witch?[28]

In such ways, any absurd dream can be made to come "true." Some absurd dreams of scientists have thus been accepted as the truth. Lamentably, the paradoxes of relativity have not been seen as mere irrational dreams, because of that theory's falsely recondite concepts and the proliferation of dodges made available to relativists by those concepts. Some metaphysical and logical analysis of space and the so-called "ether" is now in order, before we finally investigate a way out of this scientific mess.

4. On Upsetting Pi

In his book which I have already referred to, Milič Čapek denies that there is any uniform or fixed space.[29] He allows no objective reality to space at all apart from the events occurring "in" it. Denying absolute space, he ends up with no real or abiding space whatever. He would have us believe that space does not exist independently or *sui generis*. That is, space is not the medium *in* which bodies can come into existence and *through* which they can move. For Čapek, where there are no motions going on in space, there is no space at all. Einstein's later position was the same as Čapek's.[30] But in fact, it is contradictory for anyone to state that space is ontologically unreal, and then appeal to it as though it were real. For although we can imagine that there might be no bodies in motion, or that all bodies and motions in space might cease, it is impossible to imagine that space itself might cease to be. The *non-existence* of space simply cannot be conceived. How weird it seems, that the more learned some philosophers become, the more they revel in the totally incomprehensible. The denial of the objective reality of space was developed primarily by the German mathematician and philosopher G. W. von Leibniz. But the Leibnizian reduction of space to events can never possibly be honored consistently in practice. For the advocates of this theory inevitably speak of physical events occurring "in" space, while formally denying that space as a medium *in* which events can occur is ever objectively real.

To exist at all, space has to have existed always. It is inconceivable that there was a time in the past when there was no space, and that suddenly infinite space arose out of absolute spacelessness. There was never a time in the past when there was no space, nor a time in the past when there was no time. God never created space, nor did He ever originate the process of time. History never had a beginning. Space never had a beginning. It is impossible to make sense out of space and time unless we regard both as primordial categories of reality. Space and the time-process are an inherent part of God's primordial nature. For God could not create anything except through a process in time. Time has to exist before and *during* any act of creation. The time-process itself could never conceivably have come into being, for such becoming would itself be a happening in time. No one can imagine anything happening without it taking time for it to happen. Neither may we suppose that space and time existed before God existed, since the question would arise: Then who created God, and how? It would have to be another, yet more powerful, God. Such an invitation to suppose a never-ending series of ever more powerful gods accomplishes nothing but pointless confusion. Also, it inevitably would lead to theomachy, i.e., the lack of an ultimate necessary order. Thus I repeat: space and the time-process must be taken as an inherent part of God's primordial nature.

I define space in the classical way, after Isaac Newton (and Henry More): space is absolute; it cannot conceivably fail to exist. Its being is essential. Space is absolutely fixed and is everywhere the same and in every direction the same—that is, it is absolutely homogeneous and isotropic. It is immutable, eternal, infinite, all-pervasive and universal. No one can ever *do* anything to space. Neither can anyone ever do anything *with* space. Isaac Newton pointed out that it is impossible to make sense out of space without assigning to it the ontological and objective status of a primordial category of reality.[31] Immanuel Kant later did the same thing, in effect, by showing the necessity *apriori* to presuppose space in order to make sense out of the existence of objects and relations of objects as they appear in our perception. But sadly, he made the mistake of reducing space to merely a necessary subjective condition for intelligible experience of the perception of objects and their relations. Kant stopped short of making a truly logical contribution to the philosophy of space because of his inconsistencies. On the one hand, he reduced it to merely a mode of thinking, allowing it no objective status outside of the mind. He declared that, outside of the mind, "space stands for nothing whatsoever." On the other hand, he described it as having objective validity and reality, that it is an empirical reality underlying things in themselves, independently of our perception of them.[32]

Both Newton and Kant have demonstrated the *apriori* necessity that space *per se* be absolutely isotropic, homogeneous, and stationary as the medium for the existence of things and the occurrence of events. All things that exist, exist in space. Nothing ever exists outside of space, for anything that exists at all has to exist some*where*, and the concept of where-ness is unthinkable without the concept of space. Anything that happens, happens *in* space. Nothing ever happens outside of space. It is impossible to think of something happening without it happening some*where*. Space is the ultimate medium *in* which anything can come into being; for unquestionably, nothing whatever can conceivably come into being without coming into being some*where*. Without a place where it could come into being, a thing simply could not come into being at all. Space is the ultimate framework with respect to which all motion, all rotation, and all acceleration occur. However, absolute space *per se* cannot do anything to matter, nor have any effect on the existence or behavior of energy.

Philosophers and scientists who believe in the ether in space have usually made the mistake of trying to reify it. The ether in classical physics is erroneously defined as the medium *in space* in which, and through which, light travels. In place of this mistaken view, I hold that light does not move through an ether. Rather, it simply moves through space—i.e., the "absolute space" of Newton—the common-sense space of the man in the street.

The motion and behavior of matter and energy is governed by laws. As I have stated previously in this work, to make sense of these laws we have to interpret them as God Acting. The "ether" is not a thing, just as the laws of physics are not things. Just as the laws of physics are not in themselves physical, and must not be reified, so is the "ether" not in itself physical, and must not be reified. Only God, the Divine Lawmaker, can produce those *ethereal laws*, as they may be called, and inform them with a rationale essential to explain the existence and general behavior of matter and energy in space.

Positivistically oriented physicists (such as Ernst Mach) will gnash their teeth at the thought that the so-called ether is to be equated with God Acting in his space to lawfully govern the behavior of the matter and energy that He has created. Just as the laws of matter and energy can have no rationale without God, so also ethereal laws can have no rationale without God. This is simply another instance of the impossibility of making sense out of questions of physics without turning to the principles of a logical and theistic metaphysics. There is no escaping this fact: it is for the sake of intelligibility that we have to postulate the "ether," or rather the ethereal laws, as God Acting in space. This provides us with a logical solution to many theoretical problems that otherwise are in principle insusceptible to solution.

Ethereal laws as such have no physical attributes of any kind unless one is to extend the definition of the physical to include God, who is a Spiritual Agent who creates physical effects and lawfully controls them. Some bad language used by the reifiers of "ether" is, for example, the "ether wind," "contractions" and "condensations" of the ether, and conjectures of mechanical models of an ether. This is exactly the kind of nonsense that follows inevitably from leaving God out of an academic discipline, whether it be physics, chemistry, astronomy, psychology, sociology, biology, economics, or what have you. There is no philosophical system in existence leaving out God that is not polluted with a lot of meaningless language, resulting from the reification of force that simply is not there if God is not there to exert the force. The concept of exertion of force without an Exerter is simply nihilist nonsense. Even the most primitive man, totally devoid of what we now generally think of as scientific education and civilization, commonly knows better than to think in terms of general exertion in nature without an exerter (to give the exertion a rationale). Only over-educated "urbanites" can ever claim to think in such terms. Even so commendably open-minded and objective a philosopher of science as Mary Hesse is an example of the total inability of a scholar to make sense out of the ether while leaving the concept of God out of the picture.[33]

Einstein stated in 1950: "According to general relativity, the concept of space detached from any physical content does not exist. . . . There is no such thing," he said, "as an empty space, i.e., a space without [a] field."[34]

This is pure malarkey. There is no conceivable reason why there could not be some space that is empty of all things (all matter and energy), but not empty of God's Spirit. That is to say, there may be space in which God's Spirit is present but not acting for physical effects of any kind. When God starts acting in that space to create matter and to control it, then we can say that there is "ether," or rather ethereal laws, acting in that space.

Einstein denied the existence of the ether in every sense of the word in both his early and his later writings.[35] However, articles he published in 1924 and 1920 represented an interlude in time during which he affirmed part of the idea of absolute space. But he merely became an example of philosophers and scientists who have stumbled into hopelessly insoluble difficulties by equating space and the "ether." The following appeared in his 1924 article "Über den Äther":

We would not be able in theoretical physics to do without the ether, that is, without a continuum equipped with physical qualities [meaning the capacity to affect the behavior of matter and energy in space]. For the General Theory of Relativity . . . shuts out action at a distance; however, every theory of continuous action presupposes continuous fields, thus also the existence of an ether. . . . The ether of the General Theory of Relativity is distinguished from that of the Special Theory in this way: that it is not "absolute," but rather is determined in its locally variable characteristics by matter possessing mass.[36]

It is a demonstrable fact that the ethereal laws sometimes have an anisotropic effect on the propagation of light, notably in the bending and slowing of light in intense gravitational fields. Between the absolutely isotropic nature of space and the sometimes anisotropic functioning of the ethereal laws, there is a contradiction only if one equates the "ether" with space. But if one distinguishes between the two, and interprets each as I have done herein, then there is no contradiction whatever. The occasional anisotropic functioning of the ethereal laws in no way changes the absolutely isotropic nature of the space *in* which these laws function. God acts, but He could not act if He did not exist. He is infinite, and space *per se* is an inherent part of the primordial framework of his own being. Thus interpreted, the supposed paradox of variations in the functioning of the "ether" in stationary space is resolved.

Einstein was right in saying that the ether (in the sense of ethereal law) is essential for physical explanation. He was wrong in saying that the ether has "physical qualities," though in this he had the company of such undoubted luminaries as Maxwell, Fresnel, Euler, Descartes, Michelson, Morley, and Sagnac. Maxwell wrote: "The interplanetary and interstellar spaces are not empty, but are occupied by a material substance or body, which is certainly the largest, and probably the most uniform body of which we have any knowledge."[37]

It is essential to understand that space is absolute, while ethereal laws are contingent, since they are the laws relating to motion and to fields. There is no reason under the sun why God cannot alter or suspend the laws governing the behavior of matter and energy in certain areas of space, since these laws, intelligibly interpreted, must be seen in the first place as God Acting (and in many ways He can conceivably change how He wishes to act). But God can do nothing to change space, which is inherent in his own being. This is a plain point thoroughly understood by Newton (and by Kant on his more rational side) but not understood at all by Einstein and his disciples. The explanation for this lies in the fact that Einstein was a pantheist. That is, he rejected the idea of a conscious, personal, and infinite God who knows what He is doing.[38] He stated that the universe, though "unbounded" (by space) is "finite," and that there is "nothing" (i.e., no space, nor anything else) "beyond it." What was unbounded here was Einstein's confusion. Moreover, space for Einstein was "curved." But one must ask, Curved in relation to what? Light may, for all I know, travel in a great circle bigger than the visible universe and return, billions of years hence, to the back side of where it started from (as relativists have suggested). If so, that would be saying something about the way light behaves, rather than something about space. It is possible to speak meaningfully of a curve only with reference to something that is straight. One may speak of light traveling in curved lines or slowing down due to ethereal laws which qualify the light's behavior. But by his absurdity of speaking of *curved space* or *curved space-time*, Einstein became the high priest of Recondite Moronity. For one may speak meaningfully of curved bodies or objects, curved lines, curved energy fields, and curved orbits or paths of bodies *in* motion *in* space. But to speak of curved space *per se* is inimitable nonsense and pseudo-science if ever one has witnessed it.[39]

No one can imagine an edge to space beyond which there is no more space. Nor can anyone imagine "distorted" space or "curved" space as such. I have seen several so-called illustrations of "curved space" in textbooks on relativity. What is actually illustrated is an obtuse negligence of the most fundamental principles of semantics. For example, a picture of a curved geometric field (pattern of bodies related to each other in a curved manner) is senselessly labeled as "curved space." Such illustrations ignore the simple fact that nothing whatever is done to space by the curved configuration of bodies in it. Also, they ignore the fact that space is *occupied* by the bodies in it and is pervasive around all of those bodies.

Einstein went so far as to deny that anything whatever can be absolutely straight. To this end he pointed out, evidently correctly, that a disc whirling at extremely great speed would become shorter around its periphery, owing to the FitzGerald contraction. Einstein claimed that this would cause the idea of a straight line to lose all meaning. Such whirling would create "insurmountable difficulties" in the definitions of spatial co-ordinates, and hence in Euclidean geometry itself. The whirling would upset the constant ratio of *pi*, i.e., the ratio of the disc's circumference to its diameter. With the dissolution of *pi*, the Euclidean geometry which makes the calculation of *pi* possible would dissolve, and consequently so would the axioms of Euclidean geometry, including the concept of a straight line. It is nothing to the point that no experiment can be conducted with Einstein's imaginary whirling disc, in view of the fragility of all known materials at the high speed required by the experiment.[40] But this is no matter, since his argument for geometric nihilism already has been answered neatly by Herbert Ives. Ives showed that the whirling disc simply would become shaped like a cup![41]

Few men have made a greater mockery of semantics than Albert Einstein. He ignored the age-old definition of the word "space" (the medium *in* which bodies can come into existence and *through* which they can move). But he continued to use the *same word* with a radically unique meaning (the path of a body in motion, the geometric structure of an energy field, etc.), thus confusing most people to utter despair. The irony of the matter consists in the fact that it was Einstein himself who was utterly confused, but who lacked the slightest consciousness of it, and who was able to hide his confusion from the general public by a smoke-screen of what is considered to be esoteric mathematics. When I was a boy there was extant in the world a common impression that "relativity is so abstruse that only twelve people exist who can understand it." The truth is, none of them, nor anybody else, ever really understood it because it was inherently so irrational that it was in principle *un*-understandable. Einstein's main error in a nutshell was to equate *apriori* space with the contingent laws (comprising the "ether") which operate within space.

Because Einstein equated space with a reified "ether," he was unable to make any sense out of either. Finally, he claimed to be rid of the need for them both. The inevitable result of such muddled thinking on the part of so charismatic a genius was the retarding of the science and philosophy of cosmology for decades.

By now, it should be clear that the "ether," as conceived, reified, and defined by the classical physicist, no longer has any referent in reality; and consequently, the use of the word as a substantive should be avoided. Of course, it is hard not to reify it in one's head when one says the word. But most likely, the re-introduction of absolute space in physics will bring back the word "ether" where absolute space is meant. Established nebulosities generally die hard.

It is unfortunate that even J. Clerk Maxwell and Herbert Ives, both singularly great physicists, did not approach the problems of physics with the concept of God; and consequently, they used the word "ether" as though it has a physical referent in space or as something occupying space. Ives (of whom I shall say much more later) was caught up in a linguistic dilemma. He usually appeared to equate the ether with absolute space. But there was an exception: he referred to "anisotropy of the ether due to the presence of a center of gravitational attraction."[42] It would have been better simply to say that light behaves anisotropically under that gravitational condition. The ether had historically been associated with the plenum, which was taken to be a physical medium occupying all of space. Ives was usually more cautious about conceiving of the ether in this traditional, problematical respect. But he did not bring God into the picture, and hence his own concept of the ether remained ambiguous and undefined. Even the greatest physicists must ultimately fail to make sense, so long as they leave God out of physics. Physics will remain bogged down as long as it clings closely to the philosophy and methodology of positivism. The crucial error of positivism (after it denies God) is, as I have shown already, the mistaking of mere descriptions for explanations.

Here is a moral certainty: modern science and philosophy will never be able to make real sense out of *anything* as long as God is left out.

5. Round Squares

There has been another, quite different line of attack on Einstein's theories. This is the attack which criticizes the so-called *"twin paradox,"* or "clock paradox." The word "paradox," as we shall see, is in this case really only a euphemism for a contradiction. Through this contradiction we find ourselves having the same doubts about the relativists which I have already expressed. Here is Arthur Lovejoy's statement of the "paradox":

Once upon a proper time there were—or let us rather say, in the indefinite present, "there are," since, after all, these events have not yet really happened—twin brothers, Peter and Paul. Peter is a home-keeping youth, but Paul has the soul of an adventurer and busies himself with the construction of a machine for flying through space at an enormous speed. When he and Peter are twenty years of age he completes this contrivance and sets forth upon his journey. Attaining almost at once a velocity amounting to a large fraction of that of light, he continues his celestial joyride at a uniform velocity. . . . At the end of a year, as shown by the clocks he has carried with him, he is able to reverse his motion and return to earth at the same speed. Landing in his home town, he discovers that, in it, decades have passed and that his stay-at-home twin is now far older than himself. Nor would this be a conventional difference of calendars, a mere matter of bookkeeping. Paul will . . . we are told . . . be *physiologically* younger than Peter; indeed, if his speed was less by only 1/20,000 than that of light, he will, returning as a youth of twenty-two, find that 200 years have elapsed on the earth, and consequently that his twin brother has long since died of the infirmities of age. For not only the clocks . . . which Paul has carried on his voyage, but all his physical processes, the motions of the atoms composing his body, will have been retarded in proportion to the rapidity of his flight, while no such effect will have been experienced by Peter. . . . We are given to understand . . . that—though it happens to be as yet technologically impracticable for Paul to make the flight in question—if he did make it the result indicated would be literally predictable; he would, in proportion to the speed and duration of his journey, become younger than his brother born on the same day. The retardation which Paul's time underwent would confer upon him, it is true, only a somewhat equivocal benefit; as André Metz has put it: "The traveler has really lived only two years; he therefore has, from this point of view, no superiority over other men. If his stomach allows him to take only two meals a day, it is 2 times 2 times 365 meals that he will have been able to take in his projectile, and not 2 times 200 times 365. If he is an author accustomed to write a book every six months, he will have written four books, not four hundred. . . ."[43]

Now the difficulty with this conclusion is not that it is . . . extraordinarily paradoxical from the point of view of common sense. . . . The real, or at least the major, paradox does not appear until we note a further implication of the Special Theory. . . . That theory is primarily a rigorous generalization of the principle of relativity of motion; if the latter be false, the former cannot be true. And this principle [as extended by Einstein's denial of need for absolute space] asserts that the unaccelerated motion between any two systems is reciprocal, and therefore that if there *were* any modifications in durations and linear magnitudes *attributable solely to such motion*, these must affect both systems. It is, then, on relativistic principles just as true to say that the earth, and therewith Peter, has been moving away from Paul, as to say that Paul has been moving away from Peter. Hence the conclusions previously drawn for Peter must now be drawn for Paul. He too will find his time retarded, and in the same measure. As Professor [Wm. Pepperell] Montague has put it, with a kindly sense of what Peter's feelings must be in the case hitherto assumed:

"Suppose that the stay-at-home brother should feel piqued by the youthful appearance of the other who has returned from abroad. He would only have to remember that all motion is relative and that consequently he had a perfect right to regard himself as the traveler and his brother as having remained stationary. In that case it would be *he* who looked and really *was* younger. . . . But that could happen only in a universe in which squares were round and the *principium contradictionis* had been put to sleep."[44]

If, then, either twin has been in relative motion, both must have been, and with the same relative velocity; and therefore—since the direction of motion is, in the Special Theory, irrelevant to the contractions and retardations—all the benefits of rapid travel supposed hitherto to have been gained by Paul between his separation from and reunion with Peter, must equally accrue to both. Their ageing will, therefore, have been retarded in the same ratio.

Retarded, it must be asked, in comparison with what? . . . Paul's clocks will be slower than Peter's and Peter's slower than Paul's; and Paul on his return, or at any time during the voyage, will be physiologically as well as chronologically younger than Paul; and, in the extreme case, when the projectile comes back to earth, Paul will be alive while Peter is dead, and also Peter will be alive while Paul is dead—that is to say, Paul will simultaneously be both dead and alive, and Peter will simultaneously be both dead and alive.[45]

This, then, is the twin or clock "paradox." In 1918, Einstein attempted a resolution. Some years earlier, he had evidently been the first to predict that clocks in a gravitational field would slow down (a result soon confirmed by spectroscopic observations of double stars, and of the sun, and later by terrestrial atomic clocks).[46] *Of this slowing of clocks by gravitation, there can be no doubt.* To "resolve" the "twin paradox" Einstein invoked his principle of covariance, the conceptual heart of his General Theory—the theory which, unlike the Special Theory, is not restricted to uniform linear motion. Briefly stated, the principle of covariance reads: "The laws of physics must be of such a nature that they apply [alike] to systems of reference *in any kind of motion*"[47]—including even accelerated motion. The interesting application of this principle is the alleged equivalence of gravitation and acceleration—Einstein's principle of equivalence. What this comes to in the present case simply is this: the jolt you may experience in falling flat on your face is explainable not only in the conventional way, but alternatively by supposing that the earth, along with the universe, has suddenly flown up and bumped you on the head.[48] Einstein noted that Paul the traveling twin had, halfway through his voyage, to turn around and start back. In the process of slowing down, stopping, and reversing his motion, Paul would experience a strong acceleration in the reverse direction. By Einstein's principle of equivalence, acceleration is just like being in a gravitational field. And, since clocks slow down in a gravitational field, they ought also to slow down when being accelerated. Einstein's principle of equivalence in effect *equates* acceleration with gravitation. If a person were in a windowless elevator cabin being constantly accelerated in space, he would not be able to detect any difference between the effect of acceleration on him and the effect of gravity. That is, he would not be able to say that the effect of acceleration on him was not the effect of gravity instead.[49] By this principle of equivalence, Peter the stay-at-home could be regarded as being really the one who was making the trip while Paul in his space-ship stood still, thus slowing down Peter's clock some, too.[50]

This "explanation" remains orthodox at the present time and appears in numerous recent writings, both professional and popular. For instance, it appears in Martin Gardner's widely read book *Relativity for the Million*.[51] Gardner states that Peter *"the stay-at-home does not move relative to the universe"* (p. 121). And this (he declares) is the reason why "there is almost universal agreement among experts that the twin paradox will really carry through in just the manner Einstein described" (p. 120). He insists that we attend to "one gigantic fact," namely, "that when the earth moves, *the entire universe moves with it.* . . . The earth does not move relative to the cosmos," and "therefore, there is no gravitational field with respect to the earth." He declares that "when the earth executes its turnaround, the universe does also. This accelerating universe generates a powerful gravitational field." (p. 122). This gravitational field exerts no influence whatever upon Peter the stay-at-home, but enormously slows down the clock of Paul, the twin who is undergoing accelerated motion in a different inertial frame. We have to remember, Gardner says, that Peter "the stay-at-home and the cosmos do not move relative to one another" (p. 124); and consequently, Peter unavoidably will age faster than his brother Paul, no matter from which inertial frame the relative situation of both twins is viewed.

Gardner tells us that "It is always possible to choose a moving object as a fixed frame of reference without doing violence to any natural law" (p. 120). Also, he tells us that "the paradoxical difference in aging is accounted for, regardless of which twin is taken to be at rest" (p. 124). What he is really saying is this: we can select *any* moving object and *decide* that it is standing still; but then whether it is *really* standing still becomes factually an irrelevant and meaningless question and is merely a relative matter of arbitrary point of view. Gardner then says we may decide that it is the spaceship (in the twin paradox) that is standing still, that the earth and the entire universe is moving away from the spaceship, and that the earth and the entire universe then do a turnaround and start moving back toward the spaceship (p. 122). Precisely parallel statements are used to describe less spectacular matters, such as the everyday experiences of driving an automobile, pounding a nail, playing a ball game, or dropping something out of one's hand. Although the forces resulting from these events are ordinarily described as acceleration forces, they could, on the terms of Mach, Einstein, and Gardner, be equally well described as due to a kind of "gravitational field" of all the matter in the universe, which may be regarded as starting and stopping while one's hammer or car stands still, regardless of the contrary appearances.

Curiously, the physicist C. Møller has demonstrated mathematically that even an accelerated reference frame may be chosen as a reference for physical description. Møller's transformation equations generalize the laws of dynamics and of gravity so that any accelerated reference frame appears superficially adequate to describe any physical events. Even the twin or clock paradox appears resolvable in Møller's way.[52] However, Møller's demonstration entails a serious paradox of discontinuity of velocity, when the "gravitational field" changes due to acceleration. This fact was noticed and discussed by the physicists C. B. Leffert and T. M. Donahue, and was acknowledged by Møller.[53] Geoffrey Builder, Australian physicist, independently noted the same problem, and some other problems besides.[54] The paradox and its implications are too intricate to be considered here. However, I shall show that there is no need to attempt to resolve the paradox, since its presupposition of the principle of equivalence is faulty.

The politest thing I can say about such applications of the principle of equivalence is this: the movement of the *entire universe* away from, and back toward, the spaceship (or toward and away from one's hammer or auto) is *not* "one gigantic fact"; rather, it is a purely arbitrary and desperate assumption. The *whole* universe is simply not susceptible to our limited powers of observation. Moreover, I shall have much to say about the impropriety of physical descriptions that are geared to only one case at a time while there exist a multitude of cases to be covered by these mutually exclusive descriptions. Unconsciously, or at any rate without acknowledging it, Einstein and his followers, including Gardner, have reintroduced into physics an especially privileged reference frame. It is a definite frame of absolute rest, a frame (for anyone who prefers it) with reference to which all things may be said to possess their state of motion or change of motion, however much the relativists despise such a concept. By the relativists' own suppositions, they cannot now escape such a conclusion. The bodies of the universe are highly dispersed from one another. The relativists talk about accelerative (inertial) forces applying to some body when that body speeds up relative to some highly tangible reference, namely, all the mass of the universe. All that is necessary to convert this reference frame into a definite hitching post for a privileged inertial frame is to identify some representative central position for all mass, with respect to which inertial forces in accelerating bodies actually occur. Our knowledge of the universe does not at present permit one to say precisely how to define this representative central position. But one possibility that presents itself is that of the centroid of the universe (center of mass), the point at which the universe would balance if the universe could somehow be weighed. But the precise definition of this representative central position of all matter is not needed in order to suppose that it exists as physically relevant, as the reference point with respect to which all accelerations occur.

The position just reached is of course a totally unrelativistic one, but the relativists cannot avoid adopting it if they follow their own relativistic presuppositions. If any absolute rest frame is to be a part of the theory of relativity, then it certainly is time to consider a change of name for that theory. If the existence of the absolute rest frame is denied, and if Einstein's relativistic interpretation of motion is retained, then *the twin paradox is in truth a contradiction*. But when an absolute rest frame is affirmed, then there simply is no more paradox of the twins. Once it is allowed that there is such a thing as absolute motion, then one person or object may be moving absolutely while another may not be. In this case, there is no longer a logical necessity to insist that their aging or clock rate be the same. Indeed, many physicists appear to be open-minded to this fact. I will not say that they agree, for that would be déclassé! But we may now ignore Einstein's determination to prove that nothing in nature possesses "properties corresponding to the idea of absolute rest."[55] For he himself in effect denied it in his 1918 paper, referred to earlier.[56] But the question remains: Why do physicists still call their theory the theory of relativity? They may reply that the behavior of light justifies retention of this name. I shall return to this point later, to demolish it.

The discussion so far has included arguments based only on translational—i.e., straight-line—accelerations. I have argued against Einstein's relativistic description of motion, which he claimed was justified by his principle of equivalence. Actually, this principle was implicit in the thought of the nineteenth-century Austrian physicist Ernst Mach, whom Einstein much admired.[57] The problems with Einstein's principle of equivalence come out especially clearly when one considers rotations. Suppose you are on a merry-go-round or carousel. You feel that you are being pulled outward, by the "centrifugal force" of the rotation. But suppose that you consider, as Mach in effect did, that the merry-go-round could be regarded as not turning at all; but rather, the earth and the whole universe are revolving around the merry-go-round. That is, the coordinates of the frame of reference for physical descriptions are to be taken as fixed to the "motionless" merry-go-round and centered upon it. By definition, any frame of reference consists of coordinate lines and points that are fixed and are at rest. Mach is telling us that everything in the universe may be considered as moving in relation to the stationary merry-go-round and its motionless coordinates. Of course, the man with common sense would laugh at anyone taking this notion seriously. But Mach presumed to take himself quite seriously, for he insisted that the "centrifugal force" of a merry-go-round in motion can be regarded equally plausibly as *the pull of all the stars in the universe* on a merry-go-round at rest. This pull instantaneously becomes effective when the merry-go-round starts to turn—or pardon me—when the universe starts to turn around it. Relativistic physicists describe this assumed outward pull as a kind of "gravitational field."

To presume the starting and stopping of all the fixed stars and galaxies just for one's little old merry-go-round introduces an embarrassing jungle of complexities. To be explained away are the effects normally to be expected from the unheard-of accelerations and velocities projected to all the stars insofar as they tend to lie in the plane of the merry-go-round. Moreover, What is one to do when there are two merry-go-rounds, turning in opposite directions and starting and stopping at different times? Is one to apply the same "law" of attraction at the same time to each of these concurrent "alternating options"? Again, say that a cosmonaut on the moon hits his golf ball obliquely, causing it to spin. The earth, 240,000 miles away, is from the point of view of a microbe on the golf ball then to be regarded as dizzily spinning around the moon, at a speed far exceeding that of light. An analogous problem arises when one considers the light coming to the moon from heavenly objects. Imagine that the microbe on the golf ball sets up a miniature laboratory right on the ball and investigates the laws of light propagation. Further, suppose that the microbe, as a faithful relativist, declares that the coordinates he chooses to use for physical description are those that are centered upon the golf ball and stationary with respect to it (whether the ball is spinning or not, conventionally speaking). If we speak in terms of common sense and say that the ball is *in fact* spinning, the microbe would not perceive it as such; but rather, he would regard the light from the earth, the sun, and the stars as coming to him in spiral paths of many turns and at speeds far in excess of the usual value for the speed of light. The light would appear to travel in this manner unless it was emitted by stars lying in line with the axis (the poles) of the spinning golf ball; the light would travel in straight lines at the usual value for the speed of light, from these stars. But when the golf ball stopped spinning, the microbe would regard the light as coming to him directly in straight lines. The microbe should admit that all this must make for complicated statements of the laws of light propagation, especially when laboratory reports from other microbes on other spinning balls are published. But then, with a blasé expression, he simply would declare that it must be merely a matter of one's point of view.

No one can possibly verify, by observation, the relativist assumption that both Paul's frame of reference and Peter's can at the same time be regarded as equivalent reference frames. Nor can one verify that the microbe's frame of reference can be regarded as equivalent to an inertial rest frame. But there is a serious logical difficulty here which usually escapes the attention of physicists. Remember, Mach in effect described the merry-go-round as maybe not really going around at all. Rather, the merry-go-round may be regarded as in a state of rest, and the universe may be swinging around it, producing the same dizzying effect. To the strict relativist, either position is equally as tenable, equally as real, or equally as true. That is, the description of the merry-go-round as in motion is *true*. Yet, it is equally as true that it is not in motion at all, but rather is at rest. This jolting contradiction (that an object can *at once* be going around, yet not be going around at all) cannot possibly be acceptable to a person with a logical mind.

Now, there can be no quibbling about the fact that there is a contradiction here. Relativists often claim that they are not saying that *both* positions are at once equally true. But this can only be regarded as a desperate subterfuge. For if they are saying that *either* viewpoint, at a given time, can be regarded as true, then logically, *both* viewpoints at that given time can be regarded as true. Apodictically, the only way the viewpoints cannot both be true at a given time is if one of them at that time is in fact false. But if one specific option is in fact false, then plainly a logical person cannot say that *either* option that one may prefer is true. And what is Gardner's solution to this kind of problem? With no chagrin at all, he simply declares (as an exemplary relativist) that "There is no actual truth of the matter."[58] Such impudence to logic goes back to Mach, whose relativist philosophy preceded Einstein and was adopted by him. Alluding to the two logically incompatible views about a rest frame, Mach said unshamefacedly that "Both views are, indeed, equally *correct*."[59] If any relativist once acknowledges that *both* viewpoints cannot be regarded as true, then logically, he is in effect acknowledging that *there has to be* an absolute rest frame, even if he cannot determine which one it is. Gardner as much as admits this when he says that *either* frame can be regarded as the rest frame.[60] But I add: *not both!* Assuredly, not both at once. And, as a matter of practical scientific explanation, not both at different times, either. There are evidently insuperable difficulties in explaining any presumed transition from one degree of rotation of the universe, or center of rotation of the universe, to another. Thus, scientists must select one, and only one, reference frame. Which one shall it be? So far as rotation is concerned, I shall now present evidence to establish that the one and only true reference frame is absolute space, which we are able to discern after concluding that the universe as a whole is not rotating.

Isaac Newton suspended a bucket by a cord, twisted the cord, then filled the bucket with water and spun it so as to unwind the cord. When the water started to whirl with the bucket, its surface was of course no longer flat but became concave. It was not the motion of the bucket *per se* that caused the concavity, for when the water surface was flat, the water also was not rotating with respect to the surroundings. Newton presumed, as we may, that the concave water was whirling with respect to "immovable space."[61] An experiment similar in basic principle is to spin a dumbbell around in such a manner that the weights revolve in a circle. There is tensile force in the rod which connects the weights, except when the dumbbell is not spinning. When there is no tensile force in the rod, the dumbbell will not be spinning with respect to the surroundings. Again, the experimental medium, in this case the dumbbell, may be presumed to be rotating with respect to "immovable space."

Experimental evidence for absolute space generally has been swept under the scientific rug. G. Sagnac, a French physicist, discovered in 1913 an effect predicted earlier by A. A. Michelson.[62] Sagnac used an interferometer mounted on a rotating table 20 inches in diameter. The split halves of the light beam were reflected in opposite directions around an enclosed area on the table. In this way, he indeed achieved a positive result (discovery of evidence of absolute space), while the interferometer was rotating in the plane of the light paths. During this rotation, the two light beams went around a circuit and arrived back at their source at times corresponding to the same speed with reference to the stars, *not* with reference to the rotating apparatus.[63] We know it was with reference to the stars, not to the earth, because of another experiment, conducted by the aging A. A. Michelson and H. G. Gale, in 1925. Assembling a mile and a half of Chicago water-main pipe as a light-conduit and exhausting the disturbing influence of air from it, they used the Sagnac effect to detect the absolute rotation of the earth, i.e., the turning motion of the earth with reference to *absolute space*.[64] The experiments of Sagnac, and of Michelson and Gale, established conclusively that light, insofar as it travels around a closed circuit, does *not* have a constant velocity except with reference to absolute space. In this way, Einstein's relativist principle of the constancy of the velocity of light has been placed under serious embarrassment, to put it mildly.

Mach's explanation for Newton's rotating bucket was dizzy enough. But actually, C. Møller has so generalized the equations of physics as to enable the description, by means of spinning reference frames, of even the compass-like behavior of a gyroscope or of a Foucault pendulum. At the North Pole, for instance, the plane of oscillation of Foucault's long ball-and-wire pendulum would be stationary with respect to what I have called absolute space; that is, the earth would revolve under it every 23 hours and 56 minutes, which is a sidereal day. Møller can explain these phenomena on the spinning Machian relativist terms. That this can be done is a curious feature of the universe, one worthy of consideration. But why bother any more? Møller's explanations are horrendously complicated and face insuperable difficulties, as I noted previously. Furthermore, Møller's methods cannot explain the outcomes of the Sagnac or the Michelson–Gale experiments. The one simple and obvious explanation of all these phenomena is to assume the reality of absolute space, through which light travels at a constant speed (if in a vacuum and uninfluenced by gravity). This was the opinion of Sagnac and later of Herbert Ives, who found in these experiments a direct detection of the "ether."[65] The specific ethereal law so detected could be stated thus: light constrained to travel around a closed circuit has a speed measured as though it were traveling through absolute space as centered in the circuit.

Here, I pause to note that one may scan Einstein's writings in vain to find mention of the Sagnac or Michelson–Gale experiments. The same can be said of general physics textbooks and of the 1971 *McGraw-Hill Encyclopedia of Science and Technology*.[66] This is likewise true of the 1974 *Encyclopaedia Brittanica*, the 1976 *Encyclopedia Americana*, and the *Encyclopedia of Philosophy* (1967). Such an oversight in these distinguished encyclopedias constitutes a stinging indictment of professional scientific reporting.

Support for absolute space has more recently come from the direction of quantum mechanics. For example, the British physicist P. A. M. Dirac in 1951 concluded a technical note with these words: "We have now the velocity [from his equation 2] at all points of space-time, playing a fundamental part in electrodynamics. It is natural to regard it as the velocity of some real physical thing. Thus with the new theory of electrodynamics we are rather forced to have an aether."[67]

Unfortunately, such help as that offered by the above way of thinking is of spurious value until physicists can overcome their habituation to reifying the ether.

6. On Being Dumbfounded

Actually, any possibility of explaining away the twin paradox, on the basis of strict relativity, as anything but a contradiction became blocked by an experiment in 1938. The version of the twin story that has survived as *in principle true* is the tale of the twins in the simple form before anyone ever thought of the paradox. By this version, the traveling twin Paul would *in fact* age less rapidly than his stay-at-home brother Peter. As Einstein was the first to predict seriously and generally, *moving* clocks actually slow down while they are in motion.[68] Again, of this there can be *no doubt*. Paul's slower aging would be due to his extra *velocity* relative to any inertial reference frame (that is, relative to a uniformly and linearly moving reference frame). Or, to state it more specifically, the slower aging would be the result of motion relative to the earth (ignoring its various circular motions).

The slowing of moving clocks was first demonstrated experimentally by Herbert E. Ives, American physicist and television scientist, under the auspices of Bell Telephone Laboratories. His experiment (together with G. R. Stilwell) using fast, radiating canal rays (tandem hydrogen ions) as "clocks" is known to every informed physicist—although, pitiably, many physicists and philosophers of science are not adequately informed.[69] Later observations on the decay rates of fast-moving mesons and muons confirmed the retardation of clocks by the same amount.[70] A more concrete confirmation of clock retardation with motion came with the experiment of J. C. Hafele and R. E. Keating. Cesium atomic clocks were carried around the world eastward via commercial jet aircraft. After a round trip, the clocks were brought back to Washington and compared with the master clock stationed at the U. S. Naval Observatory. The clocks were found to have lost, as predicted, a fraction of a microsecond owing to their motion.[71]

Around 1960, a group of experiments were conducted by R. V. Pound, G. A. Rebka, and a British group of scientists. They found that photons (which comprise all kinds of electromagnetic radiation) when moving upward through the earth's atmosphere will slow down their *measured frequency* owing to climbing against gravity.[72] These experiments became possible with the 1958 discovery of a German physicist, Rudolf Mössbauer.[73] Mössbauer discovered that the gamma rays emitted by the nuclei of certain metallic radioactive isotopes, such as iron isotope 57, have a very sharply defined frequency as they gradually break down. Also, he discovered that the atoms in films of similar radioactive isotopes will reabsorb many of the gamma rays, but only when the contrived motion of approach or recession between the films does not have a speed greater than, say, that of a walking spider. Otherwise, the frequency of the gamma rays as received would be altered too much by the contrived motion to maintain the matching of frequencies—that is, the *tuning* of frequencies of emission and receptivity between the atoms of the emitting film and the atoms in the absorbing film. In 1964, Pound and J. L. Snider developed a more refined experimental technique. With this improvement, when one of the radioactive films approached the other or receded from the other at merely the speed of a fast snail, the emitting and receiving atoms appeared as detuned from each other enough that the receiving ones would no longer receive.[74] Gamma rays travel at the speed of light. Thus the ratio of speed of the moving film to the speed of light was about one in a hundred billion. This ratio also expresses the proportion of frequency change resulting from the contrived motion. That is, the apparatus could directly detect the motion of a snail (and, in multiple observations, an even much slower speed) merely by noting how gamma ray photons were being received in the absorbing film. The experiments consisted in placing the metallic absorber film about seventy feet above the emitter film and then in moving them slowly toward each other until the detuning caused by the "slowing" of frequency of the ascending rays was just offset by the slight relative motion. Thus, Einstein's prediction of the "slowing down" of the frequency of the gamma rays was verified to within one per cent error. However, in universal time, frequency could not logically change. One should say (unlike Einstein) that the more intense gravity near the earth slowed the lower clock more than the upper one, thus reducing the *measured* frequency during the trip.

Now, these experiments were a victory for one aspect of Einstein's principle of equivalence—in this case the equivalence of gravitational and kinetic energy.[75] Thus, his prestigious principle of equivalence still has, in some of its aspects, a definite scientific usefulness today. However, an unexpected byproduct of these experiments of Pound, et al., constitutes a fatal difficulty for the principle of equivalence in its original aspect, namely, for the claim that gravitation and acceleration have the *same* effects on physical happenings such as clock rate. In the light of some other considerations, the experimental byproduct proves conclusively that the assumption of the equivalence of acceleration and gravity is *false*. Acceleration *per se*, unlike gravity, has nothing whatever to do with the time-telling rate of a clock.

Pound and Rebka had observed that temperature affected the frequency of the gamma rays and the frequency at which they were absorbed. The higher the temperature, then the lower the frequency, or the greater the time period per cycle of the gamma rays. This effect of temperature was correctly attributed to the slowing effect of the velocities of the nuclei, resulting from random thermal bombardment. This increased mutual bombardment of the nuclei in the crystalline radioactive isotopes caused the nuclei to have a correspondingly increased to-and-fro velocity, although the metallic crystal lattices prevented the nuclei from moving far away from their normal positions. The fields which secured each nucleus did not constitute rigid limits to motion; rather, they acted as though they were springs—screen-door springs—between each pair of adjacent nuclei. Even though the temperature hardly exceeded that of a hot summer day, the thermal bombardment resulted in random to-and-fro speeds roughly that of a jet plane. It was the American physicist C. W. Sherwin who noticed that the result of the bombardment was a jiggling of the atomic nuclei at an intensity of 10^{16} (ten quadrillion) times that of the earth's gravity. Sherwin noted that this acceleration of the nuclei was "very low by atomic or nuclear standards." He stated that the Fe^{57} nuclei were "playing the role of the clocks of the 'clock paradox.'" After a detailed argument, Sherwin concluded that "In spite of the very large, randomly oriented, approximately periodic accelerations of magnitude 10^{16} g, the observed time differences are explicable . . . entirely in terms of the *velocities* of the clocks."[76] This result corroborates the experiments mentioned earlier in showing again that velocity slows clocks.[77] But the result also means that the time differences or "frequency shifts" of the gamma rays were not due at all to the mindboggling accelerations which the radiating nuclei underwent.

Thus, inertial frames of reference are privileged in the matter of simply predictable clock behavior. It is necessary to add the words "simply predictable," since physicists have argued that, even in the extreme case of the atomic nuclei of Pound, Rebka, Snider, and Sherwin, it is possible to regard the nucleus as standing still while the entire universe revolves around the mean position of the nucleus at the astounding rate of about 10^{13} (ten trillion) revolutions per second! This appears to be the orthodox position at present. It is not easy to explain the motions in these terms without a motion picture, but I will try. First, imagine that the irradiated, radioactive iron film of Pound et al. is lowered in temperature to absolute zero, where all thermal jiggling of the nuclei ceases. Of the myriad nuclei, let us choose one and call it N and call its position at that time O. Let O define the point of origin of coordinates in a conventional inertial reference frame. Let O also define the origin of coordinates in a frame that rotates at 10^{13} revolutions per second with respect to the inertial frame; this will be called the *rotational* frame. As an independent reference for describing physical happenings, it is defined as stationary, like any reference frame, even though it rotates in relation to the inertial frame.

Now let the irradiated, radioactive iron film be warmed up to room temperature, and the nucleus N with it. The nucleus and its neighbors in the atomic lattice are now vibrating at an average rate of, let us say, 10^{13} Hertz (cycles or revolutions per second). For simplicity let us say that the nucleus N is, as described in the inertial rest frame, revolving around its mean position, that is, around the position O at which it rested when at absolute zero temperature. In these terms, it is now "revolving" in such a way that it is at rest in the rotational frame. The nucleus N is not now of course at the origin of coordinates O but is removed from it by say 5 picometers (a picometer is one trillionth of a meter). It is at this small radius of thermal agitation that its speed in the inertial frame figures out to that of a jet plane.

But let us, in our imagination, stay in our rotational frame where the nucleus N does not move at all. We then see that the entire universe, the stars and galaxies, are revolving around point O. At the rate of 10^{13} Hertz, another nucleus at the relatively enormous distance of 5 microns (1/5000 inch) from point O will be circling around O at about the speed of light. If the nucleus N were in your eyeglasses, the book you are now reading would be circling around your head at better than 50,000 times the speed of light. And the farther away one traveled and paused, conventionally speaking, the faster he would (during his pause) be going with respect to the rotational reference frame and the supposedly stationary nucleus N. It is this whirling of all the matter in the universe which may be regarded as exerting a "gravitational field" upon the nucleus N and centrifugally pulling at it and keeping it away from its mean (or absolute-zero) position O. This "gravitational field" exerts about 10^{16} g's, the same as would be calculated in the inertial frame by ordinary methods. Now, our radioactive nucleus N emits a gamma ray. The ray is found to be of slower frequency than it would be if all were at rest. In the inertial frame we would attribute this slowing to the velocity of the emitter, that of a jet plane. But in the "rotating" frame, the nucleus N isn't moving; yet its gamma ray is still lowered in frequency. Why? It has to be due to the "gravitational field" induced by the whole universe swirling around approximately that point. But now, Is it not an odd kind of gravitational field that pulls away from the center and becomes stronger the farther out from the center one goes? Yet that is what the relativists call it. Like other gravitational fields, its intensity is expressed in units of acceleration, even when no acceleration is occurring (as when objects are said to be at rest on the surface of the earth, in the earth's gravitational field). So we see the principle of equivalence in its original aspect, the equivalence of gravitation and acceleration. Thus the relativist says, with a scarcely suppressed grin, that not even the Pound and Rebka experiment, with its thermally agitated nuclei, upsets Einstein's principle of equivalence. One needs only a modicum of imagination to see that gravitation and acceleration are in effect the same and that both gravitation and acceleration can be regarded as slowing clocks down, and in the same amount according to their "field," just as Einstein said it would.

Some problems with this relativistic "explanation" must now be noted. I have already mentioned the discontinuity problem noted by Builder, and by Leffler and Donahue. To my knowledge, no solution to this objection to Møller's transformations to accelerated coordinates has been put forth. Moreover, there is a new problem to be faced when thermal agitation is considered. For simplicity in the above hypothetical situation, I ignored the fact that the jiggling motions are in truth irregular. This is because the nuclei in a lattice do not all jiggle in unison, but each one goes its own way and is randomly affected by its neighbors which are also jiggling somewhat at random. Thus, there is no precise constancy in the course of any nucleus, or in its rate, or in its plane of vibration. That is, the rotational frame we have been considering with reference to the one nucleus N would in fact not permit any *real* jiggling nucleus to be considered as stationary within it. An infinity of new reference frames, shifting by infinitesimal degrees frenetically from one to another, would be required in order to regard any one nucleus as being at rest—as being a proper object of the Møller equations. This much is bad enough. But in order to be a genuine explanation, Møller's explanation would have to be repeated for each and every vibrating particle in the universe, in order to arrive at all the reference frames needed to defend the principle of equivalence from irreverent attackers. None of these infinite centillions of reference frames could jibe with each other.

The Texas cattle ranchers of my home town would dispose of this relativist theory with merely two pungent nouns. But to elaborate slightly, I return to a previous example. The reader will recall how a rotational reference frame might be chosen so as to declare a vibrating atomic nucleus in your eyeglasses as stationary (in a simplistic view of the vibration), even though the vibration is at a rate of 10^{13} Hertz. In that reference frame, the book before you would be whirling around your head at 50,000 times the speed of light. This way of viewing the matter conflicts with that of a nucleus in a page of the book. Say that you have another rotational reference frame centered near that nucleus. With respect to that frame, it is your head that is swirling around at 50,000 times the speed of light. This is again the problem of "alternating options." Can both descriptions be correct? Mach said yes. But we saw, above, how there must be an infinity of reference frames if all the jiggling nuclei in the universe are to be regarded as somehow standing still while the universe swirls around them. So we have an infinity of descriptions which, on Mach's terms, must all be equally correct. The faithful relativist says it's all in your point of view. But if one of these frames is the true one, the others cannot be true. As before, I deny that any more than one can be correct. And which frame shall it be? Of all these possible classes of frames that differ from each other with respect to rotations, only one class is stationary as commonly understood. The laws of mechanics have a unique simplicity when stated in terms of this non-rotating class of frames. Therefore, such frames have a powerful claim to our attention as exclusive, even leaving aside the experimental and logical evidence adduced earlier.

The relativists with whom I am acquainted have affirmed the validity of the above defense of Einstein's principle of equivalence —that is, of the equivalence of gravity and acceleration. One serious problem remains. In Einstein's theory, there can be no causal effect that travels at a speed faster than that of light. This restriction derives from the Lorentz transformation equations. The expression $(1 - v^2/c^2)$ becomes less than zero when the speed of light is exceeded—that is, when v is greater than c. The expression which appears in the Lorentz transformations is $(1 - v^2/c^2)^{1/2}$—that is, the square root of the quantity in parentheses. The square root of a minus number is correctly called an imaginary number. Though mathematicians and electrical engineers use such numbers, they have no direct physical applicability. Hence, for Einstein's theory, velocities greater than that of light are imaginary. They are imaginary for Ives' theory, too, since Ives also uses the Lorentz transformations.[78]

What does this fact mean for the centillions of rotating reference frames just considered? The relativists themselves admit that such reference frames have no applicability outside of the circle in which velocities so defined do not exceed the speed of light. That is, in the case of the jiggling nuclei of Pound et al., these rotating frames have no applicability farther away than 5 microns from their center! The relativists I know actually admit this. The immediate consequence of this admission is that Mach's and Møller's resort to so-called gravitational fields induced by the supposedly fast-rotating universe breaks down abjectly, totally. Consider what has happened. The relativist, trying to save Einstein's principle of the equivalence of gravitation and acceleration, has invoked rotating reference frames and centrifugal "gravitational fields" induced by all the matter of the universe rotating around the particular place of momentary interest. But then he turns around and admits that the resulting speeds of the revolving matter exerting the "gravitational field" cannot be taken seriously, since these speeds are faster than that of light. Over the doors of their classrooms one might inscribe this legend: "Abandon all logic, ye who enter here."

At this point, we may consider a way whereby we can actually obtain our true bearings in the universe. The farthest known galaxy, the radio galaxy 3C-295, in Boötes, appears to be about 5 billion light-years away. Let us select some reference frame that is centered upon the sun. Let it be so chosen as to assign to 3C-295 a velocity of revolution around the earth and sun at just the speed of light, which is the limiting attainable speed. Thus the galaxy would travel, in terms of the angle measured from the earth, at the rate of one five-billionth of a radian per year, or about a hundred millionth of a degree per year. Again, let us select another reference frame in the same way except that in this case the velocity assigned to 3C-295 is in the opposite direction in the sky. Reference frames so selected comprise the extreme limits possible for any reference frame centered upon the sun. All such possible reference frames agree, in their relative angular speeds, to within plus or minus a hundred millionth of a degree of rotation each year. Thus, for all practical scientific purposes, we may take the bearing of this galaxy in the sky (e.g., its right ascension and declination) as defining absolute space with respect to rotation. That is, this bearing will, by decision, never change. Or rather, with any conceivable further information about other possible references, the bearing of this galaxy can never change faster than a hundred millionth of a degree per year. Any movements of other celestial objects are to be reckoned in relation to the bearing of this galaxy 3C-295. On the relativists' own terms, we already have a practical definition of absolute space with respect to rotation. Let us hear no more disputation on absolute and relative rotations.

From this vantage point it is possible to settle definitively most of the questions left hanging so far. The relativists have tried to use even the Pound and Rebka experiment as evidence that Einstein's principle of equivalence of gravity and acceleration holds up, by use of centillions of conflicting rotating reference frames. But their defense cannot be maintained. Despite all the prestigious arguments, there proves to be no escape from the conclusion that the heart of Einstein's principle of equivalence has suffered a coronary attack. General relativity *as a theoretical structure* is by this fact alone vitiated.

There proves to be no way to maintain that gravity and acceleration equally slow clocks down, or equally slow the aging process. Gravity slows clocks. *Acceleration does not retard clocks.* Hence, Einstein's resolution of the twin paradox is not a factual resolution at all. Accelerated reference frames cannot as such be used for physical descriptions. Clocks slow down and people age according to their velocities in inertial reference frames. To presume that all conceivable reference frames are equally privileged, as Einstein did, is to make the twin paradox *a flat contradiction.* The contradiction vanishes when one abandons Einstein's accelerated reference frames and the principle of equivalence upon which they are based. Thus, fatally, Einstein's explanation falls flat on the ground. Or—might I use his own jargon—the ground has sprung up and smashed his explanation flat in the face.

Bypassing these impossible Machian-Einsteinian complexities, one may say simply that moving clocks slow down. But moving, one must ask, in relation to *what*? The traveling twin, we said, would return younger than his brother. Hence, he must have been moving, or moving faster, in relation to something that was of general physical significance. But what might that something be? Of all the conceivable inertial reference frames, is there one ubiquitous true frame, the trueness of which the relativists have been so concerned to rule out of existence?

In a spectacularly successful creative analysis that was, in the history of physics, second perhaps only to Newton's mechanics, J. Clerk Maxwell devised in the mid-nineteenth century a coherent theory of light as being essentially electromagnetic waves, traveling as pairs of mutually sustaining vibrations through some medium, a bit like transversely oscillating waves moving through solids. The medium was called the luminiferous ether, or simply the ether. For decades scientists strove unsuccessfully to interpret this "ether" as something mechanical that would transmit light waves. But this explanation of the transmission of light remained unbudgingly enigmatic. For scientists reasoned that the earth can hardly be stationary in this so-called ether, or in absolute space, if only because the earth revolves around the sun at a mean speed of 18.5 miles per second. That is about 1/10,000 the speed of light. If the earth is rushing through absolute space, the presence of space as absolute should, they thought, be revealed by measuring or comparing the speed of light at various angles to that motion. In the nineteenth century, the only accurate measurement, or comparison, of the speed of light then feasible required that light beams be brought back to where they came from. That is, only a measurement of the two-way speed could be made accurately. At first thought, to measure merely the two-way speed of light would not reveal the difference between the speeds going out and coming back, for they would cancel each other out. But that would not be the case on a slightly more sophisticated view of the matter. A swimmer going at constant speed relative to the water can swim straight across a stream and back quicker than he can swim the same distance upstream and then downstream. If light moved with respect to an "ether" or absolute space, its behavior ought to be similar to that of the swimmer, and any motion of a measuring apparatus through the "ether" should therefore be detectable, in principle. Maxwell had thought of all this, but he found any empirical detection of it impractical with the experimental techniques available to him in his time.[79] However, A. A. Michelson and E. W. Morley later devised an interferometer equal to the task and set it up in Cleveland. But no matter which way they turned their unique instrument, and no matter in which direction the earth was moving around the sun (i.e., which season the earth was in) the result was always "null"; that is, the velocity of light always *measured* exactly the same in any direction. This result, announced in 1887, dumbfounded scientists.[80] For it had always seemed natural to assume that light travels with reference to fixed space. That is, it will approach you faster when you are moving toward it than when you are standing still or moving away from it, just as surely as raindrops hit you faster when you are driving your car into a storm. In 1725, the English astronomer James Bradley had observed that the apparent direction of each star depends a little on the season of the year when it is observed. That is, it depends on which direction the earth is moving as it circles the sun. When the earth is moving crosswise to the direction of a star, the star *appears* to be slightly displaced in the direction of the earth's motion, as compared with its position at other times of the year. Let us say that the star's rays are raindrops in the air and that you are moving through this rain-laden air. If there is no wind, then the raindrops will seem to be coming from in front of you, no matter which way you move. And—even if there is a wind—your direction of movement will make a difference. Similarly, the star's rays seem to be coming somewhat from in front of the earth as it moves. This angle of stellar aberration, as it is called, goes up to about 20 seconds of arc, too small to be seen except with accurately mounted telescopes. A star's own velocity does not cause the apparent shift in its position as seen from the earth. We know this from observations of fast-moving double stars. It is the earth's movement and counter-movement through absolute space which explains the appearance of a shift. Rejecting space *per se*, Einstein concluded that light travels *without any reference to space or* "*ether*," and that only relative motions of the emitter of the light and its receiver are significant or meaningful. But the actual behavior of light (as above described) simply is inconsistent with relativist theory.[81]

To Einstein, the Michelson-Morley experiment indicated that light does travel without reference to absolute space or to the ether.[82] Yet logically, the actual behavior of light is contradictory without a reference to real space and ethereal laws governing light's motion. To resolve this apparent enigma, the Irish physicist G. F.

FitzGerald boldly drew the only reasonable conclusion possible. He decided that every material object, when moving through absolute space, must thereby become shorter in the direction of its movement. That includes the arms (i.e., the light paths) of the interferometer of Michelson and Morley. If such an arm is shortened by its own motion, then the light traversing it will seem to go correspondingly faster. If one objects that we could measure the contraction and thus avoid being fooled, the answer is that we cannot do so, *because our measuring instruments become shorter too*—our rulers, our interferometers, our very bodies as we are in motion. This idea of the contraction of bodies in motion did not seem odd to FitzGerald, for the new electromagnetic theory of matter conceivably could explain such unexpected behavior. In order to make FitzGerald's explanation work, it turned out that one of two other things have to happen when an object moves through absolute space. Either moving things become shorter crosswise to their own motion as well as lengthwise, or else clocks moving with the object have to slow down.[83] As I have shown, it later developed that the time-telling rate of clocks undergoes retardation when in motion. A body does not get shorter crosswise to its own motion.

Understandably, FitzGerald's explanation seemed *ad hoc*, or suspect, to some physicists back around 1900. For they asked, Why should the universe be so cunningly constructed as to *conceal* absolute motion as well as variations in the relative speed of light? Nevertheless, the Dutch physicist Hendrik Lorentz and the British physicist Joseph Larmor had already found some reason to suppose that something like the hypothesis of clock retardation was more probable than that of the crosswise shortening of rods. Accordingly, Lorentz formulated his famous transformation equations, with which one could calculate what a rod length or clock rate in one spatial frame would be, or appear to be, when measured from the point of view of a relatively moving frame. The French mathematician and physicist Henri Poincaré revised these equations but proposed that the name of Lorentz remain with them. As Lorentz told us, and as Poincaré implied, the method of arriving at these equations was one of "groping."[84] Their purpose was to accomodate the result of the Michelson-Morley and similar experiments, along with the theoretical demand of the Maxwell equations that light travel at the velocity c (the universal velocity of light in empty—and gravitation-free—space). The Lorentz transformation equations could be interpreted to account for the FitzGerald contraction of rods and the retarding of moving clocks.

Before Einstein published his "Electrodynamics" paper in 1905, Poincaré had presented the principle of relativity (*not* the Theory of Relativity), which states that nature is apparently so constituted that absolute uniform linear motion cannot be *measured* by any means whatsoever. By this principle, Poincaré meant only to deny tentatively that such motion could be measured, not to deny that it exists. Poincaré's principle may well be true.[85] The Michelson–Morley and similar experiments produced strong evidence for its validity. Maxwell's equations were verified as valid in any state of motion of the observer, allowing absolute motion to have no measurable effect. But that was not all of the evidence. For more than two centuries experiments have been made to observationally detect absolute motion. Joseph Larmor reviewed the results up to 1900. Efforts were made to detect any effect of absolute motion on the refraction of light, on its dispersion and interference, and on the polarization of light and its rotation in certain crystals.[86] Moreover, the effects of moving of electric charges or magnets did not reveal any absolute motion. In this impasse, Poincaré postulated his "principle of relativity," which is in essence a postulate of our impotence ever to *observe* motion as absolute. The principle summed up the results of many kinds of experiments in such a way as to predict what might be expected from future experiments, namely, that we can never find a way to actually *observe* the rest frame of absolute space.

However, by an illogical application of the work of Poincaré and of Lorentz, Einstein disastrously denied the existence of simultaneity and the need in physics for "absolutely stationary space."[87] No one seems to have done this explicitly before Einstein. The Michelson–Morley result generally had not been so interpreted.[88] In his early years, Einstein had a curious way of committing crashing errors and yet coming up at times with something highly important. This is a frequent peculiarity of creative people. In 1915, Einstein exemplified it in his sensationally successful explanation of the rate of advance of the perihelion of Mercury.[89] And that is not his only example. Since J. Soldner's proposal in 1801, it had been predicted that light waves, or light corpuscles, going past a gravitating body (such as the sun) would be deflected from their straight path as though they possessed mass and were gravitating according to Newton's law of gravitation. In 1911, Einstein made the same prediction on the basis of his own earlier theory. But in 1916, he doubled the amount of the expected light deflection.[90] His 1916 prediction was spectacularly confirmed in the solar eclipse of 1919. Since then, this result has been very thoroughly corroborated.[91] Recent results with radar waves have confirmed the matter beyond any question. Einstein made the prediction on the basis of his dogma of the constant velocity of light and his "curved space-time." By the early 1920s his successes (including his deserved successes in quantum mechanics) were generally accepted as phenomenal and, as textbooks prove, the scientific community began to look up to him as their master. As for counter-evidence to his *theory* (such as the logical demonstrations of its contradictions and the evidence against it from stellar aberration)—these were swept under the scientific rug in the new craze.

7. *Into the Mire*

Relativity theory has produced a morass of problems. It is now time to consider a constructive way out of these problems. Herbert Ives, in a series of meticulous studies, avoided the contradictions of Einstein by a sequence of analyses starting from the pre-Einsteinian, pre-Machian physics that I have previously described. Ives assumed, with Maxwell, that the velocity of light (c) occurred with reference to absolute space, *not* with reference to the generality of variously moving objects in space as Einstein had claimed. In his 1938 experiment on canal rays (hydrogen ions in tandem), Ives had become fully aware that the telling of time by clocks is retarded when they are in motion. By deduction from his experiment and Michelson's and Morley's, he affirmed the FitzGerald hypothesis that rods are contracted when in motion, in the direction of the motion, and along with any measuring tools. These two effects *precisely accounted* for the Michelson–Morley null result and that of similar experiments—mistakenly taken by relativists to deny the reality of space. Indeed, Ives stated that his 1938 experiment (plus FitzGerald's correct partial explanation of the Michelson–Morley result) "would have made it necessary to invent [absolute space]."[92] Ives' carefully reached opinion must be contrasted with the currently prevalent but erroneous view that the Michelson–Morley result disproved the existence of the "ether" or absolute space. One

273

can still find this error in almost any current textbook or encyclopedia.[93] Ives was aware of the self-contradictory nature of Einstein's "principle" of the absolute constancy of the velocity of light.[94] From all these facts, he became convinced that no explanation is possible without assuming that rods and clocks undergo their alterations with respect to their motion through absolute space and absolute time.[95]

Ives' experiment, and the FitzGerald contraction which was definitively deducible from it, directly verified the interpretation of the Lorentz transformation equations that moving clocks slow down and moving rods contract. Ives accepted these equations, though he subjected them to rigorous definitions not previously used.[96] Moreover, he performed the feat of deriving the FitzGerald contraction and the retardation of clocks theoretically from classical physics, including that of Maxwell, but without relying on the Michelson–Morley experiment. From there it was but one step for him to derive theoretically the Lorentz transformations also.[97] Einstein had claimed to derive the Lorentz transformations theoretically in his "Electrodynamics" paper in 1905. But his derivation was based on the untenable assumption that the velocity of light is constant to all observers independently of all conditions. In fact, Einstein committed a radical inconsistency in his derivation: he included in his equations expressions which explicitly violated his supposed principle of the constancy of the velocity of light. This is the conclusion of G. H. Keswani, among others.[98]

Ives saw fit to revise the Lorentz transformations, not because they were incorrect when properly interpreted, but because correct interpretation of the unrevised transformations meant the use of definitions which were not accessible to real physical operations.[99] Up until the Ives–Stilwell experiment in 1938, no unambiguous statement of the older hypotheses of FitzGerald, Larmor, and Lorentz could be made. Although these old hypotheses affirmed the existence of absolute space and time, they did not of themselves lead to a decision between at least three possible combinations of clock retardation and length contractions. It was the Ives–Stilwell experiment that ruled out all but one of these possibilities. From then on, one could refer to "the doubly amended ether theory" as the philosopher of science Adolf Grünbaum puts it, or to the *Ives Absolute Space and Time Theory* (as I find reason to call it, in view of Ives' voluminous experimental and theoretical work). In addition to (1) immovable three-dimensional space and (2) universal uniform time, this theory maintains that (3) moving clocks in fact slow down by a factor of $(1 - v^2/c^2)^{1/2}$ where v is the true velocity of a clock with respect to absolute space, and c is the true velocity of light with respect to absolute space (for small values of v/c the factor is about $1/2\ v^2/c^2$), (4) acceleration as ordinarily defined does not cause clocks to slow down, and (5) moving physical objects in fact contract in the direction of their motion by the same factor of $(1 - v^2/c^2)^{1/2}$.

The physics of Newton and Maxwell afford adequate grounds for the derivation of the factors in (3) and (5). The Lorentz transformations are in turn derivable from these factors. Ives' revisions of the Lorentz transformations enable apparent clock retardations to be calculated, since his formulas do not include the unknown quantities in (3) and (5). The combined operation of these numbered postulates entails a number of derived consequences. To an observer who is in uniform linear motion, all things will *appear* as though the observer's platform, whatever its absolute state of linear motion, is in the rest frame of absolute space (this amounts to Poincaré's principle of relativity). The rest frame of absolute space will be generally unidentifiable by any and all *observations*. The clocks traveling with any one uniformly moving spatial frame of reference will keep time at a uniform rate with respect to each other. This rate may be called the *proper time rate* for that reference frame, or for any other frame moving at the same absolute speed. There is no way that we can *know* whether the dial of a distant clock is set with absolute accuracy. Any clock setting can be known to be valid only for its own place. Knowledge of the accuracy of the settings of distant clocks is in practice subject to an arbitrary convention or stipulation which can never lead to the observation of true and absolute time as God perceives it. Light is always *measured* as traveling at the customary value of c, regardless of its true (absolute) velocity or the orientation of the observer's platform, or the direction or source of the light. Clocks in uniform motion relative to an observer will *appear* to run slow according to the expression in (3) above, where v is there taken as the relative velocity. However, a moving clock that is sent forth from, and returned to, a uniformly moving observer will *actually* have lost time due to its *extra velocity* (as demonstrated by Hafele and Keating). Most objects moving relative to an observer will appear distorted, at speeds close to that of light.[100]

Anyone would suppose that an acceptable theory of light, motion, space, and time would require that at some point we could somehow break Poincaré's principle of relativity long enough to *directly observe* our relation to the universe in terms of absolute space. Einstein said that there is no such relation in existence. Ives, and Poincaré before him, postulated that there is a logical necessity for such a relation but that we can never observe what it is. How, then, can Ives' program succeed? He presumed absolute space, a constant speed for light with respect to it, and the contractions of rods and retardation of clocks. Are these, then, all to be left hanging incoherently?

Fortunately, no. Ives tied it all up, despite the dismal surface appearances. On earth, in actually measuring the velocity of light over a measured course, our measuring instruments will have shrunk according to the FitzGerald contractions. Worse, as it seems, we do not know how much, because all of our measuring devices will have shrunk concomitantly and correspondingly. We could calculate how much they shrink if we knew how fast the earth were moving through absolute space. But on Poincaré's principle of relativity, accepted by Ives, this cannot be done.

Is it any better, then, with the measurement of time? No, because moving clocks slow down. Again, if we do not know how fast we are moving through absolute space, we do not know at what rate our clocks are slowing down.

The velocity of anything is the distance traversed divided by the time taken to traverse it (with close attention to definitions). Now, if we do not know absolutely how long our measuring rods are, or absolutely what time our clocks are keeping, then how can we know the absolute speed of anything—least of all, the speed of the earth moving through absolute space?

The genius of Ives brought order out of this perplexing situation. We may not know "where we are and whither we are tending," yet we are not lost. He freely grants that we have no way of observing what the absolute-space frame is or how fast we are moving with respect to it. But that is no bar to assuming that absolute space is real.[101] It turns out that all of the mathematical equations needed to make a *coherent* picture of physical reality are available without observationally knowing the particulars of the absolute space-frame or our relation to it. Through meticulous and lengthy algebra, Ives shows that our two-way measurements of the velocity of light are to be taken as true despite all these problems. Ives' equations show why we cannot observationally detect the real contractions that even our bodies undergo through their motion, or why clocks moving in any direction with respect to the earth slow down (even when the clocks must at times be moving against the real, though undetected, absolute motion of the earth). Ives shows why the measurement of the speed of light under every condition, even in a one-way measurement, will always come out c (*in vacuo* and away fram gravitational fields), and yet can be regarded as moving through absolute space at speed c. All the various contractions and additions of velocities and their concealments from us work together to achieve precisely this result—no matter which way our clocking course is pointing or how fast it is moving or in which direction. It is a beautifully coherent mathematical synthesis that Ives has reached.

But there is one complication. To measure the one-way speed of light, one must know what time it is at the far end of the clocking course. Atomic clocks are now of sufficient precision to be generally useful here. But the very carrying of the clock to the far end of the course will naturally slow it down while it is being carried. The faster it is carried, the more it will slow down over a given distance. After reaching its destination, a correction will ordinarily be made in the clock's reading. The transported clock is thereby set ahead enough to compensate for its retardation. Ives' way of stating this matter is different from mine and I think misleading.[102]

To understand Ives' theory we must perform a series of thought-experiments. In these experiments we assume (for the purpose of making our point) that (a) the rotations and revolutions of the earth are negligible, (b) the slowing effect of the atmosphere upon light is negligible, and (c) the effect of gravity upon clocks and upon light is negligible. Our first thought-experiment will assume that the earth is stationary in space, as well as non-rotating, both of which assumptions were taken as fact by the ancients. At our base of operations are two atomic clocks, synchronized. One of these clocks is transported to a distant mountain-top, by means of a jet plane which parachutes the clock down to the mountain. From our base with its stationary clock we send a light signal at a definite time, in order that a mountain-climbing observer may check the setting of the moved clock. The observer calculates the time taken by the light to travel to him, assuming that its speed wih respect to the earth is c. On this basis, he finds that the time shown on his clock during the trip has been slowed down by one billionth of a second. This result, he finds, corresponds to the prediction of Einstein that the transport of the clock would have slowed it down by about $1/2 \ v^2/c^2$ seconds per second of travel duration, where v is the velocity of the clock being transported in relation to the earth.

But what if, as is certain, the earth does *not* remain stationary in space? Einstein's theory would predict that the result of the experiment would still be the same regardless of any relative motions that may be introduced. According to Einstein, light does not travel with respect to absolute space because there is no such thing as absolute space. At this point, Ives would start a lengthy argument. To understand what the argument would be, we must think of reality as having three different levels of physical objectivity. The top level is the truly objective level, at which all events are seen with respect to the coordinates of absolute space during each moment of absolute time. This is the level which Ives infers but cannot measure. This level is now apparently inaccessible to our observation and is available only to God, though we are able to infer, with certainty, that it exists. We can call this the *divine level* of objectivity. The lowest of the three levels we may call the *Einsteinian level* of physical objectivity. This is the level I have just mentioned above. A third level is to be introduced between these two: the *options level* of objectivity. This assumes the truth of Ives' theory and all of its consequences. Ives calculates at this level and thus infers the divine level of objectivity. However, the options level turns out to be a pedagogical scaffolding. For it fails to touch the divine level (except in theory) because it does not allow us any basis for the *measurement* of absolute space and time. Nevertheless, we must work at this level in a series of thought-experiments in order to see that there exists a veiled, divine level which enables us to make sense of all of our observations.

From this point forward, I shall assume that the earth does *not* remain stationary in space. According to Poincaré's principle of relativity, accepted by both Einstein and Ives, the result of the above light-signal experiment would have to be the same as I have already stated, whether the earth is moving or not. Now Einstein's calculations remain as above, but what about Ives', at the options level of objectivity? We will find that the results of calculation are the same, regardless of what speed may be assigned to the earth's motion through space in our thought-experiment. Let us now imagine that the earth is moving through absolute space (ignoring any of its rotations or revolutions). Imagine that the absolute motion of the earth is in a direction away from the mountain as seen from our base of measuring operations. The clock is to be moved by jet plane, as before, to the mountain top. The clock's setting is to be checked by a light signal traveling from the base to the mountain top. But now, let us *imagine* that the earth is moving through space at the same absolute speed as the relative speed with which a jet plane flies through the atmosphere—say, 600 miles per hour (which is quite slow in comparison with the usual speeds of astronomical bodies). Let us suppose that the jet plane is ready to take off, on a runway pointing directly at the mountain. At that moment, the jet plane is being carried along backward (i.e., in the direction of its tail) by the 600-mile-per-hour absolute motion of the earth (as presumed in this thought-experiment at the options level of objectivity). Then, the plane becomes airborne and is heading toward the mountain at 200 miles per hour of air and ground speed (i.e., relative to the earth, *not* to absolute space). The plane is now impeded from traveling at 600 miles per hour (air speed) by its own inertia and the resistance of the atmosphere. Thus at that moment, the plane is moving *backward* at an absolute speed of 400 miles per hour. Not pondering the subtle spatial realities of his motion, the pilot thinks simply that he is going "forward" in space. But this is a perceptual error, an illusion due to his not making any distinction between relative and absolute motion. Of course, the plane has to force its way against the atmosphere. Although it is flying "into" or "through" the atmosphere, it actually is being carried along by the atmosphere faster than it is flying through it. But the plane continues to pick up air speed. The faster it goes in relation to the atmosphere and the earth, the *slower* it goes in relation to absolute space. This is true until it reaches a cruising speed of 600 miles per hour. Since the absolute speed of the atmosphere is 600 miles per hour, and the cruising speed of the plane relative to the atmosphere is 600 miles per hour, the two opposite speeds effectively cancel each other out. Consequently, the plane and the clock now are standing *still* in absolute space. Speaking conventionally, we say that the speed of the plane is 600 miles per hour, but that is in relation to the non-absolute co-ordinate system pegged to the earth and its entrained atmosphere. But speaking at the options level of objectivity in this thought-experiment, the clock and the plane are *at rest* in absolute space during the "trip" to the mountain top.

Parenthetically, some suppositions of this thought-experiment need to be restated or amplified. It is here presumed that the jet plane travels in a truly straight line, i.e., that the rotation of the earth on its axis may be ignored, as well as its revolution around its sun and the sun's revolution around the center of the Galaxy. Further, it is assumed that the curvature of the earth's surface may, over the slight distance to the mountain, be ignored as a factor determining the true path of the plane.

Would the clock actually go faster because it was standing still in absolute space? On the divine level of objectivity, it indeed would. Under that condition it would be keeping the absolute universal rate of time. But that result would appear to contradict the outcome of the Ives–Stilwell experiment, where the "clocks" were seen as slowing down due to their motion of transport relative to the earthbound apparatus of their experiment. Even his own experiment, Ives would say, did not tell the *absolute* speed of the canal rays (clustered hydrogen ions) which sped through his experimental apparatus. His canal rays might actually increase their true frequency of radiation in his apparatus if their motion were against the absolute motion of his apparatus, just as the clock while "being moved" to the mountain would appear to speed up if it were really standing still in space (relative to any moving framework). But either the canal rays or the moving clock would appear to earthbound observers as slowing down, whatever the absolute motions would be in God's view. Calculating on the options level of objectivity, the terrestrial speed of the light signal to set the moved clock would be c plus W, where W is the contrary speed of the earth through absolute space. Therefore, the light signal would arrive at the mountain clock faster than an Einsteinian calculation would indicate, for an Einsteinian calculation assumes simply a speed of c for light. Thus, on the options level, the light signal would reach the mountain clock sooner than predicted by Einsteinian calculations, and hence, would make the clock *look* slow. Full calculation on the options level of objectivity shows that the time interval by which the light signal would beat the speed of c would be just twice that which the mountain clock gained through its being stopped in space during its "trip." Subtracting the speeding-up effect from the apparent slowing-down effect leaves us, then, with a net apparent slowing down of just what the Einsteinian calculation indicated. No matter how God might perceive the actual motions and time, the experiment comes out the same for all perceiving human beings: the clock moved to the mountain *appears* to have lost the same amount of time. This fact may seem confusing, on first analysis, but the key to the explanation is simple. To understand, one has to suppose that light moves with respect to absolute space, rather than with respect to the earth. Naturally, different combinations of the assumed speed of the earth and the speed of the clock transport would yield different results. In a series of thought-experiments, one may assign to the earth any absolute velocity W one chooses, this side of c. The measured clock retardation calculated by Einstein's equation will come out the same when calculated according to the options-level calculations of Ives. Mathematically, the reason is simple. In Ives' final equations, the symbol W for the absolute velocity of the earth does not appear. It has dropped out during his derivations of the equations.

8. *Out of the Mire*

The reader will note that in our thought-experimenting we assigned, or opted for, some definite value of W, the velocity of the earth. Again, there is apparently no way we could observe the truth, or the divine evaluation of, any assigned velocity or its real consequences. We can opt for this or that linear velocity of the earth as an illustration but, whichever velocity we opt for, there is no known way our option could be validated or reveal to us the one-way speed of light as it is known by God. We can measure how much our state of motion *changes*—the aberration in the apparent position of the stars tells us that—but we do not know the absolutely preferred spatial reference frame in relation to which the earth moves. No one can tell it just like it is, because no one knows just how it is. Our last clear hope for finding out—the measurement of the one-way velocity of light—turns out to tell us nothing because an infinity of conflicting interpretations is possible on the options level of objectivity, to which we apparently are bound. If we assume that we are at rest in absolute space, or if we assume with Einstein that absolute space does not matter, then we measure the one-way velocity of light as c, on either assumption. If we assume that we are in some specific state of motion W in absolute space and adjust our measurements accordingly, then the one-way velocity of light going contrary to that motion measures as c plus W, no matter what value of W we have opted for. Thus, we learn nothing about either our absolute motion or the measured one-way speed of light, because any motion W we opt for implies some one-way measured speed of light. And that particular measured speed implies the same absolute motion W. There appears to be no escape from this circle. We still are left with no way of knowing which spatial reference frame is the one with respect to which the light moves at its standard speed.

This begins to sound like Einstein again. But this is *merely where Einstein started*. Indeed, Poincaré had stated the same argument in brief.[103] Einstein went on to stipulate that the speed of light (relative to any object) was to be assumed as the same in any direction in which it moves. This was the basis for his unfortunate denial of the existence of real simultaneity.[104]

Einstein almost snatched truth from the error in his self-contradictory stipulation. What he ought to have said was that the speed of light may *for practical purposes be regarded* as being the same in both directions or in any direction, whatever its actual speed. For that is the way our *measurements* come out (c) unless we complicate the determination of speed, etc., by assuming otherwise (c plus W) *uselessly*. Why uselessly? Because we obtain no new quantitative information thereby. What we *did* do by trying options for the absolute speed of the earth and the corresponding one-way speeds for light was to demonstrate the *coherence* of the Ives theory. Any assumption which we might make about the absolute speed and direction of the earth, about the traveling clock, or about the interpretation of light-speed measurements enabled the Ives theory to yield coherent predictions. Beyond that, we showed ourselves the practical uselessness of assuming any speed other than c for light, even in one-way speed reckonings (allowing the usual adjustments for gravity and for refractive media).[105] Assuming speeds other than c for light revealed nothing measurable that we did not already know, either with regard to absolute measurements or practical measurements.

Thus, we still cannot find out *where* the earth is going or *how fast*. Hence, one may *pretend, for practical purposes*, that the earth partakes of no absolute linear motion. Our calculations are much simpler if we do thus pretend, since we then deal with quantities as conventionally measured. The assumption or option of some definite absolute linear motion would be, not wrong, but empty —that is, it would not be practically useful. For practical purposes, we should do our clock calculations by following the operations of Einstein's examples, in which the speed of the observer does not enter into the calculations. This conclusion is one result of our thought-experiments. Yet the one great result is not absolute measurement. Rather, the thought-experiments show that the reality of absolute space and time enables us to make *coherent sense* of the physical universe *as no other theory does*.

Einstein could have had his cake and eaten it, too. He could have allowed the existence of absolute space through which light travels, while at the same time he could have said that we may, when it suits our practical convenience, pretend that the earth has no absolute linear motion. He could have held that our experiments on that assumption would cohere. He could have maintained that we may synchronize our clocks using the procedure he recommended, that is, Poincaré's way, which was to assume, or rather pretend, that a light signal takes the same time to travel out to a clock as to bounce back from it.[106] A definition of simultaneity on such assumptions would have entailed no contradiction and no flight from physical reality. In this way it would be possible to haul all of the rubbish out of Relativity—so much so, however, that the resulting theory would require a new name: the Ives Absolute Space and Time Theory. This appears to be the only theory which accounts for all of the phenomena and makes sense, i.e., logically coheres. Einstein's Special Relativity does not.

From the present vantage-point we may recall the "null cones" of Minkowski. Under Einstein's definition of simultaneity it was shown that the cones were self-destructive entities. But now, I submit that Minkowski's geometry and his cones and hyperboloids can be of continuing interest to science, provided that the concepts constituting them are carefully redefined (just as Ives' revision of the Lorentz transformations resulted in a coherent system that is fully compatible with absolute space and time). If the reader will refer back to the null-cone diagram, he will see that I have introduced "the plane of the true present." This plane of universal simultaneity always includes any observer where he is now. Thus, the universal present passes through the apex of the observer's null cone. In general, the plane of the true present will not be square with the axes of the diagram. These axes represent space and time as they appear to us, not allowing for unknown contractions of measuring rods or slowing down of clocks. This new plane would be squarely oriented with the axes of the diagram only if the observer were at rest in absolute space. The plane of the true present is a divine-level concept, since we cannot know what its slope is or what is actually going on now at a very distant location. Our knowledge of what goes on at a distance is dependent on the light signals that give us a picture of what *has* occurred. To some degree or other, the light signals always reach us *after* the event has transpired. The time that has lapsed since the event actually occurred is dependent upon how fast the light signals have moved in space to convey to us the image of the event. But, as we have seen, the speed of light in relation to an observer moving in space is not in general *c*. Plainly put, this means that we have difficulty in knowing exactly *when* a distant event occurred. In this respect, what are the limits to our ability to know when an event occurred? The limits to one's knowledge are determined by the sides of one's "null cone." Specifically, the plane of the universal present for an observer includes himself (here and now) and has a definite angular orientation or slope to the axes of the null cone diagram. But we cannot know what that orientation is. The range of theoretical possibilities for the orientation of this plane are bounded by one's null cone; that is, the plane of the true present cannot be so steeply inclined as to pass inside this cone. It passes only through the apex.

Referring again to the Minkowski diagram, a *horizontal* plane that passes through the apex of one's null cone includes of course the present where one is, but in general it does not include the true present at other places. What such a horizontal plane does include is all of those events which later appear to have been in our present provided we assume or pretend that we are at rest in absolute space and that this horizontal plane in the diagram is the plane of the true present. We say that the star Arcturus is about forty light years away. The 1933 Chicago World's Fair was opened by means of a light ray coming in from Arcturus. The ray was presumed to have left the star forty years before, in 1893. But is Arcturus really forty light years away from us? Did the ray really leave there in 1893? We don't know. What we do know is that one coherent picture, convenient for us to use, is assembled if we take some convenient reference frame such as that defined by the local surface of the earth. Or we can take the earth's center, or the sun's center. Or we can use the center of the Milky Way, or rotationally speaking, the bearings of the farthest detectable galaxies. We may choose one of these frames depending on our purposes and then pretend (1) that it is at rest in space, (2) that light moves through this space at speed c, (3) that our clocks and other clocks in this reference frame tell real time (our "proper time"), (4) that our length measurements are real, such as that of a long surveyor's base line on earth, and (5) that our triangulations from that base line out to the sun and again to Arcturus to determine its distance are valid. These are not the only coherent pictures that can be assembled on the Ives Theory. But among them, we might as well pretend one to be true. Which one we pretend to be true depends on what we are doing, for example, on whether we are designing an earthbound machine or surveying the universe. We might as well so pretend, since we can never know the difference, if Poincaré's principle of relativity holds up. Moreover, it is the simplicity of such pictures which makes physical science possible.

I shall now attempt to say what I believe Einstein *should* have said about his famous thought-experiment involving the railway train on the embankment.[107] I shall at first proceed on the divine level of objectivity; i.e., I shall pretend, contrary to fact, that we know what the rest frame of absolute space is and that the railway embankment is at rest in it. Given that much, we would know that light really travels at the usual value of c and does not merely appear to do so. Our clocks and rulers measure truthfully when they are not moving. Non-moving clocks in different places could be truly synchronized by light rays in the manner known to Poincaré and to Einstein. That is, the time for a round trip of a light ray to any mirror and back is half occupied in going out and half occupied in coming back. The embankment is absolutely at rest. An observer, a stationmaster, stands on the embankment as a train goes by. Lightning now strikes the embankment at two places at exactly the same instant. One stroke hits the embankment ahead of the train, a mile from the stationmaster. The other stroke hits behind the train, a mile from the stationmaster. The stationmaster records the flashes as reaching him at the same instant. Knowing the strokes to be equidistant from him, and knowing that light travels at speed c in his absolute reference frame, he correctly declares the strokes to be simultaneous. Meanwhile, a passenger on the train is exactly alongside the stationmaster at the instant that the lightning strokes hit. But by the time the flashes reach the train passenger, the train has moved a little. Thus the flashes do not reach him at the same instant. Will this passenger nevertheless agree with the station-master that the flashes occurred simultaneously? He will agree, provided he accepts the supposition that the embankment is at rest in absolute space. That is, he will agree, provided he calculates in the same stationary frame as the stationmaster. He can calculate the time taken by the light to reach the mid-point between the strokes, performing his calculations with reference to the station-ary frame, where the velocity of light not only *measures* to the stan-dard value c but truly has the value c. The elapsed time agrees with that figured by the stationmaster, since the passenger has taken into account the contraction of his own measuring rods and the slowing of his own clocks. He calculates how far his train has moved in the meanwhile, again calculating in the rest frame of the embankment. He finds that the distance traveled figures the same as it did for the stationmaster. In this way, he discovers for himself that the light-ning strokes were in truth simultaneous, that they struck the em-bankment at the same instant. He admits that his perception of them as being non-simultaneous was due to his not being station-ary in the rest frame of the embankment—that is, of absolute space. So far, there is no problem.

But now, let us suppose that the passenger on the train is a foot-loose young rebel, determined to overthrow old theories if he can. He decides that there is no way to know which rest frame is the true rest frame. He refuses to take this divine-level talk as the last word. Therefore, he says, the train may as well be taken as the ref-erence frame. In that case, the embankment is moving, not the train. Another experiment is conducted. But in the new experiment the lightning strokes hit in such a way that the stationmaster *sees* them as simultaneous (whatever the true state of affairs). This time it is he who must do his calculating in the frame of reference of the passenger on the train, since now it is the embankment that is mov-ing. On the train, the two strokes appear to be non-simultaneous, as before. But the passenger receives the stationmaster's report that the strokes appeared simultaneous to him. Perplexed, the passenger calculates. He notes that he was alongside the stationmaster at the instant the stationmaster said both flashes occurred. The passenger further notes that the light of the reportedly simultaneous flashes (occurring when he was midway between them) should have reached him at the same time since it would, by any measurement made from the train, travel at equal velocity with respect to the train (his reference frame). This is simply the way that we *observe* the behavior of light. The passenger correctly dismisses the idea that the motion of the lightning strokes could have affected his perception, for all physicists are correctly agreed that the velocity of light is independent of the velocity of its source. That is, the air caught in the path of the electrical discharges is ionized and heated and thus radiates light. This air is moving with the embankment. But the air's motion does not affect the speed of light radiated from it. The passenger concludes that if the flashes had occurred simultaneously, they would have reached him at the same time. But since they did not reach him at the same time, they could not have occurred simultaneously, no matter what the stationmaster might have supposed. The passenger sends a message to the stationmaster, expressing his discrepancy of perception. Then the stationmaster calculates, using the train as a stationary reference frame. The stationmaster performs his calculations in the same manner as the passenger did in the previous experiment and finds that the lightning flashes indeed were not simultaneous. He admits that his perception of them as simultaneous was an illusion.

Now, let us imagine that the stationmaster rebels and declares that his own choice of a reference frame is at least as good as that of the passenger. The stationmaster then checks his own calculations from the previous experiment. Again, he decides that the two strokes were simultaneous, on the assumption that the embankment was the rest frame in both experiments. This contradicts the passenger's report in the second experiment, which was based on the train as the rest frame of reference.

Thus, here is the predicament: when one chooses to describe the events is one inertial frame, the events *appear* to be simultaneous. But when another inertial frame is used for description of *the self-same events*, they *appear* not to be simultaneous but successive. There is no way to decide which frame ought to be used for description. This problem follows partly from the fact that light always is *measured* as moving at the same speed (minor corrections aside). In this impasse, Is it not sensible to assume (as Einstein in effect did) that light always moves at the same speed with reference to any observer? Further, Is it not sensible to assume (again, as Einstein did) that there is no such thing as simultaneity (especially between distant events)—that simultaneity is purely relative, and depends upon one's choice of reference frames? In their seeming elegance, such assumptions are devilishly tempting, as the history of physics in the twentieth century proves. Nevertheless, they cannot be maintained. At the beginning, I showed how the assumption that light always travels at the same speed leads immediately to flat contradictions, and how these in turn spawn all manner of esoteric nonsense. Moreover, I presented logical reasons why the existence of universal simultaneity (i.e., of a universal instant) could not be denied. Any argument about dynamical physics presupposes simultaneity as a *sine qua non* for a sensible discussion of time. I have shown that the universal denial of simultaneity is a self-contradictory assertion, not to mention its corrosive effects on faith and morals. Is there then "no actual truth of the matter"? To escape this predicament, all that has to be done is to adopt the Ives Absolute Space and Time Theory. In this theory, the train problem must be discussed and resolved in only one reference frame. For when we do this, no paradox arises.

It is tempting to pursue the matter through detailed examples. But that would carry us beyond my present purpose. As Lovejoy has shown beyond the ghost of a doubt, it is simply an apodictic truth that *all* events going on *anywhere* are going on now; and hence, all actually occurring events are simultaneous.[108] The fact remains, however, that we are very limited in what we can know about what is *presently* going on at great distances from us. Also, we are very limited in our ability to know at what true time (absolute time) certain past events occurred at great distances from us. As I have shown already, Minkowski's "null cones" can be used to reduce the whole of history to a universally static present. But this is the case only if one uses the cones with the mistaken assumption of the relativists that there is no absolute simultaneity throughout the universe.

In the 1952 appendix to his book *Relativity*, Einstein wrote: "Since the special theory of relativity revealed the physical equivalence of all inertial systems, it proved the untenability of the hypothesis of an aether at rest."[109]

This is a double error. First, the equivalence of all inertial systems of reference for the performance of physical experiments was shown, not by the Special Theory of Relativity, but earlier by Henri Poincaré's principle of relativity, as I have related. Secondly, the physical equivalence of all inertial systems did not prove the untenability of an "ether" or of absolute space. As has been demonstrated herein, we do not need to know which frame is the rest frame of absolute space in order to determine its logical necessity.[110]

A reader may well ask: But doesn't this replacement of Einstein's work look a bit pale when you haven't come to grips with his General Theory (the theory that deals with accelerated motion as well as uniform motion)?

Ives' theoretical work has met this challenge. Einstein used the principle of equivalence (or covariance) as a foundation for his General Theory. Ives countered Einstein's recklessly generalized principle of equivalence with his own *restricted principle of equivalence*—the equivalence of gravitational and kinetic energy. By this empirically verifiable principle, "*all* the phenomena of a gravitational field are comprised in the assumption that a body stationary in a gravitational field assumes the dimensions, clock rate, and mass of a body at the same point in a Newtonian field, moving with the velocity acquired in falling from infinity under the Newtonian law of attraction."[111]

Ives' restricted principle of equivalence was sufficient to derive what is called the Schwarzschild "metric," usually associated with Einstein's General Theory (Ives preferred to call it the Schwarzschild formula). Taking the correction factor so deduced and justifying its application to mass, Ives resolved the discrepancy in the orbit of Mercury that Einstein had first resolved in 1916. *Ives assumed no so-called "warped" or "curved" space.* Rather, he calculated the increased mass of Mercury due to its speed and to its presence in an intense gravitational field (that of the sun), both of which factors vary at different points of the non-circular orbit. Assuming *Newton's* law of gravitational attraction and the laws of conservation of energy and momentum (including angular momentum) Ives arrived at the *same* result as that of Einstein. The mathematics either way is a bit complicated, but conceptually, Ives' way is easy compared to Einstein's way.

Ives' restricted principle of equivalence readily comprehends the bending and slowing of light and radar waves, which are phenomena I have previously described. Again, *no resort is made to "curved space"* etc. Rather, Ives assumed in 1939 that the bending occurred as a result of the *slowing down* of light in gravitational fields. This was something that Eddington, though a relativist, had done in 1920.[112] Even Einstein talked this way up to around that time. The explanation for this bending of light in a gravitational field is simple. Suppose that a beam of light is going past the sun. The part of the beam that is nearer to the sun will be slowed more than the more distant part of the beam, since the gravity is more intense nearer to the sun. This disparity in retardation *tilts* the light waves, rather as though the sun were replaced by a giant lens, for light also effectively slows down in lenses. That is why lenses refract. Indeed, the process in either case can be described as one of refraction.[113]

Recently, there has been much publicity about radar tests that have measured the slowing and bending effect of the sun's gravitation on radar waves. The radar waves were sent from earth past the sun to a planet, or spacecraft, that was almost behind the sun as seen from the earth. The radar signal was bounced back or was transponded at once, and the time of transit proved to be predictably slower than that of beams passing at slightly greater distances from the sun's limb. The results corroborate both Einstein's theory and Ives' theory. But it is always only Einstein's General Theory of Relativity that is being confirmed, if one were to believe the newspapers. This very day, in 1977, as I write, a clipping from the *Washington Post* of 7 January arrived with the headline: "Einstein Relativity Theory Confirmed by Viking Test." In this article one is told that "countless physicists have tried to disprove it [Einstein's theory] and have failed." But since Ives' Absolute Space and Time Theory yields results *precisely identical* to Einstein's predictions (in the standard interpretation of Einstein) it is hard to see how Ives could have been disproved by any experiment, although the theories of other contenders may well have been. As usual, *no one seems to know of Ives' theories.* The *Washington Post* story has been often repeated, with a general lack of knowledge about Ives betrayed by most scientists in the titles of their own articles.[114]

9. On Untangling "Simplicity"

In preferring Ives' restricted principle of equivalence and its consequences over Einstein's General Relativity Theory, I do not mean to belittle Einstein's contribution. Non-creative people are apt to overlook the efforts, the skills, the time, the courage required to be the *first* to do something important—to stand where no one has stood before. Einstein was first, however odd his methods. That Ives could improve on Einstein's work is a tribute to both men.

As to Einstein's theory of gravitation, I quote a paper of his dated 1920: "The question whether gravitation theory may be set forth and established without the principle [i.e., theory] of relativity is doubtless to be answered in principle with '*Ja!*'"[115]

Einstein's assumed justification for nonetheless adhering to his theory of relativity was made in two parts. First, he said (I paraphrase him): Every nonrelativistic way of describing physical events or states of affairs in space and time entails a problem, namely, that the expressions for describing the events or states become mixed up with expressions for the means of description, i.e., with some system of spatial coordinates. The suitability of this coordinate system, Einstein continued, is presupposed along with the suitability of some definition of time. But he did not go on to tell, here or elsewhere, how one can possibly describe physical events when he himself had already ruled out any intelligible framework of space and time with reference to which events might be said to occur here or there, or before, during, or after. I pass at once, therefore, to his second objection to any non-relativistic theory. He wrote further: "Of two theories which prove correct in an actual totality of experience in an area, that one is to be preferred which has need of the fewest hypotheses that are independent of each other." Again, he stated in 1933: "Our experience hitherto justifies us in believing that nature is the realization of the simplest conceivable mathematical ideas."[116]

This issue of simplicity has often attracted philosophers of science. Adolf Grünbaum, German-born philosopher of science, attacked Ives' paper "Revisions of the Lorentz Transformations" in 1955.[117] Ives had died in 1953. However, Grünbaum's critique had already in effect been devastated by Lovejoy's forgotten 1930 article, which I alluded to earlier.[118] By 1973, Grünbaum acknowledged that the doubly amended ether theory (as he called part of what I am naming the Ives Theory) has altogether *the same predictive power* as Einstein's relativity theory. Further, in his latest position, Grünbaum retreated to claiming merely that Ives' theory is *ad hoc* in that it has an assumption (absolute space) in its foundation which he deemed it impossible ever to empirically verify. Also, he complained that Ives' theory predicts nothing in the way of feasible experiments and observable results that Einstein's theory did not already predict. Grünbaum argued that Einstein's theory is less complicated since it assumes less and therefore has less to experimentally establish or verify.[119]

All scientists and philosophers of science are familiar with the maxim that, of competing theories, the most valid theory generally turns out to be the simplest one, that is, the one that is most economical and has the smallest number of assumptions in it that are not susceptible to empirical verification. This falls under what is generally known as the principle of Ockham's Razor. Simplicity appeals to many excellent and ambitious minds in much the way that symmetry does.[120] However, the Argentinian-born philosopher of science Mario Bunge has very plainly shown, in his little book *The Myth of Simplicity*, how simplistic and naive it is to assume that the most scientifically valid theory always turns out to be the least intricate.[121] Bunge's statement of Ockham's Razor reads: "Conceptual entities should not be multiplied *in vain*."[122] Grünbaum apparently had Ockham's Razor in mind in objecting to the one postulate of the Ives theory that appeared to him arbitrary and insusceptible to scientific observation or testing, namely, the existence of absolute space.

In fact, however, Grünbaum is mistaken. I have mentioned the Sagnac and Michelson–Gale experiments, which support absolute space (with respect to rotation) as distinctly as ever could be required. Stellar aberration is plainly visible with a solidly, accurately mounted amateur's telescope and half a year's patience. Finally, we have seen that Einstein could not succeed in explaining away the commoner evidence from Newton's rotating bucket experiment and from everyday experience with accelerations. How much testing do you want, Mr. Grünbaum?

I contrast the assumption of absolute space to Einstein's *arbitrary stipulation* that the speed of light is to be taken as *in fact* the constant c under any conditions of motion whatsoever. Here is an hypothesis of the most high-handed nature—grounded in the illogical assumption that a contradiction must be accepted as the truth. Einstein is correct in stating that the velocity of light always will *show up* as c in our *measurements* of it. Or to put it as simply as possible, he states that physical realities in the real world absolutely *are* the same as they *appear to be* to the observing or measuring person. Einstein confuses what he is *actually* doing with what he believes himself to be doing. He believes that he is measuring the velocity of light directly, while he ignores the fact that the results of his measurements have to be analyzed and interpreted in the light of a logical assessment of the actual physical state of affairs in which he is conducting his measurement. Amongst experts in the psychology and methodology of testing, it is considered that the results of a test will always be affected by the stipulations of the tester about the nature of the thing that is being tested. Moreover, the results of any testing are definitely conditioned by the methodology of testing that is used. Einstein's methodology is scientific in that he calls for laboratory hardware to test out his assumptions, but it is *unscientific* in that his starting assumptions are purely *ad hoc* and not derived from the application of any scientific procedures whatever. *All* tests that presume to *directly* measure the speed of light with objective accuracy plainly are subjective and presumptuous in their nature. I can think of nothing more unscientific than the audacious assumption that things always *are*, in objective fact, the way they *appear* to be in the subject's logically unanalyzed perception of them. Equating reality with appearances is a mistake generally regarded in this twentieth century of our Lord as too naive for words. Albeit, this is precisely the naiveté resting at the very foundation of this revered theory that relativizes space and time. On the other hand, Ives' Theory of Absolute Space and Time arrives at the same results as the standard tests and measurements of the relativists but analyzes and interprets them in the context of the logical framework of absolute space and time. This leads to the construction of a *coherent* picture of the actual world of mechanics and light. Of course, by "coherent" I mean logically consistent or free from internal contradictions. Not only is Ives' theory free from internal contradictions, but also it is in conformity with all of the established facts of physics and sound theory-building methodology.

Now, Which is the more arbitrary hypothesis, that of the logically contradictory assumption that the velocity of light is universally constant and yet relative, or the empirically testable and verifiable assumption that the speed of light is governed by the ethereal laws in absolute space?

Any notion of the objective velocity of light is meaningless unless we presuppose that absolute space contains coordinates that are immobile or fixed. These coordinates are of course invisible to the eye. But they are not invisible to the mind, and in fact, it is impossible to have a theoretically sound geometry unless we turn to those truths discernible only in the mind's eye. The motion and velocity of a light beam can have an objective value only if the motion is related to coordinates having an objective status in the world—having an absolute status in absolute space. In other words, the objective value of light cannot be determined by the measurement of it unless the measurements are somehow referred to immovable spatial coordinates. Otherwise, the objective truthfulness of one's measurement is vitiated by the presumption that the velocity can be measured merely through the subjective perception of it in the observer's eye, independently of any objectively preferred spatial frame of reference. The major mistake in Einstein's theory of relativity is precisely its denial that there is any possible objectively preferred set of coordinates. That is, relativity theory denies that there are coordinates that exist in reality and are what they are, are where they are, and are spatially related to each other in an actual objective way no matter how accurately or inaccurately we may subjectively perceive them. Poincaré, originator of the original principle of relativity, may be right in having claimed that the three-dimensional coordinates of real space are not amenable to our apprehension through direct observation. However, while I of course readily grant that no one can see points in space that do not displace space as do material bodies, the fact remains that we can have no logically coherent concept of space without presupposing the objective reality of ideal coordinates. While we admittedly cannot physically observe that which is physically unobservable, the empirical result of Sagnac's experiment calls indisputably for the recognition of objective coordinates of real space by logical inference. As Newton and Kant have shown, to have an internally consistent geometry, we have to logically presuppose these fixed coordinates, *apriori*. But for those who refuse to deal in *apriori* assumptions, and presume to be governed in their thinking solely by the dictates of empirically established facts, there now can be no way to escape having to affirm absolute space. The reason for this is simple: the established results of Sagnac's experiment can be logically explained only from the standpoint of the assumption of the objective coordinates of absolute space. This is true, no matter whether we presuppose *apriori* the existence of absolute space, or arrive at the conclusion of its existence through logical inference. I now set Grünbaum's objection aside.

Poincaré's principle of relativity (the statement of our impotence to observe absolute linear uniform motion) is not here at issue. Nor is clock retardation or rod contraction here at issue. Poincaré's principle of relativity and the postulate of clock retardation in motion have had much empirical justification which clearly *implies* the validity of the postulate of rod contraction. In any case, all three of the postulates are consistent with both Einstein's and Ives' theory.

It is essential to recognize that there are many kinds of simplicity, as Bunge goes to great pains to explain. One ingredient categorically essential to true scientific simplicity is logical coherency. Ives' Absolute Space and Time Theory involves no more physically unverifiable assumptions than Einstein's, but it is logically coherent. Relativity is a logical outrage. There is no complication greater than a logical contradiction, as I have demonstrated earlier. As Lovejoy has shown, if physical reality were as illogical as Einstein portrays it to be in his Special Theory, then science itself would be impossible.[123]

Newton stated Ockham's Razor thus: "We are to admit no more causes of natural things than such as are both true and sufficient to explain their appearances."[124] Clearly, the existence of absolute space is both true and indispensable for explaining the appearances. Some will find objectionable the unusual complexity of the equations in Ives' revisions of the Lorentz transformations, published in 1951. It is not enough to retort that this is just the way nature is. To state the matter more accurately, the complexity of these revised equations (as compared to the generally accepted and limiting Poincaré version) is not the complexity of nature *per se*; rather, it results from our materially limited ability to observe objective reality directly and accurately by means of our subjective measurements. After all, we do have finite minds, finite sense organs of perception, and we have to probe nature with tools and measuring instruments containing only a finite capacity for accurately measuring reality. In any case, Einsteinians are in no position to complain of the complexity that might arise from the basic assumptions of a theory. Surely, they have set an all-time record for entanglement in that respect.

Nordenson, apropos of Einstein's mathematics and definitions in his General Theory, wrote: "Neither Einstein nor anybody else can know anything about the physical meaning of all these formulae. They are all mathematical constructions without known physical meaning."[125] On the other hand, Ives' mathematics is not only physically meaningful (associable with actual physical operations and concepts) but also is mostly accessible even to mathematically inclined 16-year-olds. Ives was attempting to be intelligible and understandable.

After a thorough analysis of the concept of simplicity, Bunge's practical advice to theory constructors is: "Occam's razor, like all razors, should be handled with care to prevent beheading science in the attempt to shave off some of its pilosities. In science, as in the barber shop, better alive and bearded than cleanly shaven but dead."[126] Bunge's book can be used as an effective answer to Grünbaum's flimsy objection to Ives' Absolute Space and Time Theory. By any appropriate concept of scientific simplicity, Ives' theory merits immediate adoption by scientists.

10. A Scientific Priesthood

At this point an alert reader may well ask: "If Einstein's critics are so smart, then why didn't they come up with the equation that $E = mc^2$?" As understood first by Einstein, the equation $E = mc^2$ asserts, in principle, an equivalence between mass and energy, with the astronomical amount of c^2 to indicate the magnitude of energy theoretically realizable from a small amount of mass. My review of the development of this equation will retrace a pattern we have observed before, namely, that Einstein was a genius at arriving at amazingly bold and correct predictions by means of wrongheaded theories.

The concept of the interchangeability of mass and energy was the work of several hands during a period of thirty years. In 1881, J. J. Thomson calculated that an electrostatically charged spherical conductor behaves, when in motion, as though it possesses an additional mass equal to 4/3 the energy of its electrostatic field divided by c^2.[127] In 1905, months before Einstein's famous paper appeared, Fritz Hasenöhrl published his calculations, which yielded the same result but with respect to electromagnetic radiation in a reflecting box.[128] As it proved, these conclusions were both wrong by the factor 4/3. However, one should note that 4/3 is a rather small factor when compared to its accompanying factor c^2 which, in conventional metric units using meters and seconds, is 90 quadrillion. Hasenöhrl's work was preceded by Poincaré's speculations in 1900, wherein he opined that light kicks backward on its source in the process of being emitted by the source, just as a cannon jumps backward when firing a projectile. Poincaré's theory was that light has only a virtual mass, some mysterious quality which acts like mass in equations of impulse and momentum. Poincaré stated his opinion in an equation of his own, from which the equation $E = mc^2$ could be derived by any alert physics student. This priority was acknowledged by Einstein in 1906.[129] In 1901 the physicist Walter Kaufmann showed experimentally that fast-moving electrons acted as though their mass had increased owing to their motion.[130] However, no one before Einstein in 1905 seems to have seriously proposed that the m in the equation could mean real mass. In his second famous paper of 1905, Einstein purported to derive the equation $E = mc^2$ (expressed by him as change of mass being equal to change of energy divided by c^2). Unfortunately, his derivation was defective, as Ives has demonstrated conclusively. There was a circularity that *entirely* nullified the mathematical work. Ives' paper should be read by all interested parties.[131] A correct derivation of $E = mc^2$ was not published until 1907, and then it came from Max Planck.[132]

It would have been generous if Einstein had given credit in print to his fellow workers on this matter. My search did not turn up such deference, except as noted above. But what primarily concerns us here is whether the equation $E = mc^2$ depends uniquely on Einstein's theories. Einstein implied that it did.[133] Ives showed clearly that it does not. In its full meaning of interchangeability of mass and energy, *the equation $E = mc^2$ is readily derivable apart from the theory of relativity.* Such a derivation has in fact been achieved. The simplest treatment was that of Wolfgang Pauli in 1920.[134]

As I have shown, it was only in 1938 that a rival theory to that of relativity matured into an unambiguous statement at the hands of Ives. By that time, Einstein was apotheosized. Speaking to a reporter, Einstein lauded the Ives–Stilwell experiment as the most direct proof that had been brought forth in support of *relativity*.[135] An editorial the same day was titled, "Einstein Triumphs Again."[136] So far as I have been able to determine, Einstein after that never again publicly mentioned Ives or his theoretical work. It cannot be said by way of excuse that Einstein was ignorant of Ives' theoretical work. A relative of Ives told me that Ives had a number of friendly meetings with Einstein, some at Princeton and others at scientific conferences, at which Ives' theoretical work was discussed.

Strictly on the face of it, the Ives–Stilwell experiment supports equally either relativity or the Absolute Space and Time Theory of Ives. Nevertheless, by discreet silences, Einstein allowed both scientists and laymen to come to believe that this experiment supported relativity and nothing else. Was this stealing? No, not actively. It is better called passive kidnaping. We have seen (from newspaper and journal reports on the radar-beam delay experiments) how such petty politics in science continues vigorously even to the present time—with Einstein long since in his grave. But it is high time that these experimental children, as it were, knew their rightful parents. Ives died in honor for his *distinctly great experimental and engineering achievements*, which included Wirephoto and the first public demonstration of television.[137] But his credit for fundamental contributions in theory evidently were quite neglected until an article by Herman Erlichson appeared in 1973. This article should be consulted by anyone who is seriously interested in studying relativity.[138]

I now vent my opinions on some standard literature. For example, Martin Gardner, a scientific journalist, published in 1962 a very popular and influential book, *Relativity for the Million*, with polished writing style and admirable illustrations. Indeed, it does contain an excellent view of the Michelson–Morley interferometer[139] Albeit, like the generality of writers, Gardner revealed no knowledge of Ives, a fact which made it easier for him to misunderstand the Kennedy–Thorndike experiment, and consequently, to falsely rule out the entire FitzGerald contraction approach, with ridicule.[140] Neither did he show any knowledge of the very consequential experiment of Michelson and Gale. Sagnac's experiment was not mentioned at all. The reviews of Gardner's book that were summarized in *Book Review Digest 1963* were all favorable. However, the book commits about all of the technical and logical errors that relativists are apt to commit. Gardner published his book two years after Pound, Rebka, and Sherwin published evidence that destroyed his hypothesis. The book remained in print for fourteen years.

Recently, Gardner has written a partly new book entitled *The Relativity Explosion* in which he repeats the same old errors of his *Relativity for the Million*.[141] He addresses himself to some new topics such as quasars, pulsars, and black holes, saying that these new data further vindicate Einstein's theory, though without explaining how. The same poor scholarship is revealed by the fact that he is still *totally* ignorant of Ives, and consequently still misinterprets the Kennedy–Thorndike experiment. At this late date, this is hard to excuse. To guarantee that future writers on the subject can no longer have any excuses for their ignorance of Ives, I have co-edited the complete collection of his works on relativity, entitled *The Ives Papers*, which is a one-volume work published simultaneously with the present book.

Gardner correctly critiques some errors in Lovejoy's attack on the twin paradox in Lovejoy's article "The Paradox of the Time-Retarding Journey." However, he does not even mention Lovejoy's 1930 article, "The Dialectical Argument against Absolute Simultaneity." That article contains the undoing of relativity theory and at the same time was equally as available for reading.

A salient example of one-sided reporting on relativity is that of Herbert Friedman, a physicist for the U. S. Naval Research Laboratory and science writer for the National Geographic Society. On the jacket of his book *The Amazing Universe*, Friedman is lauded as an experimental scientist (X-ray astronomer) of substantial stature.[142] And surely, he is quite correctly deserving of much praise. Albeit, Friedman is like many other scientists who allow their distinguished specialized expertise to blind them to certain areas of their own ignorance. From this author, the reader gets the impression that the theory of relativity is true above all question. Friedman himself appears to have carelessly swallowed the theory whole. He treats it as though it had been created, or validated, by God. In this work, he shows no awareness that Ives ever existed. He reveals no knowledge whatever of any of those experimental data and theoretical concepts that challenge the validity of relativity theory. His book is a beautiful, colorfully illustrated, remarkable volume. But this kind of impressive product only goes to prove just how much Relativity has now become effectively a *religion*. Regarding its treatment of relativity, this book may be practically described as a work of propaganda, of pretension to authority, and of ignorance that, though typical, is inexcusable. Friedman touts Einstein as a "self-effacing genius" who has "transformed mankind's understanding of the universe" (p. 176). On several occasions, Einstein did express disclaimers for much of the public acclaim he was enjoying that exceeded his merits. For example, upon receiving the One World Award (at Carnegie Hall, 27 April 1948), he declared: "In the course of my long life I have received from my fellow-men far more recognition than I deserve, and I confess that my sense of shame has always outweighed my pleasure therein." Upon receiving the Lord & Taylor Award (4 May 1953), he quipped: "As for the words of warm praise addressed to me, I shall carefully refrain from disputing them. For who still believes that there is such a thing as genuine modesty? I should run the risk of being taken for just an old hypocrite. You will surely understand that I do not find the courage to brave this danger."[143]

The fact remains, however, that Einstein showed little disposition to recognize and credit in print the work of those scientists whose experimental and theoretical accomplishments tended to threaten the validity of his theory of relativity, and hence the basis for his public apotheosis. As far as I have been able to determine, he maintained in print a studied silence regarding the damaging discoveries of Sagnac, Michelson and Gale, and the work of Ives (with the one exception mentioned a few pages back). "Self-effacing" is a naive and uninformed description of Einstein's personality and character. An historical study of the origin of the basic ideas in relativity theory shows beyond question that Einstein deliberately took personal credit for some crucial concepts which he *knew* had been originated and developed by other scientists. One example of improper crediting appears in connection with what is usually called the Einstein synchronization convention. In 1904, Poincaré clearly described the same light-ray synchronizing procedure as Einstein did in his famous "Elektrodynamik" paper of 1905.[144] Clock B at a distance from clock A is to be set on the assumption that a light ray going from clock A to clock B occupies the same time during its trip as a ray going from clock B back to clock A. Or in Einstein's way of putting it, the ray is reflected at clock B, and the delay in transmitting the light signal from A to B is presumed to be half the round-trip time for the reflected light beam as recorded at A.

However, there was a serious difference in interpretation. Poincaré's reason for suggesting light-ray synchronization of clocks was not the same as Einstein's. Poincaré presupposed absolute space although believing, as Ives later did, that there is no way to determine it.[145] Poincaré recommended light-ray synchronization of clocks because it affords consistent measurements. There is no way to know how much in error the results of any synchronizing procedure may be. On the other hand, Einstein specified the light-ray procedure as *stipulating* simultaneity under any condition, without reference to any one frame, known or unknown. Poincaré recommended light-ray synchronization because we cannot know the specifics of absolute space and time. Einstein recommended it on the basis of a flat denial of absolute space and time. If Einstein deserves credit for the light-ray synchronizing procedure, then it is merely because of his own error. The plain truth is, Einstein was very self-serving. He played the credit-merit game in a manner that was both scientifically and literarily unethical. For a further documentation of this fact, the reader may consult the historical portion of G. H. Keswani's excellent article, "Origin and Concept of Relativity."[146]

In my research, I have continually examined works like Wolfgang Rindler's book *Essential Relativity*. My most pointed remark about this particular volume, and indeed about relativity itself, is the artificiality of the conventional escape hatches therein presented, whereby relativists attempt to elude the implications of their contradiction-ridden theory. Alert teachers and students alike must surely be frustrated by the likes of Rindler's book.[147] The general quality of printed material on relativity and related matters ranges from poor to wretched, not only in popular books, but also in most physics textbooks and even textbooks on relativity. The writing often tends to be sloppy, narrow, and out of date. Ultimate sources are not mentioned nearly often enough. Ives' theoretical papers are but rarely mentioned and then only very superficially. Einstein and his theories regularly receive undeserved exclusive backing up from experimental successes which properly back up Ives' theory instead.

Controversial, unsettled matters are not presented as such, no matter how important they are—the better to keep most students pacified? Many writers pretend to understand, but simply do not. Many otherwise alert students studying relativity become logically bewildered and lose confidence in their own ability to think clearly as they slip into mysticism and become the next generation of scientific priests.

Often, one cannot learn fundamentals from the physicists, who are supposed to have expertise. There is no possible way to excuse this fact. A seeker must dig through interminable documents available only in the largest libraries in order to find what should be available from physics teachers for the asking. Nor is the large amount of physics to be known these days an adequate excuse for not knowing these most important facts.

Except for Ives in his scattered articles up to 1953, I have failed to find a single writer on the subject of relativity whose research has been adequate and up-to-date—which is, quite simply, my justification for writing this book. Even the exceptionally well-read Nordenson (whose contribution I have praised herein) erred substantially on account of not knowing about the Ives–Stilwell experiment, the Pound and Rebka experiment, and other evidences proving that the aging process is retarded by motion. On page 197 of *Relativity, Time, and Reality*, Nordenson denies that a traveling person would age more slowly than one remaining at rest. This error is costly, and can be attributed to nothing except the misfortune of being inadequately informed. I especially lament the embarrassment of this mistake, in view of the extraordinary keenness of Nordenson's mind. Some of my experiences suggest that he slipped because he could find no professional physicist who would read his writings and listen to his ideas. The generality of physicists feel as secure in their orthodoxy as did the philosophers whom Galileo invited to look through his telescope to see the moons of Jupiter; they refused to look because they had already been taught by Aristotle that the heavens were unchangeable. Or, perhaps they feared to see anything that would require them to *think*.

11. *Always and Everywhere*

My purpose in attacking relativity theory and revealing its logical replacement has been to rehabilitate absolute and uniform space

302

and time. The denial of these by orthodox relativists has become obdurately unscientific—which goes to prove how closed-minded are most scientists to logical criticisms of established scientific orthodoxies. The evidence for uniform time is simply ignored by most relativists, or else is rejected without an open hearing. For an interesting description of how *un*scientific the oracles of science can be, see Bernard Barber's article, "Resistance by Scientists to Scientific Discovery."[148]

The public has trusted the physicists, trusted them perhaps more, in this generation, than any other group. But in time, people will learn that physicists are no more immune to the perverse motivational currents of the times than any other professional people. Scientists have enormous vested interests in protecting their theories —vested energy, time, money, and indeed reputation. Like most other human beings, many are less than saintly in possessing the attributes of honesty, unselfishness, and respect for truth. And the lazy, servile adherence of many physicists to pompous, conventional dogma makes them leaders in the downward trend of civilization.

A couple of years ago I wrote to several philosophers of science in the United States and Canada, requesting their opinion of Nordenson's book, Lovejoy's article, and some notes of my own. Only two complied. Both were arrogantly disdainful of Nordenson, even though *they had not read him*. When a dissenter enters the academic citadel of physics, he obviously treads on holy ground. No one is to trifle with the mystique by which the physics profession and its hangers-on maintain their high prestige. For seventy-two years humanity has been browbeaten by an incomparably brazen bit of pseudo-science because its perpetrators have defended it by using mathematics which, though valid in itself, is not applied in relation to objective facts that are analyzed logically in the real world. Recondite kinds of higher mathematics have been falsely used to create an awesome, esoteric language whereby the initiated elite have set themselves apart from the world and have labeled all dissenters as quacks.

But physicists: Where is the theory of relativity by now? Gone is Einstein's self-consistency, and gone is the claim of relativity theory to exclusive explanatory power over the relevant experimental data. Gone is any motivation for the relativistic interpretation of Minkowski's space-time geometry, and gone is any sensible motivation for using non-inertial reference frames.

303

To be contrasted with this cerebral disaster is the Absolute Space and Time Theory of Ives which has full predictive power over all of the known experimental facts, is self-consistent, and is altogether derivable from classical physics plus Ives' restricted principle of equivalence. The result appears to be the greatest combination of coherence and explanatory power achieved in physics to the present time. For this achievement, Henri Poincaré deserves more credit than he has been accorded, in view of his numerous constructive insights.

How long will the profession of physics fill the heads of students with mind-befuddling anti-theistic nonsense while an irreproachable and practical theory already is here? How long will the profession continue to ignore the meticulous and exhaustive theoretical work of their own highly respected experimentalist Herbert Ives? Though he is now past caring about earthly glory, Ives yet most deserves to be called the successor to the greatness of Isaac Newton. The Ives Absolute Space and Time Theory fully assumes and corroborates universal simultaneity, absolute time, and immovable space. In the future, physicists would be well advised to drop Einstein's relativity and to use in its place the Ives theory. Not only does science stand to gain, but the dignity of mankind's intuitive understanding of space and time will be honored once again. The surpassing greatness of Isaac Newton is vindicated, and not simply as a physicist. He related his physics thoroughly to theology:

God . . . endures forever, and is everywhere present; and by existing always and everywhere, he constitutes duration and space. Since every particle of space is *always*, and every indivisible moment of duration is *everywhere*, certainly the Maker and Lord of all things cannot be *never* and *nowhere*.[149]

Einstein was awarded the 1921 Nobel Prize. Dignity is saved by the fact that it was for his early work in the quantum theory of the photoelectric effect, *not* for his theory of relativity.[150]

12. Science and Hope

The ultimate strategic question of modern science is this: At what point should one acknowledge that scientific explanation has gone as far as it can go? That is, at what point ought a theistic philosophical explanation be accepted as a satisfactory one where no merely empirical one appears to be possible? In the history of thought, science often has been stultified by an overzealous religious establishment whose sin was to obstruct inquiry that might threaten blind theological dogma. But now that science has uncovered so much and is, in most places, free from religious restrictions, scientists working at the boundaries of ultimate knowledge will encounter an opposite kind of problem, namely, frustration in their attempts to answer basic questions by their standard positivist methods. Lacking the theism of their ancestors in science, the positivists must eventually come to suppose that there is no rationality in the universe at bottom. But the question remains: At what point should the scientific enterprise halt, with regard to a given question or problem?

My answer is: it should halt only when a completely rational solution or explanation affords satisfaction to our need to thoroughly understand. When bare-bones hardware science fails to provide this satisfaction, then theistic philosophy must continue to seek until it finds it. Today, professional philosophers of science as a lot are morally astigmatic, suffer from a dearth of imagination, and have neither breadth nor depth in their spiritual vision of the world and the meaning and purpose of man's life within it. The main reason for this is a general positivistic hyperorthodoxy, marked by a conception of science as nothing more than the investigation and statistical description of nature as constituted merely of *accidents*. It is high time for this stiff-necked insensitivity to come to an end, to meet the fate that it has always deserved. Scientists must stop acting as though they are a class apart from that general human accountability for what we produce that affects each other's lives. Scientists, and philosophers of science, must come to see their discipline as a spiritual enterprise devoted to the search for *meaning*, for that kind of *understanding* that can lead to the fulfillment of crucial life needs. Scientists must cease to think of themselves merely as students of accidents, and come to think of themselves as seekers after greater vision and hope.

Whenever a scientist's frustrations begin to undermine his faith in ultimate order, he ought *as a scientist* to listen to the message of this book. Herein, I have attempted to present the foundation of order, that is, ultimate Rational Care, upon which both scientists and laymen can build, create, and discover in joy.

Let the doubters bury their own doubters. True science will flourish where I have been understood.

11

The Logic of Human Rights

O N SEVERAL OCCASIONS in this work I have argued that all moral distinctions would be arbitrary and meaningless unless there were some absolutely valid moral ideals inscribed in the cosmic scheme of things at large. Without such ideals there could be no logic of human rights. There could be no possible way to make objectively valid moral judgments of any kind. Consequently, I deem it essential to produce *en brève* a set of such principles herein. The logic of human rights necessarily presupposes that there are knowable objective criteria for distinguishing between true and false moral judgments, for making binding distinctions between just and unjust, right and wrong, humane and inhumane ways of thinking and acting. The criteria have to have an objective validity in principle not reducible to mere subjectivity of opinion; the criteria must transcend all reasonable doubt and hold up under all logical and factual analysis. Under any circumstances they must apply alike to all individuals, be they black, red, white, yellow or brown, male or female, young or old, rich or poor, irrespective of socio-economic and cultural conditions. Moreover, they must apply to all institutions whether they are private

307

or tax supported, democratic or otherwise. The logic of human rights is founded in two things: (1) a set of moral ideals that transcend all the changing fads and fashions, mores and customs, of every social order and generation, and (2) objective truths and facts about human nature and needs. In the chapter on Jesus, I outlined the universal, intrinsic life needs that all human beings share in common in any society, in any age. Fundamental moral ideals essential to the logic of human rights are:

1. *No one has the right to inflict needless harm or suffering on either himself or others* (valid distinctions between morally justifiable and unjustifiable kinds of suffering can be made only by the individual who understands the objective facts about his needs and the needs of others).

2. *The individual should be self-reflective, should judge himself cautiously and critically, and should judge others by the same criteria with which he judges himself under identical circumstances or when he is in the same situation.*

3. *Every individual has the right to freedom of independent and creative thinking and acting, the right to be different, as long as he recognizes and honors this same right in all others, and as long as, in his differences, he does not cause needless harm or suffering for either himself or others.*

4. *Every individual has the right to demand recognition of his needs, and to act freely to fulfill his needs, as long as he recognizes and honors this same right in all others.*

5. *Every individual should see himself as an end in himself, rather than as a means to some other person's selfish ends; and likewise, should see all others as ends in themselves, rather than as means to his own selfish ends.*

6. *Every individual has the right to defend himself from injustice or tyranny, and the duty to do so insofar as he is capable.*

7. *Every individual has the duty to fulfill himself insofar as he is capable, and to fully utilize his capacity to help others fulfill their lives.*

8. *The individual should seek that alternative to act on that will bring about the greatest amount of need fulfillment, and the least amount of need frustration, into life as a whole (i.e., the life of man, the other creatures, and God) on a long range basis.*

The difficulty of accurately assessing one's real life needs, and the needs of others, sometimes is very trying, and under complex circumstances may at the time be even impossible. But, as I pointed out in the chapter on Objectivity, the problematical nature of implementing the ideal in practice does not undermine the validity of it in principle, nor alter the fact that it is binding. It only obligates us inescapably with the duty to continue seeking after successful means of implementation.

There are three concepts that have to be understood concomitantly, for no one of them can be understood adequately without also understanding the others. They are (1) needs, (2) rights, and (3) values. The reason why every individual has a *right* to an education is because he has a *need* for an education (assuming he has not violated the right in others). The reason why an education has *value* is because the individual has a *need* for it. It is impossible that one can have a mature, enlightened philosophy of human rights unless one has a mature, enlightened understanding of human needs. Likewise, no one can really understand his intrinsic life needs unless he understands life's intrinsic values. The need for integrity can be fulfilled only by integrity. The need for health can be fulfilled only by health, etc. We can say that we have an intrinsic need for integrity because integrity is intrinsically valuable; or, we can say that integrity is intrinsically valuable because we have an intrinsic need for it. In either case, we have to think both in terms of life's intrinsic needs and intrinsic values to have a realistic philosophy of needs and values, and rights. Whole volumes could be written on practical methods of fulfilling these needs, of justifying and implementing these principles. At least, a brief statement of the logic of human rights gives us some direction.

12

Cantor's Transfinite Versus the Complete God

THROUGHOUT THIS WORK I have treated of God as The Infinite Creator. In the chapter on Jesus, I stated that the science of mathematics attests to the fact that the possibilities of creative goodness in God are infinite. As the theologically motivated Russo-German mathematician Georg Cantor discovered, there are different orders of infinity. In this discovery Cantor's contribution to philosophy of religion is simply untold. Mathematically, he laid a foundation for *hope* that can and must transcend any of the needless and final limitations that unimaginative and pikeristic philosophers of science would place upon us. There are not only different orders of infinity, but there are infinitely many orders of infinity. With its inexhaustible profusion of forms and classes, the Infinite or Transfinite shows necessarily that there is an Absolute, real limitlessness of possibilities and actualities that can be neither diminished nor depleted in time. This Super-infinity is God's goodness and glory in a fullness that reaches forever beyond our capacity to comprehend. God's creative domain is not only an "endless world," but a world unlimited in its aspects and in the variety of its goods and meanings. Cantor proved with a simple mathematical demonstration that God is inexhaustible in his aspects. Although the transfinite number "aleph" cannot be increased by mere addition or multiplication, it can be surpassed by using aleph as an exponent. Thus 2 to the aleph power is greater than aleph.

It is unfortunate, however, that Cantor contradicted himself in order to try to hold onto his theology of a complete God. Logically, a God unaugmentable in his aspects would be a static being, i.e., one who could never surpass himself by creative action. Cantor tried to put a lid on the Absolutely Infinite, by arguing that God in his completion is unaugmentable and could never enhance his own life. Fortunately, this contradiction does not plague a theology freed from the myth of omnipotence; for in principle there is no contradiction whatever between Cantor's Infinity of Infinities and the principle of God's progressive creativity. While God is already self-actualized in an infinite number of ways, there remain infinite other ways in which He can become yet more self-actualized, in his divine life without end.[1]

The most elaborate development of the concept of God as non-omnipotent and non-omniscient is found in the momentous work *The Problem of God*, by Edgar Sheffield Brightman.[2]

An excellent, voluminous analysis of the nature of God as limited is found in *Philosophers Speak of God*, by Charles Hartshorne and William L. Reese.[3] Hartshorne's brilliant book *The Divine Relativity* destroys forever the classic notion of God as immutable, impassive, and self-sufficient.[4] For a metaphysical root of the old errors, see his chapter "The Prejudice in Favour of Symmetry."[5] I knew Dr. Hartshorne at the University of Texas, and despite my great esteem of his contributions I must here temper my praise by stating tenets of his which I cannot accept. Most of my reasons appear elsewhere in the present work. (1) Hartshorne as a process philosopher denies that there are substantial, genuinely continuing souls except in the case of God. For Hartshorne, there are only thoughts and relations between thoughts; there is no thinker. There are only choices and relations between choices; there is no chooser. There are only acts and relations between acts; there is no actor. In short, there is no soul. A person is nothing but a set of relations, a sequence of related acts or occasions. (2) Similarly, Hartshorne belittles the idea of the personal immortality of creatures, claiming that God can conserve the value of our experience without conserving *us* (every person's life is terminated at the grave). (3) As though to compensate, Hartshorne holds that matter consists ultimately of myriads of micro-psyches and nothing else, primitive and evanescent though they may be. (4) He believes that they occupy a space which consists of their own relations (i.e., he denies the ontological reality of space *per se*). (5) He belittles the argument from design for God's existence.[6] He regards the ontological argument of Anselm and his own elaboration of it as alone sufficient to prove the existence of God, which I do not accept. Nevertheless, Hartshorne's elaboration of Brightman's overthrow of classical theism is of very great value, as well as many of his original insights. May his last years be peaceful.

The newer branches of Christianity have tended to shun classical theism, which explains much of their vitality. The religion of the Latter-day Saints is noteworthy. Mormon theology has incorporated the non-omnipotence and non-omniscience of God as here discussed, since the publication of the Book of Mormon, in 1830. However, Mormonism did not originate the concept of God's limited knowledge and power; it is suggested in the writings of Plato.[7] Also it is presented in F. W. J. von Schelling's book *The Ages of the World* (*Die Weltalter*), written in 1813.[8] This viewpoint about God is clearly implicit in a number of scriptures in the Old and New Testaments. Sterling M. McMurrin has supplied philosophical crosslights to this in his perceptive (though unduly pessimistic) article on "Time, History, and Christianity."[9] On Mormon theology see McMurrin's book *The Theological Foundations of the Mormon Religion*.[10] McMurrin clearly shows that to be logically coherent it is essential to see that God's existence is grounded in time, i.e., that God's life always will be creatively incomplete. One wonders, however, why anyone would want to go into such logical rigors in thinking about God while not even believing in His existence. The agnostic position expressed in the last paragraph of McMurrin's book is indeed lamentable.

Mormonism views God as inevitably delimited by the possibilities of evil in primordial reality. For an excellent exposition of this view, see the chapter on "Evil and Suffering" in Truman G. Madsen's *Eternal Man*.[11] Madsen's is the clearest statement in print on the unique Mormon position.

One sometimes hears that the German philosopher Immanuel Kant proved that God's existence cannot be deduced from the design of the universe or its laws. But actually Kant only showed that a totally omnipotent God could not be so deduced. See Kant's *Critique of Pure Reason*.[12]

Most theologians regard God as existing timelessly or outside of time; or more precisely, time simply has no reality for God; i.e., in him the past, present, and future supposedly interrelate to form just an eternal, changeless, timeless *Now*. But the fact has been established irrefutably that this viewpoint is pegged on contradictions and false assumptions about the nature of God and time. In his article "The Obsolescence of the Eternal," the American philosopher Arthur O. Lovejoy utterly devastates the notion that God, or any other entity, can exist and be totally unconnected with the passage of time. Lovejoy does not deny the reality of universals and of those things that are essential and everlasting; he does demonstrate incontestably that eternity cannot be conceived intelligibly as a mere state of timelessness, but rather, only as a process of time that is subject to no end.[13] It is unfortunate that this brilliant article from the year 1909 is generally unknown to theologians and philosophers of religion.

13

Olbers' Paradox and Infinite Creation

IN CHAPTER I, I alluded to our universe as being only one microcosm in an infinite, cosmic multiverse. In the addendum on Cantor, I argued that God must be unlimited in his creativity. In 1908, C. V. L. Charlier, a Swedish mathematician, constructed a model of the universe with dimensions increasing to infinity. Charlier's universe was static but contained an infinite extension of stars and galactic systems. Few cosmologists took this view of the cosmos seriously, for it was then generally taken practically as matter of fact that the universe could not possibly contain an infinite extension of stars. In 1720, the English astronomer Edmond Halley squarely posed the problem of how to explain why the night sky is dark. Halley demonstrated that if there was an infinite number of stars uniformly distributed throughout space, then the entire sky would be filled with their blinding light, and hence there could be no darkness. Nonetheless, Halley himself continued to believe both in an infinite number of stars and in the reality of the night sky. The discovery of this paradox traditionally has been attributed, by error, to H. W. M. Olbers; and consequently, today it is generally known as "Olbers' Paradox." Most textbooks on the subject are not historically accurate or up to date—see Stanley L. Jaki's "Olbers', Halley's, or Whose Paradox?"[1] Partly as a result of this paradox, modern astronomers almost universally concluded that the cosmos has to be finite in its number of suns. However, by applying some of Charlier's mathematical devices it can be shown that, in a theoretically infinite extension of galaxies in which a finite number of stars are clustered in non-uniformly distributed systems, the total light intensity in space will still allow for darkness in the night sky; and thus, "Olbers' Paradox" was "solved."

Charlier's model was based strictly on Euclidean space. Hardly anyone heeded him partly because at the time he developed his model another model was presented by Albert Einstein, i.e., of a universe pegged on his new definitions of the space-time of relativity. As I have shown in the coda on Einstein, his concepts of space and time are blighted with contradictions, yet have proven to mesmerize the minds of most physicists and astronomers to this day. Most cosmologists not only have been taken in by Einstein's fallacious concepts of space and time, but also have been fascinated by his notion that the universe must necessarily be finite in its contents and space. However, while relativity theory contends that "our" universe is finite, some leading protagonists of it have pointed out that it assuredly in no way precludes the possibility that other finite cosmoses might also exist. To take this position seriously, the relativist would have to give up his notion that "there is no empty space," since of necessity there would have to be real space in between other separate universes.

There have been numerous proposed solutions to Olbers' Paradox. One theory is that the galaxies are expanding away from each other at ever increasing speeds proportional to their distance from each other (Hubble's law of galactic recession). For example, the "steady-state" theory of the universe assumes such expansion. After a very great distance, galaxies begin to recede from each other at a velocity exceeding that of light; and consequently, radiation emitted by one galaxy can never reach an observer in another galaxy simply because the distance intervening between the light and the observer must continually increase. Or in other words, the observer is moving away from the light faster than the light is approaching him.[2]

We could not logically believe in an infinity of galaxies unless somehow we could solve Olbers' Paradox in a definitive and certain manner. This appears to have been accomplished by the discovery of the universal redshift, which neatly explains why we never receive light from galaxies receding from us at prodigious speeds surpassing that of light. This theory also assumes an expanding universe, with evidential data that would appear to put it beyond any viable question. As the wavelength of light received by an observer is increased and the frequency reduced, the energy carried by the photon (light quantum) is also reduced and in the same proportion, in conformity with Planck's equation. The more distant is the galaxy emitting the light, then the greater is the increase in the wavelength; and hence, as the recession of the light source from the observer is increased indefinitely, the presence of light for the observer must also be indefinitely reduced. In an indefinite shift to the red on the spectrum the intensity of electromagnetic radiation must eventually go down in principle to zero.

The expansion of the universe results in the reduced energy content of each observed photon. In addition, it decreases the rate at which photons are detectable (by separating them farther from each other in space). The separation of photons, and the reduction in their energy, results in a reduction in the quantity of light visible to the observer. The faster the galaxies move away from us, the less the light. This explains why an infinity of them would not light up an entire sky as bright as the sun, day and night. The very distant ones contribute far less light than those nearer, and the superlatively distant ones contribute no light at all.[3]

Thus, in light of the physical data now available to us, there can be no real obstacle to freedom to think big about God. We do God an injustice anytime we attribute less creative power to Him than that which is logically conceivable or possible. An infinite number of planets inhabited by persons and creatures who enjoy life is unquestionably infinitely better than only one, or a finite number.

14

Humeanism and Atomistic Psychology

IN THE CHAPTERS ON Need and Jesus, I argued that it is impossible to understand what a human being is, and to understand what one's responsibilities are, unless one sees oneself as a *self* or *autonomous agent*. For an unbelievably naive and self-contradictory denial of the reality of the self, see David Hume's *A Treatise of Human Nature*. Denying the existence of the self as an agent, Hume said:

For my part, when I enter most intimately into what I call *myself*, I always stumble on some particular perception or other, of heat or cold, light or shade, love or hatred, pain or pleasure. I never can catch *myself* at any time without a perception, and never can observe anything but the perception. When my perceptions are removed for any time, as by sound sleep, so long am I insensible of myself, and may be truly said not to exist. . . . If anyone upon serious and unprejudiced reflection thinks he has a different notion of *himself*, I must confess I can reason no longer with him. All I can allow him is, that he may be in the right as well as I, and that we are essentially different in this particular. He may, perhaps, perceive something simple and continued, which he calls *himself*; though I am certain there is no such principle in me. But setting

317

aside some metaphysicians of this kind, I may venture to affirm of the rest of mankind that they are nothing but a bundle or collection of different perceptions, which succeed each other at an inconceivable rapidity, and are in a perpetual flux and movement. . . . The mind is a kind of theatre, where several perceptions successively make their appearance, pass, re-pass, glide away, and mingle in an infinite variety of postures and situations. There is properly no *simplicity* in it at one time, nor identity [at different times], whatever natural propensity we may have to imagine that simplicity and identity. The comparison of the theatre must not mislead us. They are the successive perceptions only, that constitute the mind. . . .[1]

It should be obvious that such talk goes beyond the comical in its utter nonsensicality. Thus surely it is no wonder that the common people possess so little taste for academic philosophy when they are presented this kind of tripe as an example. No person with native good wits can think of himself as "nothing but a bundle of perceptions." Indeed, even Hume himself finally had the sensibility to have some second thoughts. Said he:

But having thus loosened all our particular perceptions, when I proceed to explain the principle of connection which binds them together, and makes us attribute to them a real simplicity and identity, I am aware that my account is very defective, and that nothing but the seeming evidence of the preceding reasoning could have induced me to entertain it. If perceptions are distinct existences, they form a whole only by being connected together. But no connections among distinct existences are ever discoverable by human understanding. We only *feel* a connection or determination of the thought, to pass from one object to another. It follows, therefore, that the thought alone finds personal identity, when reflecting on the train of past perceptions that compose a mind; the ideas of them are felt to be connected together, and naturally introduce each other. However extraordinary this conclusion may seem, it need not surprise us. Most philosophers seem inclined to think that personal identity *arises* from consciousness, and consciousness is nothing but a reflected thought or perception. The present philosophy, therefore, has so far a promising aspect. But all my hopes vanish, when I come to explain the principles that unite our successive perceptions in our thought or consciousness. I cannot discover any theory which gives me satisfaction on this head.

In short there are two principles which I cannot render consistent; nor is it in my power to renounce either of them, viz., *that all our distinct perceptions are distinct existences*, and *that the mind never per-*

ceives any real connection among distinct existences. Did our perceptions either inhere in something simple and individual, or did the mind perceive some real connection among them, there would be no difficulty in the case. For my part, I must plead the privilege of a sceptic, and confess that the difficulty is too hard for my understanding. I pretend not, however, to pronounce it absolutely insuperable. Others perhaps, or myself, upon more mature reflections, may discover some hypothesis that will reconcile those contradictions.[2]

This is indeed singularly interesting, that it should not occur to Hume—as it always does to any human being with normal common sense—that *he* is the agent who connects his own perceptions and experiences. Certainly, experiences do not organize and connect themselves; there has to be an agent organiz*er* and connect*or*: I transcend my own experiences; *I* talk about them; they do not talk about me. It is obvious to persons with common sense that there is never any thought without a thinker, never any perception without a perceiver, nor action without an actor; but then, Hume is famous for his inability to grasp the obvious. We all have our blind spots, but Hume's were simply inordinate. Any person's awareness of the continuity and unity of himself transcends the succession of events going on inside him. The self is more than just a succession of experiences or events. The self is the *agent* who accumulates the experiences in succession. It is unimaginable that a bunch of perceptions could unify themselves, or perform the act of remembering, or speak of themselves as one individual self (such as Hume repeatedly did while simultaneously denying that he could conceive of himself as actually existing). Like all of us do, Hume frequently alluded to himself with the pronoun "I," and established *de facto* the reality of his own existence as an individual perceiver, thinker, and actor. How can anyone deny that perceptions "inhere in an individual," and at the same time, by his very language, claim his unique perceptions as his own? In the world of sanity, no real individual can sensibly doubt that he is a real individual. Doubt does not doubt; doubt is always an act performed by a doubter. The atomistic psychologist denies the existence of the self as an entity endowed with a capacity for self-determination and self-transcendence. According to advocates of this school—they go by many different labels—perceptions do not *belong* to anyone, and thought requires no thinker. I could cite almost unlimited works espousing this viewpoint; suffice it to mention John Dewey (*Experience and*

Nature)[3] and one of his myriad disciples, Donald Arnstine (*Philosophy of Education: Learning and Schooling*.[4]

In no way can the abiding self be accounted for by only a succession of experiences or perceptions. There is a difference between a succession of experiences and an experience of successions. The latter is inconceivable without an abiding agent. How could Hume *talk* about *himself* after denying the existence of *himself*? How could he demand that others recognize his rights as an individual, after denying that he was an individual? Did he explain how "nothing but a bundle of perceptions" (each one distinct and unconnected from the others) could think about themselves and identify themselves, without a self to perform the act of unifying and identifying them? We can easily hush the psychological atomist by simply asking him to show one single experience or perception that does *not* belong to a definite individual. One must admit that there is a convenient escape from moral responsibility in taking the atomist view. If I do not exist as the actor who commits my own acts, then I am not responsible for my acts. If I am not the thinking agent who produces my own thoughts, then I am in no way responsible for my thoughts. I may inflict upon an innocent person a totally unprovoked and unjustifiable blow on the nose. But then, there is no reason why I should assume any accountability (either to myself or to him) for such an act, for I can simply say: "Don't blame me; I don't exist; I had no decision in the matter; you were simply hit happenstance by a bundle of disconnected perceptions!"

If it appears I am trying to make fun of atomistic psychology, indeed I am, for it is impossible for any rational man to take seriously the notion that there is no meaningful distinction between the perceiver, the act of perceiving, and the thing perceived. How can Hume speak of a "bundle" of perceptions while insisting that there is no connection at all between one perception and another? How can there be a bundle of perceptions without any agent to bundle them together? Hume claims to have no awareness whatever of himself as a perceiver, that he is only conscious of disconnected perceptions. Fortunately in the real world, few and far between are those individuals who claim never to have any self-consciousness, or a conscious distinction between oneself as the perceiving subject and the object perceived. Such persons are remarkably abnormal. I have never seen any instance of so great a philosophical ineptitude except in the college ivory tower where professional teachers are either deliberately clowning or else serving their students academic baloney sandwiches.

Hume declared, "I never can catch myself at any time without a perception, and never can observe anything but the perception." The contradiction is ribald. While denying that he could distinguish between the perceiving subject, the act of perceiving, and the thing perceived, Hume did in fact deal in such distinctions every time he uttered a sentence. He said, "I never can catch myself." In saying "I," he *de facto* recognized the reality of himself as the subject. In saying "I never can catch," he *de facto* recognized the reality of himself as an agent *performing the act* of catching. In saying "I never can catch myself," he *de facto* recognized his own self-transcendence, i.e., distinguished between himself as the subject and himself as the object of his own perception. When he said "I never can observe," he did plainly establish *de facto* a truth known always to common sense, i.e., that there is never any observation without an observer. When Hume denied that he was ever conscious of himself while being also conscious of other things, he was playing a game with himself (these days on college campuses often done by people who aren't conscious of more important things to do). As I have observed already, this can lead to only one thing when its logical implications are taken seriously—to epistemological and moral nihilism. I can think of only two possible explanations for such an indefensible position: either a gross dearth of common sense intuition of obvious truth, or else an unconscious motivation to escape from responsibility for one's thoughts and acts—or both.

Hume is directly responsible for the impracticality of much modern philosophy. The absurdity of his basic views makes it impossible for him to merit the attention focused on him in current courses in philosophy and the humanities. As required reading, he can no more likely be avoided than Aristotle or Plato. His *self*-less psychology is unsurpassed in its influence on modern philosophy of mind, e.g., in the atomistic psychology of Bertrand Russell (although, unlike Hume, Russell vacillated in his position on the relation between cause and effect, i.e., between the distinct existences of perceptions and how they are "bundled").

For an excellent criticism of soulless psychology, see the portion on "Time," *Theory of Thought and Knowledge*, by Borden Parker Bowne.[5] Also see John Elof Boodin's perceptive article, "Russell's Metaphysics."[6] An uncommonly elaborate criticism can be found in my own book *The Autonomous Man.*[7] A brilliant exposé of the self-contradiction in Hume can be found in the *Works of Thomas Hill Green.* Green pointed out that

The more strongly Hume insists that "the identity which we ascribe to the mind of man is only a fictitious one," the more completely does his doctrine refute itself. If he had really succeeded in reducing those "invented" relations, which Locke had implicitly recognized as the framework of the universe, to what he calls "natural" ones—to mere sequences of feeling—the case would have been different. With the disappearance of the conception of the world as a system of related elements, the necessity of a thinking subject, without whose presence to feelings they could not become [related] elements, would have disappeared likewise. But he cannot so reduce them. In all his attempts to do so we find that the relation which has to be explained away is pre-supposed under some other expression.[8]

Green clearly demonstrated how flagrantly Hume used himself, appealed to himself, and presupposed the reality of himself in all his efforts to deny himself. Also he showed how Hume unconsciously had to presuppose the causal relations of things in the world in order to even talk about them or try to deny them.

Hume's nihilstic agnosticism reminds me of a lyrical philosophical spoof, by the American philosopher Richard Henson:[9]

> There's little enough I'm sure of,
> And nothing at all that I know.
> But it's not because I'm stupid,
> It's *cleverness* makes me so.

15

Russell, Mathematical Truth, and Absolutes

A VERY PROFOUND STATEMENT of the reliability of mathematical truth was offered by Bertrand Russell in 1907 in "The Study of Mathematics." He declared:

Mathematics, rightly viewed, possesses not only truth, but supreme beauty—a beauty cold and austere, like that of sculpture, without appeal to any part of our weaker nature, without the gorgeous trappings of paintings or music, yet sublimely pure, and capable of a stern perfection such as only the greatest art can show. . . . Philosophers have commonly held that the laws of logic, which underlie mathematics, are laws of thought, laws regulating the operations of our minds. By this opinion the true dignity of reason is very greatly lowered: it ceases to be an investigation into the very heart and immutable essence of all things actual and possible, becoming, instead, an inquiry into something more or less human and subject to our limitations. . . . But mathematics takes us still further from what is human, into the region of absolute necessity, to which not only the actual world, but every possible world, must conform. . . . Too often it is said that there is no absolute truth, but only opinion and private judgment; that each of us is conditioned, in his view of the world, by his own peculiarities, his own taste and bias; that there is no external kingdom of truth to which, by patience, by austerity, by stern discipline, we may at last obtain admittance, but only truth for me, for you, for every separate person. By this habit of mind, one of the chief ends of human effort is denied, and the supreme virtue of candour, of fearless acknowledgment of what is, disappears from our moral vision. Of such scepticism, mathematics is a perpetual reproof; for its great edifice of truths stands unshakable and inexpugnable to all the weapons of doubting cynicism.[1]

Unfortunately, later in his life Russell changed his mind, falling victim to the very doubt he had previously described as cynical. Alluding to his earlier vision of a kingdom of absolute truth, he sighed, "All this, though I still remember the pleasure of believing it, has come to seem to me . . . nonsense. . . . Mathematics has ceased to seem to me non-human in its subject matter." He declared that "the splendid certainty which I had always hoped to find in mathematics was lost in a bewildering maze."[2]

When Russell made this decision, he turned down the only path that was open to him; for once a person definitively rejects God, it is impossible to hold that there is a kingdom of necessary and absolutely reliable truths. In reality, the inevitable and only possible alternative to God is precisely as Russell described it: "a bewildering maze"—except for those who, as Kierkegaard described so accurately in *The Sickness Unto Death*, play games by not admitting their own confusion and despair.[3]

16

Discerning the Meaning of Oneness

IN CHAPTER 3, I depreciated the vast literature available on philosophy of mathematics because of its virtually total failure to get at the rationale informing the existence of numbers. It is interesting that in Alfred North Whitehead's and Bertrand Russell's prestigious three-volume *Principia Mathematica* no mention is made of oneness as an essence or absolute principle. Whitehead and Russell never veer close to a philosophically relevant interpretation of the meaning of oneness. About the only statement they make is, "The cardinal number 1 . . . is to be regarded simply as the class of all unit classes."[1]

Of course, there are different schools of mathematical philosophy (nominalism, conceptualism, Platonism, *et al.*) in which the ultimate nature of oneness, and any other mathematical truth, is differently defined. The interested reader might begin an introductory study of these schools by consulting "Number," by Stephen F. Barker, in the *Encyclopedia of Philosophy*—with the forewarning that the author is blatantly biased and terminates his article claiming that no number theory can have a significance that has literal truth.[2] For a broader, more erudite introduction to different philosophies of mathematics, see *Philosophy of Mathematics: Selected Readings*, edited by Paul Benacerraf and Hilary Putnam.[3]

There has to be one truth that no philosophy can sanely ignore, namely, that *oneness* (or any other mathematical value) has to exist in principle (i.e., omnipresent in the absolutely rational mind of God) in order that there can exist meaningful mathematical absolutes. For oneness to exist as an absolute without an absolutely necessary and rational reason for it to be there plainly is a contradiction that would undermine any possibility of *necessarily* valid reasoning in mathematics. It is unfortunate that even the greatest mathematicians and philosophers of mathematics have had so little to offer to clarify our understanding of the ultimate nature of mathematical values. In fact, most have merely confused matters to the point of seriously discouraging students from any further pursuit of clarity in the subject. Even so great a thinker as G. Frege bogs down in so many contradictions and writes in such wearisome language that even the brightest students think of him primarily as a cure for insomnia. Straining to make a point that for all his effort remains quite nebulous, he denies that my dog has even the dimmest consciousness of oneness when he sees one thing and distinguishes it from another thing.[4] If this is supposed to add something to our understanding of the nature of numbers, it would have to do so at the cost of denying the strikingly obvious. It is both logically and psychologically a contradiction to assume a distinction between *one* thing and another if a person is unable to distinguish *oneness per se*. How could it be any different for a dog than a man? Frege's definition of the number one is as narcotizing as consuming a gallon of wine:

The number 1 belongs to a concept *F*, if the proposition that *a* does not fall under *F* is true universally, whatever *a* may be, and if from the propositions

"*a* falls under *F*" and "*b* falls under *F*"

it follows universally that *a* and *b* are the same.[5]

The practical mind is simply stymied by Frege's denial that oneness is ever the predicate of a concrete object. If a rock was not *one* rock (that is, not containing the predicate of oneness within it), then the statement, "I want only one rock showing in the garden" would mean nothing whatever. How oneness *in principle* can ingress into and out of concrete objects is indeed a mystery the finite mind can never penetrate at all. But the fact that an obvious truth is mysterious does not keep it from being a truth. My dog does not have to be able to explain how I am one being in order to *know* that I am one being. Indeed, I cannot even explain it myself. I just possess the miraculous power God endowed me with to recognize it as a fact. And so does my dog.

Today, there is a widespread relativist influence on philosophy of mathematics. As I have noted earlier, strict relativism always denies the existence of any essences; and consequently, it also denies that there are any essential truths or facts. As a result, any relativistic philosophy necessarily ends up annihilating all meaningful distinctions. In the case of mathematics, relativism destroys any meaningful objective distinction between any given number and other numbers, or between any given mathematical relation and other mathematical relations, simply by denying that there are any definite and certain truths that can be known. Even Einstein, who is reputed for his espousal of the strictest form of determinism, fell victim, in effect, to a purely nihilist metamath. Determinism interprets *all* world phenomena, including all principles of pure mathematics and mathematical physics, as being grounded in absolute, binding laws. Albeit, Einstein stated that "the series of integers is obviously an invention of the human mind, a self-created tool which simplifies the ordering of certain sensory experiences." Unmistakably, Einstein ruled against a *natural* order of mathematical and logical truths that can be known. Siding with Hume, he denied that numbers, or any other form of mathematical values or relations, can ever be found to exist in nature in any objective sense. He denied that we can have any sensory experience of anything in the world that is in fact mathematically structured or ordered. He asserted that "there is no way in which [mathematical concepts] could be made to grow, as it were, directly out of sense experience." Yet, in the same breath, he declared that the logical rules for the game of inventing mathematical concepts and symbols result merely from a "free play" of the mind. These logical rules are purely "arbitrary," and hence, can in no way be justified or maintained *apriori*.[6]

For Einstein, there appeared to be nothing in nature that corresponds either to logic or to arithmetic. Moreover, he took logic itself to be only the product of the "free play" of the human mind, having no foundation in *apriori* truth or in compelling law. The "logical homogeneity of geometry and theoretical physics," and the "concepts and fundamental principles" of either pure mathematics or applied mathematics, are "purely fictitious," and "cannot be justified either by the nature of the intellect or in any other fashion *apriori*." But lo, he then added that "this axiomatic basis of theoretical physics cannot be extracted from experience but must be freely invented." Finally, he ended this plunge into epistemological nihilism with the unbelievable remark: "I hold it true that pure thought can grasp reality, as the ancients dreamed."[7]

"Pure thought"—? How can any meaningful distinction be made between "pure thought" and impure thought, if we can have no knowledge of logical, mathematical, or physical truth either *apriori* or through sense experience? Plainly, for Einstein the truths of mathematics were grounded neither in binding laws of logic nor in the natural order of things which we can learn about through our sensory experience. As to the ultimate nature of mathematical truth, Einstein's reasoning on the subject was a hopelessly futile circle. He was often given to affirming the very thing he denied, and to denying the very thing he affirmed. The end result was a mathematical voluntarism in which truth is regarded merely as an "invention" of man. Such a position is extraordinarily egocentric, because it turns man into God, the maker of, or the locus of, Fundamental Reality. Also, it is a theoretical position that is impossible for anyone ever to successfully honor in practice. In applied mathematics, *no one* can operate literally on the assumption that mathematical laws are "purely arbitrary," "fictitious," or unamenable to certain knowledge. Like Hume, Einstein declared that we can learn nothing of mathematical truths through our sensory perception of objective representations of them in the concrete world. But this makes a mockery of the most obvious common-sense facts of perception. For example, all of us have an unmistakable intuitive apprehension *and* sensory perception of *oneness* informing the existence of things in the natural order as we experience them. It is categorically inconceivable that anyone could ever experience anything at all unless intuitively and by sense perception he could distinguish between one thing and another thing. If a person could have no direct sense experience of *oneness* in things, and no certain intuitive awareness of *oneness* in principle, then it is unimaginable that he could ever distinguish between *one* thing and another. He could never have any awareness of any single (one) experience of anything. There is no way he could ever have *one* experience of anything either concrete or abstract, and be conscious of it as *one* experience, and reflect on it as such. It is a plain truth that any child knows what *oneness* is as a predicate, long before he learns to use the symbol of the number *one* to verbally predicate oneness to a given entity or event. Very early in life, a child learns how to recognize an entity as an entity. Without the intuitive awareness of oneness, and the perception of it as a natural predication of single things, it is inconceivable that anyone could ever have an experience of the reality of an entity, either concrete or abstract. Early in life, a child learns how to distinguish one entity from other entities, knowing that each entity has in common the fact that it is *one thing*. This is made possible by the fact that in the perceivable natural order there really are entities, and by the fact that the perceiving agent can intuit the experience of *oneness* and logically extrapolate from it the abstract symbol "1" that applies to any *thing*. This natural awareness of the meaning of oneness (both intuitively and through perception) must of necessity come first in experience. The learning of a verbal symbol with which to discuss or communicate that awareness always comes *after* the experience of oneness as a fact.

Einstein declared that mathematical concepts "contain nothing of the certainty, of the inherent necessity, which Kant had attributed to them."[8] Thus unavoidably, we are forced to conclude that Einstein, taken in by Hume (whom he praised highly), ended up floundering in nihilism. Any school of thought is epistemologically nihilistic when it denies that certain knowledge is possible. Indisputably, Einstein denied that any mathematical principles can have a foundation in *apriori* reason. He also denied that any mathematical knowledge can be derived from sensory experience. What is most curious, he was on one hand the most intransigent kind of determinist, allowing no room whatever for any "free play of the mind," in any meaningful sense of these words. As I have documented earlier, he denied that man has any degree of freedom of choice. In 1930, he declared: "I do not believe we can have any freedom at all in the philosophical sense, for we act not only under external compulsion but also by inner necessity. Schopenhauer's saying—'A man can surely do what he wills to do, but he cannot determine what he wills'—impressed itself upon me in youth and has always consoled me."[9] Throughout his life Einstein contended that everything occurring in the human mind is determined by strict laws of causal necessity. But then, on the other hand, he argued that just the opposite is the truth, that there are no mathematical axioms or laws of logic that are grounded in any objective necessity whatever.

Einstein did believe that the "inventions of the mind" (i.e., the fundamental concepts and principles of either mathematics or physics) can be checked out and validated, or invalidated, by physical operations and experimentation. He chided Hume for allowing his radical scepticism to lead to a "fear of metaphysics"—a fear which he thought would paralyze the imagination and that free, creative speculation and conceptual venturing which makes progress in the sciences possible. But by the term "metaphysics," Einstein certainly did not have in mind any discipline of *apriori* truths, or necessary first principles, in which any science ultimately must be grounded in order to be sound. On the contrary, he regarded the classical conception of metaphysics (the study of first principles or necessary truths) as nothing but "empty talk."[10] His writings show that he definitely believed in a complementarity between the rational structure of the natural world order and those conceptions (constituting "pure thought" in our minds) that can hold up under sophisticated techniques of experimental verification. But while the presupposition of this complementarity is valid, and is of course *essential* to a sound philosophy of science, it nonetheless is incompatible with Einstein's denial that certain knowledge is possible either *apriori* or through our sense perception of reality. Einstein is famous for his assertion that "Science without religion is lame, religion without science is blind." By this, he clearly meant that we must have "faith in the possibility that the regulations valid for the world of existence are rational, that is, comprehensible to reason." Not reading him at first hand, many people erroneously believed that Einstein was a religious man, while in fact he was in the ordinary sense not religious at all. On the contrary, he described belief in a personal God (i.e., a conscious, feeling, knowing, caring Spirit) and belief in prayer and survival beyond the grave as "decisive weaknesses."[11] When he spoke of the universe as being "comprehensible to reason," he did not at all mean that the universe is *informed* with reason. The only way the universe could possibly be informed with reason is if a Creator exists who had in his mind a reason for creating the world and sustaining its existence. But this, Einstein specifically denied. He plainly contended that the rational structure of the world is in no way deliberate or purposeful. Logically, there is no other alternative but to assume that it is accidental. As in other issues, Einstein tried to have it both ways, which is logically impossible. His philosophy of science and mathematics is a veritable charivari of contradictions. From this most panegyrized mathematician of all time, I find scant contribution to a coherent philosophy of mathematics. He once made a remark to the effect that the most incomprehensible thing about the universe is the fact that it is comprehensible. After examining the basic assumptions in his epistemology, I can understand why he would say such a thing.

17

Singh, Peirce, and
Anthropomorphism

JAGJIT SINGH, a popular Indian writer, in his book *Great Ideas and Theories of Modern Cosmology*, describes belief in God as narcissism and madness. He declares that, "When one has cut himself off from God by a first sip from the cup of knowledge, one will not rediscover Him by drinking its dregs, no matter how hard they may be boiled." Singh sees all cosmological arguments for God's existence as nothing more than "colored phantoms of autistic souls intent on wishful dreaming."[1] Equating objectivity with agnosticism or positivistic scientism, he says: "A cosmologist may perhaps . . . be justified in dreaming about his results provided he has not allowed any human hopes and desires to bias his research," and at all events must "prevent human motivation from influencing his cosmological judgments."[2]

In reading Singh's book, a person would be uncommonly gullible not to see the obvious atheistic bias that the author projects into his own cosmological judgments. There is no mask of modesty to hide the fact that Singh deems himself a pure thinker, as though he were an ideational computer, unaffected in his scientific cogitations by his own personal purposes and desires. There can be no ques-

332

tioning the fact that all human beings allow their motivations to affect their judgments; all of us project ourselves into what we are doing, not excepting the most impartial, objective imaginable scientist. The direction and quality of any scientist's mentations and actions at work is unavoidably affected by his life motivations, and there is no reason why this should not be the case. It is not a question of whether a scientist *qua persona* is unaffected by his needs and motives, of whether he tries to have an influence on his work's results. Rather, it is a question of whether the results of his work, with all of his motivations counted, turn out to have a beneficial effect on the fulfillment of his real life needs, and the needs of others. In this respect, Singh's cosmological judgments not only are colored enormously by his own wishful thinking but betray a uniquely great misunderstanding about the nature of real objectivity. Much of his position is totally deficient in fact.

A far more realistic and honest philosophy of objectivity is expressed by the American philosopher Charles Sanders Peirce. Peirce vacillated between pragmatism and realism, but from either position he insisted that as to something

being unscientific because anthropomorphic, that is an objection of a very shallow kind, that arises from prejudices based upon much too narrow considerations. "Anthropomorphic" is what pretty much all conceptions are at bottom; otherwise, other roots for the words in which to express them than the old Aryan roots would have to be found. And in regard for any preference for one kind of theory over another, it is well to remember that *every single truth of science is due to the affinity of the human soul to the soul of the universe*, imperfect as that affinity no doubt is.[3]

Peirce strongly identified man's ability to make correct speculations in science and religion as implying an "anthropomorphic" feature of the universe, which explains why our minds can understand it. He declared that "every scientific explanation of a natural phenomenon is a hypothesis that there is something in nature to which the human reason is analogous; and that it really is so all the successes of science in its applications to human convenience are witnesses."[4]

The history of the sciences proves unabashedly the absolute necessity for anthropomorphism in man's search for intelligibility in the universe. In those cultures that have failed to see the rationality of God present in the structure of the world, the sciences simply have not developed. For a brilliant exposition of this fact, see Fr. Stanley L. Jaki's article "The Role of Faith in Physics."[5] Jaki is a uniquely commendable scholar. Read his interesting and profoundly erudite book *Science and Creation.*[6]

It is those who deny God or any anthropomorphic aspect of Him who turn out to be the real anthropomorphists. They must finally hold, with Protagoras, that "Man is the measure of all things."[7] For an exposition of this, see Charles Hartshorne's article, "Anthropomorphic Tendencies in Positivism."[8]

18

Induction and Sensibility

AS IN OTHER AREAS of philosophy, there appears to be little agreement amongst professionals on how to distinguish between sound and unsound methods of making inductive inferences. Usually, inductive reasoning is reasoning from particulars to generalities. Without induction, the sciences would be impossible. In fact, all creative and progressive disciplines would be impossible. We have an ongoing need to learn from our experiences, to extrapolate from them, to infer broad principles or general truths that can serve us effectively for making predictions and decisions. Unless we can infer general truths from our cumulative experience of particular realities, we can have no guidelines for wisely conducting our daily practical affairs.

Recently in a philosophy conference, I once again experienced that discomforting sensation of intellectual futility as one speaker after another failed to communicate agreement on the perennial questions and issues of induction, reality, and truth. As a whole, the conference veered toward nihilism, toward the doubt that any reliable basis for induction can ever be known. Those professors believing in definite canons for inductive inference were unable to convince each other as to what they are. One professor argued unabashedly that "because there are no absolutes, all inductive inferences are grounded in merely speculative assessments of probabilities, at best." Of course, this viewpoint is quite inadequate, for it is circular; it appeals to nothing but probability as the criterion for determining probability, and hence, is grossly lacking. We simply cannot rely upon the assumption that there is nothing we can always rely upon. Such an assumption is clearly self-defeating. It can afford us no sound basis for induction in any of the disciplines.

I was not surprised to find in this conference only a small element of sympathy for the notion that it is essential to start out with some absolutes. Without some absolute truths that can be understood, there can be no conceivable grounds on which to make predictions about the future, or about the behavior of the world, with any guarantee of accuracy. To this day, the professional philosophers are hobbled by Hume. In his absolute scepticism Hume concluded that no effect whatever can be reliably predicated on a cause. There simply is no known way to relate causes to effects, except as a matter of perceptual habit or expectation, in our minds. We grow accustomed to seeing B happen after A, and then in our imagination we project A as the cause of B, whereas in fact there is no demonstrable necessary connection at all. There can be no way to show for certain that an effect is caused, no way to explain how it is caused if we believe that it is caused. In short, there is no principle in reality for explaining the connections of things and events. Hume's scepticism was so extreme, he would not allow that we can predict with certainty that five minutes from now *something will be real*. Such scepticism is nonsensical, utterly unrealistic, and altogether non-productive. Not only would Hume not credit God for anything—he would not credit even himself for having the power of a flea. A flea can predict more than Hume would ever allow that he himself could safely predict. To be consistent, a Humean would need a map of the whole universe to go from Kansas City, Missouri to Kansas City, Kansas.

There has to be a set of criteria which an enlightened man would use to distinguish between sensible and unsensible inferences about scientific and philosophical matters of *lasting importance*. This must be true whether we are speaking of inferences that predicate effects on causes (predicting future events), or the connecting relations between things co-existing in a common moment. Formulated interrogatively, these criteria are: (1) What constructive reason is there for making a given inference? (2) What constructive purpose is served by making that inference? and (3) What real life need is fulfilled by making that inference? In short, what *rationale* do we have for making that inference? Then, once the inference is made, we subsequently have to provide a rationale for its verification or invalidation. There can be no justification without a rationale. Only a rationale can justify an inference, or a validation or invalidation of an inference. Practically, we have no business making inferential judgments about anything except to the extent that the quality of our lives is enhanced by the judgments that we make, including the satisfaction of our need to understand the world. The world is in much too unhappy a condition for the philosophers to continue luxuriating in abstruse pedantry that does mankind and God no good. The serious business of developing reliable canons of inference unavoidably involves much fine analysis of problems and ideas. Anyone would be simplistic to suggest that sophisticated and realistic science and philosophy is possible without finicalism in the critical analysis of reality and its laws. Albeit, finicalism is featherbrained insofar as it presumes to search for understanding while denying those epistemological and metaphysical absolutes that constitute the foundation for all true understanding.

Two of these absolutes are: (1) nature is amenable to rational comprehension because in its underlying and abiding superstructure it is informed with God's absolutely rational reason and purpose; and (2) God has endowed us with enough intelligence that, in time, we can learn progressively more about His reason and purpose if we search for it with the indefectible faith that His holy animus creates and sustains the world. Rigorous, critical reflection is an ever essential part of this search. Holy emotionality is essential, but so is *holy thinking*. Scepticism as to God's existence can never establish and justify any inductive procedures in either science or philosophy. If God—the Being Who Cannot Fail to Be, or the Being Who Cannot Fail to Love—did not exist, then *eo ipso*, there could be *no* guarantee whatever that sixty seconds from now there will be some sensible kind of reality or world. The problems of inductive science can no longer be approached without ultimately considering matters of value. Hume's sanctification of doubt has proven fruitless, in axiological matters as well as empirical.

337

Philosophers and scientists have to *justify* their thinking, and they can do it only by producing thoughts of value. There can be no value whatever in the Humean assumption that we can never certainly predict the conservation of any values or realities whatever.

Undoubtedly, some nitpickers would object to the above position on the grounds that I am using induction to arrive at the conclusion that God exists, thus using inductive procedures to establish absolute grounds for inductive procedures, which is circular. This objection is invalid. Logically, one has to *start out* with absolutes before one can *ever* make absolutely reliable judgments about anything. Using absolute truth is clearly the only possible logical way to "establish" absolute truth. If a person cannot *intuit* this fact, then no amount of inferential reasoning of any kind can lead him to an awareness of the absolute. Nothing can "establish" the absolute truth but the absolute truth itself. Absolute truth is grounded in itself. Its being is not contingent, not dependent upon anything whatever. Without God—the Necessary Being—there clearly could be no necessary truth of any kind. All necessary truth is grounded in God; it is an inherent, primordial part of His Being. Absolute truth is actually not "established" in the sense that establishing means bringing into being. Rather, it is established in the sense that it *cannot fail to be*, and in the sense that it never takes anything to establish it. Nobody can ever establish that which is already established and which has always been established.

We simply have to use God's abiding truths to come to understand Him. Without intuition, one cannot sense the validity or invalidity of any reasoning processes, be they inductive or deductive. What is wrong with using the Absolute to justify the Absolute? If we do not do this, then we end up unable to justify anything whatever. The only thing my son and daughter need in order to justify the fact that I am their father is to recognize the fact that I am their father. All I need in order to justify the Absolute is to recognize the Absolute. It is my Father, God, who enables me to justify my Father, God. Without Him, we can explain nothing for certain, predict nothing for certain, justify nothing for certain. How can anyone justify searching for grounds for certainty, after denying God, who is *the only possible ground for certainty*?

All people do undeniably deal in inductions. Indeed, it is impossible for anyone not to, if one is to act effectively to fulfill his life. Those sceptics who deny that inductive reasoning can ever be reliable cannot possibly honor their own theory in practice. Universal scepticism is a mere pretension, for no one can doubt everything in practice. If one could doubt everything then he could doubt the validity of the proposition that he can doubt everything; and hence, he would not be affirming the reality of even his own doubt. "I doubt that I ever doubt"—a statement made by one of my colleagues —is simply an utterance of dumb stubbornness.

Some critics have objected to using induction to support induction. The selfsame critics have used induction to oppose induction. Hume stated that inductive generalizations are *never* certain.[1] But clearly, this is itself a generalization about *all* generalizations and is self-contradictory. Hume admitted that he himself dealt often in generalizations; yet, he claimed that he had never come across any good reason why anyone should ever regard inductive reasoning as good reasoning. Thus, he indulged himself in doing the very thing that he blamed others for doing, but with merely a hint of self-blame.[2] He objected to inductive reasoning in religion, but used it in defense of his own irreligion. He objected to any dependence on it in the sciences, but used it in defending his own philosophy of science. In theory he undercut any possible reliable value in his own practice. How can you put on your hat after you have cut off your head? This fallacy of appealing to the selfsame thing one denies is unavoidable without some absolutes. Here is a common example of it which I have found in literature on induction:

We cannot claim that *any* inductive statement is beyond the possibility of correction or revision, or that the behavior of future unobserved instances can in *any* case of induction be unconditionally guaranteed in advance.[3]

Again: "Inductive conclusions are *never* general statements about reality." "Inductive inferences can *never* be considered as more than mere guesses based at best on considerations of probability." "Inductive inferences are *never* certain."

All of the above statements are instances of a simple logical fallacy, a paralogism. A person is guilty of this fallacy when he employs a principle in an effort to deny the validity of the selfsame principle; or, as I have stated previously, one is guilty of this when he appeals unconsciously to a truth which he consciously denies. People who deny any absolutes cannot support their integrity while dealing in absolutes themselves. For the sake of their dignity, they should never use the word "never." By undercutting all generalizations, they undercut their own generalizations, and who can profit from this? It is, of course, inevitable that all of us use absolutes in our philosophies. It is not a question of whether some philosophers do not use absolutes, for certainly there is no one who does not. Rather, it is a question of whether one's absolutes are valid or invalid, or true or false. Also, it is a question of whether one is conscious of his own absolutes, and of whether one deals in his absolutes above the board.

The prestigious analytic philosopher Max Black has demonstrated that "inductive support for induction is not necessarily circular." Objecting to Hume's extreme scepticism, Black declares that those satisfied with Hume's viewpoint "are at bottom objecting to *any* use of inductive concepts and of the language in which they are expressed unless there is deductive justification for such use. They will therefore reject *any* reliance upon induction by way of defense, however free from formal [logical] defect, as essentially irrelevant to the primary task of philosophical justification."[4] Black shows that "questions about the general or ultimate justification of induction *as such*, questions of the form 'Why should any induction be trusted?' must be recognized as senseless."[5] Nonetheless, he falls back into Hume's dark hole which he has striven so valiantly to climb out of. For he acknowledges the validity of Hume's claim that we can "never demonstrate the necessity of a cause" for any event.[6]

Hume argued (I repeat) that there is never any necessary connection between past and future phenomena, nor between any coexisting phenomena. To refute this, one would have to show that there is a connection between things, or between events, obtaining from logical necessity rather than from mere accidentality or causelessness. That is, one would have to show that the association between at least certain kinds of events and phenomena is lawful, i.e., that it arises necessarily out of a rational cosmic scheme of things which one way or another informs all reality. Black finally despairs of any satisfactory solution to Hume's "problem of induction"—the problem of showing that some logical necessity actually is in operation in the world. Hume and his army of disciples have pegged the proof of induction on the possibility of seeing the infinite long range behavior of reality. But then, they have rejected such a proof as impossible on the grounds that "the infinite long run is a chimera." Black makes the mistake of conceding to this, saying that "Hume's challenge to discover such lawfulness in experience remains as formidable as ever; no matter how many instances of joint occurrence [repeated relations] we encounter, we will never observe more than the *de facto* association and will never have ultimate, noninductive grounds for believing in a *de jure* connection."[7]

Black then declares that "The conclusion seems inescapable that any attempt to show (as Bacon and many others have hoped) that there are general ontological guarantees for induction is doomed to failure from the outset."[8] Black derides as "utopian" any of the metaphysical conceptions that religious people might draw upon as the source for such guarantees. Even so, he cannot feel at home with his own despair. He ends up defending induction, saying that Hume's problem may be a pseudo-problem simply because the very manner in which the problem is linguistically formulated makes a satisfactory linguistic solution to it impossible. He concludes: "The idea of ceasing to be an inductive reasoner is a monstrosity. The task [of solving Hume's problem] is not impossibly difficult; rather, its very formulation fails to make sense."[9]

Here, we have an exemplary case of the philosopher of science trying desperately to make sense out of reality without God—and of course inevitably failing. Black could not deride metaphysical truth if he possessed an adequate awareness of the meaning of *love* in helping us to assess the nature of reality. Aware of its own value, and hence of the necessity to believe in what is essential to its conservation, love *calls absolutely* for the analysis of all physical reality from the standpoint of metaphysical necessity. That is, it calls for believing that *love*, informed with *rational reason*, is The Ultimate Reality in which our world is grounded. Black never mentions such things, as of course also Hume did not. The giveaway in their whole argumentation is the total absence of any consideration of *value* (primarily sacred love) as a significant criterion for guiding their thinking in resolving such issues. Love—profound, committed, sacred—can never and will never predict anything less than the permanent preservation of its own precious value. Without an affirmation of the ultimate reality as Divine Reason, all philosophers inevitably contradict themselves. Without love, all philosophers are lost.

Examples of this may be found galore in the writings of all nihilists. A pristine array of them can be found on exhibit in "An Absurd

Reasoning," the first chapter of Albert Camus' book *The Myth of Sisyphus*. Using reason to ultimately undermine all reason, Camus asserted that

reason is useless and there is nothing beyond reason. . . . The world in itself is not reasonable. . . Universal reason, practical or ethical, determinism—those categories that explain everything—are enough to make a decent man laugh. . . . In psychology as in logic, there are truths, but no truth . . . there is no truth, but merely truths. . . . All true knowledge is impossible . . . no truth is absolute. . . . As soon as thought reflects on itself, what it first discovers is a contradiction. . . . The mind that studies itself gets lost in a giddy whirling . . . nothing is clear, all is chaos. . . . The tightest system, the most universal rationalism, always stumbles eventually on the irrational of human thought. . . . The world itself is but a vast irrational. . . . The mind aroused by this insistence seeks and finds nothing but contradictions and nonsense. . . . I judge the notion of the absurd to be essential and consider that it can stand as the first of my truths. . . . And carrying this logic to its conclusion, I must admit that that struggle [between the mind's efforts to be rational and the inescapability of contradictions] implies a total absence of hope.[10]

Camus devoted this whole chapter to trying to show that there can be no unifying principle in reality, that ultimately there can be no objective reason for anything to exist at all, much less a unifying reason to explain the relations between different things and events. Even so, he insisted that "without any unifying principle, thought can still take delight in describing and understanding *every* aspect of experience." This position is characteristic of those professional nihilists who deny that anything can be clearly understood, but who then proceed to write endless words to explain everything to us in order that we can understand. How can it be possible to "understand every aspect of experience" without any unifying principle? It is an indisputable fact that our various and continued experiences could never conceivably be meaningfully unified and integrated without some unifying and integrating principle. Indubitable proof of this lies in simply observing Camus' own continuous use of inductive reasoning to renounce the truthfulness or reliability of any inductive reasoning. His blatant example which I already have cited—"there is no truth, but merely truths"—is a generalization which he obviously insisted is true for all of us, while simultaneously he denied that there is any truth that is true for all of us —which is not only illogical but categorically hypocritical.

Induction and Sensibility

Camus insisted that he had "an appetite for the absolute and for unity," but simultaneously he insisted on "the impossibility of reducing this world to a rational and reasonable principle." He then lamented that he could not reconcile his desire and search for absolutes with the fact that in reality there simply are none to be found. I, for one, find no plausibility or sincerity whatever in his claim that this lamentation was real. I would be dishonest not to point out that I think his motivation was bad. Camus wanted us to think that he was an absurdist because reality is absurd and *dictates* absurdism. Clearly he attributed bad motivation to those of us who insist that rational reason calls for the affirmation of rational reason at the heart of reality. He accused us of being escapist and insincere. The truth is, Camus was by personal preference and emotional disposition a nihilist who used his attack upon reason as an escape from having to *face* those absolutes that are the only things that could bind him with the absolute responsibility to *care*.

Camus' absurdism is simply an absurd escape hatch. Denying all hope, he insisted that we are inauthentic if we allow ourselves some absolute truth or value to *appeal* to. But plainly, he himself unconsciously *appealed* to inductive reason as a tool for renouncing inductive reason. He *appealed* to absolutes to renounce all absolutes. He absolutized relativity itself. He absolutized the inescapable futility of all efforts to permanently conserve some values in life. He absolutized the irrational. He glorified the contradictory. He absolutized the absurdity of existence. The authentic man is the absurd man whose "only truth is defiance." The key words to Camus' philosophy are absurdity and defiance. Ultimately, being alive is absurd, since there is no reason to be alive, and since living adds up in the end to nothing. "Living is keeping the absurd alive. Keeping it alive is, above all, contemplating it." Since life is futile, one must live in defiance of one's own futility. Since life is meaningless, one must find meaning in defiance of one's own meaninglessness. Since existence is unreasonable, one can be reasonable only by accepting and affirming the unreasonable, i.e., by being defiantly absurd.

Does all this make sense?

Like any nihilist, Camus played a game with himself by wearing two faces. His fundamental irrationality consisted in arguing that a contradiction is the truth, that irrationality is rational, that he knew for certain that nothing is certain. Likewise, it consisted in his absolute renunciation of all absolutes, his definition of affirmation as defiance. Camus *preferred* the absurd. The absurd would save him from the responsibility to make sense. His philosophy was escapist. He did not want the world to be reasonable, because in such a world he would have an inescapable duty to be reasonable. He did not want any absolute truths to exist, because by facing such truths he would find himself absolutely accountable. Without any absolutes, he would have absolutely no responsibility to any ideal or to any person.

At the end of the chapter "An Absurd Reasoning," his final thought was about the possibility that someone might find a logical way to overcome the absurd. He rejected this thought out of hand, saying that he could make sense out of life only if he knew that ultimately it does not make sense. Camus argued that contradictions alone can sustain the authentic human being's will to live. He declared that it would be "bad to stop [living without contradictions], hard to be satisfied with a single way of seeing [having some unifying principle], to go without contradiction, perhaps the most subtle of all spiritual forces."[11]

Camus' argument that reality is ultimately unreasonable is philosophical suicide. He argued passionately that *defiance* is the only reason for not committing suicide, on the philosophical ground that there is no logical reason to remain alive, since life is absurd. I have had numerous students come into my classes who previously had become Camus' disciples (i.e., victims). The most common question they ask is, "What reason is there to believe that reality ultimately is reasonable?" The answer to this is obvious to a person with a rational mind. The rational mind acts to integrate itself, not to divide itself, as Camus did with all of his logical and axiological self-controversions. Camus divinized the contradictory, which is intellectual perfidy. The appeal to sound principles of logic to deny that there are any sound principles of logic is nihilist revel—philosophical driveling at the nose. No one can reasonably argue against reasonableness. And what is more, reasonableness must consist necessarily in being more than merely consistently logical. Reasonableness consists in dealing in value judgments that are self-supportive; i.e., no person with reasonable values will act to subvert his own values. Why put vinegar in your own milk?

Camus extolled himself as the supreme example of the "Absurd Man." Yet, not once did he show any consciousness of how incongruous he was with himself. Both his logic and axiology were self-negating. His whole philosophy was self-subversive. He argued against suicide, branding it as an escape from having to live with the truth. And what was his truth? In his own words: "there is no truth." The Absurd Man "knows that in that consciousness [of the absurdity of staying alive] and in that day-to-day revolt, he gives proof of his only truth, which is defiance."

For this kind of double talk, Camus won the Nobel Prize.

How is one to comprehend the great influence, the widespread popularity, of so irrational a man? The wreckage that comes from such destructive thinking is a sad sight to behold. Unquestionably, much of the cause of this is the confusion beriding the minds of people who do not know how to approach the solution to philosophical problems logically. But also, much of Camus' appeal is to people who want to bask in the emotional luxury of escape, i.e., to that experience of *release* which comes when suddenly they feel *unbound* by any absolute responsibility. The kind of confusion afflicting Camus' mind is inevitable to anyone seriously and critically reflecting on the problem of evil while seeing God as an omnipotent being. Camus could see that an omnipotent God cannot possibly be reconciled with the realities of evil in this world.[12] But his remarks on the subject indicate that he had no familiarity whatever with a more rational and realistic conception of God. And it is obvious that he lacked the imagination and rationality to develop such a conception on his own. Hence, his choice appeared to be between two alternatives both of which are totally implausible to the rational mind: classical theism or atheism. Camus' failure to bring love into his philosophy, plus the tendencious and aggressive nature of his espousal of anti-reason, suggests that he had little or no interest in finding a more reasonable option.

In the natural sciences, predictions can be made only on the basis of our understanding of the laws of nature and sound logical canons of inference. The laws of nature are not absolute. By laws of nature, I mean the laws of chemistry, physics, biology, astronomy, and all other disciplines wherein we have to verify or disprove assumptions by means of testing or experimental procedures. As I stated in the chapter on Evil, there is no conceivable reason why God could not create different universes characterized by different laws of nature, e.g., a world in which bodies would never grow old. All of the laws of nature operating in these universes would be contingent upon

God's will, and could be altered or suspended by Him anytime He had a rationale for changing them. On a limited basis, this may have been the case with Jesus when He produced the loaves and fishes by what appeared to be a *fiat arbitrium*. On the other hand, it may be that He did not suspend or alter any laws at all, but rather drew upon laws already present in nature which we do not yet know about or understand. Since all laws of nature are contingent, there can be no basis for making guaranteed predictions that they will always function as they now do. Nonetheless, there has to be a basis for *guaranteeing* some types of predictions. Only those laws of reality that are absolute can be certainly predicted to hold in any world order at all times. These are the laws of logic, mathematics, ontology, morality and psychology that are fixed immutably in that ultimate scheme of things which is God's Essential Being.

The reader can find an excellent treatment of the limitations on our power to scientifically predict the future in Abner Shimony's long essay "Scientific Inference."[13] This is possibly the most rigorous, sophisticated analysis of the problems of induction in print. However, his approach does not go far enough to do justice to the subject in its full breadth and depth. Like nearly all other writers on the subject, Shimony does not bring God into the picture. Neither does he see the necessity to connect the philosophy and science of induction with the philosophy of values. God is the sole basis for any conceivable conservation of values in time. He is the only basis for certainty in our predictions that *some* world will always exist in which *some* values will always be conserved. Now, we never become conscious of life's intrinsic values by ratiocinating on abstract axiological questions. Rather, we become conscious of such values *ab intra*, or through our capacity to intuit intrinsic goodness when we are the beneficiaries of it. I am speaking of unselfish love, joy, beauty, and other values which a person comes to appreciate through his capacity to *feel*. There is no way a person can experience these things by pondering the analytical issues of induction. And certainly, there would be no value in pondering such issues at all unless by so doing one arrives at a philosophy of induction that somehow might enrich his experience of these values and the joy of faith in their permanent conservation. However exact and scrupulous it might be, any philosophy of induction without God can only prove in the end to be nugatory. I realize that such statements as these are offensive to the agnostic and atheist. But then, if they clearly understand the position they are taking, they must admit that they are presenting a view of the world as ultimately unintelligible. I do not have to defend my view that intelligibility is what all philosophy must strive for in constructing a picture of the world. From my position, I can predict wholeheartedly that the sacred values in my life of love can be preserved forever, no matter what changes God might make in the laws of the universe I am now in. But the atheist and agnostic cannot wholeheartedly predict anything at all.

19
The Last Escape Hatch

ANY PERSON who is interested in an excuse to escape having to face God can find it in modern philosophy without having to look very hard. Previously in this book, I have identified several excuses for scepticism and nihilism, and have attempted to show how all such excuses end up being reducible to absurdity. There can be no doubt that the bad reputation of modern philosophy is due to the fact that it has so often violated the requirements of hoary commonsense knowledge. No person with a sharp mind can fail to realize that our commonsense perceptions of reality sometimes are illusory and mistaken and can seriously mislead us. But one perennial demand of sound common sense is that reality ultimately must make sense, and this means that the basic structure of reality must be reasonable. To say that reality is ultimately reasonable is to say that it is charged with rationality or reason, i.e., that it is free from self-vitiation by self-contradiction. Today, the nihilist or sceptic defends himself most commonly by arguing that there are "paradoxes" at the bottom of reality that are insusceptible to logical resolution. These assumed paradoxes (contradictions) and their assumed immunity to logical resolution would constitute proof that reality is ultimately irrational, and hence, that God cannot exist. A perfectly rational God would contain no inherent irrationality within Himself, and would never create a world order with any contradictions in its necessary structure. But since there are inescapable contradictions obviously informing basic reality (the nihilists tell us), the idea of God is illusory and is a false hope.

Curiously, the arguments questioning the logicality of the ultimate world ground have been originated by the professional mathematico-logicians themselves—those guardians of the innermost shrine of philosophy. For example, Cesare Burali-Forti, Jules Richard, Julius König, Kurt Grelling, and Bertrand Russell are famous for the paradoxes they have formulated that are presumed to challenge the ultimate logicality of the world order.[1]

It is odd that the questions challenging the ultimate foundations of logic have come from the logicians themselves. For it is from the logicians in their expert pursuits of rationality that one could most logically hope to find unbiased reference marks from which to rear a sound structure of knowledge. But unfortunately, the poor status of logic today has been brought about by none other than the professional logicians themselves, and the serious student in their classes is likely to end up more confused than enlightened. When students come into my classes from other teachers' philosophy courses, more often than not they carry doubts in their heads that logic has any ultimately solid foundation at all. It seems that in philosophy classes, especially in epistemology and logic, students often are led into the playing of intellectual games in which many end up losing possession of their common sense. Many students form the habit of doubting the primordial coherence of logic and the power of language to coherently express the truth. I, myself, remember my pragmatist teachers familiarizing me early in philosophy with many famous paradoxes in logic and language. In their ineptitude, my pragmatist teachers erroneously looked upon these paradoxes as insoluble. And consequently, from this viewpoint they inferred that ultimately there are no coherent laws of logic and language. Hence their dogmatic teaching that truth is finally relative and chaotic. It appeared obvious to me that the acceptance of such paradoxes as irresolvable would be irrational and self-defeating. Nonetheless, as the Oxford linguistic philosopher J. L. Mackie has put it, "These paradoxes, however artificial they may seem and however trivial their subject matter may be, constitute a challenge to the rationality of human thinking in general." Mackie himself regarded all paradoxes in logic and language as subject to rational resolution, and his writings on the topic have contributed significantly to showing that this is the case.[2]

The most famous (or infamous) of all the paradoxes is the so-called Liar paradox, attributed in origin to Epimenides of Cnossus, in the sixth century before Jesus. This is the most easily understood and entertaining of all the major paradoxes and is perpetuated to this day in many philosophy classes as though it were still a lethal challenge to the basic coherence of logic. This paradox, as we now most commonly know it, was brought into sharpened focus in the fourth century B.C. by Eubulides of Miletus, who presumably found great pleasure in inventing his paradoxes to challenge Aristotle's belief that logic is essentially a coherent discipline.

Aristotle started professional philosophy off on the right foot insofar as he clearly showed the categorical necessity for some universally binding laws of logic. One of these, e.g., is the law of identity, which simply states that something is what it is and is not what it is not. Without this law informing the scheme of things at large, it is inconceivable that any knowledge could be possible, for there could be no possible ground for identification, differentiation, and distinction. No one could recognize anything, for there simply could not be anything that is what it is and is recognizable as such. Another compelling law of logic is the principle of contradiction, which necessitates the fact that a thing cannot contain a quality and at the same time not contain that same quality. Or in other words, a proposition cannot be inherently true and false at the same time. Or in other words yet, a subject cannot have a predicate and at the same time not have that predicate.[3] For example, a person cannot make a single simple statement and at the same time be telling the truth while he is telling a falsehood. Another law close to these is the law of excluded middle, which states that, at a given time, a subject either has a definite predicate or it does not. For example, either Abraham Lincoln is dead or he is not; either I am the author of this book or I am not.

Now, in some modern schools of philosophy these fundamental laws of language and logic are regarded as having no necessary binding power at all. For example, in the language philosophy known as "general semanticism"—which is grounded in the assumption that there is no fixity in nature whatever (due to the alleged omnipresence of change)—all three of the above-mentioned laws of logic are set aside as based on the erroneous assumption that there are beings and essences in reality, and on the assumption that there are some universal and absolute truths. Some widely influential advocates of this school are Count Alfred Korzybski, Stuart Chase, and S. I. Hayakawa. The overwhelming majority of courses in semantics taught in departments of communication and departments of English in our colleges today familiarize the students almost exclusively with the viewpoints in this relativistic philosophy of language, at the great expense of ignoring the general history of semantics and the essential principles of a realistic philosophy of language and logic. Right and left, I encounter students in my classes who have taken these courses and found in them all the excuses they need to rationalize nebulous and contradictory ways of thinking—and to escape from having to face some clear and definite responsibilities to ultimate truth and ideals.

A person with a rational mind can readily see through the fallacies and self-deception involved in clinging to the epistemological nihilism of this "general semanticist" school. While they deny the validity of any of Aristotle's simple and essential principles of logic, they nonetheless constantly appeal to them in the very acts of making their attacks against them. For example, they employ the principle of "either/or" in trying to undermine the principle of "either/or." It is obvious that, in effect, they are taking the position that *either* the principle of "either/or" is not valid, or else it is valid; and then, they conclude that one is not justified in employing the principle because it is not valid, while they themselves at the very time are actively but unconsciously employing the selfsame principle.

Intellectual *hipocresía sin igual.*

I shall now return to the Liar paradox as started by Epimenides. A semi-legendary prophet of the island of Crete, Epimenides made a remark about Cretans that, as it was phrased, in effect condemned himself as an inveterate liar. For he said, *"All* Cretans are liars," which was a sweeping condemnation of Cretans that included himself. The Apostle Paul picked this up in his Epistle to Titus, which shows how widely known the paradox was at the time. Paul remarked, "It was a Cretan prophet, one of their own countrymen, who said, 'Cretans are always liars, vicious brutes, lazy gluttons'— and he told the truth!"[4] It is uncertain whether Paul saw the apparent paradox in Epimenides' remark, although he did call for a return to "sane beliefs" on the part of the whole Cretan society. In this case I shall show that the term paradox is simply an honorific term for a contradiction, and a contradiction can never be true. Those philosophers who argue that Epimenides was speaking truthfully and falsely at the same time are speaking up only to put themselves down. If Epimenides had been asked whether he meant to include himself in the word "all," at least on this occasion, he no doubt would have said "no"—and the so-called paradox of the Liar would perhaps never have arisen. But Epimenides did not think to exclude himself as the subject of his own predicate, or as the object of his own reference, in his own statement about all Cretans being liars. This being the case, he could be accused of committing a paralogism, or of plugging his mouth with his foot.

As his statement stands, it is not necessarily a contradiction. The ridiculousness of it could be brought out more sharply if one reworded it to show the paradox in clear focus: "Anything any Cretan ever says anytime is a lie." Or to put it another way, which is implicit in the original statement: "I lie all the time; nothing I ever say is true." Or as Eubulides of Miletus put it (still bringing out what is implicit in Epimenides' statement): "What I am now saying is false," or simply, "I am lying." No matter how one may reword the original statement, unless one changes it to exclude Epimenides as either the subject or object of his own reference, it appears impossible to decide whether the statement is true or false. It is pathetic that many philosophy teachers see it as an instance of irrationality in the foundations of logic and of language, and hence perpetuate in their classes their irrational notion that reality in the last analysis must in some ways be basically absurd.

Now, ordinarily, we understand a statement as meant to be true by the person who made it. But if the kind of statement made by Epimenides is taken to be true, then it follows that it is false because the statement refers to itself, includes itself, and is about itself. But if we decide that the statement is false, then it follows that it is true because of its self-reference. In effect, Epimenides is calling himself a liar. If, as a liar, he tells us that his statement is true, then his statement is false, because he is lying. But if he thus tells us that his statement is false, then as a liar he is really telling us that his statement is true. Thus because his statement is true it is false, and because it is false it is true and so on, in an infinite regression forever, like the images in barber-shop wall mirrors that face each other. If we fed the Epimenides statement into a computer programmed to analyze and decipher propositions from the standpoint of the laws of logic, the computer would go on flip-flopping forever without settling on a conclusion as to whether the statement is true or false—until someone pulled the plug.

Some logicians have declared that Epimenides' statement is meaningless because it ends up saying nothing. But merely meaningless sentences cannot interact with a computer as true or false, whereas the Epimenides statement can be programmed into a computer and thus preserved from the frequent charge of being logically meaningless, i.e., of being neither true nor false. The Austrian philosopher Karl Popper has argued that to suppose that such sentences are meaningless does not succeed in getting rid of the paradox. According to Popper, if we get the Liar out of the front door —by declaring that his statement is neither true nor false—then immediately he comes back again through the window.[5] The endless indecision of the logical computer, the futile bouncing between truth and falsity during the attempt to decipher the sentence, "What I am saying is a lie"—this is an intolerable condition to any logician who is concerned to use ordinary language as an effective instrument for communicating and preserving truth.

A Polish logician, Alfred Tarski, has presented an argument to try to show that it is impossible to resolve such paradoxes by the use of ordinary language. According to Tarski, there are two types of language. The first type is called "object language." Object language is simply ordinary language—say standard English—when it is used to talk about anything except statements or language. For example, if I say "I am awake," this is object language, or ordinary language, because I am making a statement, but my statement is not *about* a statement or part of one. That is, I am using language to talk about something but not about language. Tarski called the second type of language "metalanguage." We speak in metalanguage when we are talking *about* ordinary language. Metalanguage may consist of, say, standard English, plus arithmetic, plus special symbols of set theory. The last four statements in this paragraph would be classified by Tarski as metalanguage because they are all *about* language.

Tarski tells us that there can be metalanguage, and meta-meta-language (statements about statements about statements about statements) *ad infinitum.*[6] For instance, "I rebutted his comment on my paper," or "I rebutted his comment about John's comment about my comment," etc. Consider the question of Pontius Pilate, "What is truth?" This *sentence* is in the metalanguage because it is language used to talk *about* language—in this case, about the meaning of the word "truth." The *word* "truth" is, in this context, in ordinary language, or the object language. Again, consider the sentence: "The statement 'The truth is hard to discover' is a true statement." In this sentence, the first use of the word "statement" is in the metalanguage, since it is used to evaluate a quotation in ordinary language. The second use of the word "statement" is in the ordinary language.

Now, let me return to the Liar paradox in a different form. Consider the following two statements:

PLATO: What Socrates is about to say is false.
SOCRATES: Plato has just spoken truly.

Although the above paradox consists of two distinct statements, rather than a single statement referring to itself, it creates the same type of problem for logical analysis as the notorious statement of Epimenides. For if Socrates' statement is false, as Plato said it would be, then it follows that Plato's statement is false, which in turn makes Socrates' statement true, and so on, flip-flopping forever, without either statement ever ending up as decisively true or false. Plato's statement may be taken as being in the object language, since Socrates' ensuing statement speaks of it. Socrates' statement then is to be seen as in the metalanguage. But Socrates' language is ordinary language for Plato's statement. Yet, since Socrates' statement is, as I have shown, already in the metalanguage, then Plato's statement must be in the meta-metalanguage. But I have already said that it is in the ordinary language—which it is, but it is in both languages at once. If we carry this on (as Tarski implies), then we discover that the one statement is similarly a member of all odd-numbered language levels all the way through an infinity of language levels. Likewise, we discover that the other statement is similarly a member of all even-numbered language levels through infinity. Each statement becomes alternatively true and false as one progresses up this infinite language hierarchy. Albeit, since each is in a different language all by itself, there is no final, discernible contradiction involved. To my knowledge, Tarski did not

354

discuss this particular version of the Liar paradox, but applying his procedures to it would lead to this as his own "resolution" of that paradox.

What Tarski did discuss was the same kind of paradox rendered in a different way. Consider the following:

The sentence between these ruled lines is not true.

The above is an example of a paradox similar to the kind Tarski used instead of Epimenides' sentence. But clearly, it is the Liar paradox all over again, but without the full-blooded Liar. No speaker is specified for the sentence used in between the ruled lines, although the sentence is clearly *somebody's* idea. On first glance, the sentence in between the ruled lines may be taken as being in the ordinary (object) language. But then, one sees that the selfsame sentence is referring to itself. Hence, the sentence is at the same time in the metalanguage, for it is in the same line of words in the same line of print, and refers to itself as its own object. Yet, the distinction between ordinary language and meta-language is to be maintained, simply for the reason that this is the only way in which a contradiction between successive attempts to interpret the Liar statement can be avoided. A sentence in the ordinary (object) language would be the object for the same string of words taken as being in the metalanguage of the next highest level, which in turn would be the object for the sentence in the next highest level, and so on through an infinite number of such upward hops. As Tarski sees it, truth cannot be expressed in any semantically closed system. It is essential to use infinite levels of language to resolve a paradox, since a paradox is not resolvable in any closed semantical system. Tarski would have us believe that the Liar sentence is linguistically decipherable into an infinite number of sentences. Contradiction is avoided by the fact that each successive sentence, which ordinarily would be thought to contradict the one next to it, is preserved from that fate by the fact that each sentence is in a separate, logically distinct metalanguage all by itself. That is, each statement (in a pair of contradictory statements) is lifted *out* of its logical and linguistic context with respect to its contradictory statement. Thus, the contradictions ostensibly disappear.

But now, not even Tarski would in point of fact maintain that we ever actually find anything like this in the world as we experience it. The only justification for this flight of fantasy is to skirt or evade the paradoxes. We do not need an infinite order of different languages in order to define truth. Moreover, no one can escape from the binding power of the simple fundamentals of logic by proposing that we can have no compelling language laws at all unless our semantical system is infinite. One gets the feeling from reading Tarski that his process of avoiding paradoxes amounts to dynamiting butterflies. Nevertheless, I have before me at this moment Irving Copi's widely used textbook *Symbolic Logic*, which tells us that "The source of the trouble is generally agreed to lie in the attempt to formulate the truth conditions of a language within that language itself."[7] This probably is not an overstatement, for Tarski's theory as a way to escape the paradoxes does appear to be dominant at the present time.

Tarski's theory of language and metalanguage arose from a suggestion by Bertrand Russell.[8] Russell had discovered a paradox that bears his own name. In an effort to find a resolution to it, as well as to other paradoxes, he devised his theory of logical types. I shall not go into this here, since its multiple problems render it mainly of historical interest, at least so far as language is concerned, and since Russell himself at length described his work as chaotic and unfinished.[9] Russell's influence on academic Western philosophy has been extraordinary indeed. But his inveterate habit of switching his positions, and of ignoring and abusing his own rules of the philosophical game, has resulted mostly in merely the spreading of useless doubt and confusion.

A mortal criticism of the weaknesses of Russell and Tarski's theory of linguistic logic is presented by the psychologist Henry Winthrop, in his brilliant article "Metalypsis and Paradox in the Concept of Metalanguage."[10] Winthrop clearly demonstrates that the philosophy of infinite levels of language appeals *unconsciously* to the assumption that everything intelligible in each level can be comprehended and expressed by statements in a language that is common to all of the levels. That is, Tarski's philosophy presumes to say something intelligible regarding the very thing about which it insists that nothing whatever intelligible can be said. In arguing that the concept of metalanguage is a logical necessity, the metalinguist must admit (to be consistent) that "every discussion of *any object language* assumes that the discussion proceeds only on the level of its corresponding metalanguage about whose structure *nothing can be said.*"[11] Why try to say something sensible about something you yourself are insisting nothing sensible can be said about? Why claim to understand that which you yourself claim cannot be understood? Why try to communicate something you yourself insist cannot possibly be communicated? Why try to clarify what you yourself insist cannot be clarified? Here again, we find an entire philosophical theory constructed on the basis of that fallacy I have previously pointed out as being most common in philosophy: appealing covertly to what is overtly denied. To my knowledge, no one has exposed this fallacy in the "logic" of metalanguage more lucidly—and engagingly—than Winthrop.

In his "Concept of Truth in Formalized Languages," Tarski tells us that *"The attempt to set up a structural definition of the term 'true sentence,' applicable to colloquial language, is confronted with insuperable difficulties. . . . The very possibility of a consistent use of the expression 'true sentence' which is in harmony with the laws of logic and the spirit of everyday language seems to be very questionable, and consequently the same doubt attaches to the possibility of constructing a correct definition of this expression.*"[12] For a stinging comment on the futility of such thinking as that expressed above, see Dennis Anthony Rohatyn's article "Against the Logicians: some Informed Polemics." Rohatyn sees Tarski and his followers as exerting strenuous effort only to accomplish a highly academicized return to logical nihilism in disguise. A rational and practical approach to

the problem of Truth has not even been broached. The deep issues have been left aside in favor of an easy and convenient, and ultimately self-deceptive, brand of symbol-mongering. Not only is the formulation philosophically trivial, it is of no help in trying to do something, however modest or humble, about the philosophically inescapable problem or problems of life, in small or in capital letters. Tarski and his followers, as well as his detractors, have nothing to say to *men*. They have neither explored nor exploited Truth, but merely debased and degraded it. . . . One cannot imagine Tarski offering his definition as a reply to Pilate's question.[13]

No subtle and complicated theory of types, or of language levels, is needed to resolve the paradox of the Liar and other paradoxes.

It can be shown easily that all Liar-type paradoxes are flat contradictions from the start. Careful attention reveals the fact that any statement, including any paradoxical statement, presupposes one or more suppressed statements as part of its meaning. Firstly, any overt statement entails, as part of its meaning, the covert assertion that the main statement is true.[14] Secondly, every statement implies that some person said it. That is, language is communication, which is inconceivable without somebody communicating some message to somebody. For example, the suppressed or covert part of a statement might say, "I say that," or "He asserts that," or "Someone claims that," or "I write that," etc. And needless to say, the subject who is doing the communicating must be in a conscious state. A suppressed remark communicated in detail might read: "I, an existing and conscious person, assert that . . ." In fact, a person usually asserts himself this fully in his last will and testament. Lawyers are well conscious of the problems that can arise when covert assumptions are not overtly communicated in writing—in order to resolve in advance any possible problem of doubt or confusion regarding what meaning is intended.

Epimenides declared: "All Cretans are liars." If we say that "I, a Cretan, am telling you truthfully that . . ." is the suppressed statement in Epimenides' communication, then his whole remark would read, "I, a Cretan, am telling you truthfully that all Cretans are [always] liars." In this case, it is simply obvious that Epimenides has made an irrational statement because it is immediately self-contradictory, and there is no paradox at all. Epimenides has simply spoken irrationally. On the other hand, if the suppressed statement in his remark is "Except for myself," then his communication as a whole would read, "Except for myself, Cretans are liars." Or, his remark could read, "All Cretans, other than myself, are liars." In this case, there would be neither a contradiction nor a falsehood in the communication, if it were a true statement. And of course, no paradox. If Epimenides' own statement was false, then it would be only a falsehood, not a paradox. In the latter part of Arthur Pap's chapter "Analytic Truth and Ostensive Definition," the reader can find an interesting explanation of this approach to resolving paradoxes without the cumbersome problems in the drastic solutions proposed by Russell and Tarski.[15]

There are many other kinds of paradoxes that raise challenges to language, logic, and the rationality of the universe. As this book is already too long, I shall not pause to raise them here. The reader further interested in these problems would do well to consult J. L. Mackie's incisive and creative article, "What Can We Learn from the Paradoxes?"[16] There he will find answers sufficient in quantity and generality to support the faith that logical reason, properly understood, supports the rationality of the universe and does not negate it. The reader will find some helpful suggestions in Karl Popper's clever dialogue, "Self-Reference and Meaning in Ordinary Language."[17]

Fortunately, most writers in logic are cautious about openly applying their anti-logic to anything outside of games in their logic classes. But the fact remains, the nonsense which they have made available for their classroom use has at least inhibited many of their followers from affirming any necessary truths and has spread pungent fertilizer on the fast-growing brambles of unreason. Many laymen and inept students have been rendered helpless to use their powers of reason with confidence, being caught as they are in the thickets of unreason. The matter is serious because the perpetrators of such confusion often are subtle and recondite people. Ordinary persons do not have time to track down the cause of the trouble raised by such games, nor do they usually suspect that it lies in the phony logic, or anti-logic, of many logicians themselves.

In some writings of serious importance, the American philosopher Henry B. Veatch and the Canadian philosopher F. F. Centore have illumined a basic and subtle perversity in modern logic (i.e., mathematical logic) when it is interpreted ontologically, i.e., as saying what is real and what is unreal.[18] This is the logic that received its main formulation in *Principia Mathematica*, a three-volume work by A. N. Whitehead and Bertrand Russell. At the present time, this logic is usually regarded as having superseded the traditional or "intentional" logic stemming from Aristotle. Traditional logic presumes to deal not only with bare symbols and abstract relations between them, but with real things and their essential qualities and relations. Veatch and Centore have shown that there is an important place for both logics, since each is useful in its own different way. The two different kinds of logic "are not interchangeable," and neither can be regarded as the father of the other. Centore and Veatch admire the abstractness of mathematical logic, that is, its inherent freedom from all content and meaning, and its efficient handling of relations. They admire it for the same reasons that they admire mathematics. But to rely exclusively upon it in ontology, as Russell would have us do, is to make the very kind of metaphysical commitment that Russell himself was concerned to rule out. Russell called himself a logical atomist (at least part of the time). He saw reality as made up of data of immediate experience in a complex batch of logical relations lacking any existential structure or essential reality. His first commitment, implicit in his mathematical logic, was to deny metaphysically that conceptual entities ever represent anything actually existing. For example, in mathematical logic there is no way to speak of *oneness* as having any reality aside from the abstract, featureless things of the world which are each somehow unitary. Oneness is not a *real* quality or predicate inhering in real things. Russell's second metaphysical commitment was that of relying exclusively upon the symbols of mathematical logic as a way of talking rationally about reality. And consequently, by staying within the confines of mathematical logic, we can never say or know what a thing actually is. That is, we can never say or know what essences ingress into a thing, or constitute it, or inform it. Fortunately, A. N. Whitehead (co-author of *Principia*) did not agree with Russell's reductionistic, simplistic notion that all reality can be formulated, studied, and understood mathematically. Russell's way of describing the world was indeed simple, but was too parsimonious and academic to do justice to reality. Realizing the limitations of mathematical logic, Whitehead said: "The justification of the rules of inference in any branch of mathematics is not properly part of mathematics; it is the business of experience or of philosophy. The business of mathematics is simply to follow the rule. . . . The conclusion is that Logic, conceived as an adequate analysis of the advance of thought, is a fake. It is a superb instrument, but it requires a background of common sense."[19]

Veatch and Centore brilliantly exposed the unrealism in Russell's denial that subjects and objects exist (and real persons!) which have a reality going beyond what can be expressed in mathematical logic. These writers show that the traditional or "intentional" logic avoids the problems of mathematical logic by allowing for real identities, i.e., real people and things having essential predicates and real ethical predicaments. As such, traditional logic has a definite place just as mathematical logic has its own place, and neither can displace the other. Thus, Russell's most ingenious and

The Last Escape Hatch

subtle thrust to tear down everything real and meaningful has been blunted.

It is said that someone once uttered the toast, "To pure logic— may it never be of any use to anybody." This legendary toaster, said to be a man from Cambridge, may have understood the extent to which logic has been twisted to persuade people that reality is irrational, and that religion and ethics are a waste. Of course, few logicians who are aptly described by the preceding sallies would admit to twisting logic or to having nihilist motivations. And probably very few are suspected by many students. But in failing to identify the self-destructive contradictions in much modern philosophy, and in sparing them from the derision they deserve, logicians and philosophers have held open the door to ultimate escape from moral responsibility. Too few logicians have spoken up. And amongst those who have, the contribution often has been more harmful than good. Professional logicians must bear indirectly much of the blame for the inhumane aberrations of the twentieth century.

20
Gödel and Metasystems

DEFENDERS OF TARSKI'S metalanguage theory may suggest that his infinite regress of metalanguage is, in its open-endedness, justified or even demanded by the well-known "incompleteness theorem" of the Austrian mathematician Kurt Gödel. The falsity of this claim is readily shown, even though Gödel's incompleteness theorem is fully accepted, and evidently rightly so. Gödel's theorem, published in 1930, concerns closed formal systems (i.e., symbolizable or ideational systems) such as arithmetic, geometry, and mathematical logic, all built up from axioms by definite rules of inference. Gödel's theorem states that the full consistency of a mathematical system cannot be proven without at some point going outside of the system and using rules of inference that are not originally in the system. That is, if one were to arrive at a strictly arithmetical "proof" of the impossibility of any contradiction appearing within arithmetic, then that "proof" would itself entail a contradiction in a manner somewhat similar to that of the Liar "paradox." On the other hand, a "proof" of the reality of a contradiction within arithmetic would entail a contradiction within that proof itself; and consequently, a contradiction in the system also

362

Gödel and Metasystems

could not be proven. What Gödel's theorem establishes is that in any mathematical system there is always a formula whose validity cannot be decided within the limited formal procedures of that system. This general undecidability means that arithmetic as a system which is deduced from axioms and rules is essentially incomplete or not fully systematized within itself. The philosophers Ernest Nagel and James R. Newman state in their valuable little book *Gödel's Proof*: "Given *any* consistent set of axioms, there are true arithmetical statements that cannot be derived from the set."[1] Neither would the addition of new axioms or rules to the set enable one to escape the incompletion of the set. For there would be some new arithmetical statements, derived from the added axioms and rules, that likewise turn up as undecidable. As Nagel and Newman put it, in the solving of mathematical problems there is always "a fundamental limitation in the power of the axiomatic method."[2]

In addition to strictly arithmetical statements such as "$2 + 3 = 5$," there are statements to be made *about* arithmetic. For example, a definition of squaring would tell us what 5^2 meant and how to arrive at its quantity as squared. Or again, "$1 + \frac{1}{2} + \frac{1}{4} + \frac{1}{8} \ldots$ implies an infinite series." Further talk about arithmetic carries over into discussion and theorizing, such as the unproved statement: "Every even number is the sum of two prime numbers." Statements *about* arithmetic are made in syntactically ordinary language and use words from ordinary language. Such statements are regarded by linguistic philosophers as metamathematical. Evidently, there is no reason to quarrel with Gödel's theorem up to this point. It is about some interpretations of his theorem that questions must be raised. For instance, in the opinion of the philosopher J. van Heijenoort, Gödel's theorem means that since "mathematics cannot be formalized in one formal system," it follows that "some hierarchy of systems is necessary."[3] This opinion is reminiscent of Tarski's move to evade the Liar paradox by superimposing an infinity of metalanguages upon ordinary language.

Gödel's theorem does suggest that any full proof of the consistency of knowledge, at least in formalized systems, can be obtained only through resorting to an ever receding, ultimately infinite regress of such systems, arranged in a hierarchy. Each system in the hierarchy would contain some statements which would enable the system next below it to attain consistency and completeness. This ideal of perfect knowledge has fascinated some powerful minds.

As I have intimated with respect to arithmetic, such a hierarchy of systems would evidently have to be in essence linguistic. Now, consider the "system" of ordinary language. As with arithmetic, ordinary language can be commented upon by means of language about language, or talk about talk about talk, etc. Should these levels be treated as distinct languages? Tarski thought so. As I have indicated, the language to be talked about was called by him the object language, and the commenting languages were metalanguages. Since the superimposing of a potentially infinite number of metalanguages upon ordinary language does go outside of ordinary language, and since this superimposing does avoid or evade paradoxes, some philosophers believe that Tarski's metalanguage theory is a paradigm of the supposed universal applicability of Gödel's theorem to any closed symbolical or ideational system. This belief is analogous to that expressed by van Heijenoort in his article "Gödel's Theorem," especially since metamathematics is a matter of language, at least in its syntax.[4]

Now, ordinary language is not and cannot be a completely formalized system, as is evidenced by the countless ambiguities in the meanings of words. Some philosophers—e.g., Bertrand Russell—have argued that ordinary language can be reconstructed into a fully formalized system. But the analytic philosopher Max Black has cogently argued that the full formalization of language is impossible. Indeed, Russell later stated, "I have never intended to urge seriously that such a language should be created, except in certain fields and for certain problems. The language of mathematical logic is the logical part of such a language. . . . The language of theoretical physics is a *slightly* less abstract part of what I should regard as a philosophical language."[5]

This restricted room for reconstruction will always leave us with language as something that is less than a fully formalized system. As van Heijenoort suggests, it is very hard to say what, if anything, Gödel's theorem might mean for a less than fully formalized system such as ordinary language.[6] As to language, the most that Gödel's theorem might do would be to suggest that even a formalized language would at some point be incapable of having its consistency absolutely proven, and that to become complete in this sense it would be necessary for something to be expressed outside of the known language—which simply means that it could not be expressed at all by us. But there is no problem here, since the systematization of human language in a complete set of logical rules and symbols is impossible both in theory and in practice.

But even if a completely formalized language system were possible, then what would it mean? Would Gödel's theorem prove that there is of necessity an inconsistency or paradox in language that can be resolved only through somehow going outside of a formalized object language for its resolution? Not at all. It is important to understand what Gödel's theorem does *not* do. Gödel's theorem does not establish that our arithmetical system, or any other system, is inconsistent or paradoxical merely because the theorem raises *questions* the answers to which lie outside of the formalized system under study. The fact that something cannot be either proven or disproven does not imply a contradiction or paradox. In Gödel's theorem, there is no *paradox* to avoid. There are countless things in philosophy and in the world generally which cannot be absolutely proven. Until Gödel's theorem appeared, no one but a nihilist would use this kind of fact as an occasion for a general wringing of hands or for resorting to obscurantism about the ultimate rationality of mathematics. Moreover, Gödel's theorem is relevant only to systems which start out with axioms that are by definition unproven and which are taken for granted. Thus, even if Gödel's theorem had never been discovered, systems such as geometry and arithmetic would still rest upon assumptions which everyone has always recognized as *apriori* or "unproven." One wonders what all the extramathematical flap regarding Gödel's theorem has been about. And as a matter of fact, the consistency of arithmetic was established by the German mathematician Gerhard Gentzen in 1936, and since then by others in various ways. These mathematicians have used logical and mathematical techniques outside of arithmetic proper, and their proofs appear to have satisfied most investigators.[7]

The occasion for Tarski's introduction of his metalanguages was his attempt to resolve the Liar "paradox." It is true that the Liar paradox needed to be resolved somehow, lest logic and the truth-transmitting power of language become subverted. But Tarski's attempted resolution has been shown to be hopelessly awkward and impractical. There are other ways to resolve the Liar paradox, as I have shown. Can Tarski's metalanguage theory justifiably be considered as a paradigm of the general applicability of Gödel's theorem? Do the questions left hanging in any formal system by Gödel's theorem justify Tarski's infinite regress of metalanguages?

Commitment to Care

The answer is definitively no. Of course, it would be pleasant to find answers to all of the questions that arise in the problem of how to understand and use metamathematical systems in practical ways to fulfill our real life needs. It also would be pleasant to know everything that we need to know. But that is not "in the cards" for human beings, at least not in this world. If the business of linguistic philosophy and mathematics is to fulfill the real life needs of Man, then we must address ourselves to solving the practical problems that are now related to these needs, rather than inventing paradoxes and seeking their solutions in something so lunatical and useless as an infinite regress of languages that no one can speak.

Notes and Library Key

CHAPTER ONE: Care in Objectivity

Epigraph: from "Two Tramps in Mud Time," *The Poetry of Robert Frost*, copyright 1936 by Robert Frost. Copyright © 1969, Holt, Rinehart & Winston. Reprinted by permission of Holt, Rinehart & Winston, Publishers.

1. For an explanation of the possibility of an infinite, cosmic multiverse, see Chapter 13: Olbers' Paradox and Infinite Creation.

2. For an excellent essay treating of the idea that God experiences suffering and tragedy, see Charles Hartshorne's "Whitehead and Berdyaev: Is There Tragedy in God?" (*Journal of Religion* 37 [1957]: 71–84). The article will lead the reader to an abundance of rich literature on the subject.

3. An awareness of this fact is essential to any sound system of psychology, especially in counseling and psychotherapy. William Glasser partly bases his theory and practice of therapy on it in his valuable book *Reality Therapy: A New Approach to Psychiatry*. Says he:

> Therapy will be successful when [patients] are able to give up denying the world and recognizes that reality not only exists but that they must fulfill their needs within its framework. A therapy that leads all patients toward reality, toward grappling successfully with the tangible and intangible aspects of the real world, might accurately be called a therapy toward reality, or simply *Reality Therapy*. . . .
> It is not enough to help a patient face reality; he must also learn to fulfill his needs (New York: Harper & Row, 1965, p. 6).

4. *The Letters of William James* (Two volumes, Boston: Atlantic Monthly Press, 1920, Volume II), p. 213.

5. Dickinson S. Miller, "James's Doctrine of 'The Right to Believe' " (*Philosophical Review* 51 [1942]: 541–558, at pp. 553–555). Italicization of "need" is mine.

6. *Thoughts*, by Blaise Pascal, "Infinity-Nothing."

7. William James, *The Will to Believe* (New York: Longmans, Green & Co., 1896), pp. 94*n*–95*n*. Or in *Mind* o.s.v. 4 [1879]: 317–346. Italicization of "risk" is mine.

8. In theory, pragmatism denies that any definite or certain truth ever can be *known* about needs. I.e., there are no necessarily valid criteria for distinguishing between knowing and merely believing. Even so, all pragmatists (Dewey, James, Peirce) inevitably appeal deviously to need, and to the practicality of satisfying need, as the basis for sound philosophy and psychology. But it is senseless for them to talk about the "satisfying" of needs while denying that certain knowledge of real needs is possible. Rejecting intrinsic truths and values, pragmatism denies the existence of any *necessary* criteria or conditions for distinguishing between good and bad kinds of personal "satisfaction" (Dewey's tool for making value judgments). Pragmatism leads inevitably to anti-intellectualism and moral nihilism because it renders the very concept of truth meaningless. A consistent pragmatist could never presume to deal in any reliable understanding of reality simply because there could never be any definite or certain truths for him to understand. Nonetheless, pragmatists continue to write endless volumes of philosophy appealing to their readers to share all of the understanding of the facts about the human condition offered in their pages. The pragmatist's fakery consists in his always appealing unconsciously to those necessary truths which he consciously denies. The most outstanding contemporary example of this fakery is pragmatist Joseph Fletcher, former Dean of St. Paul's Cathedral, Cincinnati. Philosophizing spiritedly and proudly in his best-selling *Situation Ethics: The New Morality* (Philadelphia: Westminster Press, 1966), he denies categorically that philosophy can ever in any way serve to bridge the gap between faith and doubt (see p. 41, Chapter 2). He clearly denies that anything at all certain can ever be known. Reducing Christianity to ethical relativism, Fletcher falls victim to all of the fallacies in such thinking exposed by Socrates, 2300 years ago, in Plato's classic work *Theaetetus*. Unfortunately, *Situation Ethics* has done untold damage by the notion it has spread that nothing whatever can be *known* about how to make valid and binding distinctions between true and false, and right and wrong. For a systematic dissection of the inconsistencies in the pragmatic concept of necessity or need, see my book *The Autonomous Man* (St. Louis: Bethany Press, 1970). Also see Arthur O. Lovejoy's *The Thirteen Pragmatisms* (Baltimore: The Johns Hopkins Press, 1963), especially pp. 18 through 25. See Paul Crosser's highly penetrating, devastating criticism in *The Nihilism of John Dewey* (New York: Philosophical Library, 1955; now available only from Xerox University Microfilms, Ann Arbor, Michigan, 1974). While attempting

to extricate himself from the inconsistencies of pragmatism, James only mires himself hopelessly in "Humanism and Truth Once More" (*Mind*, n.s.v. 14 [1905]: 190–198).

CHAPTER TWO: Care in Atomic Action

Epigraph: *Plain Truth* (Pasadena), June 1976, p. 21.

1. The first clause quoted is from Huxley's *Evolution in Action* (New York: Harper & Brothers, 1953, p. 7). The second clause is from his *Man Stands Alone* (New York: Harper & Brothers, 1941), p. 277. The final two clauses are from *Religion Without Revelation* (New York: Harper & Brothers, 1957), pp. 24, 121.

2. To make sense out of purpose, it is essential to regard purpose as a primordial category of reality. For a most interesting and convincing argument to this effect, see pages 104–116 of *Theory of Thought and Knowledge*, by Borden Parker Bowne (New York: Harper & Brothers, 1897; reprinted by Kraus Reprint Corp., 1970).

3. Bertrand Russell, *Religion and Science* (New York: Oxford University Press, 1968), p. 222.

4. Russell, "The Free Man's Worship," paragraph 5 (*Independent Review* [*Albany Review*] December 1903). Later reprinted, slightly altered, in his *Mysticism and Logic* (London: George Allen & Unwin, 1917). Italics mine.

5. Alan Wood, *Bertrand Russell: The Passionate Sceptic* (London: George Allen & Unwin, 1957), pp. 236–237. The television quotation is from the article on Russell in the *Encyclopedia of Philosophy*, near the end.

6. As indicated in Job 23, God as a complete entity is never biblically presented as an empirical observable. Neither Jesus nor the prophets regarded God as reducible to mere empirics.

7. Hoyle, *The Nature of the Universe*, revised edition (New York: Harper & Row, 1960), notably Chapter 6.

8. George Gaylord Simpson, *The Meaning of Evolution* (New Haven: Yale University Press, 1949), p. 344.

9. Some of the most recondite physicists are beginning to experience at least a faint awareness of the impossibility of ever constructing a comprehensibly intelligible theory of energy without turning to God. For example, Freeman J. Dyson, of the Institute for Advanced Study, asserts: "It would not be surprising if it should turn out that the origin and destiny of the energy in the universe cannot be completely understood in isolation from the phenomena of life and consciousness. . . . As we look out into the universe and identify the many accidents of physics and astronomy that have worked together to our benefit, it almost seems as if the universe must in some sense have known that we were coming" ("Energy in the Universe," *Scientific American*, September 1971, 50–59, at pp. 51, 59).

CHAPTER THREE: Care in the Cosmic Order

Epigraph: Ralph Waldo Emerson, *Monadnoc*, Stanza 12.

1. For an argument to this effect, see Sidney Hook's sophomoric book *The Quest for Being* (New York: St. Martin's Press, 1961). While denying that anything exists, Hook appeals to the existence of something in every sentence he writes! He could have saved himself and his readers much wasted energy if only he had read and understood Plato's *Cratylus*, in which Socrates refutes the dogma of the omnipresence of change once and for all—putting the prestigious pragmatist 2300 years behind the times. The *Cratylus* dialogue may be found in *Plato with an English Translation*, vol. 6, translated by H. N. Fowler (Loeb Classical Library, New York: G. P. Putnam's Sons, 1926), pp. 439–440. Or see *Great Books of the Western World*, vol. 7 (Chicago: Encyclopaedia Brittanica, 1952). Compare Plato, *Theaetetus*, 179–180.

For a consummate refutation of this pragmatic dogma of ceaseless and universal change, see *The Principles of Scientific Thinking*, by Rom Harré, Chapter 9 (Chicago: University of Chicago Press, 1970), pp. 234–256. Also see my book *The Autonomous Man*, especially Chapter 1 (St. Louis: Bethany Press, 1970). Generally, pragmatism confounds past, present, and future, and would annihilate any meaningful conception of time. This is especially the case with John Dewey and his disciples. For an exposé of Dewey's fallacies in this regard, see Arthur O. Lovejoy's article "Time, Meaning, and Transcendence" (*Journal of Philosophy* 19 [1922]: 505–515, 533–541). Also see my book mentioned above, especially Chapter 4.

2. Bethany Press, Box 179, St. Louis, Missouri 63166; 1970.

3. See Chapter 15: Russell, Mathematical Truth, and Absolutes.

Even a celebrated agnostic like Morris R. Cohen to make sense out of the world demands absolute truths. For example, the laws of logic and the laws of mathematics are categorical necessities, existing independently of the individual's perception or understanding. It is unfortunate, however, that Cohen's universals are accidental in essence, since they are not informed with any necessary reason or purpose. An accidental essence cannot in any meaningful sense be said to be essential and is a contradiction in terms. For since accidents are by definition non-essential, then how can they be regarded as *essential or absolute*? Cohen obviously accepts these laws as simply *given*, but for no *reason*. While he is of this bent, there is no reason why he could not also accept the existence of God, as simply *given*, since there is no call for a reason.

Cohen does not address himself to absolutes intelligibly. See his *Reason and Nature* (New York: Harcourt, Brace & Co., 1931), Book II, Chapter 1, pp. 202–205.

4. See Chapter 10: Einstein, Simultaneity, and Scientific Orthodoxy.

5. This is a verbatim quotation from one of my pragmatist graduate professors. Pragmatism relativizes all mathematical truth as hypothetical and tentative, or as "true only while it works."

6. See Chapter 16: Discerning the Meaning of Oneness.

7. Until recently, some physicists were convinced that evidence for symmetry in the atomic structure of the world was inconclusive. Evidence was lacking that the basic building blocks of the world were truly symmetrical in terms of their charge and mass. However, the evidence for total, ultimate symmetry in physics has now been established conclusively, and once and for all, by recent discoveries of the nature and behavior of anti-particles. See Chapter 3 of *Worlds-Antiworlds* by Hannes Alfvén (San Francisco: W. H. Freeman, 1966).

8. The idea that the universe is purposeless inevitably has an unrealistic influence on how we define objectivity. For a more elaborate statement on this, see Chapter 17: Singh, Peirce, and Anthropomorphism.

CHAPTER FOUR: Care in the Cell

1. *The Logic of Personal Knowledge: Essays Presented to Michael Polanyi on His Seventieth Birthday* (London: Routledge & Kegan Paul, 1961. Reprinted in Eugene P. Wigner's *Symmetries and Reflections*, Bloomington: Indiana University Press, 1967, pp. 200–208). See also Chapter 9 of the present work.

2. J. Bronowski, "New Concepts in the Evolution of Complexity," *Synthese* (Dordrecht, Netherlands) 21 (1970): 228–246.

3. Ibid., pp. 232, 245.

4. For an interesting treatment of this idea, see Charles Hartshorne's article "The Reality of the Past, the Unreality of the Future," *Hibbert Journal* 37 (1939): 246–257. See also his article "The Meaning of 'Is Going to Be,'" *Mind* 74 (1965): 46–58.

5. *Beyond Reductionism* (The Alpbach Symposium, 1968), edited by Arthur Koestler and J. R. Smythies (New York: Macmillan Co., 1970, p. 71). Copyright © 1969 by Hutchinson Publishing Group Ltd. Italics mine. The earliest suggestion of counter-entropy or negentropy known to me is in *The Way of Things*, by the theistic philosopher Wm. Pepperell Montague (New York: Prentice-Hall, 1940), pp. 119–123. See also Erwin Schrödinger, *What Is Life?* (Cambridge, England: At the University Press, 1944), Chapter 6.

6. J. Bronowski, "New Concepts," p. 243.

7. *Chance and Necessity*, translated by Austryn Wainhouse (New York: Alfred A. Knopf, 1971, p. 14).

8. *General Biology and Philosophy of Organism* (Chicago: University of Chicago Press, 1945).

CHAPTER FIVE: Care in Evil

Epigraph: *Echoes*, iv, "In Memoriam R. T. Hamilton Bruce, 1846–99," *Poems* (1904).

1. This statement is not a quotation. Rather, for purposes of effective representation, it is a summary in my own words of the strongest and most common objections made by my students to the idea of God.

2. This is the only manner in which the Sermon on the Mount can be coherently interpreted. See Matthew, Chapters 5, 6, and 7. Also see I John, the entire fourth chapter; and Revelations 3:20.

3. I would not wish my viewpoint to be confused with that of G. W. von Leibniz (seventeenth century German philosopher). Leibniz insisted that we live in the best possible universe, that any other possible universe would contain more evil than now exists in ours—which definitely is not my view. Leibniz did not understand freedom and used the word in tricky, illogical ways. He contended that God predetermines man to choose however he chooses, which is a bald contradiction. Thus, he strained himself to the point of self-parody to justify all the evils in the world. This is inevitably the bind one gets into when he ascribes complete dominion to God while simultaneously ascribing freedom to man (see Leibniz's *Theodicy*).

Voltaire is justly credited for demolishing this viewpoint of Leibniz's in his famous satire *Candide*. Unfortunately, however, Voltaire's tale ends up as little more than a bald travesty, since his own view of God is nothing more than that of a detached, deistic being who is above good and evil and about whom we can know nothing. He went even so far as to question God's goodness, implying that He has no particular care about the needs and affairs of men.

4. I would not credit myself for originating this idea. Perhaps the most elaborate formal treatment of it is found in Immanuel Kant's philosophy (*Critique of Pure Reason*, A811 = B839; *Critique of Practical Reason*, translated by Lewis White Beck, Indianapolis: Bobbs-Merrill Co., 1956, pp. 126–128, or 121–124 in the Prussian Academy edition).

Kant found reason to suppose that there is an infinite moral progression in the afterlife of every person. His writing indicates that he knew there were other thinkers before him who had seen intelligibility in the idea of restitution only on the *long range*. The idea is explicit in both the Old and New Testaments. The reader can find a comprehensive exposition of this viewpoint from a Christian perspective in my book *Lonely God, Lonely Man* (New York: Philosophical Library, 1960), out of print but now available from Xerox University Microfilms, Ann Arbor, Michigan.

5. Innumerable instances could be cited of atheists exploiting the idea of God's callousness, i.e., that He is omnipotent but does not use his power to prevent evil in the world. And rather than believe in a callous God, they deem it wiser simply to drop the idea that He exists. Ordinarily, atheists take the position that a God who is less than omnipotent would be only a behemoth magnification of Man. Bertrand Russell declared that if an omniscient God really existed, He would have known better than to produce a creature of such petty value as a human being. See his cynical *Religion and Science* (New York: Oxford University Press, 1968), p. 222.

6. For a uniquely rational discussion of the problem of good and evil in the afterlife, as implied by the concept of a non-omnipotent and non-omniscient God, see Chapters 5 through 8 of F. R. Tennant's *Philosophical Theology*, Volume 2 (Cambridge, England: Cambridge University Press, 1930).

7. There probably is no better treatment of the psychology and metaphysics of despair than Søren Kierkegaard's little book *The Sickness Unto Death*, translated by Walter Lowrie (Garden City, New York: Doubleday & Company, Inc., Anchor Books edition, 1954). Especially interesting is his description and explanation of unconscious despair.

CHAPTER SIX: Care in Need

Epigraph: *The Stoic and Epicurean Philosophers*, edited by Whitney J. Oates (New York: Random House, 1940), pp. 49–50, fragment 54, copyright 1940 by Random House Inc. Two words have been changed for smoother reading.

1. The concept of need is at the basis of even the ontological argument for God's existence; i.e., joyful existence is better, more valuable and *needful*, than non-existence. Charles Hartshorne, leading protagonist of the ontological argument, appeals obliquely to *need* as a primordial category of reality. See his book *Anselm's Discovery* (La Salle, Illinois: Open Court Publishing Co., 1965), pp. 172–173. See also his "Rejoinder to Purtill" (*Review of Metaphysics* 21 [1967]: 308–309).

2. *The Denver Post*, 9 May 1973.

3. For a very interesting documentation of man's latent preternatural psychical capacities, see Colin Wilson's book *The Occult* (New York: Random House, 1973).

4. Probably the most elaborate and scholarly analysis of the nature of the *self* ever printed is that of Christopher John Bittner in *The Development of the Concept of the Social Nature of the Self* (Iowa City: Fred Hahn Co., 1932, privately printed, originally a Ph.D. dissertation, now available only as an electrostatic reproduction from Xerox University Microfilms, Ann Arbor, Michigan).

5. Alburey Castell presents an uncommonly good argument, indeed cogent proof, of the fact that a person is a *spiritual agent* transcending his body and environment. See his little book *The Self in Philosophy* (New York: Macmillan Co., 1965).

6. In modern philosophy and psychology the concept of the self as a pure subject, or as an irreducible spiritual agent, not only is generally very misunderstood but often is disdained and mocked. See Chapter 14: Humeanism and Atomistic Psychology.

7. For a demolishing and incomparably funny criticism of behaviorist dogmas, see Harvey Wickham's *The Misbehaviorists* (New York: Dial Press, 1929). For an equally clever and lethal criticism, see Arthur O. Lovejoy's

article "The Paradox of the Thinking Behaviorist" (*Philosophical Review* 31 [1922]: 135–147). In much modern philosophy the existence of persons as subjects has been held to be a meaningless question. Lovejoy has refuted this view with his usual finesse. See his essay "On the Criteria and Limits of Meaning" in *Philosophical Essays in Honor of Edgar Arthur Singer, Jr.* (Philadelphia: University of Pennsylvania Press, 1942), pp. 3–23.

8. I treat the Nihilism of Sartre, Camus, and Russell in critical detail in *The Autonomous Man* (St. Louis: Bethany Press, 1970)—my intention being to show that their nihilist ideologies would make any rational concept of personal autonomy theoretically impossible. Any person who rejects God will unconsciously, if not consciously, proceed to substitute something else in His place. For an eye-opening exposé of the inadequacies of any substitutes, see Vincent P. Miceli's *The Gods of Atheism* (New Rochelle, N.Y.: Arlington House, 1971). Miceli has the weakness of being too unimaginative in his conception of God, but he effectively treats of atheism's gods historically, focusing especially revealing attention on Feuerbach, Nietzsche, Marx, Comte, Camus, Sartre, Heidegger, and Merleau-Ponty. Also, he systematically criticizes theologians who have depersonalized God, and hence, who also should be properly classified as atheists.

9. For an interesting critique of Maslow's deficient concept of freedom, see Peter Bertocci's and Richard Millard's book *Personality and the Good* (New York: David McKay Co., 1963), especially Chapter 5. Maslow's principal book is *Motivation and Personality* (New York: Harper & Brothers, 1954. A second edition appeared in 1970).

CHAPTER SEVEN: Care in Jesus of Nazareth

Epigraph: *The Destiny of Man* (London: Geoffrey Bles, 1937), pp. 28–29.

1. B. F. Skinner, *Beyond Freedom and Dignity* (New York: Alfred A. Knopf, 1971). This book is an exemplary instance of a work undeserving of public attention, of a purely gratuitous intellectual accolade. It reminds me of John Beloff's description of behaviorism as "methodologically misleading, philosophically false and ideologically pernicious. But in the end, perhaps its most glaring fault is simply a certain unmistakable *silliness* which qualifies it, surely, as one of the oddest intellectual aberrations of the twentieth century" (*The Existence of Mind*, London: Macgibbon & Kee, 1962, p. 49). Equally accurate is C. D. Broad's description of it as an example of "the numerous class of theories which are so preposterously silly that only very learned men could have thought of them." He then explains the popularity of the theory among gullible-minded people by pointing out that it is "put forward in highly technical terms by learned persons who are themselves too confused to know exactly what they mean" (*The Mind and its Place in Nature*, London: Kegan Paul, 1925, p. 623). Brand Blanshard describes behaviorism as an ideological "travesty" that "makes nonsense of human life." See his excellent article "Critical Reflections on Behaviorism" (*Proceedings of the American Philosophical Society* 109 [1965]: 22–28).

2. Jesus' attitude toward the Pharisees and Sadducees is disclosed sharply in Chapters 5, 7, 15, 16, 22, 23 of Matthew, and 13, 16, 18 of Luke.

3. Matthew 5:48 (King James Bible).

4. *A Place to Stand* (New York: Harper & Row Publishers, 1969), pp. 56, 80. Chapter 3, "The Living God," is an invaluable, edifying essay on the reality of God as a caring, divine Person.

5. Matthew 7:21, 5:13 (King James Bible). Italics added.

6. Matthew 5:43–47, 5:20 (King James Bible. Punctuation is here altered for smooth reading.)

7. In Catholic Bibles, Psalm 138.

8. It can be shown logically that to create at all, God has to have been creating always, in an indefinite past with no beginning. For demonstrations of this, see my book *Lonely God, Lonely Man* (New York: Philosophical Library, 1960, out of print; now available in 1974 xerographed edition by Xerox University Microfilms, Ann Arbor, Michigan); Edgar S. Brightman's book *A Philosophy of Religion* (New York: Prentice-Hall, 1940), Chapter 10, p. 335; and Rom Harré's "The Ultimate Structure of the World," Chapter 10 of his book *The Principles of Scientific Thinking* (Chicago: University of Chicago Press, 1970).

9. (1525) Translated by Philip S. Watson and Benjamin Drewery, in *Luther's Works*, volume 33, Philadelphia: Fortress Press, 1972.

10. See Chapter 12: "Cantor's Transfinite Versus the Complete God."

11. New York: Harper & Row, 1964.

12. Undoubtedly, Albert Schweitzer had this in mind when he wrote: "For the work which the American missionaries began here and the French have continued, I feel a hearty admiration. It has produced among the natives human and Christian characters which would convince the most decided opponents of missions as to what the teaching of Jesus can do for primitive man. . . . In proportion as he becomes familiar with the higher moral ideals of the religion of Jesus, he finds utterance for something in himself that has hitherto been dumb, and something that has been tightly bound up finds release. . . . Thus redemption through Jesus is experienced by him as a two-fold liberation; his view of the world is purged of the previously dominant element of fear, and it becomes ethical instead of unethical." See *On the Edge of the Primeval Forest* (New York: Macmillan Co., 1956, pp. 112, 104. London: A. & C. Black, 1922, pp. 167, 155. Copyright 1931 by Macmillan Publishing Co., Inc.).

13. I Corinthians 15:32.

14. Lamont (New York: G. P. Putnam's Sons, 1935), Chapter 6, pp. 243–244.

15. Ibid., Chapter 5, p. 174.

16. Ibid., Chapter 7, p. 228.

17. "What I Believe," *Forum*, October 1930, pp. 193–194. Reprinted in Albert Einstein, *Ideas and Opinions* (New York: Crown Publishers, 1954) p. 11.

18. Lamont, ibid., Chapter 5, p. 162.

CHAPTER EIGHT: *Chance and Necessity* Reviewed

Epigraph: *Faith and Education* (New York: Abingdon-Cokesbury Press, 1952), p. 124.

1. Translated by Austryn Wainhouse (New York: Alfred A. Knopf, 1971. Copyright © 1971 by Alfred A. Knopf Inc.). This book is almost matchless in its unreadability. Of the twelve graduate students I had study it, not one was able to make sense out of it.

2. For example, see the formidable case made against Monod's type of doctrine in *Cell and Psyche: The Biology of Purpose*, by Edmund W. Sinnott, former president of the American Association for the Advancement of Science (Chapel Hill: University of North Carolina Press, 1950). Though this work is earlier than Monod's, nothing has changed *in principle* concerning the nature of true biological explanation.

See also J. H. Woodger's *Biological Principles* (London: Routledge & Kegan Paul, 1929), Chapter 5, especially pp. 264–272.

For an interesting scientific criticism of the doctrine of evolution by chance, see Duane T. Gish's book *Evolution: The Fossils Say No!* second edition (San Diego: Creation-Life Publishers, 1973).

3. 15 October 1971, p. 39.

4. Page 172. Italics mine.

5. Arthur S. Eddington, *The Nature of the Physical World* (Cambridge, England: At the University Press, 1928), p. 71.

6. *Ibid.*, pp. 72–73. Italics with clause are mine, with "might" are Eddington's.

7. Evan Esar, *20,000 Quips & Quotes* (Garden City, New York: Doubleday & Co., 1968), p. 48.

CHAPTER NINE: Hume and Contemporary Physicists

Epigraph: *Collected Papers of Charles Sanders Peirce* (Cambridge, Massachusetts: Havard University Press, 1935), 6.12.

1. One of Hume's contemporary admirers is the Australian philosopher John Passmore. In his book *Hume's Intentions*, he praises Hume's agnosticism as though he regards doubt as an intrinsic value. Passmore ends his book declaring: "To be a Humean, precisely, is to take no system as final, nothing as ultimate except the spirit of inquiry" (revised edition, New York: Basic Books, 1968, p. 159). Passmore reminds me of the Unitarian bumper-sticker: "The question is the answer." If the purpose of philosophy is merely to conduct endless explorations never leading to any reliable and obligating truths, then—why

bother! As a matter of fact, the spirit of intellectual inquiry actually decreases in virtually exact ratio as agnosticism spreads across the world. Nothing more dampens the will to discover than the belief that there are no definite and reliable truths that can ever be discovered.

2. *Dialogues Concerning Natural Religion* (Indianapolis: Bobbs-Merrill Co., Library of Liberal Arts, 1947. Copyright © 1947 by Thomas Nelson & Sons Ltd.; reprinted by permission of the Bobbs-Merrill Co., Inc).

3. Sentences are arranged by me to shorten and clarify Hume's position.

4. The same can be said for Antony Flew (contemporary Englishman) whose agnosticism is both as proud and shaky as Hume's. See his *God and Philosophy* (New York: Harcourt, Brace & World, 1966).

5. Probably no one in history has created more academic philosophical perversions than Hume. One that is most noteworthy is his so-called "Fork" theory of truth, i.e., that there are two realms: (1) truths of reason, and (2) truths of fact. Hume thought that he had established an ultimate dichotomy between these two separate realms of truth, that is, that there ultimately is no intelligible relationship between truths of reason and truths of fact. His theory contains a hoof-in-mouth contradiction, namely, that it is intelligible to say that there is an inherent *un*intelligibilty in the relationship between reason and fact in the ultimate structure of reality. For an effective refutation of Hume's "Fork," see Brand Blanshard's "Necessities in Nature," which is Chapter 10 of his *Reason and Analysis* (La Salle, Illinois: Open Court Publishing Co., 1962). Charles Hartshorne refutes it abstractly and tidily in his article "Hume's Metaphysics and Its Present-day Influence" (*New Scholasticism* 35 [1961]): 152–171).

6. For an interesting and effective support of this point, read Henri Poincaré, mathematician and philosopher of science, in his book *Science and Method*, in various translations, Chapter 1. This is included in Poincaré's *The Foundations of Science* (New York: Science Press, 1913).

7. Some of these nine points were covered by F. R. Tennant in 1930 in his *Philosophical Theology*, vol. 2 (Cambridge, England: At the University Press). I came by most of these conclusions on my own, but am happy to have very recently discovered some of them in the thinking of earlier writers. However, the need to bring them up to date, to unify them, and to treat of them at length as I have done in this work, is unquestionably crucial. The reader may also find a strong presentation of some similar points in R. G. Swinburne's "The Argument from Design" (*Philosophy* 43 [1968]: 199–211). I have through my own thought concluded the need for a Cosmic Agent to explain the existence of natural laws. However, I find the same thought expressed by an eighteenth century English clergyman, the much maligned William Paley (*Natural Theology*, abridged by Frederick Ferré, Indianapolis: Bobbs-Merrill Co., 1963, Chapters 1, 23, 24; pp. 6, 38, 47–48). Paley's most voluminous argument for design in the universe was that of the designs of creatures in their physical and instinctual aspects. Later, Darwin was thought to have undercut Paley and his successors on this, a matter now substantially

in doubt (see Duane T. Gish's book *Evolution: The Fossils Say No!* second edition, San Diego: Creation-Life Publishers, 1973).

Be this as it may, Paley's weaker argument for design raised so much dust that his stronger argument was in effect lost from view. During my life I must have read thirty discussions mentioning Paley, but not one of them had a good word for him or mentioned his lucid statement of the argument that natural laws clearly imply a cosmic lawgiver. A contemporary case in point is that of J. J. C. Smart in the oft-mentioned *New Essays in Philosophical Theology*, edited by Antony Flew and Alasdair MacIntyre (New York: Macmillan Co., 1955, pp. 42 ff.). M. H. Carré repeats the same omission in his otherwise useful historical article entitled "Physicotheology" (*Encyclopedia of Philosophy*, New York: Macmillan Publishing Co., 1967).

There is some opinion that Paley's argument may not have been original. Paley was born in 1743. An argument making the same points was presented by Robert Boyle in his book *The Christian Virtuoso*, in 1690 (included in his *Works*, 1772, vol. 5, pp. 508 ff. Reprinted at Hildesheim, West Germany: Georg Olms, 1966, at pp. 520–521). It was a pleasure to have recently discovered Paley's argument deriving laws from a lawgiver, a sadness to have found it totally neglected or ignored in all previous allusions to him.

8. London: Routledge & Kegan Paul, 1957. Bohm's thought is mentioned favorably by the Argentine-born philosopher Mario Bunge in his book *Causality* (Cambridge: Harvard University Press, 1959). See especially the last few pages. See also *Quantum Theory and Reality*, edited by Bunge, which is Volume 2 in the series *Studies in the Foundations, Methodology and Philosophy of Science* (New York: Springer-Verlag, 1967). The articles by Bunge and by the philosophers Karl R. Popper and Henry Mehlberg are especially noteworthy. For another effective refutation of the indeterminist dogma, see Rollin W. Workman's article, "Is Indeterminism Supported by Quantum Theory?" (*Philosophy of Science* 26 [1959]: 251–259).

9. Ryle's celebrated book *The Concept of Mind* (London: Hutchinson, 1949) is merely pathetic, for it was thoroughly refuted nineteen years before it was written. Arthur O. Lovejoy, a most astute critic, had in 1930 published his great work *The Revolt Against Dualism* (Chicago: Open Court Publishing Co.). Ryle could have learned much from Lovejoy's orderly, gentlemanly, but mortal attack against the monisms of Russell, Whitehead, and others. But Ryle does not refer to Lovejoy. If philosophers and their publishers would read more before rushing into print with sophistic literature, then not only would much paper be saved, but the reputation of philosophy would improve. Instead, the intellectual community flounders in nonsense and malaise, having lost its way in the search for true philosophy. It is not only physics, psychology, and biology that stand in need of philosophical enlightenment, but religion and ethics above all.

See Harvey Wickham's *The Unrealists* (New York: Dial Press, 1930) for another devastating and exceedingly witty criticism of monistic ideologies. Though they obviously are not even slightly conscious of it, all despair-mongering monists such as Ryle must cling obdurately to a metaphysical psychasthenia. See Ryle's doctrine laid to ruins in John Beloff's *The Existence of Mind* (London: Macgibbon & Kee, 1962).

10. Berkeley and Los Angeles: University of California Press, 1944. Part III, Section 33, "Suppression of Causal Anomalies through a Three-valued Logic." See especially the third from last paragraph of this section, p. 166. See also Bunge's *Quantum Theory*, p. 115. Vast literature is available which treats of the philosophical problems of quantum mechanics. The reader may find a broad spectrum of the topical subjects discussed *en brève* in Max Jammer's *The Philosophy of Quantum Mechanics: The Interpretations of Quantum Mechanics in Historical Perspective* (New York: John Wiley & Sons, Inc., 1974).

Unfortunately, *none* of the literature heretofore published has shown a consciousness of the necessity to bring God into theoretical consideration to make sense out of the existence and behavior of quanta. Physicists normally grit their teeth at any theoretical postulations that "smack of metaphysics." Promptly rejected are any hypotheses not susceptible to direct sense observation or measurement by physical operations. Yet these same physicists—who would purge science of all metaphysical assumptions—do continuously, and indeed unavoidably, deal unconsciously in metaphysical presuppositions in every theory they devise and put forth. The reader will find this to be true of every theoretician studied by Jammer in his book. The only question is: Does the scientist deal in his metaphysical assumptions consciously and out in the open, or dishonestly and beneath the board? In this field, the first discovery an alert observer makes is how much theory has been accepted without any legitimate empirical verification whatever. Yet, the same theoreticians would keep God out of the picture solely on the grounds that His existence is empirically unprovable (i.e., by a *physical* demonstration).

11. See Niels Bohr, *Atomic Theory and the Description of Nature* (New York: Macmillan Co.; Cambridge: At the University Press, 1934), Essay III, pp. 99–101. On Einstein see Jerome Frank, *Fate and Freedom* (New York: Simon & Schuster, 1945), p. 162.

12. Elmer E. Anderson, *Modern Physics and Quantum Mechanics* (Philadelphia: W. B. Saunders Co., 1971), p. 99. Italics mine.

13. Kenneth W. Ford, *The World of Elementary Particles* (Waltham, Massachusetts: Blaisdell Publishing Co., 1963), p. 209. After Richard Feynman.

14. Bertrand Russell, *Religion and Science* (New York: Oxford University Press, 1968), p. 243.

15. London: Pergamon Press, 1958. Out of print—stated at the publisher's request.

16. Oxford: At the Clarendon Press, 1949. Quoted by permission of the Clarendon Press.

17. Interesting reflections on Born's type of subjectivism can be found in *Quantum Theory and Reality* (footnote 8 herein).

18. For two deadly criticisms of determinism, see Jerome Frank's *Fate and Freedom* (New York: Simon & Schuster, 1945); and Isaiah Berlin's *Historical Inevitability* (London: Oxford University Press, 1959).

19. Even the agnostic philosopher Ernest Nagel recoils at the thought of ultimate lawlessness. See his attack on indeterminism in Chapter 10 of his book *The Structure of Science* (New York: Harcourt, Brace & World, 1961). It is unfortunate that he treats the laws of nature ultimately as accidents, thus bogging down in the same quicksand as the indeterminists but proudly without awareness.

20. "New Concepts in the Evolution of Complexity" (*Synthese* [Dordrecht, Netherlands] 21 [1970]: 228–246, at p. 242). Italics mine. There are earlier references to Bronowski in Chapter 4.

The reader may find similar objections to Bronowski expressed most effectively by the philosopher F. F. Centore, in his article "Mechanism, Teleology, and 17th Century English Science." This essay is a gentle, but crushing, criticism of the anti-teleological metaphysics in Ernest Nagel's *The Structure of Science*. Centore's article appeared in *International Philosophical Quarterly* 12 (1972): 553–571.

Centore's critical reflections on the theory of evolution are very recommendable reading. See *The Thomist* 33 (1969): 456–496, 718–736; ibid. 35 (1971): 113–142.

CHAPTER TEN: Einstein, Simultaneity, and Scientific Orthodoxy

The Ives Papers: Alternative to Relativity is published simultaneously with this volume. Numerous journal references to the papers of Ives appear below, all correlated to *The Ives Papers* volume. That volume is recommended to serious students as a companion to the present volume. It is published by Institute for Space-Time Studies, Box 7123, University Station, Provo, Utah 84602.

Einstein's *Collected Writings* were issued in 1960 on opaque microcards by Readex Microprint Corporation, New York, with an index book. The references to Einstein's works that appear below can generally be found there.

J.O.S.A. in the notes refers to the *Journal of the Optical Society of America.*

1. *Space, Time, Matter,* translated by Henry L. Brose (London: Methuen & Co., 1922), p. 174. Italics are in the original.

2. *Albert Einstein: Philosopher-Scientist,* edited by Paul A. Schilpp, Evanston, Illinois: Library of Living Philosophers, 1949, p. 245. Margenau later retreated partially from this remark; see *Philosophy of Science* 24 (1957): 297–307, at p. 303.

3. *Albert Einstein: Philosopher-Scientist,* p. 587.

There has been some argument as to whether Einstein actually said that the velocity of light is in fact the same for all observers under all circumstances (minor corrections aside). Whatever Einstein may have implied to the contrary, this conclusion follows directly from (1) his denial of absolute space or "rest," and (2) his clock synchronization convention. That is, a ray from clock

A travels to clock *B*, where it is reflected back to clock *A*. The elapsed time for the round trip is noted at *A*. Einstein stipulated that half of this interval is to be taken as the time occupied by the trip from *A* to *B*, even though nobody knows this to be either true or false. Moreover, Einstein's denial of absolute space (as something through which and with reference to which light travels) blocks even the conceivability of such knowledge. Thus, Einstein leaves no room for distinction between objective speeds for light and our measurement of the speed of light, which always comes out to the same value. In any event, this is the way the matter has generally been understood by scientists. As to (1), see "Electrodynamics," the second paragraph. As to (2) see "Electrodynamics," section 1. See note 4.

4. *Relativity: The Special and the General Theory*, fifteenth edition, New York: Crown Publishers, 1961, Chapter 7, p. 23. Hereinafter this volume is referred to as *Relativity*. See also the famous 1905 paper "Zur Elektrodynamik bewegter Körper" ("On the Electrodynamics of Moving Bodies"), *Annalen der Physik*, fourth series, 17 (26 September 1905): 891–921, in section 1, at p. 894; hereinafter the article is referred to as "Electrodynamics." A stilted English translation appears in *The Principle of Relativity*, by Hendrik A. Lorentz et al., New York: Dover, 1952, p. 40; hereinafter the book is referred to as *Principle*.

5. P. 120. In this connection the physicist Geoffrey Builder is noteworthy (*Australian Journal of Physics* 11 [1958]: 457–480).

6. See also summaries on pp. 120, 193, and 214. Most of the value of the book lies here and in the first 67 pages. Elsewhere, Nordenson went too far, as explained later herein. Notably, he erred in denying all physical meaning to the Lorentz transformation equations, a trap into which many have fallen, both critics and defenders.

7. *Albert Einstein: Philosopher-Scientist*, p. 587.

8. *Journal of Philosophy* 27 (1930): 617–632, 645–654, mostly reprinted in *The Ives Papers*, pp. 205 ff. Sections 3 to 5 (pp. 648–652) of Lovejoy's otherwise superb article must be dismissed as non-cogent. I cannot dwell at length upon his error, which requires intricate exposition. I will only say that the complexity which he hoped to eject through the front door re-enters through the back door. Fortunately, the rest of his article in no way depends upon these sections. For Lovejoy's further philosophizing on relativity, see *The Revolt against Dualism*, second edition (La Salle, Illinois: Open Court Publishing Co., 1960), pp. 111–116, 174–182, 345–347.

9. Ibid., pp. 624, 652–654. Also *Philosophical Review* 41 (1932) at p. 503 only.

10. "Electrodynamics," section 2, p. 897, or in *Principle*, pp. 42–43, here retranslated. Italics are added.

11. *Relativity, Time, and Reality*, Chapters 2, 3, and 4, especially Chapter 4.

12. "Space and Time," section 1, in *Principle*, p. 75.

13. Ibid., section 2, p. 83.

14. Ibid., section 3.

15. *Monist* 15 (January 1905): 1–24, at p. 16. See note 103.

16. See Weingard's article in the *British Journal for the Philosophy of Science* 23 (1972): 119–121. See also Putnam, *Journal of Philosophy* 64 (1967): 240–247.

17. E. Cunningham, *The Principle of Relativity* (Cambridge, England: At the University Press, 1914), p. 191, also p. 213. This is the only reference herein to this book; do not confuse with *The Principle of Relativity* by Lorentz, Einstein, et al., frequently referred to herein.

18. See the *Oeuvres de Henri Poincaré* (Paris: Gauthier-Villars, 1954), "Sur la Dynamique de l'Electron," volume 9, pp. 494–550, section 4 on pp. 513–515, also section 9. This is reprinted from *Circolo Matematico di Palermo, Reconditi* 21 (1906): 129–175, the most relevant pages being 144–146. On Minkowski's side see the *Gesammelte Abhandlungen von Hermann Minkowski* (Leipzig: B. G. Teubner, 1911), volume 2, the footnotes in "Die Grundlagen für die elektromagnetischen Vorgänge in bewegten Körpern," pp. 352–404, which is reprinted from *Akademie der Wissenschaften* (Göttingen) *Nachrichten, Mathematisch-physikalische Klasse*, 1908, p. 53–111.

19. See Lorentz's "Deux Memoirs . . ." in the *Oeuvres de Henri Poincaré*, volume 11, pp. 247–261, the first section, notably pp. 254–255. This is reprinted from *Acta Mathematica* 38 (1921) 293–308, notably pp. 300–301.

20. I was made conscious of the relevance of the law of contradiction by an interesting historical and analytical article of Martha Hurst: "Can the Law of Contradiction Be Stated without Reference to Time?" (*Journal of Philosophy* 31 [1934]: 518–525). References to earlier literature are to be found there. For the classic statement of the law of contradiction see Aristotle, *Metaphysica*, Book Gamma, 1005–1008. This is in *The Works of Aristotle*, Volume 8, translated by W. D. Ross (Oxford: At the Clarendon Press, 1908).

21. See Chapters 3 and 12 of Capek's *Philosophical Impact of Contemporary Physics* (New York: D. Van Nostrand Co., 1961).

22. *The Direction of Time* (Berkeley: University of California Press, 1956), section 30, p. 269.

23. Adolf Grünbaum, "Relativity Theory, Philosophical Significance of," *Encyclopedia of Philosophy* (New York: Macmillan Publishing Co., 1967), paragraph 1.

24. P. 126 of *The Nature of the Physical World* (Cambridge, England: At the University Press, 1929).

25. P. 108 (Garden City, New York: Doubleday & Co., 1964).

26. *The Collected Papers of Charles Sanders Peirce* (Cambridge, Massachusetts: Harvard University Press, 1932–1958), 5.520.

27. Compare Irving M. Copi, *Symbolic Logic* (New York: Macmillan Co.), in various editions, in the chapter "The Method of Deduction" and the section "The Rule of Indirect Proof." The philosopher Clarence Irving Lewis has been

credited with this discovery, in the first edition (only) of his book *A Survey of Symbolic Logic* (Berkeley: University of California Press, 1918), Chapter 5, pp. 335–339.

28. The opera libretto is by Adelheid Wette; the translation is here reproduced by courtesy of Angel/EMI Records (Karajan knew how to conduct it!).

29. Chapters 10 and 11 of *Philosophical Impact*.

30. *Relativity*, additions to fifteenth edition in 1952, pp. vi and Appendix 5.

31. *Mathematical Principles of Natural Philosophy* (*Principia*), "Definitions," (Scholium).

32. *Critique of Pure Reason*, A23 = B38 to A28 = B44. Two cogent general critiques of Kant are offered by Arthur Lovejoy, in *Archiv für Philosophie* 19 (1906): 380–407 (in English); also *Philosophical Review* 16 (1907): 588–603. Professional philosophers often flaunt their knowledge of Kant to browbeat the uninitiated. One may armor himself by reading Lovejoy's articles.

33. "Ether," *Encyclopedia of Philosophy*, 1967.

34. *Scientific American*, April 1950, pp. 13–17, at p. 15. *Relativity*, Appendix 5 (1952), p. 155.

35. See Einstein, "Electrodynamics," introduction, or in *Principle*, p. 38. *Jahrbuch der Radioaktivität* 4 (1907): 411–462, at p. 413. *Forum Philosophicum* 1 (1930): 180–184. *Relativity*, Appendix 5 (1952): pp. 149–150.

36. Translated from *Schweizerische naturforschende Gesellschaft, Verhandlungen*, 105 (1924): 85–93, at pp. 92–93. This view is affirmed in Einstein's book *The World as I See It*, New York: Covici Friede, 1934, "Relativity and the Ether" (1920), pp. 121–137.

37. *Scientific Papers of James Clerk Maxwell*, New York: Dover Publications, 1965, "Ether, pp. 763–775, at p. 775.

38. *Out of My Later Years*, New York: Philosophical Library, 1950, pp. 26–27.

39. Einstein did not always hold dogmatically to curved space. In 1932 there appeared a joint article by him and W. de Sitter, which stated: "We must conclude that at the present time it is possible to represent the facts without assuming a curvature of three dimensional space" (*Proceedings of the National Academy of Sciences* [Washington] 18 [1932]: 213–214).

40. Einstein, *Relativity*, Chapter 23, pp. 81–82.

41. Ives, *J.O.S.A.* (*Journal of the Optical Society of America*) 29 (1939): 472–478; reprinted in *The Ives Papers*, pp. 58 ff.

42. *J.O.S.A.* 29 (1939): 183–187, at p. 187; in *The Ives Papers*, p. 49.

43. *La Relativité*, Paris: Editions Chiron, 1923, p. 26n.

44. *Philosophical Review* 33 (1924) at p. 156.

45. Lovejoy, "The Paradox of the Time-Retarding Journey," *Philosophical Review* 40 (1931): 48–68, 152–167, at pp. 48–55. Some other parts of this

article must be rejected where Lovejoy's usual invincibility slipped. Lovejoy listened to Einstein too trustingly where Einstein failed to distinguish the true one-way velocity of light from the round-trip velocity ("Electrodynamics," section 1). Having missed this distinction, Lovejoy was bound to be sucked into a swamp of unresolvable arguments where formidable-looking mathematical expressions are used as smoke screens to cover ambiguity or contradiction. We may forgive Lovejoy for finally becoming impatient with the relativists who, he erroneously implied, didn't know what they were talking about with regard to contractions and retardations. Lovejoy even suggested (with some relativists) that these effects were illusions, as Henri Bergson had concluded. Nevertheless, Lovejoy's 1930 article had provided the tools for draining the swamp, to leave the relativists to wiggle about as best they might.

46. Walter S. Adams, *Proceedings of the National Academy of Sciences* 11 (1925): 382–387. Ives, *J.O.S.A.* 27 (1937): 305–309, at p. 309n; in *The Ives Papers*, p. 20.

On terrestrial atomic clocks, see later references to R. V. Pound et al.

47. *Principle*, pp. 99–101, 113, 117. Italics are added.

48. Compare *Relativity*, Chapters 18 to 20.

49. *Relativity*, Chapter 20. *Jahrbuch der Radioaktivität* 4 (1907): 411–462, at pp. 454–458. Also see Einstein's 1911 paper in *Principle*, pp. 97 ff.

50. *Naturwissenschaften* 6 (1918): 697–702. For a fuller exposition, see Lovejoy in *Philosophical Review* 40 (1931), pp. 157 to top of p. 161 only.

51. New York: Macmillan Co., 1962.

52. Møller, *The Theory of Relativity*, Oxford: At the Clarendon Press, 1952, e.g., sections 20 and 98.

53. *American Journal of Physics* 26 (1958): 515–523. Ibid., 27 (1959): 491–493.

54. *Australian Journal of Physics* 10 (1957): 246–262, 424–428. Ibid., 11 (1958): 279–297.

55. "Electrodynamics," introduction.

56. See note 50.

57. Mach, *The Science of Mechanics*, fourth edition, translated by Thomas J. McCormack, Chicago: Open Court Publishing Co., 1919, e.g., Chapter 2, sections 5 and 7, pp. 231–234; Appendix 20, 542–543.

58. *Relativity for the Million*, p. 43.

59. *The Science of Mechanics*, Chapter 2, section 5, p. 232. Italics are mine.

60. *Relativity for the Million*, pp. 124, 120.

61. *Principia*, "Definitions," (Scholium).

62. *Philosophical Magazine* (London), sixth series, 8 (1904): 716–719.

63. *Comptes Rendus . . . de l'Académie des Sciences* (Paris) 157 (1913): 708–710, 1410–1413; translated into English for *The Ives Papers*, pp. 191 ff.

Journal de Physique et le Radium, fifth series, 4 (1914): 177–195. See also E. J. Post, *Reviews of Modern Physics* 39 (1967): 475–493. Sagnac may have been killed in World War I. I have been unable either to verify or disprove this.

64. *Astrophysical Journal* 61 (1925): 137–145; reprinted in *The Ives Papers*, pp. 195 ff. A summary appeared in *Nature* (London) 115 (1925): 566.

65. *J.O.S.A.* 28 (1938): 296–299; reprinted in *The Ives Papers*, pp. 41 ff. *J.O.S.A.* 43 (1953): 217–218; reprinted in *The Ives Papers*, pp. 186 f.

66. The editor of the *McGraw-Hill Encyclopedia* writes me that the offending article, and also an abominable article on the "ether," are rewritten for the pending 1977 edition, though Sagnac, and Michelson and Gale, still go unmentioned.

67. *Nature* (London) 168 (1951): 906–907.

68. "Electrodynamics," section 4, in *Principle* at pp. 48–50. *Annalen der Physik*, series 4, 23 (1907): 197–198. For history see Ives, *J.O.S.A.* 37 (1947): 810–813; reprinted in *The Ives Papers*, pp. 128 ff.

69. *J.O.S.A.* 28 (1938): 215–226; ibid. 31 (1941): 369–374; reprinted in *The Ives Papers*, pp. 29 ff., 85 ff. Even the very most prestigious writers generally are not up to current information on important experimental findings. For example, Milič Čapek (whom I mentioned earlier) in his book *Philosophical Impact of Contemporary Physics* showed no knowledge of the Ives-Stilwell experiment. Harald Nordenson, in his often illuminating book *Relativity, Time, and Reality*, unfortunately did not know of this experiment. Note pp. 100, 123, 137, and 197 in Nordenson.

70. David H. Frisch and James H. Smith, *American Journal of Physics* 31 (1963): 324–355.

71. For details refer to *Science* 177 (1972): 166–170. See Ives' related prior analysis in *Nature* (London) 168 (1951): 246, which responds to W. H. McCrea, *Nature* 167 (1951): 680; both are reprinted in *The Ives Papers*, pp. 161 ff.

72. The interested reader may consult *Physical Review Letters* in 1959, 1960, and 1964 under the names of R. V. Pound, J. P. Schiffer, and T. E. Cranshaw.

73. The Mössbauer effect is further explained by L. Marder in his book *Time and the Space Traveler* (Philadelphia: University of Pennsylvania Press, 1971), pp. 154–161. Whatever my disappointments with Marder (and there are some), he has done considerable reading and reported on it clearly. See also *McGraw-Hill Encyclopedia of Science and Technology* on the Mössbauer effect.

74. *Physical Review* 140 (1965): B788–B803.

75. Einstein's prediction appeared in *Jahrbuch der Radioaktivität* 4 (1907): 411–462, at pp. 458–459. His 1911 amplification appears in *Principle*, pp. 97–108.

76. Sherwin, *Physical Review* 120 (1960): 17–21. Compare F. S. Crawford, *Nature* (London) 179 (1957): 35–36. Even Ives appears to have slipped a mite in the present matter; see *J.O.S.A.* 38 (1948): 413–416, at p. 416n, note 6; in *The Ives Papers*, p. 135.

77. Or more concisely (and for small values of $\Delta v/c$), the slowing Δt of the clock that experiences extra motion during a round trip will vary in proportion to the square of its speed Δv relative to one's own (inertial) frame of reference. We arrive at the total retardation Δt by integrating (i.e., summating) Δv^2 over all the infinitesimal instants dt from time o to T (in proper time) during an entire trip at various speeds, and then supplying some constants. That is,

$$\Delta t = \frac{1}{2c^2} \int_{O}^{T} (\Delta v)^2 \, dt$$

There is nothing here about acceleration *per se*. This equation itself is not new, but the interpretation becomes unambiguous only with Ives and with Builder.

78. For a further introduction to c as a limiting velocity, see Edmund Whittaker's book *A History of the Theories of Aether and Electricity*, volume 2 (London: Thomas Nelson & Sons, 1953), pp. 38 and before; also see pp. 48 and before.

79. *Scientific Papers*, p. 769.

80. *American Journal of Science*, third series, 34 (1887): 333–345. The same article appeared in *Philosophical Magazine* (London), fifth series, 24 (1887): 449–463.

81. See Herbert Ives, *J.O.S.A.* 27 (1937): 263–273, at p. 271; in *The Ives Papers*, p. 13. *J.O.S.A.* 27 (1937): 305–309, at pp. 308–309; in *The Ives Papers*, pp. 19–20. *J.O.S.A.* 40 (1950): 185–191, at p. 190n; in *The Ives Papers*, p. 152.

82. It is sometimes said that Einstein did not know of the Michelson-Morley experiment when he wrote his famous "Electrodynamik" paper of 1905. Einstein did say somewhere that he did not depend on the Michelson-Morley result to arrive at his own conclusions. Be this as it may, G. H. Keswani was able to show that Einstein had previously read *Science et Hypothèse*, by Henri Poincaré (New York: Science Press, 1905, as translated). In the index of that book, Michelson is mentioned four times, all in connection with the Michelson-Morley experiment. In view of this fact, it is reasonable to suppose that Einstein did know of a well published and much discussed work of this kind that was eighteen years old when Einstein published. See the first installment of Keswani's paper in the *British Journal for the Philosophy of Science* 15 (1965): 286–306, especially pp. 296–297. For the 1887 report of Michelson and Morley see the reference appearing two notes above.

83. Ives, *J.O.S.A.* 27 (1937): 177–180; reprinted in *The Ives Papers*, pp. 1 ff.

84. *Proceedings of the American Philosophical Society* 95 (1951): 125–131; reprinted in *The Ives Papers*, pp. 154 ff.

85. See note 100 for further discussion of this point. The English translation of Poincaré's paper appears in the *Monist* 15 (1905): 1–24, e.g., at p. 5. Edmund Whittaker pushed Poincaré's priority back to 1899, in *A History of the Theories of Aether and Electricity*, volume 2, pp. 30–31. See also the previous note. Students by and large as well as the general public are of the erroneous opinion that the *principle* of relativity was discovered by Einstein. A terminological confusion early in the century was partly responsible for this. Nevertheless, the sad fact is that textbooks usually fail to place this credit where it belongs. An example chosen at random appears in *Essential Relativity* by Wolfgang Rindler (New York: Van Nostrand Reinhold Co., 1969), p. 11, where one reads, "At that time of lively debate (1905), Einstein cut the Gordian knot by asserting, in his famous *relativity principle* that 'all inertial frames are totally equivalent for the performance of all physical experiments.' " For the facts, refer to G. H. Keswani in *British Journal for the Philosophy of Science* 15 (1965): 286–306; ibid. 16 (1965): 19–32, ibid. 16 (1966): 242–248, 273–294; ibid. 17 (1966): 149–152, 234–236. Pp. 284–292 in volume 16 are an attempt at a new theory not in conformity with the present work.

86. Joseph Larmor, *Aether and Matter* (Cambridge, England: At the University Press, 1900), notably Chapter 2. An attempt to detect absolute motion was made with a longitudinally vibrating metal rod in various orientations, being subject to the FitzGerald contraction and other effects. But A. B. Wood et al. in this experiment simply confirmed once more Poincaré's principle of relativity (*Proceedings of the Royal Society of London*, Series A 158 [1937]: 606–633).

87. "Electrodynamics," introduction; the same is in *Principle* at p. 38.

88. Ives, *J.O.S.A.* 38 (1948): 879–884, at 880n; in *The Ives Papers*, p. 137.

89. *Akademie der Wissenschaften* (Berlin) *Sitzungsberichte*, 18 November 1915: 831–839.

90. See *Principle*, pp. 108 and 163.

91. See summary graph of many results compiled by Robert H. Dicke, in *Gravitation and the Universe*, Philadelphia: American Philosophical Society, 1970, pp. 26 ff. Recently, waves from celestial radio sources have been shown to be similarly deflected by the gravity of the sun; e.g., see G. A. Seilstad et al., *Physical Review Letters* 24 (1970): 1373–1376.

92. *Scientific Proceedings of the Royal Dublin Society*, new series, 26 (1952): 9–26a, at p. 25; in *The Ives Papers*, p. 179. Also see *J.O.S.A.* 38 (1948): 879–884, at p. 880n; in *The Ives Papers*, p. 137.

93. A typical example of textbook misguidance of students is that of M. Paul Hagelburg's *Physics*. On p. 479, after his discussion of the experiment of Michelson and Morley, Hagelburg says: "One can only conclude that there is no absolute frame of reference for light propagation" (Englewood Cliffs, New

Jersey: Prentice-Hall, 1973). The *Encyclopedia Americana* (1976) in the article on "Light, History of Theories" states, "Negative results of the experiment revealed the nonexistence of the ether." Ives refuted all such statements not only experimentally and logically, but also historically. See *Scientific Proceedings of the Royal Dublin Society,* new series, 26 (1952): 9–26a, at pp. 24–25; in *The Ives Papers,* pp. 178–179. Also see *J.O.S.A.* 38 (1948): 879–884, at p. 880n; in *The Ives Papers,* p. 137.

94. *Proceedings of the American Philosophical Society* 95 (1951): 125–131; reprinted in *The Ives Papers,* pp. 154 ff. *Scientific Proceedings of the Royal Dublin Society,* new series, 26 (1952): 9–26a; reprinted in *The Ives Papers,* pp. 163 ff.

95. Important definitions of Ives appear in *J.O.S.A.* 38 (1948): 879–884, at p. 880; in *The Ives Papers,* p. 137. Also see *J.O.S.A.* 27 (1937): 263–273, 310–313, 389–392; reprinted in *The Ives Papers,* pp. 5 ff, 21 ff., 25 ff.

96. *Proceedings of the American Philosophical Society* 95 (1951): 125–131; reprinted in *The Ives Papers,* pp. 154 ff. *J.O.S.A.* 38 (1948): 879–884, at p. 880n; in *The Ives Papers,* p. 137.

97. *Philosophical Magazine* (London), seventh series, 36 (1945): 392–403; reprinted in *The Ives Papers,* pp. 112 ff. Also *J.O.S.A.* 39 (1949): 757–761; reprinted in *The Ives Papers,* pp. 142 ff. *J.O.S.A.* 40 (1950): 185–191, 883; reprinted in *The Ives Papers,* pp. 147 ff.

98. "Electrodynamics," section 3; in *Principle* at pp. 44–45. Note Einstein's expressions $(c - v)$ and $(c + v)$ and the context. Compare G. H. Keswani's paper in *British Journal for the Philosophy of Science* 16 (1965): 19–32, toward the end, especially p. 32.

99. *Proceedings of the American Philosophical Society* 95 (1951): 125–131; reprinted in The Ives Papers, pp. 154 ff. *Scientific Proceedings of the Royal Dublin Society,* new series, 26 (1952): 9–26a; reprinted in *The Ives Papers,* pp. 163 ff.

100. Stars are not the only objects whose apparent position is affected by the motion of the observer. For example, Neil Ashby and Glenn Brink (University of Colorado, Boulder) programmed a computer with the same formulas that are used in calculating the aberration of stellar positions due to the motion of the earth. They then undertook to compute how a rectangular solid object would appear in perspective, when the solid approached the speed of light. They found the same distortions that James Terrell had noted in 1959 (*Physical Review* 116 [1959]: 1041–1045). Ashby and Brink also noted a distortion of depth perspective. But they also found a shrinkage in the apparent size of an observed object when the observer is moving along with the object at a constant distance from the object. If this computed extrapolation from known facts proves to be valid, then the result would be a tidy circumvention of Poincaré's principle of relativity. That is, the *absolute* motion of two objects moving together would be directly detectible from each to the other. However, this method of detecting absolute motion appears to be of

interest only at speeds near to that of light. The results are presented graphically in an unpublished paper by Ashby and Brink.

101. *J.O.S.A.* 38 (1948): 879–884, at p. 880*n;* in *The Ives Papers,* p. 137.

102. In several places Ives makes much of that measured variation from the usual value of c which results when the speed of transport of a moved clock slows it down. Ives derives a formula for the speed of light in absolute space as reached by a one-way measurement with a transported and uncorrected clock (*J.O.S.A.* 38 [1948]: 879–884, especially p. 883; p. 140 in *The Ives Papers*). I may demur that a speed measurement with an uncorrected clock is of little interest, when a simple formula for making the correction is at hand. That formula was presented for this purpose by Einstein in "Electrodynamics," section 4: a moving clock will run slow by about $1/2 \ v^2/c^2$ seconds per second (*Annalen der Physik,* fourth series, 17 [1905]: 891–921, or *The Principle of Relativity* by H. A. Lorentz et al., New York: Dover Publications, 1952). Ives used that formula himself in predicting the result of his own 1938 experiment on canal rays (*J.O.S.A.* 28 [1938]: 215–226; *J.O.S.A.* 31 [1941]: 369–374; reprinted in *The Ives Papers,* pp. 29 ff., 85 ff.) My inspection concludes that the use of Einstein's formula (or his longer, exact formula) would result in the same correction as the complicated method of Ives. When the Einstein correction is made, the speed comes out to the usual value of c. The same value would result with Ives' method if he permitted the correction factor to be used. Ives preferred his procedure even though the uncorrected time caused the velocity so calculated to differ from the usual value of c. He did this in order to adhere strictly to operationally definable concepts, inferring nothing beyond (*J.O.S.A.* 40 [1950]: 185–191, at p. 189; p. 151 in *The Ives Papers*). Moreover, his method enabled him to use absolutely parallel operational definitions of three kinds of conventional speed measurements, or rod-clock quotients as he called them.

But to have a variable value for c, contingent on the circumstances of measurement, seems a high price to pay for a purely operational definition of a measured quantity. It appears to me that Ives went too far toward operationism and would have done well to suggest the use of the Einstein clock correction and, with it, the universally predictable and constant measured velocity of light at the conventional value of c (*in vacuo* etc.) In any event, my demurral does not touch the main body of Ives' thinking; the matter is hardly more than semantical.

103. *Monist* 15 (1905): 1–24, at pp. 10–11. Translated from *Bulletin des Sciences Mathématiques* 28 (1904): 302–324.

104. *Relativity,* Chapter 8, p. 23; "Electrodynamics," sections 1 and 2. In an otherwise excellent article, "The Constancy of the Velocity of Light," Geoffrey Builder has argued that Einstein did not mean to affirm the constancy of the velocity of light to all observers (*Australian Journal of Physics* 11 [1958]: 457–480). Although Einstein is hardly clear or consistent, I do not read Einstein the way Builder did. Moreover, Builder stretches language too far in retaining the name "relativity" for what is in reality a quite different theory. Neverthe-

less, Builder's articles should be read by the serious student of relativity, for
his conclusions are similar to those of Ives. For references to other articles of
Builder's see note 54 herein. As to Einstein, see note 3 herein.

105. G. Burniston Brown reminds us that the first determination of the
speed of light was a one-way measurement, namely, that of the seventeenth-
century Danish astronomer Ole Rømer. Rømer timed the eclipses of Io, one of
Jupiter's moons, with respect to the varying orbital motion of the earth. He
correctly attributed the residual observed variation to the time taken by the
light to travel from Jupiter to the earth, which varied wih the distance of Jupiter. The period of revolution of Io was assumed to be constant, except for the
calculated effect of one other moon. Rømer's work was remarkably accurate.

Rømer's work was repeated with modern apparatus by R. T. A. Innes from
1908 to 1926. Small sources of the residual variation in both sets of observations have been calculated by Samuel J. Goldstein and others (*Astronomical
Journal* 78 [1973]: 122–125; ibid., 80 [1975]: 532–539). Goldstein assumed
that the one-way speed of light was the same as the accepted two-way speed.
However, an inspection of his results suggests that any variation in the measured one-way speed that might result from the light's various absolute directions of travel would have been obvious, had such variation been as great as
one part in 200 of the speed of light.

Robert Vessot and the National Aeronautics and Space Administration put
an atomic-hydrogen maser into a rocket and sent it up hundreds of miles and
back. The maser constituted a very accurate clock. Although measurement of
the one-way speed of light was not the primary aim of the experiment, a reading of this speed was a byproduct. Since the rocket was sent quickly in only
one direction (before the earth could rotate much), the velocity measurement
was only in one direction with respect to the stars. The results have yet to be
published. But I understand that, unless the choice of direction was most in-
opportune, the one-way velocity of light appears to be the same as the two-
way velocity within far less than one part in a billion.

Current technology has enabled the planning of a spectacular experiment
for the early 1980s. N.A.S.A. is to place into orbit around the sun an artificial
satellite for several purposes. One of them will be that of vastly improving the
accuracy of Rømer's results, primarily in order to test theories of gravitation.
The satellite will orbit close to the sun, well inside the orbit of the planet
Mercury. To maintain its orbit at this short distance, the satellite will have to
revolve quite rapidly around the sun. The satellite will contain a radio beacon
which will "flash" at some precisely uniform interval. On earth, the number
of radio flashes will be counted, and the time will be recorded from the arrival
of the first flash in a series to the arrival of the last flash. The distance of the
satellite's recession, or approach to, the earth in the meanwhile will be determined. Dividing this distance by the total time deviation and applying the
Einstein clock correction will yield a very precise value for the measured one-
way velocity of light. For reasons I have stated, the value so measured and
corrected may be expected to be the same as the accepted two-way value of
the velocity of light c (with minute adjustment for the effect of gravity).

106. Poincaré, *Monist* 15 (1905): 1–24, at pp. 10–11. See note 103.

107. *Relativity*, Chapters 8 and 9.

108. *Journal of Philosophy* 27 (1930): 617–632, 643–654. But omit sections 3, 4, and 5 on pp. 648–652. To make clear Lovejoy's error in these pages would require another tedious kinematic exposition. The reader, having understood the foregoing text, can trace the error for himself if he so desires. See note 8.

109. *Relativity*, Appendix 5, p. 149.

110. *J.O.S.A.* 38 (1948): 879–884, at p. 880n; reprinted in *The Ives Papers*, p. 137.

111. *J.O.S.A.* 38 (1948): 413–416, e.g., p. 416; in *The Ives Papers*, p. 135. *J.O.S.A.* 29 (1939): 183–187; reprinted in *The Ives Papers*, pp. 45 ff. *Physical Review* 72 (1947): 229–232; reprinted in *The Ives Papers*, pp. 124 ff. Compare a note by Oliver Lodge, *Nature* (London) 104 (1919): 334. See further a letter by Joseph Larmor, *Nature* 142 (1938): 1035. Both are reprinted in *The Ives Papers*, p. 205.

112. *Space, Time, and Gravitation* (Cambridge, England: At the University Press, 1920), p. 107.

113. *J.O.S.A.* 29 (1939): 183–187, at p. 184; in *The Ives Papers*, pp. 45 ff.

114. See *Physical Review Letters* 24 (1970): 1377–1380. Ibid. 26 (1971): 1132–1135.

115. Translated from *Naturwissenschaften* 8 (1920): 1010–1011.

116. "On the Method of Theoretical Physics," in *The World as I See It* (New York: Covici Friede, 1934), p. 36.

117. *American Journal of Physics* 23 (1955): 450–464, at p. 458.

118. *Journal of Philosophy* 27 (1930): 617–632, 645–654; mostly reprinted in *The Ives Papers*, pp. 205 ff. See note 8.

119. *Philosophical Problems of Space and Time*, second edition (Dordrecht, Holland): D. Reidel Publishing Co., 1973), pp. 721–726. "Relativity Theory," *Encyclopedia of Philosophy*, 1967. As is usual, neither the experiment of Sagnac nor that of Michelson and Gale are mentioned.

120. See "The Prejudice in Favour of Symmetry," by Charles Hartshorne, in his *Creative Synthesis and Philosophic Method* (La Salle, Illinois: Open Court Publishing Co., 1970), pp. 205–226 (also pp. 96–97).

121. *The Myth of Simplicity* (Englewood Cliffs, New Jersey: Prentice-Hall, 1963), especially section II: "Simplicity and Truth."

122. Ibid., p. 75.

123. *Journal of Philosophy* 27 (1930): 617–632, especially at pp. 630–631; in *The Ives Papers*, pp. 218–219.

124. *Principia*, "Rules of Reasoning in Philosophy," Rule 1.

125. *Relativity, Time, and Reality*, p. 117. A French physicist, Léon Brillouin, correctly criticized Einstein with the statement that he "introduced a very heavy mathematical structure that goes much beyond any physical need" (*Relativity Reexamined*, New York: Academic Press, 1970, p. 31).

126. *Myth of Simplicity*, p. 115.

127. Edmund Whittaker, *A History of the Theories of Aether and Electricity*, volume 2, pp. 44–54, at p. 51.

128. *Annalen der Physik*, series 4, 16 (14 March 1905): 589–592. See also Whittaker's *History*, ibid., pp. 51–52. Refer also to Ives in *J.O.S.A.* 42 (1952): 540–543. A biography by a noted scientist that also includes personal data is in *Great Men of Science* by Philipp Lenard (New York: Macmillan Co., 1933), pp. 371–382.

129. See Ives' summary and reference, *J.O.S.A.* 42 (1952): 540–543, at pp. 540–541. The full reference of Ives is *Archives Néerlandaises des Sciences Exactes et Naturelles* (The Hague) second series, volume 5 (1900): 252–278. Einstein's reference to Poincaré's priority appears on the first page of an article in *Annalen der Physik*, series 4, 20 (1906): 627–633.

130. *Akademie der Wissenschaften* (Göttingen) *Nachrichten, Mathematisch-physikalische Klasse*, 1901 (published 1902), pp. 143–155; and 1902, pp. 291–296.

131. The serious student must consult Ives' main paper, *J.O.S.A.* 42 (1952): 540–543. An exchange of letters follows: *J.O.S.A.* 43 (1953): 618–619. Ives refers to earlier papers of his: *J.O.S.A.* 33 (1943): 163–166; ibid., 34 (1944): 222–228. All these are reprinted in *The Ives Papers*, pp. 182 ff., 188, 101 ff., 105 ff.

132. *Akademie der Wissenschaften* (Berlin) *Sitzungsberichte*, 13 June 1907: 542–570, e.g., p. 566. Referred to by Ives, *J.O.S.A.* 43 (1952): 540–543.

133. *Relativity*, Chapter 15, p. 45. "Relativity . . ." in *Grolier Encyclopedia*, 1947. "Relativity . . ." in *American People's Encyclopedia*, 1948. The error is so deeply entrenched everywhere that one almost despairs of ever seeing it much corrected. An example at random is that of Patrick Moore in *The Atlas of the Universe* (New York: Rand McNally & Co., 1970), p. 31: "Einstein's special theory of relativity showed him that mass and energy were interchangeable."

134. See summary and reference in Ives, *J.O.S.A.* 43 (1952): 540–543, at p. 542. The reference by Ives is *Encyklopädie der mathematischen Wissenschaften*, volume 5, part 2, section 19 (1922): 539–775, at pp. 679–681.

135. *New York Times*, 27 April 1938, p. 25.

136. Ibid., p. 22.

137. Ibid., 8 April 1927, p. 1. Ibid., 15 November 1953, p. 88. *J.O.S.A.* 43 (1953): 1228–1229; reprinted in *The Ives Papers*, p. xi. See further biography in the front of *The Ives Papers*.

Encyclopedia Americana (1976) has 27 lines on Ives but does not mention either the Ives-Stilwell experiment or Ives' basic theoretical work on light, space, and time. Other negative examples could be mentioned. Evidently, Ives' prying into such holy matters was thought to be indiscreet.

138. *American Journal of Physics* 41 (1973): 1068–1077.

139. Gardner (New York: Macmillan Co., 1962), pp. 22–23.

140. Ibid., p. 29. For a correct interpretation of the Kennedy-Thorndike experiment see Ives, *J.O.S.A.* 27 (1937): 177–180; reprinted in *The Ives Papers*, pp. 1 ff. The Kennedy-Thorndike interferometer had decidedly unequal arms, unlike the Michelson-Morley interferometer. Both experiments gave null results. See also *J.O.S.A.* 28 (1938): 215–226, at p. 226, in *The Ives Papers*, p. 40. Also *J.O.S.A.* 38 (1948): 879–884, at 880n, note 3; in *The Ives Papers*, p. 137.

141. New York: Random House, 1976.

142. Washington: National Geographic Society, 1975.

143. *Collected Writings*, Readex edition.

144. Poincaré, *Monist* 15 (1905): 1–24, at pp. 10–11. Einstein's views appear in "Electrodynamics," section 1, and in *Relativity*, Chapter 8.

145. In his 1904 address in St. Louis, Poincaré (on pp. 10–11 of the English version) clearly implied his affirmation of the reality of absolute space (see the previous note and note 103). However, in 1908 in his book *Science et Méthode* he obviously has fallen victim to Einstein's belief that space is relative. On page 93 of the 1914 English version (the first page of Book II) he states that "Whoever speaks of absolute space uses a word devoid of meaning." Making the same mistake as Einstein, he concludes that things simply *are* the same as they *appear*. Obviously, Poincaré had forgotten about such things as stellar aberration and the multiple problems of attempting to explain rotation with relativity physics.

146. See note 85, the reference to *British Journal for the Philosophy of Science*.

147. *Essential Relativity*, pp. 48–59.

148. *Science* 134 (1961): 596–602.

149. *Principia*, "General Scholium." The interested reader should seek out a rarely beautiful literary piece which is in resonance with this passage of Newton's. It is by Joseph Addison in *The Spectator* no. 565 (1714).

150. Nordenson, *Relativity, Time, and Reality*, p. 214.

CHAPTER TWELVE: Cantor's Transfinite Versus the Complete God

1. See Georg Cantor, *Gesammelte Abhandlungen*, edited by Ernst Zermelo (Berlin: Julius Springer, 1932), Chapter 4, especially pp. 405–406. See also

James Thomson, "Infinity in Mathematics and Logic," *Encyclopedia of Philosophy* (New York: Macmillan Publishing Co., 1967).

2. New York: Abingdon Press, 1930. Currently available from Ann Arbor, Michigan: Xerox University Microfilms.

3. Chicago: University of Chicago Press, 1953.

4. New Haven: Yale, 1948.

5. In Hartshorne's *Creative Synthesis and Philosophic Method* (La Salle, Illinois: Open Court Publishing Co., 1970), pp. 205–226, also pp. 96–97.

6. E.g., in *Man's Vision of God* (New York: Harper & Brothers, 1941), pp. 253–254.

7. E.g., *The Republic*, 379.

8. For excerpts see Charles Hartshorne and William L. Reese, *Philosophers Speak of God* (Chicago: University of Chicago Press, 1953), especially pp. 238–241.

9. *Proceedings of the Utah Academy of Sciences, Arts, and Letters* 44 (1967): 421–437.

10. Salt Lake: University of Utah Press, 1965.

11. Salt Lake: Deseret Book Co., 1966.

12. A620 = B648 to A630 = B658.

13. *Philosophical Review* 18 (1909): 479–502.

CHAPTER THIRTEEN: Olbers' Paradox and Infinite Creation

1. *American Journal of Physics* 35 (1967) 200–210. Physicists present differing interpretations of Charlier's model of an infinite universe. For example, Hannes Alfvén, in *Worlds-Antiworlds*, understands Charlier to be saying that the total *mass* of the universe is infinite, i.e., that there is an infinite number of stars (San Francisco: W. H. Freeman & Co., 1966, pp. 95–96). Stanley L. Jaki states, apparently cogently: "Alfvén claims that in Charlier's universe the total mass is infinite. As a matter of fact, the whole purpose of the hierarchical distribution of mass in an infinite space was to make the total mass finite and avoid thereby the gravitational and optical paradox" (*Science and Creation*, New York: Science History Publications, 1974, p. 360, footnote 107). In a book entitled *The Paradox of Olbers' Paradox*, Jaki explains why Charlier's proposed solution to Olbers' paradox eventually lost the support of both theoretical and observational cosmology (New York: Herder & Herder, 1969), pp. 198–209.

2. See Martin Harwit, *Astronomical Concepts* (New York: John Wiley & Sons, 1973), pp. 458–461.

3. For a sophisticated mathematical exposition of this, see D. H. Menzel, F. L. Whipple, and G. de Vaucouleurs, *Survey of the Universe* (Englewood Cliffs, New Jersey: Prentice-Hall, 1970), pp. 761–763.

CHAPTER FOURTEEN: Humeanism and Atomistic Psychology

1. Oxford: At the Clarendon Press, 1888, Book I, Part 4, Section 6, pp. 252–253. Slight changes in spelling and punctuation are made by me for readibility in modern English.

The main historical antecedent for the denial of personal identity is Buddhism. Buddhist metaphysics is strictly relativistic and denies the existential reality of any entities. In Buddhism, the self is only a compilation of relations, and the individual is only an abstraction. See for instance *Buddhism: Its Essence and Development*, by Edward Conze (Oxford: Bruno Cassirer, 1951).

2. *A Treatise of Human Nature*, appendix to Book I, pp. 635–636. I have changed three words and some punctuation marks in order to make the reading more natural to contemporary English.

3. Chicago: Open Court Publishing Co., 1925.

4. New York: Harper & Row, 1967, especially pp. 100–110.

5. New York: Harper & Brothers Publishers, 1897, pp. 66–70.

6. In *The Philosophy of Bertrand Russell*, edited by Paul A. Schilpp (Evanston, Illinois: Northwestern University, 1944), pp. 475–509.

7. St. Louis: Bethany Press, 1970.

8. Volume I, fifth impression (London: Longmans, Green, and Co., 1906), p. 297, paragraph 345.

9. "Little Philosophical Verses," *Western Humanities Review* 17 (1963): 213.

CHAPTER FIFTEEN: Russell, Mathematical Truth, and Absolutes

1. *New Quarterly*, November 1907, paragraphs 4, 14, 17. Later reprinted, slightly altered, in Russell's *Mysticism and Logic* (London: George Allen & Unwin, 1917).

2. "The Retreat from Pythagoras," *My Philosophical Development* (New York: Simon & Schuster, 1959, pp. 211–212. Also in *The Basic Writings of Bertrand Russell* (New York: Simon & Schuster, 1961), pp. 254–255.

3. The book is translated by Walter Lowrie (Princeton: Princeton University Press, 1941. Reprinted at Garden City, New York: Doubleday & Co., 1954).

CHAPTER SIXTEEN: Discerning the Meaning of Oneness

1. Second edition (Cambridge, England: At the University Press, 1925) Vol. I, p. 347.

2. New York: Macmillan Publishing Co., 1967.

3. Englewood Cliffs, New Jersey: Prentice-Hall, 1964.

4. *The Foundations of Arithmetic*, translated by J. L. Austin (New York: Philosophical Library, 1950), p. 42e.

5. Ibid., p. 67e.

6. See his article, "Russell's Theory of Knowledge," in *The Philosophy of Bertrand Russell*, edited by Paul A. Schilpp (Evanston, Illinois: Northwestern University, 1944), pp. 285–291.

7. *The World as I See It* (New York: Covici Friede, 1934), pp. 33–37.

8. "Russell's Theory of Knowledge," p. 285.

9. See note 18, Chapter 9. The quotation on freedom is from his essay "What I Believe," *Forum*, October 1930, pp. 193–194, at p. 193. Reprinted in Albert Einstein, *Ideas and Opinions* (New York: Crown Publishers, 1954), pp. 8–11, at p. 8.

10. "Russell's Theory of Knowledge," p. 289.

11. *Out of My Later Years* (New York: Philosophical Library, 1950), pp. 26–27.

CHAPTER SEVENTEEN: Singh, Peirce, and Anthropomorphism

1. New York: Dover Publications, 1961, p. 257.

2. Ibid., pp. 257–258.

3. *Collected Papers of Charles Sanders Peirce*, edited by Charles Hartshorne, Paul Weiss, and Arthur W. Burks (Cambridge, Massachusetts: Harvard University Press, 1931–1958), 5.47. Italics are mine.

4. Ibid., 1.316. See also volumes and sections 1.80, 5.47, 5.591–5.592, 6.12, 6.553, and 7.46–7.48.

5. *Zygon* 2 (1967): 187–202.

6. New York: Science History Publications, 1974.

7. Plato, *Theaetetus*, 152.

8. *Philosophy of Science* 8 (1941): 184–203.

CHAPTER EIGHTEEN: Induction and Sensibility

1. Hume treats the subject at considerable length. The historically minded reader may consult *A Treatise of Human Nature* (Oxford: At the Clarendon Press, 1888), Book I; and *Enquiries Concerning the Human Understanding*, second edition (Oxford: At the Clarendon Press, 1902), especially Sections 4 and 7.

2. *A Treatise of Human Nature*, Book I, Part 4, Section 1, pp. 186–187.

3. *The Meaning of Philosophy*, by Joseph Gerard Brennan (New York: Harper & Row, 1967), p. 115.

4. "Induction," *Encyclopedia of Philosophy* (New York: Macmillan Publishing Co., 1967), Volume 4, at pp. 173–174. Italics are mine.

5. Ibid., p. 179. Italics are Black's.

6. Ibid., p. 171.

7. Ibid., p. 171.

8. Ibid., p. 175.

9. Ibid., p. 179.

10. New York: Random House, 1955. Sentences are rearranged so as to bring Camus' points emphatically into clear focus.

11. Ibid.

12. Ibid., paragraph 73.

13. In *The Nature and Foundation of Scientific Theories*, edited by Robert G. Colodny (Pittsburgh: University of Pittsburgh Press, 1970), pp. 79–172. Those who are uninitiated into inductive logic will wish to consult also an introductory survey, such as *The Foundations of Scientific Inference* by Wesley C. Salmon (Pittsburgh: University of Pittsburgh Press, 1967). Salmon's book is altogether common. It adequately familiarizes the reader with the fundamental assumptions of different schools of thought on induction; but unfortunately, it also contains the virtually ubiquitous bias against *apriori* knowledge as applicable in the sciences. Salmon labels himself an "unregenerate frequentist" (p. 128)—reducing all predictions exclusively to probability and hence eventually to guesswork. He aligns himself with the empiricist claim that all knowledge of the world is grounded exclusively in observational evidence, i.e., that factual understanding is confined to what we can observe and infer therefrom. Of course, he never imagines that questions of inductive science are nugatory when they are pondered independently of any considerations of value. Needless to say, God is not mentioned in his index; neither is the term "absolute," nor the term "value." Here is just another example of how casually philosophers of science exclude God from the world which they could not possibly understand were His reason not present within it.

CHAPTER NINETEEN: The Last Escape Hatch

1. The reader may find an extensive bibliography treating of the descriptions of these paradoxes, and proposed solutions to them, in the article "Logical Paradoxes" by the Dutch logician John van Heijenoort, in the *Encyclopedia of Philosophy* (New York: Macmillan Publishing Co., 1967).

2. "What Can We Learn from the Paradoxes?" *Critica: Revista Hispanoamericana de Filosofía* (Mexico City) 5 (1971): 35–54, 85–108. The quotation is from p. 88.

3. Aristotle, *Metaphysica*, Book Gamma, 1005–1008. In *The Works of Aristotle*, Volume 8, translated by W. D. Ross (Oxford: At the Clarendon Press, 1908).

4. Titus 1:12.

5. "Self-Reference and Meaning in Ordinary Language," *Mind* 63 (1954): 162–169, at p. 167. Reprinted in Popper's *Conjectures and Refutations* (New York: Harper & Row, 1965), pp. 304–311, at p. 309.

6. "The Semantic Conception of Truth and the Foundations of Semantics," *Philosophy and Phenomenological Research* 4 (1944): 341–375, especially sections 7, 8, and 9 (pp. 347–351), notably p. 350.

7. Several editions (New York: Macmillan Co.), chapter, "A Propositional Calculus," section, "Object Language and Metalanguage."

8. Preface to Ludwig Wittgenstein's *Tractatus Logico-Philosophicus* (London: Routledge & Kegan Paul, 1922), p. xxii.

9. In *A Hundred Years of Philosophy*, by John Passmore, revised edition (New York: Basic Books, 1966), p. 224. For the specific problems see the article "Types, Theory of," by Yehoshua Bar-Hillel in the *Encyclopedia of Philosophy*. See also therein the article "Categories," by Manley Thompson, "Logical Paradoxes," by John van Heijenoort, and the article on Bertrand Russell.

10. *Philosophical Review* 54 (1945): 607–610.

11. Ibid., p. 608, italics mine.

12. In *Logic, Semantics, Metalanguage* (Oxford: At the Clarendon Press, 1956), pp. 152–278, at pp. 164–165. Italics are Tarski's.

13. *Dialectica* (Switzerland) 28 (1974): 87–102, at p. 100.

14. Arthur N. Prior, "Some Problems of Self-Reference in John Buridan," *Proceedings of the British Academy, 1962,* 48 (1963): 281–296, notably at p. 292. See also C. S. Peirce, *Collected Papers* (Cambridge, Massachusetts: Harvard University Press, 1931–1958), 5.340. Paul Finsler traces this idea back to A. Geulincx in the year 1663; see "Gibt es unentscheidbare Sätze?" *Commentaire Mathematici Helvetici* (Zürich) 16 (1944): 310–320, note 6.

15. *Semantics and Necessary Truth* (New Haven: Yale University Press, 1958), Chapter 5, especially pp. 261–268. Similar considerations underly an article on Descartes by Jaako Hintikka: "Cogito, Ergo Sum: Inference or Performance?" *Philosophical Review* 71 (1962): 3–32.

16. See note 2.

17. See note 5.

18. Henry B. Veatch, *Two Logics* (Evanston, Illinois: Northwestern University Press, 1969). F. F. Centore, "The Metalogic of Mathematical Logic," *Philosophical Studies* (Ireland) 20 (1972): 124–138. See also Centore's article "There Are Two Logics," *New Scholasticism* 45 (1971): 343–347.

19. *A Treatise on Universal Algebra* (Cambridge: At the University Press, 1898), p. vi. *The Philosophy of Alfred North Whitehead*, edited by Paul A. Schilpp (Evanston, Illinois: Northwestern University, 1941), p. 700.

CHAPTER TWENTY: Gödel and Metasystems

1. *Gödel's Proof* (New York: New York University Press, 1958), pp. 58–59.

2. Ibid., p. 94. Compare p. 60.

3. "Gödel's Theorem," *Encyclopedia of Philosophy* (New York: Macmillan Publishing Co., 1967), "Influence of Gödel's Results," sub-section "Intuitionism."

4. Ibid.

5. *The Philosophy of Bertrand Russell* (Evanston, Illinois: Northwestern University, 1944), Max Black, "Russell's Philosophy of Language," pp. 227–255, especially pp. 251–254. See further Russell's "Reply to Criticisms," pp. 691–695, at pp. 693–694.

6. "Gödel's Theorem," ibid., "Epistemological Significance."

7. See Ernest Nagel's and James R. Newman's book *Gödel's proof*, referred to above, pp. 96–97. Also see J. van Heijenoort's article "Gödel's Theorem," referred to above, the last four pages. Some objections to the cogency of Gentzen's proof are countered by Alonzo Church in a review in the *Journal of Symbolic Logic* 30 (1965): 357–359, especially p. 359.

Glossary and Index

Glossary and Index

Glossary and Index

Glossary and Index

404

Glossary and Index

Glossary and Index

Glossary and Index

Glossary and Index

Glossary and Index

409

Glossary and Index

410

Glossary and Index

Chance as ordinarily defined). The inevitable connection between a thing and the ground or cause of its being.

Need. That which makes something meaningful or sensible and which makes thought and action possible; that which is requisite to any intelligible action or being. That which is required but lacking.

Need
  complementary to care, 56
  vs. desire, 14–18, 29
  and epistemology, 167–68
  and induction, 336–38
  per James, 15–18
  need for need, 125, 139
  at heart of reality, 102
  for things of value, 10, 111
Needs, essential life, 8–20, 124, 140–44, 150–51, 157, 167, *et passim.*
  See also Values; Essences
  lists, 168–69, 307–09, 140, 144
  and value, 140–44
  as unconscious, 140
Negentropy and life, 91–94, 371
Neumann, J. von., 209–11
Neurosis, metaphysical, 123
Newman, J., 363
Newton, I.
  on rotations, 258–59
  on space, 243–44, 247, 294
  on theology, 304
Nietzsche, F., 374
Nihilism. *See* Atheism; Relativism; Pragmatism
Nordenson, H., 224, 228, 302, 381
Nothing, as creative, 23–25, 33–38, 148–49. *See also* Monod; Hume
Nowness, 51. *See also* Simultaneity
Null cones. *See* Cones, null

Objectivity, 3–20. *See also* Truth; Needs
  criterion of, in need and care, 9–14
  levels of, in space and time, 278
  Monod on, 183, 192–200
Occult, the, 373
Ockham's Razor, 292–96
Olbers, H., and paradox, 314–16, 394
Oneness, 51–59, 325–29, 360.
  See also Platonism

Ontological. Expressing an ontology or ontological viewpoint. Informed by ultimate truth or reality.

Ontology. That branch of philosophy that studies the nature and essential properties of being.

Operationism, 210, 389
Options level of objectivity, 278
Order, *passim. See also* Invariance; Laws; Necessary truths
  not to be absolute, 88–91
  Hume on, 201–07
  Monod on, 187–200
  without an orderer, 68–69
Ordered arguments against order, 6
Organizing in biology, 75–86, 92–93
Ought, 107, 151

Paley, W., 377–78
Palomar telescope, and chance, 76
Panpsychism, 62, 312
Pap, A., 358, 398
Paradoxes, logical, as escapes, 348–66, 397–98
Parapsychology, 127, 131–32
Parmenides, 233
Particles, subatomic. *See* Electrons
Parts and wholes, harmony of, 206
Pascal, B., 18–19
Passmore, J., 376–77
Past facts as real, 44–47, 52, 371.
  See also Time, cumulative
  and pragmatism, 47
Paul the Apostle, 351–52, 173
Pauli, W., 297
Peirce, C. S.
  on anthropomorphism, 333
  on laws, 201, 376
  on philosophers, 239
Pendulum, Foucault, 259
Perception, extra-sensory, 127, 131–32
Perfection, divine, 161
Person, existence of, implied in every statement made, 398
Personalism, 125, *et passim*
Personhood, 42–47, 104–39. *See also* Identity; Freedom of Choice; Mind
  denial of by
    Arnstine, 320
    Dewey, 319
    Hume, 317–22
    Lovejoy on, 374

Glossary and Index

Personhood (*cont.*)
  dependent on reasonableness in the
    structure of reality, 46–47
Persons
  conservation of. *See* Immortality;
    Values, conservation of
  as good or bad, 48, 102
  need for, 125–26
  origin of, in God, 125
  reduction to physics, 184–85. *See also*
    Indeterminism
Petitio principii. Begging the question;
  a fallacy in which a premise is
  assumed to be true without an adequate basis; a fallacy in which
  what is to be proved is implicitly
  taken for granted.
Petitio principii in justifying need,
  11–20
Philo Judaeus, 161–62
Philosophy
  failings of method, current, 122, 239,
    321, 337, 348, 378
  and science, 6, 35, 214–15, 220,
    304–06, 379
  use of, Epicurus on, 124
Physicists, responsibility of, 302–03
Physics,
  laws of, as God's will, 212
  and metaphysics. *See* Philosophy and
    science
Pilate, Pontius, 354
Planck, M., 62, 220, 297
Plane of the true present, 283–85
  in diagram, 230
Plato, 312, 370
Platonism. The viewpoint established
  by the Greek philosopher Plato that
  all true knowledge originates in
  the mind, rather than through sense
  impressions and conforms to eternal
  essences that have always existed
  in a perfect world predating and
  transcending Man and his natural
  order.
Platonism, 325–331. *See also* Mathematics; Cantor; Essences; Oneness
Poincaré, H.
  on clock synchronization, 283, 300–01
  on null cones, 304, 233
  on esthetic structure of reality, 377

on Lorentz transformations, 271, 282,
  295
on mass-energy equivalence, 297
on principle of relativity, 272, 275–
  78, 288–89, 294–95, 387
on absolute space, 301, 393
Popper, K., 353, 359, 378
Positivism, 210, 304–06
  Lovejoy on, 374
  in Monod, 183
Possibility, 88–91. *See also* Future
Pound, R., *See* below
Pound-Rebka experiment, 261–68
Pound-Snider experiment, 262
Power, as behavior criterion, 143–44
Pragmatism, 43, 47, 368–70, *et passim*
  of James, 15–20
Prayer, 116
Predestination, 90. *See* Determinism
Predictability, 6. *Also see* Laws
Preferred configurations in nature, 221
Principle of relativity. *See under*
  Poincaré
Principles, without power to act, 94
Prior, A., 398
Probability as ultimate, 217. *See also*
  Indeterminacy
Process. That aspect of reality which
  involves activity, that is, becom-
  ing and unbecoming.
Protagoras, 334
Psychology, atomistic, 317–22
Psychopath, 151
Psychotherapy, 47–49, 175
Purpose, 8, 29–30. *See also* Creation;
  Reason; Meaning; Care; Life;
  Moral ideal; Need; *et passim*
  biology of, 376
  and evolution, 27, 38, 220–21. *See*
    Monod on, 181–200
  ground of, in need, 29–30
  from purposelessness, 64, 197
Putnam, H., 231–33, 326

Quanta and God, 214
Quanta and law, 212
Quantum theory, 207–15, 223, 379
  and Einstein, 223, 273
  and life, 78–80

Radar tests of General Relativity, 290

412

Glossary and Index

Glossary and Index

A Note About the Author

Dean Turner was born in Tyrone, Oklahoma, and was raised in Stratford, Texas. He now teaches in the University of Northern Colorado, and is an ordained minister in the Disciples of Christ Church. He received a B.A. degree from the *Centro de Estudios Universitarios* in Mexico, and a Ph.D. degree from the University of Texas. He served in the U.S. Army in the Korean War. The author of five books, he has given over three hundred television, radio, and after-dinner addresses. He taught in Mexico, the University of Maryland, the Azores, Labrador, Newfoundland, Greenland, and Bermuda. Also he taught in Sullins Women's College, and in five American high schools. Presently, he lives in Greeley, Colorado. He is married and has a daughter and son.